MostUsedWords.com presents

French Frequency Dictionary

Master Vocabulary

7501-10000 Most Common French Words

Book 4

First Printing, 2018

Jolie Laide LTD
12/F, 67 Percival Street, Hong Kong

www.MostUsedWords.com

Contents

Why This Book?

Hello, dear reader.

Thank you for purchasing this book. We hope it serves you well on your language learning journey.

Not all words are created equal. The purpose of this frequency dictionary is to list the most used words in descending order, to enable you to learn a language as fast and efficiently as possible.

First, we would like to illustrate the value of a frequency dictionary. For the purpose of example, we have combined frequency data from various languages (mainly Romance, Slavic and Germanic languages) and made it into a single chart.

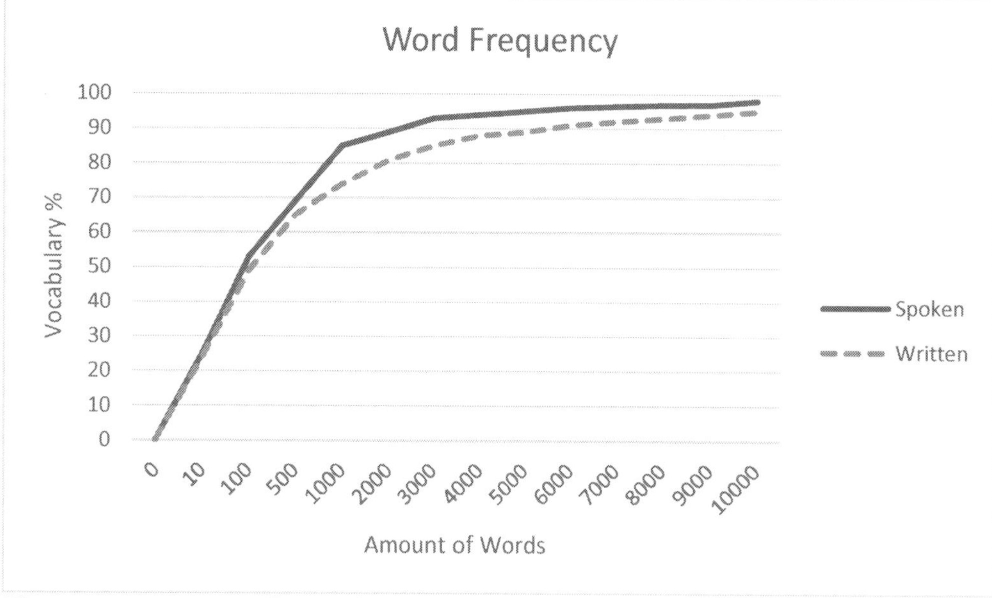

The sweet spots, according to the data seem to be:

Amount of Words	Spoken	Written
• 100	53%	49%
• 1.000	85%	74%
• 2.500	92%	82%
• 5.000	95%	89%
• 7.500	97%	93%
• 10.000	98%	95%

Above data corresponds with Pareto´s law.

Pareto's law, also known as the 80/20 rule, states that, for many events, roughly 80% of the effects come from 20% of the causes.

In language learning, this principle seems to be on steroids. It seems that just 20% of the 20% (95/5) of the most used words in a language account for roughly all the vocabulary you need.

To put his further in perspective: The Concise Oxford Hachette French Dictionary lists over 175.000 words in current use, while you will only need to know 2.9% (5000 words) to achieve 95% and 89% fluency in speaking and writing. Knowing the most common 10.000 words, or 5.6%, will net you 98% fluency in spoken language and 95% fluency in written texts.

Keeping this in mind, the value of a frequency dictionary is immense. Study the most frequent words, build your vocabulary and progress naturally. Sounds logical, right?

How many words do you need to know for varying levels of fluency?

While it's important to note that it is impossible to pin down these numbers and statistics with 100% accuracy, these are a global average of multiple sources.

According to research, this is the amount of vocabulary needed for varying levels of fluency.

1. 250 words: the essential core of a language. Without these words, you cannot construct any sentence.
2. 750 words: those that are used every single day by every person who speaks the language.
3. 2500 words: those that should enable you to express everything you could possibly want to say, although some creativity might be required.
4. 5000 words: the active vocabulary of native speakers without higher education.
5. 10,000 words: the active vocabulary of native speakers with higher education.
6. 20,000 words: what you need to recognize passively to read, understand, and enjoy a work of literature such as a novel by a notable author.

Caveats & Limitations.

A frequency list is never "The Definite Frequency List."

Depending on the source material analyzed, you may get different frequency lists. A corpus on spoken word differs from source texts based on a written language.

That is why we chose subtitles as our source, because, according to science, subtitles cover the best of both worlds: they correlate to both spoken and written language.

The frequency list is based on analysis of roughly 20 gigabytes of French subtitles.

Visualize a book with almost 16 million pages, or 80.000 books of 200 pages each, to get an idea of the amount words that have been analyzed for this book. A large base text is vital in order to develop an accurate frequency list.

The raw data included over 1 million entries. The raw data has been lemmatized; words are given in their root form.

Some entries you might find odd, in their respective frequency rankings. We were surprised a couple of time ourselves. Keep in mind that the frequency list is compiled from a large amount of subtitle data, and may include words you wouldn't use yourself.

You might find non-French loanwords in this dictionary. We decided to include them, because if they´re being used in subtitle translation, it is safe to assume the word has been integrated into the French general vocabulary.

We tried our best to keep out proper nouns, such as "James, Ryan, Alice as well as "Rome, Washington" or "the Louvre, the Capitol".

Some words have multiple meanings. For the ease of explanation, the following examples are given in English.

"Jack" is a very common first name, but also a noun (a jack to lift up a vehicle) and a verb (to steal something). So is the word "can" It is a conjugation of the verb "to be able" as well as a noun (a tin can, or a can of soft drink).

This skews the frequency rankings slightly. With the current technology, it is unfortunately not possible to rightly identify the correct frequency placements of above words. Luckily, these words are very few, and thus negligible in the grand scheme of things.

If you encounter a word you think you won't need in your vocabulary, just skip learning it. The frequency list includes 25 extra words to compensate for any irregularities you might encounter.

The big secret to learning language is this: build your vocabulary, learn basic grammar and go out there and speak. Make mistakes, have a laugh and learn from them.

We hope you enjoy this frequency dictionary, and that it helps you in your quest of speaking French.

How To Use This Dictionary

abbreviation	*abr*
adjective	*adj*
adverb	*adv*
article	*art*
auxiliary verb	*av*
conjunction	*con*
interjection	*int*
noun	*f(eminine), m(asculine)*
numeral	*num*
particle	*part*
phrase	*phr*
prefix	*pfx*
preposition	*prp*
pronoun	*prn*
suffix	*sfx*
verb	*vb*
singular	*sg*
plural	*pl*

Word Order

The most common translations are generally given first. This resets by every new respective part of speech. Different parts of speech are divided by ";".

Translations

We made the decision to give the most common translation(s) of a word, and respectively the most common part(s) of speech. It does, however, not mean that this is the only possible translations or the only part of speech the word can be used for.

International Phonetic Alphabet (IPA)

The pronunciation of foreign vocabulary can be tricky. To help you get it right, we added IPA entries for each entry. If you already have a base understanding of the pronunciation, you will find the IPA pronunciation straightforward. For more information, please visit www.internationalphoneticalphabet.org

French English Frequency Dictionary

Rank	French Part of Speech [IPA]	English Translation(s) French Example Sentence -English Example Sentence
7501	**irriter** vb [iʁite]	**irritate** Je n' aime pas irriter mes collègues en les interrompant, mais je réclame votre coopération. -I do not like to irritate colleagues by interrupting them, but I must appeal for your support.
7502	**répugnant** adj [ʁepyɲɑ̃]	**repugnant** Le terrorisme, quelles que soient ses manifestations est répugnant. -Any manifestation of terrorism is abhorrent.
7503	**synthétique** adj; m [sɛ̃tetik]	**synthetic; synthetic** L'étude tentera d'utiliser les données pour présenter une image synthétique et identifier les lacunes. -The study will attempt to blend the various data into a synthesized picture and identify gaps.
7504	**trotter** vb [tʁɔte]	**trot** Je vais trotter, galoper, pendant une heure. -I'm going to trot then gallop for an hour.
7505	**cynisme** m [sinism]	**cynicism** Le Parti réformiste a aidé à perpétuer ce cynisme. -The Reform Party has contributed to the continuation of this cynicism.
7506	**traumatique** adj [tʁomatik]	**traumatic** Non, c'était plutôt traumatique. -No, it was pretty traumatizing.
7507	**énervant** adj [enɛʁvɑ̃]	**annoying** C'est énervant. -That's annoying.
7508	**paternité** f [patɛʁnite]	**paternity** En fait, il s'agit surtout du père sur lequel pèse une présomption de paternité. -Mostly, these concern the father for whom there is a presumption of paternity.
7509	**trompeur** adj; m [tʁɔ̃pœʁ]	**misleading; deceiver** L'exemple souvent n'est qu'un miroir trompeur. -The example often is only a misleading mirror.
7510	**artisan** m [aʁtizɑ̃]	**artisan** À l'œuvre, on connaît l'artisan. -One recognizes the craftsman by his work.
7511	**lésion** f [lezjɔ̃]	**lesion** Les tests ne révèlent aucune lésion médullaire ou cérébrale. -Tests show no spinal cord injury, no cerebral lesions, no hemorrhage.
7512	**téléviseur** m [televizœʁ]	**TV** Les jeunes passent beaucoup de temps devant le téléviseur ou l'ordinateur. -Young people spend a lot of time in front of television screens or computer monitors.
7513	**sodomie**	**sodomy**

f C'est dangereux, la sodomie.
[sɔdɔmi] -It's a hazardous business, sodomy.

7514 **charrue** **plow**
f Le bond entre la charrue et le tracteur n'est pas du tout le bond approprié.
[ʃaʁy] -The leap from plough to hi-tech tractor is not at all an appropriate one.

7515 **lande** **moor**
f Ne traversez pas la lande seul.
[lɑ̃d] -You're not going to cross the moor alone, Sir Henry.

7516 **négociateur** **negotiator**
m Vous êtes un négociateur avisé.
[negɔsjatœʁ] -You're one savvy negotiator.

7517 **pâturer** **graze**
vb Empêcher le bétail de pâturer le gazon traité avec BASAGRAN herbicide liquide.
[patyʁe] -Do not allow livestock to graze on BASAGRAN Liquid Herbicide treated turf.

7518 **bourdonnement** **buzz|hum**
m Plus de bourdonnement dans nos têtes.
[buʁdɔnmɑ̃] -No more buzzing inside our heads.

7519 **déraper** **skid**
vb Mais c'est là qu'on commence à déraper vers l'irréalisme, le pharisaïsme et l'intégrisme.
[deʁape] -This, however, is the start of the sideslip into lack of realism, self-righteousness and fundamentalism.

7520 **troc** **barter|bartering**
m Tout gouvernement se fonde sur le compromis et le troc.
[tʁɔk] -All government is founded on compromise and barter.

7521 **mystérieusement** **darkly**
adv Le contenu des conversations enregistrées circule mystérieusement dans les médias.
[misteʁjøzmɑ̃] -The contents of recorded conversations mysteriously circulate in the media.

7522 **attrister** **sadden**
vb Pour nous, ton départ ne peut que nous attrister.
[atʁiste] -We are simply saddened by your leaving.

7523 **dessinateur** **designer|draftsman**
m Ton prédécesseur était un grand dessinateur.
[desinatœʁ] -Guy who used to sit there was a great cartoonist.

7524 **éradiquer** **eradicate**
vb Pour ce qui est de la tuberculose, le calcul est identique, mais la maladie est plus difficile à éradiquer.
[eʁadike] -As regards TB, the mathematics are similar but it is more difficult to eradicate.

7525 **pamplemousse** **grapefruit**
m J'ai mangé un demi-pamplemousse pour le petit-déjeuner.
[pɑ̃pləmus] -I had half a grapefruit for breakfast.

7526 **ravager** **ravage|destroy**
vb On a pu aussi parvenir à l'équilibrer en ravageant le régime de soins de santé.
[ʁavaʒe] -The other way to balance the budget was to devastate the health care system.

7527 **autruche** **ostrich**
f[otʁyʃ]
C'est la plus belle autruche que j'ai jamais vue. -This is the most beautiful ostrich I've ever seen.

7528 **courroux** **wrath**
m
[kuʁu]
De même l'usage impropre de l'internet a suscité le courroux de beaucoup.
-Likewise, the misuse of the Internet drew the wrath of many.

7529 **magnat** **magnate**
m
[magna]
Lionel Shabandar, magnat de la communication, collectionneur et véritable brute épaisse.
-Lionel Shabandar, media tycoon, art collector and an absolute brute of a fellow.

7530 **corpus** **corpus**
m
[kɔʁpys]
Cette phrase et peut être quelques autres, doivent être retirées du corpus.
-These and perhaps other sentences need to be removed from the corpus.

7531 **formuler** **formulate|express**
vb
[fɔʁmyle]
Il pourrait ensuite soit présenter une série de solutions soit formuler une seule proposition claire.
-He could either present a series of options or formulate one clear proposal.

7532 **imposture** **imposture|fraud**
f
[ɛ̃pɔstyʁ]
La politique régionale européenne est surtout une imposture économique.
-European regional policy is, above all, an economic sham.

7533 **transpercer** **pierce|penetrate**
vb
[tʁɑ̃spɛʁse]
J'ai senti une épée de glace me transpercer le coeur.
-I felt a shard of ice pierce my heart.

7534 **embobiner** **bamboozle**
vb
[ɑ̃bɔbine]
Mais, mon chou, qui crois-tu embobiner ?
-But, sweetie... who the fuck do you think you're kidding?

7535 **troisièmement** **thirdly**
num
[tʁwazjɛmmɑ̃]
Troisièmement, le commerce international doit servir de moteur de développement.
-Thirdly, international trade must be harnessed as an engine for development.

7536 **gendarmerie** **police**
f
[ʒɑ̃daʁməʁi]
Entre-temps, je préviens la gendarmerie.
-In the meantime, I'm calling the police.

7537 **grognon** **grumpy; grumbler**
adj; m
[gʁɔɲɔ̃]
Tu es grognon.
-You're grumpy.

7538 **épingler** **pin**
vb
[epɛ̃gle]
Et je voudrais épingler un certain nombre d'éléments qui me paraissent importants.
-I would like to draw attention to a number of points which I think are important here.

7539 **anchois** **anchovy**
m
[ɑ̃ʃwa]
Toutefois, selon la rapporteure, le stock d'anchois n'a pas retrouvé son niveau.
-However, according to the rapporteur, the anchovy stock has not yet recovered.

7540 **stabiliser** **stabilize**

vb[stabilize] | En matière de politique énergétique en Europe, nous devons stabiliser l'accès à l'énergie. -When it comes to energy policy in Europe, we must stabilise access to energy.

7541 **esquive** **dodge**
f
[ɛskiv]
Madame la présidente, voilà une esquive intéressante.
-Madam Chairman, that is an interesting dodge.

7542 **hospitaliser** **hospitalize**
vb
[ɔspitalize]
Vingt-deux pour cent de la population de l'échantillon avaient été hospitalisés précédemment.
-"Twenty two per cent of the sample population had been previously hospitalized.

7543 **postérité** **posterity**
f
[pɔsteʁite]
Cela restera dans les annales de cette organisation pour la postérité.
-This is going to be noted in the records of this Organization for posterity.

7544 **pignon** **pinion|gear**
m
[piɲɔ̃]
Thomas conduit un vélo à pignon fixe.
-Thomas rides a fixed-gear bicycle.

7545 **cornet** **horn|screw**
m
[kɔʁnɛ]
Voulez-vous un cornet?
-Do you want a bag?

7546 **fourcher** **pitchfork**
vb
[fuʁʃe]
L'étiquette n'arrive qu'au moment de la fourchette et la bonne solution serait que ce soit au moment de la fourche!
-The label only comes along when the fork is poised; but the best solution would be to label when the pitchfork is poised.

7547 **charte** **charter|convention**
f
[ʃaʁt]
La Convention renforce la Charte, et la Charte complète la Convention.
-The Convention reinforces the Charter and the Charter supplements the Convention.

7548 **jaillir** **flow**
vb
[ʒajiʁ]
Les canalisations crevées laissent jaillir de l'eau qui forme des torrents de saleté.
-Torrents of filthy water spewed out of crushed pipe work.

7549 **qualification** **qualification**
f
[kalifikasjɔ̃]
Une qualification bien insignifiante pour gouverner.
-It's a qualification that is meaningless in terms of government.

7550 **cacao** **cocoa**
m
[kakao]
Les graines de cacao sont moulues et réduites en «pâte» (encore appelée «pure pâte» de cacao ou «masse» de cacao).
-The nibs are milled to give a fine cocoa "liquor" (also called cocoa "paste", or cocoa "mass").

7551 **savoureux** **tasty|savory**
adj
[savuʁø]
Il y a des extraits savoureux dans cette loi.
-There are some really juicy parts to this bill.

7552 **condor** **condor**
m
[kɔ̃dɔʁ]
Le condor de Californie a toujours captivé les gens.
-The California Condor has always captured the imagination.

7553 **constructeur** **builder**
m[kɔ̃stʁyktœʁ]
Nous fournissons des pièces détachées au constructeur automobile. -We supply parts to the auto manufacturer.

7554 **intégration** **integration**

f
[ɛ̃tegʁasjɔ̃]
L'intégration professionnelle est ainsi associée à l'intégration sociale.
-Professional integration is therefore associated with social integration.

7555 **résistant** **resistant**
adj
[ʁezistɑ̃]
Ils sont virtuellement insolubles dans l'eau et hautement résistant à la dégradation.
-They are virtually insoluble in water and highly resistant to degradation.

7556 **lunatique** **lunatic**
adj
[lynatik]
À l'exception de la frange lunatique des libéraux néerlandais, l'avis du Parlement est le même.
-Parliament is still of the same view with the exception of the lunatic fringe of the Dutch liberals.

7557 **survoler** **fly|fly over**
vb
[syʁvɔle]
J'ai eu le privilège discutable de survoler Haïti et le Chili à quelques semaines d'intervalle.
-I had the dubious privilege to fly over Haiti and Chile, within a couple of weeks of each other.

7558 **argenter** **silver**
vb
[aʁʒɑ̃te]
Le schiste n'est pas seulement noir, le schiste est blanc et argenté et gris.
-Slate doesn ' t have to be just black, it can be white or silver or grey.

7559 **border** **border|rim**
vb
[bɔʁde]
Cours « Border Security First Response Training », tenu à Nuevo Laredo (Tamaulipas).
-Course on border security first response training, Nuevo Laredo, Tamaulipas.

7560 **algèbre** **algebra**
f
[alʒɛbʁ]
T'es fâché avec l'algèbre de Boole ?
-Are you at odds with Boolean algebra?

7561 **dénouement** **outcome**
m
[denumɑ̃]
Mais contre Uesugi, impossible de prédire le dénouement.
-But, against Uesugi's Echigo army... it's impossible to predict the outcome.

7562 **dissiper** **dispel|clear**
vb
[disipe]
On s'efforce de dissiper les peurs, les inquiétudes et les doutes par la discussion.
-Fears, anxieties and doubts are dealt with through reassurance and discussion.

7563 **supportable** **bearable|tolerable**
adj
[sypɔʁtabl]
Peu de centres ont des activités qui rendraient la détention plus supportable.
-Very few of the centres offered activities to make imprisonment more bearable.

7564 **dépotoir** **dumping ground; refuse dump**
m; vb
[depɔtwaʁ]
Il semble apparemment acceptable d'utiliser l'Afrique comme dépotoir.
-It is apparently acceptable to use Africa as a dumping ground.

7565 **tunique** **tunic**
f
[tynik]
Crabtree, boutonnez cette foutue tunique.
-And Crabtree, do up that bloody tunic!

7566 **inconsciemment** **unconsciously**
adv[ɛ̃kɔ̃sjamɑ̃]
Les hommes aspirent inconsciemment à connaître l'excitation de l'aventure qu'apportent les conflits. -Men may even subconsciously wish for the excitement of adventure that conflicts present.

7567 **patio** **patio**

m
[pasjo]
Avez-vous une table dans le patio ?
-Do you have a table in the patio?

7568 **indécent**
indecent|improper
adj
[ɛ̃desɑ̃]
C'est antidémocratique, indécent, en conflit avec le principe d'égalité et, par conséquent, illégal.
-It is undemocratic, improper, in conflict with the principle of equality and, therefore, illegal.

7569 **empester**
stink
vb
[ɑ̃pɛste]
Entassée, elle empeste, mais dispersée, elle fait des merveilles.
-It stinks in a heap, but brings rich blessings when widely spread' .

7570 **berge**
bank
f
[bɛʁʒ]
Alice commençait à être très fatiguée d'être assise à côté de sa sœur sur la berge et de n'avoir rien à faire : une ou deux fois, elle avait jeté un coup d'œil dans le livre que sa sœur était en train de lire, mais il ne contenait aucune image ni conversation, « et à quoi sert un livre », pensait Alice, « sans images ni conversations ? »
-Alice was beginning to get very tired of sitting by her sister on the bank, and of having nothing to do: once or twice she had peeped into the book her sister was reading, but it had no pictures or conversations in it, 'and what is the use of a book,' thought Alice 'without pictures or conversation?'

7571 **solennel**
solemn
adj
[sɔlanɛl]
C'était un moment solennel; c'était un moment particulier; c'était un moment fort.
-It was a solemn moment; it was a special moment; it was a potent moment.

7572 **ballot**
bundle; clownish
m; adj
[balo]
Cela a dû tomber de votre ballot.
-This must have fallen out of your bundle.

7573 **mûrir**
mature|ripen
vb
[myʁiʁ]
Seules les institutions qui préservent l'expérience collective peuvent mûrir."
-Only institutions that preserve the collective experience can mature.'

7574 **froisser**
offend|crease
vb
[fʁwase]
J'espère ne froisser personne en affirmant que les choses ne sont pas aussi simples.
-I hope I am not shocking anyone by saying that it is not as easy as that.

7575 **brasserie**
brewery
f
[bʁasʁi]
Une brasserie qui a une capacité de production de 3,2 millions d'hectolitres par an compte 600 employés.
-A brewery with a production capacity of 3.2 million hectolitres per year has 600 employees.

7576 **fiole**
flask
f
[fjɔl]
Laisser déposer, puis décanter dans une autre fiole au moyen d'un petit papier filtre.
-Allow to clear and decant through a small filter paper into a flask.

7577 **certifier**
certify
vb[sɛʁtifje]
Il faut certifier la qualité, l'origine, les conditions de production et de transformation. -There must be a system of certificates of quality, origin and production and processing conditions.

7578 **mite**
moth
f
[mit]
Peut-être que la mite va se retransformer.
-It's possible we could get the moth to transform back.

7579 **éveil**
awakening

	m [evɛj]	Le rapport du Secrétaire général mentionne la création de « conseils de l'Éveil ». -The report of the Secretary-General talks about the creation of "Awakening Councils".
7580	**émoi**	**stir|emotion**
	m [emwa]	Monsieur le Président, Mesdames et Messieurs, honorable Assemblée vide, c' est avec émoi que j' ai écouté M. -Mr President, ladies and gentlemen, honourable empty Chamber, I have listened to Mr Poettering with excitement.
7581	**texture**	**texture**
	f [tɛkstyʁ]	La texture granuleuse de cette purée de pommes-de-terre est fort déplaisante. -The grainy texture of these mashed potatoes is deeply unpleasant.
7582	**dérailler**	**derail**
	vb [deʁaje]	Cela a fait dérailler nos plans d'élargissement des services de lutte contre le VIH/sida. -That has derailed plans to expand HIV/AIDS services.
7583	**geôlier**	**jailer**
	m [ʒolje]	Vous vous êtes querellée avec le geôlier et enfuie pour chercher de l'aide. -You quarreled with the jailor and I fled for help.
7584	**intentionnellement**	**intentionally**
	adv [ɛ̃tɑ̃sjɔnɛlmɑ̃]	L'instigateur est celui qui a intentionnellement convaincu un tiers de commettre le crime. -Abettor is the one who has deliberately persuaded somebody else to commit the crime.
7585	**préventif**	**preventive**
	adj [pʁevɑ̃tif]	Il faut également promouvoir le « journalisme préventif ». -There is also a need to promote "preventive journalism".
7586	**nébuleux**	**nebulous**
	adj [nebylø]	Ce point reste nébuleux également, et si vous la déposer trop tard, elle sera complètement inutile. -This too is unclear, and if you table it too late it will be utterly useless.
7587	**venimeux**	**venomous**
	adj [vənimø]	En outre, ce langage venimeux est en soi complètement incompréhensible, en dépit des explications fournies hier par la Commission lors du débat en plénière. -As a matter of fact, this venomous language is, in itself, quite incomprehensible, in light of the explanations given by the Commission yesterday during the debate in plenary.
7588	**insaisissable**	**elusive**
	adj [ɛ̃sezisabl]	La communauté internationale, insaisissable, porte une lourde responsabilité à cet égard. -The elusive international community bears a heavy responsibility for this.
7589	**entorse**	**sprain|strain**
	f [ɑ̃tɔʁs]	Je me suis fait une entorse. -I pulled a muscle.
7590	**rebondir**	**bounce|start up**
	vb [ʁəbɔ̃diʁ]	Je parle de quelque chose que tu peux faire rebondir. -I'm talking about something you can bounce.
7591	**mets**	**dish**
	m [mɛ]	On n'a pas préparé ce mets depuis des années. -We haven't prepared that dish in years.

7592 **garrot** **tourniquet**
m
[gaʁo]
Laissez-lui le garrot jusqu'au bloc.
-Don't touch the tourniquet until he's on the table.

7593 **électromagnétique** **electromagnetic**
adj
[elɛktʁɔmaɲetik]
Un robinet électromagnétique est employé pour admettre ou suspendre à distance l'arrivée du GPL.
-An electrical solenoid valve is used to switch the LPG flow on and off remotely.

7594 **Tchao!** **Ciao!**
int
[tkao!]
Mais tu ne seras pas là pour le voir. Tchao!
-Pity you won't be around to enjoy it. Bye!

7595 **libido** **libido**
f
[libido]
Mais ça semble augmenter sa libido.
-But it just seems to rev up her libido.

7596 **cortex** **cortex**
m
[kɔʁtɛks]
Cette matrice temporelle fonctionne avec un cortex.
-That's a temporal matrix running within a cortex.

7597 **fertilité** **fertility**
f
[fɛʁtilite]
Je pencherais pour un symbole de fertilité.
-That's one way of guess is it's some sort of fertility symbol.

7598 **quotidiennement** **daily**
adv
[kɔtidjɛnmɑ̃]
Cette information est actualisée périodiquement, parfois quotidiennement.
-The information is updated on a regular basis, sometimes daily.

7599 **cadran** **dial**
m
[kadʁɑ̃]
Ne touchez pas à ce cadran !
-Don't touch that dial.

7600 **enfler** **swell|inflate**
vb
[ɑ̃fle]
La dette enfle lorsque la personne à besoin de nourriture et de transport, et les taux d'intérêt sont tels que le remboursement devient impossible.
-The debt becomes inflated through charges for food, transport and interest on loans, making it impossible to repay and trapping the worker in a cycle of debt.

7601 **stipuler** **stipulate**
vb
[stipyle]
Il doit stipuler les mêmes obligations et responsabilités pour tous les États.
-It must stipulate the same obligations and responsibilities for all States.

7602 **déplorable** **deplorable**
adj
[deplɔʁabl]
Il est déplorable que des vies innocentes soient réduites à l'état de chiffres.
-It is deplorable that the lives of innocent people have become mere statistics.

7603 **inquisition** **inquisition**
f[ɛ̃kizisjɔ̃]
C'est McCarthy, ce sont les sorcières de Salem, c'est l'Inquisition!!! -It is McCarthy, the witches of Salem, the Inquisition!

7604 **trinité** **trinity**
f
[tʁinite]
En célébrant l'Incarnation, nous fixons notre regard sur le mystère de la Trinité.
-In celebrating the Incarnation, we fix our gaze upon the mystery of the Trinity.

7605 **buveur** **drinker**
m
[byvœʁ]
Le problème, c'est le récidiviste, le buveur chronique, celui qui conduit toujours en état d'ébriété.

-The problem is the repeat offender, the chronic drinker, the drinker who drinks and drives repeatedly.

7606 **paillasson** m [pajasɔ̃]
mat
Jack essuya ses pieds sur le paillasson.
-Jack wiped his feet on the doormat.

7607 **renouveau** m [ʁənuvo]
renewal
Le renouveau du vieux prussien a commencé au début des années quatre-vingt.
-The Old Prussian language revival began in the early 80's.

7608 **corbeille** f [kɔʁbɛj]
basket
Elle avait une corbeille pleine de pommes.
-She had a basket full of apples.

7609 **unanime** adj [ynanim]
unanimous
S'il faut pour ce faire obtenir le consentement unanime, alors je demande le consentement unanime.
-If it requires unanimous consent, then I would ask for unanimous consent.

7610 **pénitentiaire** adj [penitɑ̃sjɛʁ]
penitentiary
Le Président du Turkménistan a constaté la nécessité de réformer le système pénitentiaire.
-The President of Turkmenistan has noted the need for reform of the penal system.

7611 **mufle** m; adj [myfl]
oaf; caddish
Allez-vous-en, espèce de mufle français !
-Get out of the way, you big French oaf!

7612 **diversité** f [divɛʁsite]
diversity
A l'heure actuelle, 25 langues disparaissent chaque année ! Comprenez bien une chose : je ne me bats pas contre l'anglais ; je me bats pour la diversité.
-Currently, 25 languages are disappearing every year! Understand one thing: I'm not fighting against English, I fight for diversity.

7613 **math** m [mat]
math
Jack est bon en math.
-Jack is good at math.

7614 **interférer** vb [ɛ̃tɛʁfeʁe]
interfere
La Convention est sacrée ; nous ne pouvons pas interférer dans ses travaux.
-The Convention is sacrosanct: even minimal interference is out of the question.

7615 **alchimie** f; adj[alʃimi]
alchemy; alchemic
Il y avait une bonne alchimie entre eux. -They had good chemistry.

7616 **anarchiste** adj; m/f [anaʁʃist]
anarchist; anarchist
Ceux qui commettent ces attaques sont des anarchistes: ils utilisent le nom de l'Islam pour atteindre leur but anarchique, qui est de restaurer la dictature et de s'installer au pouvoir.
-Those who are carrying out these assaults are anarchists: they misuse the name of Islam for their anarchical aim to restore dictatorship with themselves in power.

7617 **alphabétique** adj [alfabetik]
alphabetical | alphabet
No 9 Code alphabétique pour la représentation des monnaies, février 1978
-No.9 Alphabetic code for the Representation of Currencies, February 1978

7618 **canif** m [kanif]
penknife
Je me suis coupé avec mon canif.
-I cut myself with my penknife.

7619 **paumé** **lost|godforsaken**
adj
[pome]
Il a l'air paumé.
-He looks lost.

7620 **allocation** **allocation|allowance**
f
[alɔkasjɔ̃]
La loi sur l'allocation de logement crée un droit à une telle allocation.
-The Housing Allowance Act provides a legal claim to a housing allowance.

7621 **rééducation** **re-education**
f
[ʁeedykasjɔ̃]
Il existe à Lipcani une colonie de rééducation par le travail réservée aux garçons.
-The Republic of Moldova has a Boys Colony of re-education through labour in Lipcani.

7622 **guérillero** **guerrilla**
m
[geʁijeʁo]
Il doit donc accepter son affirmation selon laquelle ses activités en faveur du PKK et sa présentation en tant que candidat guérillero lui faisaient courir un tel risque.
-It should therefore accept his claim that his activities for the PKK and his introduction as a guerilla candidate place him at such risk.

7623 **pourchasser** **chase**
vb
[puʁʃase]
Les policiers pourchassent et arrêtent des criminels violents.
-Police officers chase and catch violent criminals.

7624 **répercussion** **repercussion**
f
[ʁepɛʁkysjɔ̃]
La dépendance accrue envers les nouvelles technologies a une répercussion sur les opérations.
-An increasing reliance upon new technology is having an impact on operations.

7625 **métamorphoser** **metamorphose**
vb
[metamɔʁfoze]
La proportion des ressources propres dites traditionnelles ne cesse de s'amenuiser. Le système tout entier se métamorphose d'un réel financement autonome à une forme de transfert forfaitaire.
-The proportion of what are termed traditional own resources is decreasing all the time, and the whole system is mutating from genuine self-financing into the transfer of lump sums.

7626 **monologue** **monologue**
m[mɔnɔlɔg]
Je dois apprendre un monologue de Shakespeare, Richard III. -I have to memorize a monologue from Shakespeare's Richard 3.

7627 **icône** **icon**
f
[ikon]
Pour cela, la barre d' instruments contient l' icône Formulaire.
-The Form icon of the main toolbar opens a floating toolbar by long clicking the icon.

7628 **incomplet** **incomplete**
adj
[ɛ̃kɔ̃plɛ]
Des soins sont-ils prévus pour les femmes qui ont subi un avortement incomplet ?
-What provisions are made for the care of women with incomplete abortions?

7629 **intérim** **interim**
adj
[ɛ̃teʁim]
François Bon-temps, Premier Secrétaire, exercera les fonctions de chargé d'affaires par intérim.
-During his absence, Mr. François Bon-temps, First Secretary, is acting as Chargé d'affaires a.i.

7630 **sélectionner** **select**

	vb [selɛksjɔne]	Si le service technique le juge nécessaire, il peut sélectionner un échantillon supplémentaire. -If the Technical Service deems it necessary, it may select a further sample.
7631	**militant**	**activist**
	m [militɑ̃]	Kenyon Richards est un militant communautaire influent à Crenshaw. -Well, Kenyon Richards is an influential community activist in Crenshaw.
7632	**électrochoc**	**electroshock**
	m [elɛktʁoʃɔk]	L'invention concerne des technologies qui réalisent un système d'arme à électrochoc pour un dispositif mobile. -The technologies disclosed herein introduce an electroshock weapon system for a mobile device.
7633	**herpès**	**herpes**
	m [ɛʁpɛs]	L'herpès ano-génital est causé principalement par le virus herpès simplex de type 2. -Anogenital herpes is caused mainly by herpes simplex type 2 virus (HSV2).
7634	**pipeline**	**pipeline**
	m [pajplajn]	This is a reference to the Yamal-Europe natural gas pipeline and the 'Friendship' oil pipeline. -Il faisait référence au gazoduc Yamal-Europe et à l'oléoduc de l'"amitié".
7635	**perfusion**	**drip**
	f [pɛʁfyzjɔ̃]	Doribax est reconstitué puis dilué avant perfusion. -Doribax is reconstituted and then further diluted prior to infusion.
7636	**pollen**	**pollen**
	m [pɔlɛn]	Les abeilles aident les plantes à répandre le pollen. -Bees help plants spread their pollen.
7637	**grève**	**strike**
	f [gʁɛv]	La grève a nui à l'économie nationale. -The strike affected the nation's economy.
7638	**ponctuel**	**punctual**
	adj[pɔ̃ktɥɛl]	Elle a aussi établi un système d'enregistrement ponctuel et systématiquement mis à jour des livraisons d'armes interceptées sur le territoire national. -It also maintains an accurate and updated record of arms shipments seized in the national territory.
7639	**échelon**	**echelon**
	m [eʃlɔ̃]	Les aliments importés n'ont pas atteint cet échelon de la structure du commerce de détail. -Imported foods have not reached this level of the retail structure.
7640	**saligaud**	**bleeder|creep**
	m [saligo]	Elle m'a pris pour un saligaud. -She thought I was a creep.
7641	**frivole**	**frivolous**
	adj [fʁivɔl]	Monsieur le Président, le dernier rappel au Règlement est frivole et donc irrecevable. -Speaker, the last point of order was frivolous and therefore non-receivable.
7642	**circulaire**	**circular; circular**
	adj; f [siʁkylɛʁ]	La seconde plaque est sensiblement circulaire. -The second plate is substantially circular in shape.
7643	**centenaire**	**centenary; centenary**
	adj; m/f [sɑ̃tnɛʁ]	Il est possible que je sois centenaire, ou plus ; mais ne saurais le dire parce que je n'ai jamais vieilli comme les autres hommes, pas plus que je me

souviens d'une quelconque enfance.
-Possibly I am a hundred, possibly more; but I cannot tell because I have never aged as other men, nor do I remember any childhood.

7644 **sérénade** f [seʁenad] **serenade**
Une sérénade pour mon numéro un, si vous préférez.
-A serenade to my number one, if you will.

7645 **prêche** m [pʁɛʃ] **preaching**
Il est extrêmement important que le gouvernement pratique ce qu'il prêche.
-It is crucially important that the government practice what it preaches.

7646 **imprimeur** m [ɛ̃pʁimœʁ] **printer**
Cette opération sera réalisée par l'imprimeur lors du tirage.
-This process will be carried out by the printer during the print run.

7647 **aubaine** f [obɛn] **boon|windfall**
Considère que de ne pas obtenir ce que l'on veut est parfois une grande aubaine.
-Remember that not getting what you want is sometimes a wonderful stroke of luck.

7648 **dompter** vb [dɔ̃pte] **tame**
Nous ne pouvons les dompter, mais ensemble, nous pouvons modérer les dégâts qu'elles causent.
-We cannot tame them, but we can collectively mitigate their devastation.

7649 **puma** m [pyma] **puma**
Tu avais raison pour le puma.
-I guess you were right about that puma.

7650 **lux** m [lyks] **lux**
Dr Weaver, j'obtiens un résultat de 500 lux.
-Dr. Weaver, I'm getting a reading of 500 lux.

7651 **zeppelin** m [zɛplɛ̃] **zeppelin**
Le zeppelin ne finira pas aux mains ennemies.
-We cannot let ze zeppelin fall into enemy hands.

7652 **invraisemblable** adj [ɛ̃vʁɛsɑ̃blabl] **unlikely|incredible**
Il est invraisemblable et terrifiant que l'on en soit encore là en l'an 2000.
-It is incredible and horrific that this should still be happening in the year 2000.

7653 **coqueluche** f [kɔklyʃ] **whooping cough**
Est décrite la préparation d'un vaccin contre la coqueluche selon ce procédé.
-Preparation of a vaccine against pertussis in accordance with the method is illustrated.

7654 **acre** m [akʁ] **acre**
Pour une exploitation de 4000 acres, les coûts fixes ne sont que de 15 $ l'acre.
-On a 4,000-acre farm, the fixed cost is only $15 an acre.

7655 **alto** adj; m [alto] **alto; alto**
On ne peut pas improviser à l'alto.
-You can't improvise the viola.

7656 **limier** m [limje] **bloodhound**
C'est le limier de l'autre côté du couloir.
-She's the bloodhound from across the hall.

7657 **gothique** adj; m [gɔtik] **Gothic; Gothic**
La cathédrale de Cologne est la plus grande cathédrale gothique des pays germaniques.

-Cologne Cathedral is the largest gothic cathedral of the Germanic countries.

7658 **alléger** **alleviate**
vb
[aleʒe]
Je ferai tout ce que je peux pour alléger vos soucis.
-I'll do everything I can to alleviate your worries.

7659 **museau** **muzzle**
m
[myzo]
Le museau de la clé s'est cassé.
-The tip of the key broke.

7660 **ponte** **spawn**
f
[pɔ̃t]
Les femelles, affaiblies par la ponte, deviennent alors des proies faciles...
-The females, weakened by laying, make easy prey.

7661 **équivaloir** **amount**
vb
[ekivalwaʁ]
Le pays se situe au niveau cinq de sa catégorie (0,70), ce qui équivaut au rang de l'Italie.
-The Bahamas was fifth in its tier (0.70) which was equal to that of Italy.

7662 **privilégier** **privilege**
vb
[pʁivileʒje]
Bien au contraire, elles ont contribué à privilégier la "ruée vers le tribunal".
-On the contrary, they have helped to encourage the so-called 'rush to court'.

7663 **titulaire** **holder; titular**
m/f; adj
[titylɛʁ]
Elle en informe le titulaire du certificat.
-It shall notify the holder of the certificate to that effect.

7664 **hebdomadaire** **weekly; weekly**
adj; m[ɛbdɔmadɛʁ]
« Florile dalbe », magazine hebdomadaire destiné aux enfants et aux adolescents. -"Florile dalbe" is a weekly magazine for children and teenagers.

7665 **préoccupation** **concern|preoccupation**
f
[pʁeɔkypasjɔ̃]
Ma deuxième préoccupation concerne le développement d'une monoculture intensive.
-My second concern relates to the development of an intensive monoculture.

7666 **amadouer** **coax**
vb
[amadwe]
Nous pourrions espérer qu'en nourrissant le fauve, nous allons peu à peu l'amadouer.
-We may hope that by feeding the beast we can gradually tame it.

7667 **bouder** **sulk**
vb
[bude]
C'était un endroit parfait pour bouder.
-This was a good place to sulk.

7668 **épileptique** **epileptic; epileptic person**
adj; m/f
[epilɛptik]
Il était épileptique, et n'avait reçu aucun traitement depuis qu'il était détenu.
-He was epileptic, and had not received any medical help since his detention.

7669 **pagaie** **paddle**
f
[pagɛ]
Le MAINC ressemble à un canot qui descend rapidement une rivière, mais qui est sans pagaie.
-DIAND is like a canoe heading down a fast moving river but without a paddle.

7670 **folklore** **folklore**
m
[fɔlklɔʁ]
Dans le folklore japonais, les bakenekos sont des chats possédant des pouvoirs magiques.
-In Japanese folklore, bakeneko are cats with magical powers.

7671 **décadence** **decadence|decay**

	f [dekadɑ̃s]	L'Europe peut connaître rapidement une forme de décadence dangereuse. -Europe may swiftly slip into a dangerous form of decadence.
7672	**protestant** adj; m [pʁɔtɛstɑ̃]	**Protestant; Protestant** Nombre de princes catholiques d'Europe veulent briser votre règne protestant. -Most of the Catholic princes of Europe seek to topple you... and end your Protestant reign.
7673	**dinar** m [dinaʁ]	**dinar** Je vous fais une ristourne d'un dinar. -I suppose I could knock a dinar off the price for you.
7674	**absolution** f [apsɔlysjɔ̃]	**absolution** À ces dernières, on donne l'absolution totale et on fait en sorte de ne pas trop les achaler. -The Liberals give big business a sort of total absolution, they try not to bother it too much.
7675	**intérimaire** adj; m/f [ɛ̃teʁimɛʁ]	**interim; deputy** Cette proposition se veut une solution intérimaire. -Our proposal is meant to be an interim solution.
7676	**tranquillisant** m; adj [tʁɑ̃kilizɑ̃]	**tranquilizer; tranquilizing** Les effets du tranquillisant vont bientôt disparaître. -The effects of the tranquilizer should be nearly gone.
7677	**émerger** vb[emɛʁʒe]	**emerge** La vieille Europe doit se montrer capable de faire émerger la vision d'un nouveau monde. -Old Europe must prove itself capable of setting out a vision of a new world.
7678	**malchanceux** adj [malʃɑ̃sø]	**unlucky|unfortunate** Monsieur le Président, l'Afrique est un continent malchanceux. -Mr President, Africa is an unfortunate continent.
7679	**varier** vb [vaʁje]	**vary** Il y a deux scénarios de base, qui peuvent varier d'un État membre à l'autre. -There are two basic scenarios, which may vary from one Member State to another.
7680	**remise** f [ʁəmiz]	**delivery|remission** La remise des données d'événement est confirmée au moyen d'un service de transactions. -Delivery of events is confirmed using a transaction service.
7681	**usure** f [yzyʁ]	**wear** Les employés eux-mêmes épargneraient beaucoup d'usure à leur véhicule. -The employees would save a tremendous amount of wear and tear on their vehicles.
7682	**gîte** m [ʒit]	**home|shelter** J'ai cherché un gîte. -I looked for a place to crash.
7683	**lasso** m [laso]	**lasso|noose** Avec les bracelets pare-balles et le lasso de vérité. -Complete with bulletproof bracelets and lasso of truth.
7684	**inapte** adj [inapt]	**unfit** Et cela vaut également pour les personnes inaptes à donner leur consentement. -That also applies with regard to persons who are incapable of giving consent.

7685 **doré** **golden|coated**
adj
[dɔʁe]
À cette époque, les amplis Marshall sont dotés d'une face avant en plastique doré.
-This era of Marshall's amps had a plastic gold front panel.

7686 **maxime** **maxim**
f
[maksim]
Cette maxime est valable dans le cadre de la conduite des affaires internationales.
-That is a valid maxim for the conduct of international affairs.

7687 **bijoutier** **jeweler**
m
[biʒutje]
On vérifie auprès du bijoutier en ce moment.
-We're just following up with the jeweler now.

7688 **soudoyer** **bribe|tamper**
vb
[sudwaje]
Elle rejette l'allégation selon laquelle elle aurait tenté de soudoyer un témoin.
-She rejects the allegation that she tried to bribe a witness.

7689 **escapade** **escapade**
f
[ɛskapad]
Voyez-vous un inconvénient à ce que je me joigne à votre escapade à la campagne ?
-Do you mind if I join your trip to the country?

7690 **amande** **almond**
f[amɑ̃d]
Pour les amandes blanchies, la mention du calibre ou crible porte sur l'amande avant blanchiment. -In blanched almond kernels, the size or screen reference is related to the almond kernel before blanching.

7691 **éprouvant** **testing**
adj
[epʁuvɑ̃]
Plusieurs détenus ont observé des grèves de la faim particulièrement éprouvantes.
-Several prisoners have been on particularly stressful hunger strikes.

7692 **typhus** **typhus**
m
[tifys]
Le pays est fréquemment frappé par des épidémies de paludisme, de méningite, de typhus et de choléra.
-Frequent epidemics occur of malaria, meningitis, typhus and cholera.

7693 **colosse** **colossus; colossal**
m; adj
[kɔlɔs]
Sami est un colosse égyptien de 260 livres.
-Sami is a colossal 260 pound Egyptian guy.

7694 **narcotique** **narcotic; narcotic**
adj; m
[naʁkɔtik]
Ils ont observé des effets typiques d'un mode d'action narcotique : réaction de frayeur retardée ou absente et anorexie.
-Trout showed responses indicative of a narcotic mode of action, such as delayed or absent startle response and reduced feeding.

7695 **lacer** **lace**
vb
[lase]
Je me suis arrêté pour lacer ma chaussure...
-I stopped to tie my shoelace.

7696 **carrelage** **tiles**
m
[kaʁlaʒ]
Il faudra mieux nettoyer le carrelage.
-You have to do a better job on the tile.

7697 **albinos** **albino**
m
[albinos]
L'autre avait l'air d'un albinos.
-And the other guy was like an albino.

7698 **radicalement** **radically**
adv
[ʁadikalmɑ̃]
L'épidémie de VIH/sida a radicalement changé le monde dans lequel vivent les enfants.

-The HIV/AIDS epidemics have drastically changed the world in which children live.

7699 **vertical** **vertical**
adj
[vɛʁtikal]
Si vous cliquez sur le symbole Vertical, les dessins se voient attribuer une ombre verticale.
-Click Vertical to apply a vertical shadow behind the individual text characters.

7700 **genèse** **genesis**
f
[ʒənɛz]
La chambre de genèse est activée.
-Genesis chamber coming online, sir.

7701 **éphémère** **ephemeral; ephemeral**
adj; m
[efemɛʁ]
Les techniques sont particulièrement utiles pour la diffusion d'information éphémère par les nœuds.
-The techniques are particularly useful for the broadcast of ephemeral information by the nodes.

7702 **destinée** **destiny**
f[dɛstine]
Dans ce processus, c'est le peuple du Myanmar qui détermine sa propre destinée. -In this process, it is the people of Myanmar who will determine their own destiny.

7703 **prouesse** **prowess**
f
[pʁuɛs]
Cette prouesse a été réalisée par des hommes courageux et épris de liberté.
-This was a feat achieved by brave men, by men of freedom.

7704 **intoxication** **poisoning|addiction**
f
[ɛ̃tɔksikasjɔ̃]
Je parle à tout le monde de l'intoxication au mercure.
-I talk to anybody about mercury poisoning.

7705 **alcoolisme** **alcoholism**
m
[alkɔlism]
Les frais consécutifs aux maladies de l'alcoolisme sont énormes.
-The costs resulting from alcoholism are enormous.

7706 **chaman** **shaman**
m
[ʃaman]
Mon père était chaman chez les Chinook.
-My father was a shaman among the Chinook.

7707 **lucratif** **lucrative**
adj
[lykʁatif]
C'est un marché très lucratif, à l'heure actuelle, dans le secteur privé.
-There is a lucrative market for such information right now in the private sector.

7708 **appendicite** **appendicitis**
f
[apɛ̃disit]
J'ai l'appendicite.
-I have appendicitis.

7709 **tresser** **braid|twine**
vb
[tʁese]
J'ai pris le drap, je l'ai tressé.
-I took the bed sheet, braided it.

7710 **Antéchrist** **Antichrist**
m
[ɑ̃tekʁist]
Bolkestein est devenu le sauveur pour les uns, l'antéchrist pour les autres.
-Mr Bolkestein has become the saviour for some, and the Antichrist for others.

7711 **oméga** **omega**
m
[ɔmega]
Vous avez vu ce qui arrive à un oméga.
-You saw what happens to an omega.

7712 **joug** **yoke**
m
[ʒu]
Je ne vivrai pas sous ce joug.
-And I will not live under that yoke.

7713 **purification** **purification**
f
[pyʁifikasjɔ̃]
Nous répandons du sel en signe de purification.
-We sprinkle salt for purification.

7714 **insubordination** **insubordination**
f
[ɛ̃sybɔʁdinasjɔ̃]
Vous avez été viré pour insubordination.
-You know, you were fired for insubordination.

7715 **dédommager** **compensate**
vb
[dedɔmaʒe]
Il semblerait que le gouvernement de la Saskatchewan s'apprête à le dédommager.
-It would seem the Government of Saskatchewan is getting ready to compensate him.

7716 **tamisé** **screened|sifted**
adj
[tamize]
Il doit être parfaitement sec et tamisé avant de l'utiliser.
-It should be completely dry and sifted before using it

7717 **prédicateur** **preacher**
m
[pʁedikatœʁ]
Je cherche ce prédicateur aveugle, Hawks.
-I'm lookin' for that blind preacher named Hawks.

7718 **balayer** **sweep|scan**
vb
[baleje]
Une fois par jour, Kozon Komlan quittait la cellule pour balayer le bureau et les alentours.
-Once a day, he left the cell to sweep the office and the area around the post.

7719 **exigeant** **demanding|exacting**
adj
[ɛgziʒɑ̃]
En fait, le traité type d'extradition de l'Organisation des Nations Unies impose aux États une obligation beaucoup plus exigeante.
-In fact, the United Nations Model Treaty on Extradition places a more exigent obligation on Governments.

7720 **transfusion** **transfusion**
f
[tʁɑ̃sfyzjɔ̃]
À Sao Tomé-et-Principe, il existe un risque élevé de contamination par transfusion.
-In Sao Tome and Principe, there is a high risk of contamination by transfusion.

7721 **joyeusement** **merrily**
adv
[ʒwajøzmɑ̃]
Nous voterons joyeusement ce programme aujourd' hui ou demain.
-We will now formally adopt this programme today or tomorrow.

7722 **extradition** **extradition**
f
[ɛkstʁadisjɔ̃]
On peut distinguer entre « extradition déguisée » et « extradition de facto ».
-A distinction may be drawn between a “disguised extradition” and a “de facto extradition”.

7723 **hippodrome** **hippodrome**
m
[ipodʁom]
Tu marcheras le long de l'hippodrome.
-You shall walk along the Hippodrome.

7724 **couturière** **seamstress**
f
[kutyʁjɛʁ]
Il concerne la couturière Anni Münch.
-It concerns the seamstress, Anni Meunch.

7725 **garnement** **rascal**
m
[gaʁnəmɑ̃]
Quel garnement !
-What a rascal!

7726 **enfantin** **infantile**
adj
[ɑ̃fɑ̃tɛ̃]
Dans l'éducation enfantine la gratuité est étendue pour permettre aux parents de choisir librement l'établissement qui convient le mieux à leurs

attentes ou à leurs croyances.
-In the education of young children, free education is being extended in order to enable parents to choose freely the establishment that is best suited to their expectations or beliefs.

7727 **vitalité** f [vitalite] — **vitality|vigor**
La langue française favorise grandement la vitalité artistique francophone.
-The French language is a major stimulant of Francophone artistic vitality.

7728 **bastion** m [bastjɔ̃] — **bastion**
Ce bastion du mal affecte le délicat équilibre écologique.
-This bastion of evil upsets the delicate ecological balance.

7729 **geindre** vb[ʒɛ̃dʁ] — **whine|moan**
Florus, ton tour viendra dans une minute, alors arrête de geindre et de ronchonner! -Florus, you will get your chance in a minute, so stop whining and belly-aching at the back.

7730 **resplendissant** adj [ʁɛsplɑ̃disɑ̃] — **resplendent**
La contribution de la communauté bougainvillaise dans son ensemble est un exemple resplendissant pour le monde entier.
-The contribution of the Bougainvillean community in general is a shining example to the world as a whole.

7731 **Siam** m [sjam] — **Siam**
La Thaïlande, jadis connue sous le nom de Royaume de Siam, est située au cœur de l'Asie du Sud-Est.
-Thailand, formerly known as the Kingdom of Siam, lies in the heart of South-East Asia.

7732 **hippopotame** m [ipɔpɔtam] — **hippopotamus**
Les esclaves du Conseil le frappèrent avec leurs fouets en cuir d'hippopotame.
-The Council slaves whipped him with their hippopotamus hide whips.

7733 **abstrait** adj; m [apstʁɛ] — **abstract; abstract**
Le bonheur est un concept vraiment abstrait.
-The idea of happiness is extremely abstract.

7734 **pétrolier** m [petʁɔlje] — **tanker|oilman**
Un pétrolier géant vient de quitter le bassin.
-A huge tanker just pulled out from the dock.

7735 **défigurer** vb [defigyʁe] — **disfigure**
Les dépôts de suie défigurent les bâtiments et provoquent leur noircissement.
-Deposits of soot disfigure buildings and cause blackening.

7736 **profane** adj; m/f [pʁɔfan] — **profane; layman**
Vous mêlez avec désinvolture l'amour sacré et le profane.
-You mix sacred and profane love too casually.

7737 **suspens** m [syspɑ̃] — **suspense**
Si vous voulez sauver l'union économique et monétaire, ne laissez pas les obligations européennes en suspens.
-If you want to save the economic and monetary union, do not leave European treasury bonds hanging in the air.

7738 **disgrâce** f [disgʁas] — **disgrace**
Cela l'a finalement obligé à démissionner et à quitter en disgrâce les premières banquettes.
-This led ultimately to his resignation and retirement in disgrace to the backbenches.

7739 **colonial** — **colonial**

	adj [kɔlɔnjal]	Dans le passé colonial, ce pillage s'est fait de façon ouverte et éhontée. -In the colonial past, pillaging was carried out in an open and shameless fashion.
7740	**immigrer**	**immigrate**
	vb [imigʁe]	Les enfants mineurs peuvent immigrer avec leurs parents. -Minor children can immigrate with their parents.
7741	**bureaucrate**	**bureaucrat**
	m/f [byʁokʁat]	Alors il faut penser en bureaucrate. -So you got to think like a bureaucrat.
7742	**reconsidérer**	**reconsider**
	vb [ʁəkɔ̃sideʁe]	Il a recommandé au Royaume-Uni de reconsidérer son interprétation de l'article. -It recommended that the United Kingdom reconsider its interpretation of the article.
7743	**tricoter**	**knit**
	vb [tʁikɔte]	C' est ce qui arrive, Monsieur Prodi, quand Pénélope, contrairement à ce que lui enseigne l' Odyssée, détricote au lieu de tricoter! -That is what happens, Mr Prodi, when Penelope goes against the teaching of the Odyssey and unravels instead of knitting.
7744	**corsage**	**blouse|corsage**
	m [kɔʁsaʒ]	Si Fi défait un bouton de son corsage, tout va bien. -If Fi is wearing one button down on her blouse, everything's groovy.
7745	**tartiner**	**spread**
	vb [taʁtine]	La pâte à tartiner ne peut prétendre être bénéfique pour les enfants seulement parce qu' elle est pleine de vitamines et de substances minérales. -Chocolate spreads cannot claim to be good for children just because they are full of vitamins and minerals.
7746	**béret**	**beret**
	m [beʁɛ]	Dimanche dernier, j'avais mon béret. -Last Sunday, I had my beret.
7747	**déroutant**	**disconcerting**
	adj [deʁutɑ̃]	Dans notre cas, cette expérience est d'autant plus déroutante qu'elle a frappé notre petite société avec une soudaineté et une ampleur inattendues. -In our case that experience is all the more unnerving in that it has struck our small society with unexpected suddenness and magnitude.
7748	**psychanalyse**	**psychoanalysis**
	f [psikanaliz]	Appelons-le juste le parrain de la psychanalyse moderne... -Let's just call him the godfather of modern psychoanalysis...
7749	**pesanteur**	**gravity**
	f [pəzɑ̃tœʁ]	Un gradiomètre de pesanteur est combiné à un système d'isolation activement commandé à deux étages. -A gravity gradiometer is combined with a two-stage actively controlled isolation system.
7750	**artériel**	**arterial**
	adj [aʁteʁjɛl]	La prévalence de l'hypertension artérielle a été de 36,3 %. -The figure for the prevalence of arterial hypertension was 36.3 per cent.
7751	**phosphore**	**phosphorus**
	m [fɔsfɔʁ]	Est-ce que les engrais contiennent du phosphore ? -Do fertilizers contain phosphorus?
7752	**schizophrène**	**schizophrenic**

	adj	La politique communautaire en matière d'immigration reste schizophrène.
	[skizɔfʁɛn]	-Community policy on immigration continues to be schizophrenic.
7753	**aspiration**	**aspiration**
	f	L'élément allongé délimite un passage d'aspiration longitudinal.
	[aspiʁasjɔ̃]	-The elongated member defines a suction passageway which extends longitudinally therethrough.
7754	**débit**	**debit|output**
	m	Le débit autorisé est supérieur au débit limité.
	[debi]	-The permitted flow rate is greater than the restricted flow rate.
7755	**souplesse**	**flexibility|suppleness**
	f	Sa délégation apprécie la souplesse affichée par la délégation japonaise.
	[suplɛs]	-Her delegation appreciated the flexibility shown by the delegation of Japan.
7756	**rapprochement**	**reconciliation|link**
	m	Le rapprochement du compte courant est effectué chaque année depuis 1970.
	[ʁapʁɔʃmɑ̃]	-The reconciliation of the current account has been undertaken each year since 1970.
7757	**toxico**	**junkie**
	m/f	Je ne suis pas une toxico.
	[tɔksiko]	-I'm not a drug addict.
7758	**irakien**	**Iraqi**
	adj	Le dictateur irakien nargue une fois encore la communauté internationale.
	[iʁakjɛ̃]	-The Iraqi dictator is flouting the international community once more.
7759	**simulateur**	**simulator**
	m	Le simulateur fournit une répartition de probabilités.
	[simylatœʁ]	-The simulator generates an output in the form of a probability distribution.
7760	**habitat**	**habitat**
	m	Leur habitat est menacé par la déforestation.
	[abita]	-Their habitat is threatened by deforestation.
7761	**renier**	**deny|renounce**
	vb	Enfin, l'Afrique doit renier ses dettes.
	[ʁənje]	-Finally, Africa must disown its debts.
7762	**grièvement**	**severely**
	adv	Un élève a été grièvement blessé et évacué vers un hôpital de Jérusalem.
	[gʁijɛvmɑ̃]	-One student was seriously injured and evacuated to a Jerusalem hospital.
7763	**hardi**	**bold|daring**
	adj	Projet indubitablement hardi, l'Union est pourtant indispensable.
	[aʁdi]	-The proposed African Union is without doubt a bold but indispensable undertaking.
7764	**législation**	**legislation**
	f	Les compagnies de la liste Fortune 500 furent les plus durement touchées par la récente législation.
	[leʒislasjɔ̃]	-Fortune 500 companies were the hardest hit by recent legislation.
7765	**neiger**	**snow**
	vb	Les températures à Vienne à la fin de l'automne sont souvent basses, et il peut neiger.
	[neʒe]	-Late autumn in Vienna often features low temperatures, and snow is also possible.
7766	**logiquement**	**logically**

	adv [lɔʒikmɑ̃]	C'est l'unique recours, aussi bien logiquement et techniquement que juridiquement. -That is the only recourse logically, technically and legally remaining.
7767	**attirail**	**paraphernalia**
	m [atiʁaj]	On n'a pas trouvé de drogues dans son appartement, aucun attirail. -There was no drugs found in her apartment, no paraphernalia.
7768	**assortir**	**set**
	vb[asɔʁtiʁ]	De plus, la communauté internationale doit commencer à assortir les paroles d'actes. -The international community must furthermore begin to match rhetoric with action.
7769	**festivité**	**festivity**
	f [fɛstivite]	L'intérieur somptueux du restaurant Musala Palace crée une ambiance de festivité et de glamour. -The rich interior of Musala Palace Restaurant creates an ambience of festivity and glamour.
7770	**timidité**	**timidity**
	f [timidite]	Les hésitations et la timidité de ce Parlement face au Conseil constituent un obstacle énorme. -The timidity and shyness of this Parliament before the Council is a huge obstacle.
7771	**juvénile**	**juvenile**
	adj [ʒyvenil]	L'établissement du rapport sur la mortalité infantile et juvénile se poursuit. -Work has continued on the preparation of the report on infant and child mortality.
7772	**accroc**	**snag|infraction**
	m [akʁo]	Tout a fonctionné sans accroc. -Everything worked without a hitch.
7773	**pavé**	**paved; pavement**
	adj; m [pave]	Tu cherches un emploi, pas vrai ? Ne devrais-tu pas être en train de battre le pavé ? -You're looking for a job, aren't you? Shouldn't you be out pounding the pavement?
7774	**saga**	**saga**
	f [saga]	Le référendum de ce week-end mettra, je l'espère, un terme à cette saga. -The referendum at the end of this week will hopefully bring an end to the saga.
7775	**désireux**	**eager**
	adj [deziʁø]	Son gouvernement est désireux de trouver une solution globale à la dispute. -His Government was eager to find an overall solution to the dispute.
7776	**injure**	**insult|affront**
	f [ɛ̃ʒyʁ]	Et c'est faire injure à leur intelligence que d'avoir une attitude semblable. -It is an insult to their intelligence to show such an attitude.
7777	**épanouir**	**light up**
	vb [epanwiʁ]	Mais le talent ne peut éclore et s'épanouir en vase clos. -However, talent cannot bloom and flourish in a vacuum.
7778	**insérer**	**insert|slot**
	vb [ɛ̃seʁe]	Dans le deuxième sous-titre et au i) et au j), insérer ", wagon" après "véhicules" -In the second sub-heading and in (i) and (j) insert ", wagon" after "vehicles".
7779	**bis**	**bis; twice; repeat**

	m; adv; adj [bis]	Sans les difficultés objectives, je dirais bis. -If it wasn't for the objective difficulties, I would say bis.
7780	**myope** adj; m/f [mjɔp]	**short-sighted; myope** Une personne sur dix est myope. -One in ten people have myopia.
7781	**perversion** f [pɛʁvɛʁsjɔ̃]	**perversion** L'exemple le plus flagrant de cette perversion concerne les fonds structurels. -The most flagrant example of this perversion concerns the Structural Funds.
7782	**mégère** f [meʒɛʁ]	**shrew|vixen** Dommage qu'il soit marié à une mégère. -Too bad he's married to that shrew.
7783	**toison** f [twazɔ̃]	**fleece** Les moutons sont élevés pour leur toison et leur viande. -Sheep are bred for their fleece and their meat.
7784	**bouilloire** f [bujwaʁ]	**kettle** Elle quitta la cuisine avec la bouilloire. -She left the kitchen with the kettle boiling.
7785	**hamac** m [amak]	**hammock** Mindy dans un hamac et moi, avec une bière fraîche. -Mindy in a hammock and me with an ice-cold beer.
7786	**klaxonner** vb [klaksɔne]	**honk|sound** Qui est ce poisseux assez pour klaxonner là-bas? -Who is that tacky enough to honk out there?
7787	**bénéficiaire** m/f; adj [benefisjɛʁ]	**beneficiary; profitable** Puis-je écrire le nom du bénéficiaire en russe ? -Can I write the name of the beneficiary in Russian?
7788	**rizière** f [ʁizjɛʁ]	**paddy field** Les crabes grouillent dans la rizière. -Crabs are all over the paddy.
7789	**déviation** f [devjasjɔ̃]	**deviation** D'autres régions de la surface de raffinage peuvent également être décalées pour compenser la déviation. -Other regions of the refining surface can also be offset to compensate for deviation.
7790	**réintégrer** vb [ʁeɛ̃tegʁe]	**reinstate** Au point B), réintégrer la phrase précédemment supprimée. -In section (B), reinstate the sentence that had previously been deleted.
7791	**designer** m [dəziɲe]	**designer** Elle veut devenir designer. -She hopes to become a designer.
7792	**clignoter** vb [kliɲɔte]	**flash** Dans le cas d'un freinage d'urgence, les feux-stop peuvent clignoter. -In the case of an emergency braking the stop lamps may flash.
7793	**cavité** f [kavite]	**cavity** Plusieurs tubes concentriques relient la surface à la cavité. -A plurality of concentric pipes extend from the surface into the cavity.
7794	**napalm**	**napalm**

	m [napalm]	Corps calcinés au napalm, grenades lâchées par des gamins... -Napalm-charred bodies, children leaving grenades in your boots.
7795	**vandalisme**	**vandalism**
	m [vɑ̃dalism]	Les deux premières séries de vandalisme étaient classiques. -The first two rounds of vandalism, they were typical.
7796	**inceste**	**incest**
	m [ɛ̃sɛst]	L'inceste est un tabou que l'on rencontre dans presque toutes les cultures. -Incest is a taboo found in almost all cultures.
7797	**circoncire**	**circumcise**
	vb [siʁkɔ̃siʁ]	Dans certaines régions, les filles ne sont pas considérées comme mariables tant qu'elles n'ont pas été circoncises. -In some areas, girls are not considered marriageable unless they have been circumcised.
7798	**rempart**	**rampart**
	m [ʁɑ̃paʁ]	Dans cet appartement, je peux créer un rempart de stabilité et de prédictibilité. -In this apartment, I can create a rampart of stability and predictability.
7799	**recourir**	**resort**
	vb [ʁəkuʁiʁ]	Le couteau était si émoussé que je ne pus couper la viande avec et je dus recourir à mon couteau de poche. -The knife was so blunt that I could not cut the meat with it and I resorted to my pocket knife.
7800	**persécution**	**persecution**
	f [pɛʁsekysjɔ̃]	Évidemment, ces actes relèvent également d'une persécution religieuse, notamment la persécution de chrétiens. -Of course, these acts include religious persecution, namely the persecution of Christians.
7801	**faucheur**	**mower|reaper**
	m [foʃœʁ]	Chaque faucheur a son propre style. -Every reaper has their own style.
7802	**précepteur**	**tutor**
	m [pʁesɛptœʁ]	Je vais te désigner un précepteur. -Yes, I'm sending you to a tutor.
7803	**macaroni**	**macaroni**
	m [makaʁɔni]	C'est une des raisons pour lesquelles ils se nourrissent de Coca Cola et de macaroni. -That is partly why they are living on Coca-Cola and macaroni.
7804	**vigoureux**	**vigorous**
	adj [viguʁø]	Ses efforts de paix méritent l'appui vigoureux de l'Organisation des Nations Unies. -Its peacekeeping efforts deserve vigorous support from the United Nations.
7805	**logeur**	**landlord**
	m [lɔʒœʁ]	Ni d'argent, sauf quelques shillings qu'il devait à son logeur. -Nor any money, except a few shillings which he owed in rent to his landlord.
7806	**partiellement**	**partially**
	adv [paʁsjɛlmɑ̃]	Je ne peux pas m'empêcher de me sentir partiellement responsable. -I can't help but feel partly responsible.
7807	**déjouer**	**foil**
	vb [deʒwe]	Elle n'a ni le mandat ni la compétence pour traquer des terroristes ou déjouer leurs plans.

-It has neither the mandate nor the expertise to hunt down terrorists or to foil terrorist plots.

7808 **fautif** **incorrect|culprit**
adj; m[fotif]
À l'évidence, la sécheresse est la grande fautive dans la corne de l'Afrique. -Clearly, drought is the major culprit in the Horn of Africa.

7809 **amulette** **amulet**
f
[amylɛt]
Où est l'amulette ?
-Where's the Buddha amulet?

7810 **assignation** **summons|subpoena**
f
[asiɲasjɔ̃]
Cette assignation est soumise à l'approbation des autorités intéressées.
-Such assignment shall be made with the agreement of the competent authority.

7811 **injustement** **unfairly**
adv
[ɛ̃ʒystəmɑ̃]
Je ne crois pas que son discours soit injustement interrompu par le bruit.
-I think his speech perhaps is not being unduly interrupted by the noise in the House.

7812 **accidentel** **accidental|incidental**
adj
[aksidɑ̃tɛl]
Cet idéal canadien n'est pas accidentel.
-And that Canadian idea is not accidental.

7813 **prélèvement** **sample; compensatory**
m; adj
[pʁelɛvmɑ̃]
Cette invention concerne un dispositif à main de prélèvement ainsi que le procédé correspondant.
-A hand-held sampling apparatus and method are provided.

7814 **chapelet** **beads|rosary**
m
[ʃaplɛ]
C'est un chapelet d'îles éparses... dans l'immense océan cosmique.
-It's a sparse and rather typical chain of islands... in the immense cosmic ocean.

7815 **asticot** **maggot**
m
[astiko]
La digestion de l'asticot peut générer une chaleur de 50° C.
-Maggot digestion can generate heat up to 125 degrees.

7816 **dissoudre** **dissolve|deactivate**
vb
[disudʁ]
Le tribunal peut dissoudre le mariage à la demande de l'un ou de l'autre époux.
-Court may dissolve marriage following the application of one or both spouses.

7817 **tapisserie** **tapestry**
f
[tapisʁi]
Chaque famille apporte une nouvelle couleur à la grande tapisserie canadienne et l'embellit de sa présence.
-Each family brings new patterns to the varied Canadian tapestry and enriches it by their presence.

7818 **contravention** **violation**
f
[kɔ̃tʁavɑ̃sjɔ̃]
J'ai reçu une contravention.
-I got a traffic ticket.

7819 **blocus** **blockade**
m
[blɔkys]
Le blocus par la Grande-Bretagne et les autres alliés fut couronné de succès.
-The blockade by Britain and the other allies was very successful.

7820 **caddie** **caddy|trolley**
m
[kadi]
Vider les produits du caddie actuel.
-Empty all products from the current shopping cart.

7821 **tombola** **raffle**

	f	J'ai gagné la tombola.
	[tɔ̃bɔla]	-I won the raffle.
7822	**sillage**	**wake**
	m	La cité tremblait dans son sillage.
	[sijaʒ]	-The city trembling in his wake.
7823	**croupier**	**croupier**
	m	C'est un croupier.
	[kʁupje]	-He's a casino dealer.
7824	**cellier**	**cellar**
	m	Si je pouvais retourner au cellier...
	[selje]	-If I could just go back to the cellar...
7825	**éducatif**	**educative**
	adj	Nous avons discuté la question d'un point de vue éducatif.
	[edykatif]	-We discussed the matter from an educational point of view.
7826	**scier**	**saw**
	vb	Selon les règles de l'Office des forêts, 25 % des arbres abattus devraient être sciés dans le pays.
	[sje]	-According to FDA rules, 25 per cent of the volume of logs felled should be sawn in the country.
7827	**remous**	**swirl**
	m	Le milieu est introduit pour un échange intensif de matière pratiquement exclusivement dans la région de ces remous de courant liquide.
	[ʁəmu]	-The medium is introduced for an intensive material exchange substantially exclusively in the area of said liquid stream eddy.
7828	**cloison**	**partition**
	f	La cloison présente une pluralité de trous.
	[klwazɔ̃]	-The partition has a plurality of holes formed therein.
7829	**instantané**	**instant; snapshot**
	adj; m	Tout en agitant le café instantané, elle lui ajoutait du lait.
	[ɛ̃stɑ̃tane]	-She stirred the instant coffee and poured in milk.
7830	**dissertation**	**dissertation**
	f	J'avais besoin de travailler sur une dissertation.
	[disɛʁtasjɔ̃]	-I had to work on an essay.
7831	**miaou**	**meow**
	m	Disons juste "miaou" et restons-en là.
	[mjau]	-Well, let's just say "meow" and leave it at that.
7832	**improvisation**	**improvisation**
	f	Actuellement, la part d' improvisation est encore beaucoup trop importante.
	[ɛ̃pʁɔvizasjɔ̃]	-There is still too much improvisation going on at the moment.
7833	**broyeur**	**crusher**
	m	Le robot à chenilles existant a été modifié et il lui a été ajouté un collecteur, un broyeur, un agitateur amélioré et un groupe motopompe hydraulique.
	[bʁwajœʁ]	-The existing deep sea crawler was being modified with the addition of a collector, crusher, enhanced slurry pump and hydraulic power pack.
7834	**cocon**	**cocoon**
	m	J'étais enveloppée dans mon cocon...
	[kɔkɔ̃]	-I was wrapped up in my cocoon...
7835	**rocker**	**rock musician**
	m	D'après le fabricant, il est customisé pour un rocker en particulier.
	[ʁɔke]	-According to the manufacturer, it's custom-made for one particular rocker.
7836	**échographie**	**ultrasound|scan**

f[ekogʁafi] Faites faire une échographie et appelez la chirurgie. -Page Radiology to come do an ultrasound and get Surgery down here.

7837 **bordure** **border**
f
[bɔʁdyʁ]
Pour définir une bordure, vous pouvez également utiliser l' icône Bordure dans la barre d' objets.
-To set a border, you can also use the Borders icon on the object bar.

7838 **mortuaire** **mortuary**
adj
[mɔʁtɥɛʁ]
Puis l'ambulance est partie, laissant le corps qui devait être emmené par un fourgon mortuaire.
-The ambulance then left, leaving the body to be collected by a mortuary van.

7839 **fidèlement** **faithfully**
adv
[fidɛlmɑ̃]
À quoi sert-il de suivre fidèlement la recette du Fonds monétaire international ?
-Why should we faithfully comply with the recipe of the International Monetary Fund?

7840 **galère** **galley**
f
[galɛʁ]
La galère est la représentation héraldique conventionnelle du bateau.
-The galley is the conventional heraldic representation of a ship.

7841 **surréaliste** **surrealist**
m/f
[syʁealist]
Ça avait un certain charme surréaliste.
-There was a certain surreal quality to it.

7842 **incitation** **incitement**
f
[ɛ̃sitasjɔ̃]
Le moindre signe de faiblesse ou d'hésitation de notre part sera interprété comme une incitation.
-The least sign of weakness or hesitation... will be interpreted as incitement.

7843 **donation** **donation**
f
[dɔnasjɔ̃]
Il fit donation d'innombrables pièces au musée.
-He donated countless pieces to the museum.

7844 **guirlande** **garland|string**
f
[giʁlɑ̃d]
Une fois un ivrogne est venu dans notre maison avec une guirlande.
-Once a drunkard barged in our house with a garland.

7845 **Vlan!** **Whack!**
int
[vlɑ̃!]
Et vlan! Encore une porte qui claque !
-Bang! Another door slamming!

7846 **saxo** **sax**
m
[sakso]
Vous savez, je joue du saxo ténor.
-You know, I play tenor sax.

7847 **languir** **languish**
vb
[lɑ̃giʁ]
Un ancien enfant soldat canadien continue de languir à Guantanamo Bay.
-A former Canadian child soldier continues to languish at Guantanamo Bay.

7848 **décliner** **decline|refuse**
vb
[dekline]
Il regrette de devoir décliner cette invitation en raison d'obligations professionnelles.
-He was sorry to have had to decline the invitation because of work commitments.

7849 **scierie** **sawmill**
f[siʁi]
La société DARA s'est engagée la même année dans la production industrielle en construisant une scierie à Mangina. -The same year, DARA

engaged in industrial production with the construction of a sawmill in Mangina.

7850 **consentir** **consent**
vb
[kɔ̃sɑ̃tiʁ]
La deuxième restriction tient à ce que la famille doit consentir au mariage d'un mineur.
-The second restriction is that the family must consent to the marriage of a minor.

7851 **divulguer** **disclose**
vb
[divylge]
On appelle « être objectif » le fait de ne pas divulguer le côté duquel on est.
-Being objective means not telling everybody whose side you are on.

7852 **mixte** **mixed**
adj
[mikst]
Le système électoral macédonien est de type mixte.
-The electoral model in the Republic of Macedonia is of mixed character.

7853 **messagerie** **messaging|courier service**
f
[mesaʒʁi]
La messagerie texte interentreprise est utilisée depuis quelques années déjà.
-Inter-carrier text messaging has been in place for the last few years.

7854 **indicateur** **indicator**
m
[ɛ̃dikatœʁ]
Une chaleur inhabituelle est un indicateur de mouchard.
-Why? Unusual heat is an indicator of... spyware.

7855 **rumba** **rumba**
f
[ʁɛ̃ba]
You better cancel that rumba lesson.
-Tu ferais mieux d'annuler ton cours de rumba.

7856 **triade** **triad**
f
[tʁijad]
Voilà une triade dont il ne faut pas s'approcher.
-There is a triad from which we certainly want to keep our distance.

7857 **écuyer** **squire**
m
[ekɥije]
Votre écuyer était tellement ivre la veille qu'il...
-Your squire had gotten so drunk the night before that he threw up.

7858 **armurerie** **armory**
f
[aʁmyʁʁi]
Nous n'avons que deux personnes assignées à l'armurerie.
-We only have two crewmen assigned to the Armory full-time.

7859 **confrère** **colleague**
m
[kɔ̃fʁɛʁ]
Je voudrais féliciter le rapporteur, mon confrère M. Fjellner, pour son travail sur ce rapport.
-I should like to congratulate the rapporteur, my colleague Mr Fjellner, on his work on this report.

7860 **épique** **epic**
adj
[epik]
Nous devons tous mener cette bataille épique, ensemble, en alliés et en partenaires.
-We must all fight this epic battle together as allies and partners.

7861 **braqueur** **raider|robber**
m
[bʁakœʁ]
Pouvez-vous nous dire à quoi ressemblait le braqueur ?
-Can you tell us what the bank robber looked like?

7862 **détritus** **litter**
m
[detʁitys]
Le travail consiste essentiellement à débroussailler et évacuer les détritus.
-The work mostly consists of removing undergrowth and clearing away litter.

7863 **transmetteur** **transmitter**
m[tʁɑ̃smɛtœʁ]
La CPAC est le transmetteur officiel de nos messages. -CPAC is the official transmitter of our messages.

7864 **clarinette** **clarinet**

	f [klaʁinɛt]	La clarinette réussirait peut-être à me tirer de la rue. -He said that if the piano didn't keep me off the streets...... maybe the clarinet would.
7865	**clavicule** f [klavikyl]	**clavicle** La clavicule intercostale d'un brontosaure. -That's the intercostal clavicle of a brontosaurus.
7866	**chevreuil** m [ʃəvʁœj]	**roe|deer** Les chiens se rapprochaient du chevreuil. -The dogs were closing in on the deer.
7867	**lyncher** vb [lɛ̃ʃe]	**lynch** Nous ne lynchons pas les assassins du Rwanda - nous les jugeons! -We are not going to lynch the murderers in Rwanda - we are bringing them to trial!
7868	**opposant** adj; m [ɔpozɑ̃]	**opponent; oppositionist** Alexander Kazulin, un opposant notoire de M. Lukaszenko. -She is the wife of Mr Alexander Kazulin, a prominent opponent of Mr Lukaszenko.
7869	**poussiéreux** adj [pusjeʁø]	**dusty** Ou s'agira -t-il d'une résolution de plus destinée à terminer dans quelque placard poussiéreux? -Or will this be yet another UN resolution for filing in some dusty cabinet.
7870	**amender** vb [amɑ̃de]	**amend** Nous souhaiterions donc le modifier ou l'amender. -Consequently, we would like to amend it.
7871	**cachemire** m [kaʃmiʁ]	**cashmere** Pithoragarh est communément appelé le "petit cachemire". -Pithoragarh is popularly known as the "little Kashmir".
7872	**immersion** f [imɛʁsjɔ̃]	**immersion|diving** L'invention porte sur un équipement d'immersion à sec. -The invention relates to a dry immersion equipment.
7873	**ethnique** adj [ɛtnik]	**ethnic** L'identité ethnique d'une personne est fonction de son origine ethnique. -The ethnic identity of a person is traced through his/her ethnic origin.
7874	**islamique** adj [islamik]	**Islamic** Il y aura une condition : ces femmes seront obligées de respecter la loi islamique. -There will be one condition: these women will have to respect the law of Islam.
7875	**survenir** vb [syʁvəniʁ]	**occur|arise** Nous envisageons toutes les situations hypothétiques qui pourraient survenir. -We are looking at whatever hypothetical possibilities might arise.
7876	**interface** f [ɛ̃tɛʁfas]	**interface** L'unité interface entrée/sortie communique avec les équipements domestiques. -The input/output interface unit communicates with the home appliances.
7877	**convenance** f[kɔ̃vənɑ̃s]	**convenience** Dans ce cas, par convenance politique. -In this case, it was done out of political convenience.
7878	**amorce**	**bait**

	f [amɔʁs]	Le ministre ira-t-il voir le premier ministre pour lui demander d'amorcer ce programme avant que quelqu'un soit tué ? -Would the minister please go to the Prime Minister and ask him to initiate the program before we have a death?
7879	**emplir**	**fill**
	vb [ɑ̃pliʁ]	En me débattant pour me dégager, j'ai aggravé ma situation, et la neige a commencé à m'emplir la bouche, alors que je peinais déjà à respirer. -As I struggled I became more and more immersed, snow began to fill my gasping mouth.
7880	**ténor**	**tenor**
	m [tenɔʁ]	Au second... derrière un ténor. -In the second act... behind a tenor.
7881	**insatiable**	**insatiable**
	adj [ɛ̃sasjabl]	De surcroît, les firmes pharmaceutiques étrangères, dont l'appétit est insatiable, consomment plus de la moitié du budget de mon pays consacré à la santé. -On top of that, the insatiable and greedy foreign pharmaceutical corporations are consuming more than half of my country's health budget.
7882	**sonate**	**sonata**
	f [sɔnat]	Elle donna une sonate. -She played a sonata.
7883	**niais**	**simpleton; simple**
	m; adj [njɛ]	Il est un peu niais. -He's a bit naive.
7884	**hirondelle**	**swallow**
	f [iʁɔ̃dɛl]	Une hirondelle vole très vite. -A swallow flies very swiftly.
7885	**capitulation**	**capitulation**
	f [kapitylasjɔ̃]	Aimer veut dire abandonner le pouvoir, c'est une capitulation mutuelle. -Loving someone means we have to relinquish power, it's mutual surrender.
7886	**extravagant**	**extravagant**
	adj [ɛkstʁavagɑ̃]	C'est juste que tout ça est trop extravagant. -It's just this is all so extravagant.
7887	**dominant**	**dominant**
	adj [dɔminɑ̃]	Celle-ci deviendra le langage dominant du futur. -This will be the dominant language of the future.
7888	**pardessus**	**overcoat**
	m [paʁdəsy]	Un bouton du pardessus est tombé. -A button from his overcoat fell off.
7889	**nuance**	**shade|nuance**
	f [nyɑ̃s]	Tout se passe comme si le mot «nuance» était banni du discours des députés ministériels. -Things are happening as if the word nuance was prohibited in ministers' speeches.
7890	**caboche**	**noggin**
	f[kabɔʃ]	Lui coller un pruneau dans la caboche. -Put a bullet right in his noggin.
7891	**saper**	**undermine**
	vb [sape]	Des pirates informatiques ont été en mesure de s'introduire dans le système informatique de l'entreprise et de saper la sécurité de son réseau.

-Hackers were able to break into the company's computer system and undermine its network security.

7892 **murmurer** vb [myʁmyʁe]
murmur
Il nous faut quelqu'un pour lui murmurer à l'oreille.
-We need someone just to whisper in his ear.

7893 **carillon** m [kaʁijɔ̃]
carillon
On a entendu le carillon cette nuit.
-We heard the carillon last night.

7894 **pat** adj; m [pat]
stalemate; stalemate
Et tu sais pourquoi c'est un pat ?
-And you know why it's a stalemate?

7895 **humer** vb [yme]
smell
Je pense que les gens devraient s'arrêter et humer l'odeur des roses.
-I think people should stop and smell the roses.

7896 **originalité** f [ɔʁiʒinalite]
originality
Le talent provient de l'originalité, qui est une manière spéciale de penser, de voir, de comprendre et de juger.
-Talent comes from originality, which is a special way of thinking, seeing, understanding, and judging.

7897 **sténo** f [steno]
shorthand|stenographer
Mais ne me demandez pas de faire sténo.
-Just don't ask me to do shorthand.

7898 **repêcher** vb [ʁəpeʃe]
recover
Les aéronefs à voilure fixe ne peuvent pas descendre des treuils pour repêcher des naufragés.
-Fixed wing aircraft cannot lower winches to recover people out of the sea.

7899 **spontanément** adv [spɔ̃tanemɑ̃]
spontaneously
Elles n'ont pas été prises spontanément et volontairement par les Iraquiens.
-They are not something that came forward willingly and freely from the Iraqis.

7900 **incorrect** adj [ɛ̃kɔʁɛkt]
incorrect
Désormais, il ne sera plus possible de les tromper avec un étiquetage incorrect.
-From now on, it will no longer be possible to deceive them with incorrect labelling.

7901 **verge** f [vɛʁʒ]
yard|rod
Ce tissu est vendu à la verge.
-This cloth is sold by the yard.

7902 **aigri** adj [egʁi]
embittered
Je ne veux pas ressortir aigri de cette expérience.
-I don't want this to make me bitter.

7903 **originel** adj[ɔʁiʒinɛl]
original
Selon l'ordre du jour originel, on devrait passer aux rapports sur la concurrence. -According to the original agenda, the competition reports should now follow.

7904 **bulldozer** m [byldɔzɛʁ]
bulldozer
Vous ne réussirez aucune réforme du marché avec ces tactiques de bulldozer.
-You will not achieve market reform with those bulldozer tactics.

7905 **déguster**
savor

vb
[degyste]
À déguster avec un vin pétillant canadien.
-Enjoy with a glass of Canadian bubbly.

7906 **réglementaire** **regulation**
adj
[ʁɛgləmɑ̃tɛʁ]
Le Gouvernement entend faire de son utilisation une obligation réglementaire.
-The government intends to introduce a statutory obligation to use the reporting code.

7907 **présomptueux** **presumptuous**
adj
[pʁezɔ̃ptɥø]
Monsieur le Président, essayer de commenter le sommet de Copenhague en deux minutes serait présomptueux.
-It would be arrogance to attempt to sum up the Copenhagen Summit in two minutes.

7908 **osseux** **bony|angular**
adj
[ɔsø]
Un test DEXA de densité du tissu osseux est assuré tous les 2 à 5 ans aux femmes de plus de 50 ans.
-A DEXA bone density check up is provided to women over 50 every 2-5 years.

7909 **revendeur** **dealer**
m
[ʁəvɑ̃dœʁ]
Cette règle a pour but d'exonérer le revendeur de responsabilité pour contrefaçon.
-The rule serves to immunize a reseller from infringement liability.

7910 **décontracter** **relax**
vb
[dekɔ̃tʁakte]
Boire du vin, tu vas te décontracter.
-We'll have wine, you can relax.

7911 **malt** **malt**
m
[malt]
Le dispositif susdit convient particulièrement pour broyer le malt.
-Said device is designed in particular for the crushing of malt.

7912 **gospel** **gospel**
m
[gɔspɛl]
Nous devons vous enseigner les principes du gospel.
-We must teach you the gospel principles.

7913 **rave** **rave**
f
[ʁav]
Les résultats pourraient nous mener à la rave.
-Results might lead us to the rave.

7914 **administratif** **administrative; executive**
adj; m
[administʁatif]
L'article 214b, selon mon opinion une des dispositions encore plus étranges du Code administratif général du Land de Schleswig-Holstein, semble stipuler que quelqu'un qui voit un éléphant rose doit lui délivrer un reçu.
-Section 214b, in my opinion one of the stranger provisions of the Land of Schleswig-Holstein's General Administrative Code, seems to imply that somebody who sees a pink elephant must give it a receipt.

7915 **enlacer** **embrace**
vb[ɑ̃lase]
Veux-tu toujours m'enlacer ? -Do you still want to give me a hug?

7916 **fourneau** **furnace**
m
[fuʁno]
Comme une fougère à côté d'un fourneau.
-Like a fern by the furnace.

7917 **recaler** **fail**
vb
[ʁəkale]
Lorsque l'on parle d'Europe, cela me rappelle d'une certaine manière l'école, où nous disions toujours "j'ai réussi" ou "je me suis fait recaler".
-When we talk about Europe, it reminds me a bit of school, where we always said 'I have passed' or 'they have failed me'.

7918 **flatterie** **flattery**

f La flatterie ne te mènera nulle part.
[flatʁi] -Flattery will get you nowhere.

7919 **distingué** **distinguished**
adj Il avait les traits d'un étudiant universitaire distingué.
[distɛ̃ge] -His features were of the type of a distinguished College student.

7920 **flamber** **blaze|flame**
vb Disons, que j'ai les moyens de flamber.
[flɑ̃be] -You could say... I've got money to burn.

7921 **panoramique** **panoramic**
adj L'écran LCD couleur haute résolution offre un retour visuel complet des positions de panoramique et des autres fonctions actives.
[panɔʁamik] -The high-resolution color LCD gives you rich visual feedback of your pan positions and other onscreen functions.

7922 **hindou** **Hindu; Hindu**
adj; m Ils sont liés au meurtre d'un dirigeant hindou que la police attribue aux maoïstes.
[ɛ̃du] -This is connected with the murder of a Hindu leader, a crime that the police blame on Maoists.

7923 **féministe** **feminist; feminist**
adj; m/f Il est bien meilleur féministe que toi.
[feminist] -He's a much better feminist than you are.

7924 **surcharge** **overload**
f Un contrôleur détermine si une condition de surcharge de la première source d'alimentation existe.
[syʁʃaʁʒ] -A controller determines whether an overload condition of the first power source exists.

7925 **approfondir** **deepen**
vb Les échanges personnels sont essentiels pour approfondir cette reconnaissance.
[apʁɔfɔ̃diʁ] -Personal exchanges are essential in order to deepen such recognition.

7926 **lavette** **mop; wet**
f; adj Maintenant mon sous-vêtement est trempé de jus de lavette.
[lavɛt] -Now my undershirt is wet with mop juice.

7927 **hyène** **hyena**
f Le jappement de la hyène résonne comme un rire.
[jɛn] -The hyena's bark sounds like laughter.

7928 **fracasser** **smash**
vb[fʁakase] Personnellement, je crains que ceci ne soit que la partie visible de l'iceberg contre laquelle le navire de l'Union européenne va immanquablement se fracasser. -I myself fear that this is only the tip of the iceberg against which the ship of the European Union is bound to shatter into pieces.

7929 **déporter** **deport**
vb En 1755, l'Angleterre a décidé de déporter les Acadiens, les chassant de leurs terres.
[depɔʁte] -In 1755, England chose to deport the Acadians from their lands.

7930 **ingénierie** **engineering**
f Je pourrais aider Trip en ingénierie.
[ɛ̃ʒeniʁi] -I could give Trip a hand in Engineering.

7931 **chaotique** **chaotic**
adj Quand l'univers devient chaotique, rien ne vaut une assiette de sardines.
[kaɔtik] -When the universe is being chaotic, there's nothing like a good old-fashioned plate of sardines.

7932 **armistice** **armistice|truce**
m
[aʁmistis]
Horthy va annoncer un armistice avec les Russes.
-Horthy is about to announce an armistice with the Russians.

7933 **serviable** **helpful**
adj
[sɛʁvjabl]
Je pense que vous seriez plus serviable.
-I thought you'd be more helpful.

7934 **piraterie** **piracy**
f
[piʁatʁi]
Nous devons agir contre la piraterie et contre les facteurs qui la sous-tendent.
-We need to act against piracy, as well as the roots of piracy.

7935 **estrade** **platform|stage**
f
[ɛstʁad]
Plus tard, un microphone et un haut-parleur avaient été installés sur la place, sur une estrade.
-Later, a microphone and loudspeakers were installed on a podium in the square.

7936 **fonte** **melting|font**
f
[fɔ̃t]
La construction est en matériaux réfractaires traditionnels, voire en fonte.
-The construction is made with standard refractory materials, i.e. cast iron.

7937 **gaga** **gaga**
adj
[gaga]
Merci, je ne suis pas encore gaga.
-Thank you, but I'm not gaga yet.

7938 **choucroute** **sauerkraut**
f
[ʃukʁut]
On retrouve, entre autres mets traditionnels, l'anguille marinée, le boudin noir et la choucroute à la viande de porc.
-Among the traditional dishes are marinated eel, blood sausage and sauerkraut stew with pork.

7939 **administrer** **administer**
vb
[administʁe]
Il a pour tâche d'appliquer la loi et d'administrer les affaires du pays.
-The prime minister exercises regulatory power and may delegate certain of his powers to ministers.

7940 **assemblage** **assembly**
m
[asɑ̃blaʒ]
Il existait un assemblage inhabituel d'organismes dans ces évents.
-There was an unusual assemblage of organisms in those vents.

7941 **retoucher** **retouch|touch**
vb[ʁətuʃe]
Les logiciels nécessaires pour retoucher les images sont disponibles dans tous les magasins spécialisés et à des prix et des niveaux de qualité divers. -Software for retouching pixel graphics is widely available; the quality and price of the software tends to vary.

7942 **succéder** **succeed**
vb
[syksede]
Une de ses geishas devra lui succéder.
-One of her own geisha to succeed her.

7943 **incomber** **behove**
vb
[ɛ̃kɔ̃be]
Incombe à l'État d'encourager l'habitude des sports et de la culture physique ».
-It is incumbent on the State to encourage the habit of sports and physical culture.

7944 **spéculation** **speculation**
f
[spekylasjɔ̃]
Projection restante interdit toute spéculation utile.
-Remaining projection is not open to useful speculation.

7945 **loch** **loch**

	m	Sur le loch, en face de notre distillerie.
	[lɔkx]	-It's across the loch from our distillery.
7946	**farcir**	**stuff**
	vb	Bien laisser égoutter la mozzarella avant de farcir les fleurs de courge pour ne pas trop les mouiller.
	[faʁsiʁ]	-Leave the mozzarella to drain well before stuffing the pumpkin flowers to prevent them becoming too wet.
7947	**immatriculer**	**register**
	vb	Seules les personnes physiques ou morales chiliennes peuvent immatriculer un bateau au Chili.
	[imatʁikyle]	-Only a Chilean natural or juridical person may register a vessel in Chile.
7948	**confédérer**	**confederate**
	vb	Il y a un pistolet de confédéré sur ses genoux, sous son châle... et elle te tuera en un clin d'œil.
	[kɔ̃fedeʁe]	-There's a Confederate pistol in her lap under her shawl, and she'll kill you quick as look at you.
7949	**étiré**	**spread|stretch**
	adj	Lorsque je me suis réveillé ce matin, j'ai baillé, me suis étiré, j'ai frotté le sommeil de mes yeux et j'ai enfilé une paire de pantoufles.
	[etiʁe]	-When I woke up today, I yawned, stretched, rubbed the sleep out of my eyes, and put on a pair of slippers.
7950	**tangible**	**tangible**
	adj	Ces institutions sont l'expression la plus tangible de l'autonomie culturelle.
	[tɑ̃ʒibl]	-These institutions constitute the most tangible result of cultural autonomy.
7951	**appétissant**	**appetizing**
	adj	L'Afrique est un fruit très appétissant.
	[apetisɑ̃]	-Africa is a most appetising fruit.
7952	**assureur**	**insurer**
	m	Ces incidents doivent être déclarés à l'assureur.
	[asyʁœʁ]	-Such events must be reported to the insurer.
7953	**bit**	**bit**
	m	Ainsi, un bit d'information peut être transmis par puce.
	[bit]	-Thereby, one data bit ban be transmitted per chip.
7954	**hémisphère**	**hemisphere**
	m	L'éclipse totale du Soleil de demain sera visible depuis l'hémisphère sud.
	[emisfɛʁ]	-Tomorrow's total eclipse of the sun will be visible from the southern hemisphere.
7955	**exterminateur**	**exterminator; exterminating**
	m; adj	Nous devons amener ici un exterminateur...
	[ɛkstɛʁminatœʁ]	-We need to get an exterminator in here...
7956	**restreindre**	**restrict|narrow**
	vb	Si nous devons restreindre la démocratie, faisons -le au moins démocratiquement.
	[ʁɛstʁɛ̃dʁ]	-If we are to limit democracy, let it at least be done democratically.
7957	**traceur**	**stud|teat**
	m	Cette composition pyrotechnique convient comme composant combustible de traceur infrarouge.
	[tʁasœʁ]	-The pyrotechnic composition is useful as the combustible component of an infrared tracer.
7958	**mamelon**	**nipple|hill**
	m	Cette boule sous le mamelon est un carcinome.
	[mamlɔ̃]	-The lump under your nipple is a stage two breast carcinoma.

7959 **sniffer** **sniff**
vb Si tu en as, j'aimerais la sniffer.
[snife] -If you've got some, I'd like to sniff it.

7960 **anal** **anal**
adj Les viols consistaient en pénétration vaginale, anale et orale et en fellation.
[anal] -The rapes included vaginal, anal and oral penetration and fellatio.

7961 **averse** **shower**
f Je fus pris sous une averse.
[avɛʁs] -I was caught in a shower.

7962 **sensuel** **sensual**
adj Cette cour va maintenant écouter le témoignage très sensuel... de l'ex petite-
[sɑ̃sɥɛl] amie du président, Turanga Leela.
-This court will now hear some very sensual testemony... from this court's ex lover, Turanga Leela.

7963 **peupler** **populate**
vb Pour être certain que ces filles trouveraient à se marier et aideraient à
[pœple] peupler la Nouvelle-France, le gouverneur...
-To make sure these people were married off and that they would help populate New France, the governor…

7964 **épouvante** **dread**
f L'épouvante de la troisième sera décisive.
[epuvɑ̃t] -The horror of the third war will be decisive.

7965 **mortellement** **fatally|mortally**
adv Il semblerait que ce soit cela que les autorités nord-coréennes craignent
[mɔʁtɛlmɑ̃] littéralement mortellement.
-It would appear that this is the thing that the North Korean authorities literally mortally fear.

7966 **calligraphier** **calligraph**
vb[kaligʁafje] Ce nouveau métier permet au joueur de calligraphier des glyphes, qui servent à modifier sorts et compétences. Les maîtres qui l'enseignent se trouvent dans les villes et capitales et vous pouvez d'ores et déjà atteindre le niveau 375. -The inscription profession, which allows players to create glyphs that modify spells and abilities, can now be learned in cities and trained up to 375 skill level.

7967 **bureaucratie** **bureaucracy**
f Nous assistons plutôt à une expansion de la bureaucratie au service de la
[byʁokʁasi] bureaucratie.
-What we see is that the bureaucracy is expanding to service the needs of the bureaucracy.

7968 **incompris** **misunderstood**
adj Nous sommes trop souvent ignorés ou incompris.
[ɛ̃kɔ̃pʁi] -We scientists are too often ignored or misunderstood.

7969 **vadrouiller** **bum around**
vb Avez-vous vu le chien ? Il est parti en vadrouille il y a quelques minutes.
[vadʁuje] -Have you seen the dog? He wandered off a couple of minutes ago.

7970 **désapprouver** **disapprove**
vb Il m'arrive de désapprouver une chose ou l'autre, mais je ne condamne
[dezapʁuve] jamais rien.
-I may disapprove of one thing and another, but I never condemn anything.

7971 **gangrène** **gangrene**
f Un des détenus avait un doigt atteint de gangrène pour lequel il ne
[gɑ̃gʁɛn] bénéficiait d'aucun soin.

-One of the detainees had a finger affected by gangrene for which he was receiving no medical attention.

7972 **colossal** **colossal|huge**
adj
[kɔlɔsal]
Mais mon projet colossal reste tel quel
-But my colossal scheme remains as it was.

7973 **jugeote** **savvy|gumption**
f
[ʒyʒo]
Tu as anticipé, fait des recherches et montré de la jugeote.
-Well, you anticipated, did research and showed gumption.

7974 **blizzard** **blizzard**
m
[blizzaʁ]
Toi, derrière le volant dans le blizzard.
- You, behind the wheel in a blizzard.

7975 **démentir** **deny|contradict**
vb
[demɑ̃tiʁ]
Les premiers résultats chiffrés semblent pourtant déjà démentir les ambitions qui sont affichées.
-Nevertheless, the first figures seem to deny the ambitions declared.

7976 **bifteck** **steak**
m
[biftɛk]
On ne peut pas s'offrir de bifteck.
-Not all of us can afford steak.

7977 **provisoirement** **tentatively**
adv
[pʁɔvizwaʁmɑ̃]
Le Président considère que ce paragraphe peut donc être adopté provisoirement.
-The Chairperson said he took it that the paragraph could therefore be adopted provisionally.

7978 **désobéissance** **disobedience**
f[dezɔbeisɑ̃s]
La désobéissance civile s'est soldée par de nombreuses arrestations et mises en détention. -Civil disobedience had led to the arrest and imprisonment of many.

7979 **éclore** **hatch**
vb
[eklɔʁ]
Bahrein a fait éclore sa culture, comme un écho à la richesse de ses sources artésiennes.
-Bahrain's culture has blossomed, nourished by the richness of these roots.

7980 **acrobate** **acrobat**
m/f
[akʁɔbat]
Être un acrobate est l'ambition de presque tout garçon.
-To be an acrobat is the ambition of almost every boy.

7981 **pillard** **plunderer; predatory**
m; adj
[pijaʁ]
Et grâce aux salariés d'Interface, je suis devenu un pillard repenti.
-And thanks to the people of Interface, I have become a recovering plunderer.

7982 **perpétuel** **perpetual**
adj
[pɛʁpetɥɛl]
Ce problème a été la cause de nombreuses guerres et a conduit à un cycle perpétuel de violence.
-It was the cause of many wars and has led to a continuous cycle of violence.

7983 **guilde** **guild**
f
[gild]
Ces officiers doivent pouvoir gérer la guilde en votre absence.
-These players need to be able to control the guild while you're not around.

7984 **paperasserie** **red tape**
f
[papʁasʁi]
Je vous laisse à votre paperasserie.
-I'll let you get back to your paperwork, then.

7985 **hygiénique** **hygienic**

adj [iʒjenik] | La vérité est qu'ils veulent imposer leur volonté hygiénique à tout le monde. -The truth is that they want to impose their hygienic will on all of us.

7986 **podium** **podium**
m [pɔdjɔm]
C'était incroyable de voir nos garçons sur le podium.
-To see our boys on the podium was unreal.

7987 **recyclage** **recycling**
m [ʁəsiklaʒ]
Pratiques-tu le recyclage ?
-Do you recycle?

7988 **serpillière** **mop|swab**
f [sɛʁpijɛʁ]
Et vous devriez amener une serpillière...
-And you might want to bring a mop.

7989 **expérimentation** **experimentation**
f [ɛkspeʁimɑ̃tasjɔ̃]
Expérimentation du service de communication multimédia à large bande.
-Experimentation with wide-band multimedia communication service.

7990 **thorax** **thorax; bust**
m; f [tɔʁaks]
Un coussin doit être placé entre le thorax du mannequin et la combinaison.
-A cushion must be positioned between the chest of the manikin and the overall.

7991 **gazer** **zap|gas**
vb[gaze]
Les murs de la vieille ville sont ornés de graffitis obscènes et racistes (par exemple, «il faut gazer tous les Arabes»). -Obscene, racist graffiti (for example, "Gas the Arabs") adorns the walls of the old city of Hebron.

7992 **fornication** **fornication**
f [fɔʁnikasjɔ̃]
Si toute votre vie vous vous abstenez du meurtre, du vol, de la fornication, du parjure, du blasphème et de l'outrecuidance envers vos parents, votre église et votre roi, on vous considérera conventionnellement comme digne d'admiration morale, même si vous n'avez jamais fait un seul geste gentil ou généreux.
-If throughout your life you abstain from murder, theft, fornication, perjury, blasphemy, and disrespect toward your parents, your church, and your king, you are conventionally held to deserve moral admiration even if you have never done a single kind or generous or useful action.

7993 **exorciste** **exorcist**
m [ɛgzɔʁsist]
C'est un exorciste.
-He's an exorcist.

7994 **marqueur** **marker|scorer**
m [maʁkœʁ]
C'est comme le cholestéryl, il y a un marqueur positif et un marqueur négatif.
-It is like cholesterol: there is a positive marker and a negative marker.

7995 **clonage** **cloning**
m [klonaʒ]
Préparons-nous pour le clonage.
-Let's get ready for the cloning.

7996 **orque** **orc|orca**
m/f [ɔʁk]
C'est une orque, Benjamin.
-She is an orca, Benjamin.

7997 **videur** **bouncer**
m [vidœʁ]
Des slogans forts tels que : « Le videur a dit à Abdel "soirée privée".
-Some strong slogans were very instructive — for instance, "The bouncer said to Abdel, `exclusive party'.

7998 **écolier** **schoolboy**

m
[ekɔlje]
Liberté. Sur mes cahiers d'écolier. Sur mon pupitre et les arbres. Sur le sable de neige. J'écris ton nom.
-Freedom. On my school notebooks. On my school desk and the trees. On the sand of the snow. I write your name.

7999 **contrefaçon** **counterfeit**
f
[kɔ̃tʁəfasɔ̃]
Normalement, c'est le titulaire des droits qui déclare qu'il y a contrefaçon.
-Normally, the statement that the goods are counterfeit is made by the right holder.

8000 **matou** **tomcat**
m
[matu]
Regardez ce que le matou nous emmène.
-Well, look what the cat dragged in.

8001 **Chypre** **Cyprus**
f
[ʃipʁ]
Une compagnie maritime basée à Chypre.
-It's a shipping company based in Cyprus.

8002 **traîtrise** **treachery**
f
[tʁɛtʁiz]
Trudeau et Axworthy ne seraient sûrement pas capables de traîtrise.
-Trudeau and Axworthy would surely not be capable of treachery.

8003 **tentacule** **tentacle**
m[tɑ̃takyl]
Ils avaient le diagramme d'un tentacule. -They even had a diagram of a tentacle.

8004 **aiguiser** **whet|hone**
vb
[egize]
L'ONU doit continuer d'affiner sa stratégie et sa synergie et d'aiguiser sa concentration afin de répondre aux aspirations des milliards d'habitants de la planète.
-The United Nations must continue to hone its strategy and synergy and to sharpen its focus in order to fulfil the aspirations of the billions of people of the globe.

8005 **professionnellement** **professionally**
adv
[pʁɔfesjɔnɛlmɑ̃]
Depuis 25 ans, je suis engagée professionnellement dans la protection des droits de l'homme.
-I have been involved professionally for 25 years in protecting human rights.

8006 **faisan** **pheasant**
m
[fəzɑ̃]
C'est un faisan.
-It's a pheasant.

8007 **essayage** **fitting**
m
[esejaʒ]
Larry le demande pour un essayage.
-Larry needs to see him for a fitting.

8008 **romancier** **novelist**
m
[ʁɔmɑ̃sje]
J'ai un ami dont le père est un romancier célèbre.
-I have a friend whose father is a famous novelist.

8009 **chimère** **chimera**
f
[ʃimɛʁ]
L'animal chimère est utile pour étudier les maladies hépatiques humaines.
-The chimeric animal is useful in the study of human hepatic diseases.

8010 **affirmation** **affirmation**
f
[afiʁmasjɔ̃]
La valeur de vérité d'une affirmation peut être une valeur de probabilité.
-The truth value of an assertion may be a probability value.

8011 **gravir** **climb|ascend**
vb
[gʁaviʁ]
La ratification est une montagne qu' il faut encore gravir.
-Ratification is a mountain still to climb.

8012 **spasme** **spasm**

	m [spasm]	Cette horrible tragédie a provoqué un spasme flagrant dans le processus politique en cours en Afghanistan. -That brutal tragedy marked a palpable spasm in Afghanistan's evolving political process.
8013	**parodie**	**parody|skit**
	f [paʁɔdi]	C'est une parodie. -It's a travesty.
8014	**géomètre**	**land surveyor**
	m/f [ʒeɔmɛtʁ]	Le Géomètre principal s'est installé à Asmara le 15 novembre 2001. -The Chief Surveyor took up residence in Asmara on 15 November 2001.
8015	**déformer**	**deform|distort**
	vb [defɔʁme]	Nul ne peut compromettre l'enquête ou en déformer les résultats (art. -No one shall interfere with the inquiry or misrepresent the result of inquiry (art.
8016	**implanter**	**implant**
	vb[ɛ̃plɑ̃te]	Les réseaux du terrorisme international sont profondément implantés en Asie du Sud-Est. -International terrorist networks are deeply embedded in Southeast Asia.
8017	**confiserie**	**confectionery**
	f [kɔ̃fizʁi]	Quelle est ta confiserie préférée ? -What's your favorite kind of candy?
8018	**globule**	**globule**
	m [glɔbyl]	Un globule de soudure est placé à l'autre extrémité du trou. -A solder ball is placed on the other end of the hole.
8019	**nuageux**	**cloudy|misty**
	adj [nyaʒø]	La première étape, consacrée à la comparaison de modules chimiques de la transformation du mercure dans un milieu nuageux, s'est achevée en février 2001. -The first stage was devoted to the comparison of chemical modules of mercury transformation in a cloud environment.
8020	**parisien**	**Parisian**
	adj [paʁizjɛ̃]	On peut transformer ta cour en bistrot parisien. -We can set up your courtyard like a Parisian bistro.
8021	**solidaire**	**solidary**
	adj [sɔlidɛʁ]	Les réfugiés palestiniens peuvent compter sur notre soutien solidaire. -The Palestinian refugees can count on our support and our solidarity.
8022	**aboi**	**barking**
	m [abwa]	Un chien qui aboi, des gens qui regardent dans l'oeilleton de la porte, des rumeurs sur Hanky. -I got barking dogs, people looking through peepholes... drug talk about Hanky.
8023	**populace**	**populace|mob**
	f [pɔpylas]	Quelle populace ! -What people!
8024	**salve**	**salvo|salute**
	f [salv]	Votre salve d'introduction était certainement impressionnante. -Your opening salvo was certainly impressive.
8025	**normand**	**Norman**
	adj [nɔʁmɑ̃]	Des démonstrations d'artisans ponctuent cet itinéraire autour du patrimoine rural normand.

-The craftsmanship displays mark this itinerary on the Norman rural heritage.

8026 **chronométrer** vb [kʁɔnɔmetʁe]
time
Tu pourrai en chronométrer beaucoup toi-même, même si tu comptes dans ta tête.
-You could time a lot of this yourself, even if it's counting in your head.

8027 **dispenser** vb [dispɑ̃se]
dispense|exempt
Une commission peut décider de se dispenser de l'interprétation dans certaines langues.
-A committee may dispense with certain language interpretations.

8028 **parloir** m [paʁlwaʁ]
parlor
Ta mère est en bas, dans le parloir.
-Your mother's downstairs in the visiting room.

8029 **requête** f[ʁəkɛt]
request
Merci d'avance pour toute la considération que vous porterez à notre requête. -Thank you very much for the consideration you will give to our request.

8030 **chalumeau** m [ʃalymo]
blowtorch
Le chalumeau est destiné de préférence au soudage d'articles de grande épaisseur.
-The torch is intended preferably for welding articles of a big thickness.

8031 **biologiste** m/f [bjɔlɔʒist]
biologist
Il travaille actuellement comme biologiste à Hay River (territoires du Nord-Ouest).
-He is presently employed at Hay River, Northwest Territories, as a biologist.

8032 **philosophique** adj [filɔzɔfik]
philosophical
La ligne philosophique de la Commission, c'est le malthusianisme.
-The Commission's philosophy is Malthusian.

8033 **appendice** m [apɛ̃dis]
appendix
Cette partie était peut-être comme un appendice.
-Maybe it's a part you don't need anymore, like an appendix.

8034 **roumain** adj; m [ʁumɛ̃]
Romanian; Romanian
Il est prévu de restructurer le secteur roumain de production d'électricité.
-The Romanian electricity sector is supposed to be transformed to a new structure.

8035 **sodium** m [sɔdjɔm]
sodium
L'hydroxyde de sodium est utilisé dans la fabrication des savons.
-Sodium hydroxide is used in making soaps.

8036 **gamelle** f [gamɛl]
lunch box
De qui est-ce la gamelle ?
-Whose lunch box is this?

8037 **mythique** adj [mitik]
mythical
C'est une caisse aussi mythique que les licornes et les coffres au trésor.
-It is as mythical as leprechauns, as mythical as that pot of gold.

8038 **spartiate** adj [spaʁtjat]
Spartan
Tu as utilisé un moyen spartiate de persuasion: le courage.
-My good Trojan, you have used a Spartan persuasion on me: courage.

8039 **acné** f [akne]
acne
Elle s'est moquée de mon acné.
-She made fun of my acne.

8040 **bâtonnet** **rod**
m
[batɔnɛ]
Le bâtonnet à humer facilite l'apport et la consommation individualisés de parfum.
-The sniffing stick facilitates the delivery and individualized consumption of fragrances.

8041 **changeur** **converter**
m
[ʃɑ̃ʒœʁ]
Tout changeur agréé qui contrevient à l'article 30.1 commet une infraction passible d'une amende pouvant atteindre 100 000 ringgit.
-A licensed money-changer who contravenes this section shall be guilty of an offence and upon conviction be liable to a fine not exceeding RM100,000.

8042 **beagle** **beagle**
m[bigl]
J'ai trouvé un magnifique beagle. -And I found another gorgeous beagle.

8043 **stratagème** **stratagem|ploy**
m
[stʁataʒɛm]
L'auteur de l'enlèvement ne peut échapper à la compétence du tribunal par un tel stratagème.
-The kidnapper cannot escape the jurisdiction of the court by such a stratagem.

8044 **rayonnement** **influence|radiance**
m
[ʁɛjɔnmɑ̃]
La performance de rayonnement est également améliorée.
-At the same time the radiation performance is improved.

8045 **inaudible** **inaudible**
adj
[inodibl]
De fait, l'Union européenne était quasiment inaudible lors des ultimes négociations.
-In fact, the EU was virtually inaudible during the final negotiations.

8046 **stimulation** **stimulation**
f
[stimylasjɔ̃]
Tous les enfants ont besoin de stimulation.
-All children need stimulation.

8047 **engourdir** **numb**
vb
[ɑ̃guʁdiʁ]
C'est pour engourdir le secteur.
-This is to numb the area.

8048 **endurcir** **harden**
vb
[ɑ̃dyʁsiʁ]
Susan Ross a besoin de s'endurcir, Abby.
-No, Susan Ross needs to toughen up, Abby.

8049 **rénovation** **renovation**
f
[ʁenɔvasjɔ̃]
Avant la rénovation, la maison était dans un état désastreux.
-Before the renovation the house was in a disastrous state.

8050 **camionneur** **truck driver**
m
[kamjɔnœʁ]
C'est bizarre pour un camionneur.
-That's odd for a trucker.

8051 **prothèse** **prosthesis**
f
[pʁɔtɛz]
Jill a une prothèse de bras.
-Jill has a prosthetic arm.

8052 **consumer** **consume**
vb
[kɔ̃syme]
Il s'agit, entre autres, des catastrophes naturelles, telles les sécheresses; du coût élevé de l'énergie; et de la dette extérieure, qui continue de consumer une grande part du revenu du pays.
-They include natural calamities such as droughts; the high cost of energy; and external debt, which continues to use up much of the country's revenue.

8053 **étonnement** **astonishment; surprisingly**

	m; adv [etɔnmɑ̃]	Mon étonnement n'était pas dû à votre personne, mais simplement à votre temps de parole ! -The cause of my astonishment was merely your speaking time, not you personally.
8054	**différer**	**differ|vary**
	vb [difeʁe]	Les chiffres réels pourraient différer considérablement de ces estimations. -Actual results could significantly differ from those estimated.
8055	**boueux**	**muddy; bin man**
	adj; m [buø]	On devrait avoir un printemps boueux. -It's supposed to be a muddy spring.
8056	**satanique**	**satanic|ghoulish**
	adj [satanik]	Il était possible que tout était une illusion, ou pire, une illusion satanique? -It was possible that everything was illusion, or worse, satanic illusion?
8057	**faille**	**break**
	f [faj]	Jack a tiré avantage d'une faille juridique. -Jack used a legal loophole.
8058	**mimer**	**mimic|gesture**
	vb [mime]	Quelque 1056 réfugiés (femmes, hommes et enfants) ont assisté aux spectacles des TFD et 395 réfugiés ont participé au mime. -1056 refugees (women, men and children) attended TFDs and 395 refugees participated in Mime Theatre.
8059	**pensionnaire**	**boarder|pensionary**
	m/f [pɑ̃sjɔnɛʁ]	J'envisage de prendre une pensionnaire. -I'm considering taking in a boarder.
8060	**autrichien**	**Austrian**
	adj [otʁiʃjɛ̃]	Le Gouvernement autrichien a proposé de soutenir financièrement cette initiative. -The Austrian Government has offered to financially support this arrangement.
8061	**respectueusement**	**with respect**
	adv [ʁɛspɛktɥøzmɑ̃]	Respectueusement soumis, Le vice-président, NICK SIBBESTON Des voix : Bravo ! -Respectfully submitted, NICK SIBBESTON Deputy Chair Some Hon. Senators: Hear, hear!
8062	**iode**	**iodine**
	m [jɔd]	Dans certains systèmes et procédés, l'iode peut être régénéré. -In certain systems and methods, the iodine may be regenerated.
8063	**adoration**	**worship**
	f [adɔʁasjɔ̃]	Vous semblez peu réceptif à l'adoration, moi je le suis. -I'm sorry you didn't enjoy the adoration of the masses but I do.
8064	**conférer**	**confer|lend**
	vb [kɔ̃feʁe]	La participation de l'ONU à ces processus peut leur conférer la légitimité voulue. -United Nations involvement can confer legitimacy on the process.
8065	**échafaud**	**scaffold**
	m [eʃafo]	Louis XVI mourut sur l'échafaud. -Louis XVI died on the scaffold.
8066	**saucisson**	**sausage**
	m [sosisɔ̃]	Et mon nouveau saucisson que je viens d'inventer. -And I brought some of that sausage I been workin' on.
8067	**préhistorique**	**prehistoric**

adj
[pʁeistɔʁik]
La principale raison expliquant leur choix est que l'ancienne directive est inapplicable et, d'un point de vue environnemental, préhistorique.
-The main reason why they do so is that the old directive is unworkable and, in environmental terms, pre-historic.

8068 **botanique** **botanical; botany**
adj; f
[bɔtanik]
Quelle préparation scientifique détiennent-elles en chimie, physique, botanique, zoologie ?
-What scientific preparation do they have in the fields of chemistry, physics, botany and zoology?

8069 **furet** **ferret**
m
[fyʁɛ]
Mettez une perruque blonde à un furet et il ressemble à Jessica Simpson.
-You could put a long, blonde wig on a ferret and it would look like Jessica Simpson.

8070 **morose** **morose**
adj
[mɔʁoz]
Pour éviter son utilisation, il a été proposé de remplacer les ABS par des mélanges de polyoxyde de phénylène et de polystyrène choc ignifugés au RDP (Morose, 2006).
-To avoid their use in ABS applications, poly (phenylene oxide) / high impact polystyrene (PPO / HIPS) blends flame retarded with resorcinol diphosphate (RDP) have been proposed (Morose, 2006).

8071 **inefficace** **ineffective|inefficient**
adj
[inefikas]
J' estime que c' est une injustice et que cette mesure est de surcroît inefficace.
-I believe that this is unjust and that, furthermore, it has no effect whatsoever.

8072 **révolter** **appal|revolt**
vb
[ʁevɔlte]
Aucun peuple au monde ne saurait accepter éternellement le joug de la domination sans se révolter.
-No people in the world could be expected to live in eternal subjection without rebelling.

8073 **tabou** **taboo; taboo**
adj; m
[tabu]
Ce sujet est tabou.
-This subject is taboo.

8074 **vicomte** **viscount**
m
[vikɔ̃t]
Le Vicomte, qui est le chef de l'administration de la Royal Court, exerce les fonctions de Coroner.
-The Viscount, who is the Chief Executive Officer of the Royal Court, exercises the functions of coroner.

8075 **turban** **turban**
m
[tyʁbɑ̃]
Dessin 12: Un dessin d'un homme portant des lunettes et un turban dans lequel se trouve une orange.
-Drawing 12: A drawing of a man wearing glasses and a turban with an orange in it.

8076 **pompeux** **pompous**
adj
[pɔ̃pø]
Louée dans des discours pompeux, la subsidiarité n'est jamais respectée dans les politiques mises en œuvre.
-Subsidiarity is hailed in grand speeches but is never respected in the policies put into practice.

8077 **pompon** **tassel|cake**
m
[pɔ̃pɔ̃]
Comme il est grand, ça ne ferait pas bien avec un petit pompon.
-This is a big beret, a small pom-pom wouldn't look nice.

8078 **négresse** **nigger**

f | On a jeté une petite négresse morte chez Patterson.
[negʁɛs] | -Somebody just threw a dead nigger girl on Patterson's lawn.

8079 **orienter** | **guide|orient**
vb | Certaines agences utilisent ces cours pour orienter les nouveaux employés.
[ɔʁjɑ̃te] | -Some of the agencies use them to help orient new staff.

8080 **désinfectant** | **disinfectant; disinfectant**
adj; m[dezɛ̃fɛktɑ̃] | L'invention concerne un désinfectant buccal pour animaux domestiques. -The present invention is generally related to an oral disinfectant for companion animals.

8081 **astre** | **star**
m | En théorie, il pourrait arrêter la fusion d'un astre.
[astʁ] | -In theory, it could stop all fusion within a star.

8082 **framboise** | **raspberry**
f | Cette tarte babeurre framboise est super.
[fʁɑ̃bwaz] | -That raspberry buttermilk pie turns out real nice.

8083 **incarcération** | **incarceration**
f | Nous ne croyons pas à l'incarcération totale pour le principe de l'incarcération.
[ɛ̃kaʁseʁasjɔ̃] | -We do not believe in complete incarceration just for the simple reason of it.

8084 **infériorité** | **inferiority**
f | Ils ont adopté un complexe d'infériorité qui est devenu une risée nationale.
[ɛ̃feʁjɔʁite] | -They have bought into this inferiority complex that has become a national joke.

8085 **astronome** | **astronomer**
m/f | Pour être un astronome, on a besoin d'étudier, mais pour être un astrologue, il suffit juste d'être un raté et un grand menteur.
[astʁɔnɔm] | -To be an astronomer, you have to study, but to be an astrologer, it is sufficient to be a loser and a big liar.

8086 **poivron** | **pepper**
m | J'adore le poivron.
[pwavʁɔ̃] | -I like peppers very much.

8087 **irrationnel** | **irrational; irrational**
adj; m | Dans un accès d'optimisme irrationnel.
[iʁasjɔnɛl] | -I did... in a fit of irrational optimism.

8088 **déodorant** | **deodorant**
m | Voici un peu de déodorant.
[deɔdɔʁɑ̃] | -Here's some deodorant.

8089 **fusionner** | **merge**
vb | Pour être compétitif, il faudrait fusionner.
[fyzjɔne] | -To be competitive on a global level, we must merge.

8090 **lupus** | **lupus**
m | Il n'y a rien dans ses antécédents médicale qui suggère le lupus.
[lypys] | -There's nothing in her medical history that suggests lupus.

8091 **narcissique** | **narcissistic**
adj | Un con narcissique comme Richard... ne s'intéresse qu'à lui-même.
[naʁsisik] | -A narcissistic prick like Richard doesn't care about anyone but himself.

8092 **conduite** | **conduct|driving**
f | Jack a donné un cours de conduite à Jill.
[kɔ̃dɥit] | -Jack gave Jill a driving lesson.

8093 **mousson** | **monsoon**

m | La plus grande partie de ce système devient fonctionnelle après l'arrivée de la mousson.
[musɔ̃] | -After arrival of the monsoon, most of the irrigation system becomes functional.

8094 **divisionnaire** **divisional**
adj[divizjɔnɛʁ] Les appels d'ordonnances concernant les sommes d'argents supérieures à 500 $ sont interjetés devant la Cour divisionnaire. -An appeal lies to the Divisional Court from an order for the payment of money in excess of $500.

8095 **bolide** **bolide|high end car**
m On est quelques-uns à faire une virée en bolide.
[bɔlid] -A bunch of us guys... are chipping in on a hot rod.

8096 **vandale** **vandal; vandal**
adj; m/f Tu sais qui est le vandale.
[vɑ̃dal] -You know who the vandal is.

8097 **mélodrame** **melodrama**
m Comme le méchant dans un mélodrame.
[melɔdʁam] -Like a villain in a melodrama.

8098 **acceptation** **acceptance**
f Cette information est retournée au terminal local pour acceptation.
[aksɛptasjɔ̃] -This information is sent back to the local terminal for acceptance.

8099 **dégradation** **degradation|deterioration**
f « Amnesty International » a déclaré que le procès de Sergeï Magnitsky, assassiné dans une prison russe, « ouvrirait un chapitre entièrement nouveau de la dégradation des droits de l'homme en Russie. »
[degʁadasjɔ̃] -Amnesty International said the trial of Sergei Magnitsky, assassinated in a Russian prison, would "open a whole new chapter in Russia's worsening human rights record".

8100 **insinuation** **insinuation**
f Le sénateur Boudreau: Sans insinuation... Une voix: Jamais !
[ɛ̃sinɥasjɔ̃] -Senator Boudreau: Not with innuendo — An Hon. Senator: Never!

8101 **miraculeusement** **miraculously**
adv À la suite de la victoire de la gauche en 2006, le problème a miraculeusement disparu.
[miʁakyløzmɑ̃] -Following the victory of the left in 2006, the problem miraculously disappeared.

8102 **vraisemblablement** **in all likelihood**
adv Il faudra vraisemblablement prévoir des mesures d'accompagnement transitoires.
[vʁɛsɑ̃blabləmɑ̃] -This will likely require measures for temporary mitigation.

8103 **breuvage** **beverage**
m Je préfèrerai ce breuvage avec du sucre.
[bʁœvaʒ] -I think I would prefer this beverage with sugar.

8104 **veto** **veto**
m Le recours au veto a malheureusement anéanti ces espoirs.
[veto] -Unfortunately, the use of the veto has dashed those hopes.

8105 **recueil** **collection**
m Ledit dispositif comprend un substrat de recueil planaire doté d'un matériau absorbant.
[ʁəkœj] -The device includes a planar collection substrate having an absorbent material.

8106 **aimant** **magnet**

m
[ɛmɑ̃]

La Terre est comme une espèce de balle avec un grand aimant à l'intérieur.
-The Earth is like a ball with a large magnet inside.

8107 **boursier**
m[buʁsje]
scholar|stock market
L'indice boursier a atteint des sommets. -The stock price index soared to an all-time high.

8108 **carafe**
f
[kaʁaf]
carafe|jug
Vous avez versé votre carafe d'eau, et j'ai cru...
-Well, sir, I saw you pour it from your water carafe, I assumed...

8109 **légèreté**
f
[leʒɛʁte]
lightness
Tout dans la simplicité et la légèreté.
-It's all about simplicity, lightness.

8110 **mélasse**
f
[melas]
treacle|molasses
Autant remplir les réservoirs de mélasse.
-I might as well fill up those fuel tanks with molasses.

8111 **tisonnier**
m
[tizɔnje]
poker
Garde-feu, tisonnier, chenets et brasero figurent également sur cette image.
-Fender, poker, andirons and fire basket are also displayed on this image.

8112 **hache**
f
[aʃ]
ax
Piratage populiste comme si l'on visitait un jardin botanique la hache à la main.
-Populist hacking, as though going at a botanical garden with an axe.

8113 **archéologie**
f
[aʁkeɔlɔʒi]
archeology
Le Comité tient un colloque spécial sur le thème "L'espace et l'archéologie".
-The Committee held a special symposium on the theme "Space and Archaeology".

8114 **transcription**
f
[tʁɑ̃skʁipsjɔ̃]
transcription
As-tu vu la transcription ?
-Did you see the transcript?

8115 **corrida**
f
[kɔʁida]
bullfight
Ce divertissement sanglant s'appelle la corrida.
-And this bloody form of amusement... is bullfighting.

8116 **cordialement**
adv
[kɔʁdjalmɑ̃]
cordially
Le vernissage sera suivi d'une réception à laquelle vous êtes tous cordialement invités.
-The opening will be followed by a reception, to which everyone is cordially invited.

8117 **java**
f
[ʒava]
rave
Il adore faire la java.
-He loves to party.

8118 **recteur**
m; adj
[ʁɛktœʁ]
rector; rectorial
Demain, petit-déjeuner avec le recteur qui m'avait aidé pour mon livre.
-Tomorrow a breakfasting with the rector who'd helped me with my book.

8119 **irréfutable**
adj
[iʁefytabl]
irrefutable
Telle est la réalité absolue et irréfutable sur le terrain aujourd'hui en Afghanistan.
-This is the stark and irrefutable reality on the ground of present-day Afghanistan.

8120 **accoutrement**
m
[akutʁəmɑ̃]
regalia
Elle est issue de pur sang bleu, voyez-vous. Malheureusement, ce n'est pas une sorte d'accoutrement, mais sa véritable nature.

-She's pure bred blue-blood you see. Unfortunately that's no sort of put-on but her natural self.

8121 **argot** m [aʁgo] **slang**
C'est déjà de l'argot.
-Well, "iffy" is already slang.

8122 **asperger** vb [aspɛʁʒe] **spray**
Étant donné qu'elles étaient très vulnérables aux infestations par des parasites, il fallait les asperger de produits chimiques.
-Because they were highly susceptible to pest infestation, they required extensive spraying of chemicals.

8123 **pacifiste** m/f [pasifist] **pacifist**
Le désaccord concernait la position pacifiste de Woodsworth au sujet de la Seconde Guerre mondiale.
-Those two had a disagreement over Woodsworth's pacifist stand on world war two.

8124 **sexiste** adj [sɛgzist] **sexist**
Au sein de la famille, on observe divers stéréotypes de nature sexiste.
-A number of different stereotypes of a sexist nature are observed within the family.

8125 **mandarin** m [mɑ̃daʁɛ̃] **Mandarin**
Il disait que parler le mandarin est comme de manger de l'ananas. Ça le démange partout.
-He said that speaking Chinese is like eating pineapple. It makes him itchy all over.

8126 **furtif** adj [fyʁtif] **furtive|slinking**
Néanmoins, l'introduction furtive et déguisée de questions controversées sous couvert de ces sujets devient une fâcheuse habitude.
-Nevertheless, the furtive and back-handed introduction of divisive issues under cover of these very topics is turning into a regrettable habit.

8127 **passoire** f [paswaʁ] **strainer**
Non, tu ne peux pas te mettre la passoire sur la tête ; tu feras l'astronaute après que j'aurai égoutté les pâtes.
-No, you may not put the strainer on your head; you can be an astronaut after I drain the pasta.

8128 **ballerine** f [balʁin] **ballerina**
Je prends des leçons de ballet depuis l'âge de trois ans et j'espère devenir une ballerine.
-I have been taking ballet lessons since I was three and hope to be a ballerina.

8129 **verdure** f [vɛʁdyʁ] **greenery|greenness**
Je ne veux pas d'animaux domestiques ou de verdure.
-I don't want to see any domesticated animals or greenery.

8130 **majestueux** adj [maʒɛstɥø] **majestic|stately**
La vérité est humble, non majestueuse, républicaine en quelque sorte.
-Truth is humble, non-majestic and republican to a certain extent.

8131 **cerisier** m [səʁizje] **cherry**
Un cerisier poussait dans le jardin.
-There was a cherry tree growing in the garden.

8132 **compression** f [kɔ̃pʁesjɔ̃] **compression**
La compression vidéo numérique (CVN) est une autre technologie révolutionnaire.
-Another revolutionary technology is digital video compression (DVC).

8133 **manquant** adj[mɑ̃kɑ̃]
missing
Un enfant est manquant. -A child is missing.

8134 **rapace** adj; m [ʁapas]
rapacious; predator
L'aigle est un rapace comme le faucon et le vautour.
-The eagle is a predator, like the falcon and vulture.

8135 **traumatiser** vb [tʁomatize]
traumatize
Vous allez le traumatiser, laissez-le tranquille.
-You are going to traumatize him, leave him alone.

8136 **trimballer** vb [tʁɛ̃bale]
cart around
Ils ne vont pas trimballer tous ces bocaux.
-They can't lug all these jars.

8137 **croustillant** adj; m [kʁustijɑ̃]
crispy; crispness
Le produit ainsi obtenu peut être chauffé au four à micro-ondes tout en demeurant croustillant.
-The resultant product can be heated in a microwave oven but still remains crispy.

8138 **contusion** f [kɔ̃tyzjɔ̃]
contusion
Le suspect est sorti avec une contusion au visage.
-The suspect emerged with a facial contusion.

8139 **mémorial** m [memɔʁjal]
memorial
Au moins tu ferais partie du mémorial.
-Then at least you'd be a part of the memorial.

8140 **habiliter** vb [abilite]
empower|enable
Le Pakistan a suggéré plusieurs mesures concrètes pour habiliter l'Assemblée générale.
-Pakistan has suggested several concrete steps to empower the General Assembly.

8141 **claustrophobe** adj [klostʁɔfɔb]
claustrophobic
Il a été renvoyé chez lui plutôt qu'en prison sous prétexte qu'il est claustrophobe.
-The reason he was sent home instead of to jail is because he is claustrophobic.

8142 **déménageur** m [demenaʒœʁ]
mover
Ça pourrait être un déménageur professionnel.
-Whoever did this could have been a professional mover.

8143 **moisissure** f [mwazisyʁ]
mold|mouldiness
Il y a de la moisissure sur le pain. Ça veut dire qu'on ne peut plus le manger.
-There's mold on the bread. This means that we can't eat it anymore.

8144 **posé** adj [poze]
laid
Le moment où Julia a posé les yeux sur moi.
-It was out of your hands the moment Julie laid eyes on me.

8145 **pulvériser** vb [pylveʁize]
spray|pulverize
Je n'ai alors plus besoin pulvériser de l'insecticide - ce qui présente un avantage écologique.
-There would then be no need to spray insecticides - good news for the environment!

8146 **jonction** f[ʒɔ̃ksjɔ̃]
junction
L'invention concerne un dispositif magnétorésistif comportant une jonction magnétique. -According to embodiments of the present invention, a magnetoresistive device having a magnetic junction is provided.

8147 **éminence**
eminence|height

	f [eminɑ̃s]	Merci, Votre Éminence, pour votre discours ici, au Parlement européen. -Thank you, Your Eminence, for your address to us here in the European Parliament.
8148	**alternatif**	**alternative**
	adj [altɛʁnatif]	Un mode de réalisation alternatif de l'invention concerne un procédé consistant à synthétiser un nanocomposite. -An alternative embodiment of the disclosure provides a method of synthesizing a nanocomposite.
8149	**mutilation**	**mutilation**
	f [mytilasjɔ̃]	C'était sa troisième mutilation en quelques mois. -This was his third mutilation in about as many months.
8150	**cylindre**	**cylinder**
	m [silɛ̃dʁ]	Clark ne pourra pas démagnétiser le cylindre. -Only Clark won't be able to demagnetize the voice cylinder.
8151	**styliste**	**stylist**
	m/f [stilist]	Votre veste en cuir a été dessinée par un styliste européen mais a été confectionnée en Turquie. -Your leather jacket is by a European designer, but it was made in Turkey.
8152	**jaquette**	**jacket**
	f [ʒakɛt]	Avec la jaquette, ça ira. -With the jacket, it will be fine.
8153	**fictif**	**fictional**
	adj [fiktif]	Je félicite le rapporteur et le rapporteur fictif ainsi que le commissaire. -I congratulate the rapporteur and the shadow rapporteur as well the Commissioner.
8154	**menuisier**	**carpenter**
	m [mənɥizje]	Dans une région donnée, il se peut qu'un menuisier gagne en général 25 $ l'heure. -The prevailing wage in an area for a carpenter might be $25 an hour.
8155	**symphonique**	**symphonic**
	adj [sɛ̃fɔnik]	Chaque année l'Orchestre symphonique national de Lettonie donne des concerts de charité. -Every year the Latvian National Symphonic Orchestra gives charity concerts.
8156	**phénoménal**	**phenomenal**
	adj [fenɔmenal]	Au cours du quart de siècle écoulé, les pays du Sud ont connu un développement économique et social phénoménal. -The past 25 years had seen phenomenal economic and social development in the South.
8157	**médiocrité**	**mediocrity**
	f [medjɔkʁite]	Elles sont extrêmement coopératives et sont parfaitement conscientes que leur soutien fait la différence entre médiocrité et qualité de l'enseignement. -They were extremely supportive and understood fully that their support meant the difference between poor and quality education.
8158	**balourd**	**oaf; awkward**
	m; adj[baluʁ]	Un balourd qui se croit profond est encore pire qu'un balourd de base. -A nudnik who believes he's profound is even worse than just a plain nudnik.
8159	**abîme**	**abyss|gulf**
	m [abim]	Nous sommes tombés dans un abîme de contradictions et d'incohérences. -This has caused us to fall into an abyss of contradictions and inconsistencies.
8160	**documentation**	**documentation**

f
[dɔkymɑ̃tasjɔ̃]
Le Gouvernement vérifie actuellement cette documentation.
-The documentation is now being studied by the Government for accuracy.

8161 **veilleur**
m; adj
[vɛjœʁ]
watchman; watchful
Si le veilleur avait reconnu le type qui s'enfuyait.
-I sure wish that watchman could describe the guy he almost caught.

8162 **déchéance**
f
[deʃeɑ̃s]
decline
Le droit indien ne prévoit pas la déchéance de la nationalité ni l'expulsion des nationaux.
-Indian law did not provide for deprivation of nationality or for expulsion of nationals.

8163 **alouette**
f
[alwɛt]
lark
Colajanni est la vieille recette du pâté d'alouette, mi-cheval/mi-alouette, un cheval pour une alouette.
-Mr Colajanni's objectivity reminds me of the old recipe for lark pâté: half horse, half lark, one of each.

8164 **révolu**
adj
[ʁevɔly]
gone
Le temps des simples déclarations de principes et d' exigences est révolu.
-It is no longer enough to simply make a statement of principles and requirements.

8165 **moue**
f
[mu]
pout
Et tu as la moue parfaite.
-Besides, your pout is perfect.

8166 **mausolée**
m
[mozɔle]
mausoleum
Vous devez sortir de ce mausolée.
-You need to get out of that mausoleum.

8167 **dépraver**
vb
[depʁave]
pervert
La possession de matériels pornographiques est davantage répandue et le caractère des matériels plus dépravé qu'il y a dix ans.
-Possession occurs on a larger scale and the nature of the material is more depraved than a decade ago.

8168 **tuyauterie**
f
[tɥijotʁi]
piping
Le système comprend au moins deux composants de tuyauterie et un dispositif d'étanchéité.
-The system comprises at least two piping components, and a sealing device.

8169 **fable**
f
[fabl]
fable
Monsieur le Président, je suis certain que vous connaissez cette fable latine.
-I am sure you are familiar with this Latin fable, Mr President.

8170 **agacer**
vb[agase]
annoy|aggravate
Cependant, si ces mesures d'inspection sont bel et bien nécessaires, celles - ci ne soient pas être exagérément bureaucratiques, car c'est là un problème qui agace les agriculteurs au plus haut point. -But while we must have inspection measures, they must not be overly bureaucratic, because that is one of the problems that aggravates farmers most.

8171 **appréciation**
f
[apʁesjasjɔ̃]
appreciation
Nous avons gagné l'appréciation et l'admiration de la communauté internationale.
-This has earned us the appreciation and admiration of the international community.

8172 **grossièreté**
f
[gʁosjɛʁte]
rudeness
Je ne pouvais supporter sa grossièreté.
-I couldn't put up with his rudeness.

8173	**irréversible**	**irreversible**
	adj	Elle est définitive et irréversible.
	[iʁevɛʁsibl]	-It is final and non-reversible.
8174	**ineptie**	**ineptitude**
	f	Il tenta de dissimuler son ineptie dans un tour de passe-passe pas très adroit.
	[inɛpsi]	-He tried to conceal his ineptitude in a not-so-deft sleight of hand.
8175	**commanditaire**	**silent partner|sponsor**
	m	Le CN est devenu un important commanditaire de Lorie Kane en 2006.
	[kɔmɑ̃ditɛʁ]	-CN became a major sponsor of Lorie Kane in 2006.
8176	**arcade**	**arcade**
	f	C'est les clés de l'arcade.
	[aʁkad]	-These are the keys to the arcade.
8177	**réputé**	**renowned|reputed**
	adj	Observation: Dans certaines régions éloignées, les montants du tableau sous la colonne revenu réputé sont majorés de 20p.
	[ʁepyte]	-Note: For certain remote regions, the amounts listed under the "reputed income" column are increased by 20%.
8178	**questionnaire**	**questionnaire**
	m	Le questionnaire suit la structure présentée dans le questionnaire ordinaire.
	[kɛstjɔnɛʁ]	-The questionnaire follows the structure outlined for the regular questionnaire.
8179	**faussaire**	**forger**
	m/f	J'utilise sciemment le terme de falsificateur de produits, pour ne pas utiliser le terme trop dur de faussaire.
	[fosɛʁ]	-I am quite deliberately saying product counterfeiter, rather than refer to a peddler of phoney products, which sounds very harsh.
8180	**dactylo**	**typist**
	m/f	Elle est dactylo.
	[daktilo]	-She is a typist.
8181	**bigleux**	**cross-eyed|four-eyed**
	adj	Vaut mieux pas être un bigleux dans le quartier ouest aujourd'hui.
	[biglø]	-Not a good day to be cross-eyed in West Baltimore.
8182	**scarabée**	**beetle**
	m[skaʁabe]	Comme le disait Schopenhauer: "N'importe quel crétin de gamin peut écraser un scarabée, mais tous les professeurs du monde ne peuvent en créer un". -Schopenhauer said 'Any stupid boy can crush a beetle, but all the professors in the world cannot create a new beetle.'
8183	**shah**	**shah**
	m	Only the shah may end an audience.
	[ʃa]	-Seul le Shah peut mettre fin à une audience.
8184	**moite**	**moist**
	adj	Excusez moi, pendant que je me change, le hola boogie ma rendu tout moite.
	[mwat]	-Excuse me I have to change, the bogey sweater made me sweaty
8185	**précipitamment**	**hastily|precipitately**
	adv	La solution au problème n'est pas de jeter précipitamment cette institution aux orties.
	[pʁesipitamɑ̃]	-The answer to the problem is not to precipitously trash the institution.
8186	**abruti**	**jerk; stupid**
	m; adj	Jack est clairement un abruti.
	[abʁyti]	-Jack is obviously a jerk.

8187 **métabolisme** **metabolism**
m
[metabɔlism]
J'ai un problème de métabolisme.
-No, I have a metabolism thing, and I...

8188 **néfaste** **harmful**
adj
[nefast]
Il serait effectivement insensé et néfaste d'intervenir dans ce cas en octroyant des aides publiques.
-It would in fact be nonsensical and damaging to use State aid to intervene in such situations.

8189 **cligner** **wink|blink**
vb
[kliɲe]
Il pouvait juste cligner des yeux.
-All he could do was blink.

8190 **remarquablement** **remarkably**
adv
[ʁəmaʁkabləmɑ̃]
Le nombre d'années de scolarité a remarquablement progressé dans les minorités ethniques.
-The years for ethnic minorities to receive education have remarkably extended.

8191 **unisson** **unison**
m
[ynisɔ̃]
Il est donc important pour l'Union européenne de parler et d'agir à l'unisson.
-It is therefore important for the European Union to speak and act in unison.

8192 **préservation** **preservation**
f
[pʁezɛʁvasjɔ̃]
Il a consacré sa vie à la préservation de la nature.
-He has dedicated his life to the preservation of nature.

8193 **incinérer** **incinerate**
vb
[ɛ̃sineʁe]
En effet, le volume des déchets à incinérer va être considérablement augmenté.
-The volume of waste to be incinerated is going to be significantly increased.

8194 **vallon** **small valley**
m[valɔ̃]
Il est allé chasser dans le vallon. -He went hunting in the valley.

8195 **accoupler** **mate**
vb
[akuple]
Ces animaux ont été enlevés, une fois de plus, par un groupe d'action qui s'occupe de protéger et de conserver cette espèce, dans le but de les accoupler.
-These hamsters were spirited away by a campaign group for the protection and preservation of this species who believed that, if they abducted the hamsters, they could get them to mate.

8196 **hibernation** **hibernation**
f
[ibɛʁnasjɔ̃]
Si vous considérez l'objectif de l'hibernation, je pense que c'est la réponse des animaux qui essaient de survivre d'une manière ou d'une autre à la saison hivernale avec son manque de nourriture.
-If you consider the objective of hibernation, I think it's the response of animals trying to somehow survive the winter season with its lack of food.

8197 **pathologie** **pathology**
f
[patɔlɔʒi]
Je crois reconnaître une pathologie criminelle particulière.
-When I saw it on the news I recognized a certain type of criminal pathology.

8198 **dioxyde** **dioxide**
m
[djɔksid]
Analyseurs NDIR pour la détermination du monoxyde et du dioxyde de carbone.
-NDIR analysers for the determination of carbon monoxide and carbon dioxide.

8199 **enchaînement** **sequence|linking**
m
[ɑ̃ʃɛnmɑ̃]
Un enchaînement ne peut s' effectuer que dans le sens antécédent vers dépendant.
-Linking is only possible from one frame to the next.

8200 **dégueuler** **puke**
vb
[degœle]
Ouais, ils paient pour pratiquement dégueuler.
-Yeah, they pay money so they can almost puke.

8201 **indescriptible** **indescribable**
adj
[ɛ̃dɛskʁiptibl]
En effet, le peuple burundais vit aujourd'hui dans une misère indescriptible.
-Indeed, the people of Burundi are now living in unspeakable poverty.

8202 **ardemment** **ardently**
adv
[aʁdamɑ̃]
Cette motion propose des lignes de conduite similaires et nous devrions la soutenir ardemment.
-This motion proposes something along similar lines and we should ardently support it.

8203 **énergique** **energetic**
adj
[enɛʁʒik]
Nous poursuivons également une politique de développement énergique dans notre pays.
-We are also pursuing an vigorous development policy at home.

8204 **canasson** **nag**
m
[kanasɔ̃]
En réalité, ce n'était qu'un vieux canasson.
-In reality, it was an old nag.

8205 **simplifier** **simplify**
vb
[sɛ̃plifje]
Le reste est la vérification, que Mme le commissaire devra simplifier.
-The remainder is made up by the verification the Commissioner is called upon to simplify.

8206 **bazooka** **bazooka**
m[bazɔɔka]
Le rocket L.A.W.S... est un bazooka à un coup. -The L.A.W.S. Rocket: For all purposes... a one-shot disposable bazooka.

8207 **nervosité** **nervousness**
f
[nɛʁvozite]
L'homme silencieux semblait encore plus maladroit que d'ordinaire et il but du champagne avec régularité et détermination, par pure nervosité.
-The silent man seemed even more clumsy than usual, and drank champagne with regularity and determination out of sheer nervousness.

8208 **yogi** **yogi**
m
[jɔʒi]
Ma mère sort avec un yogi qui ne mange que cru.
-My mom is dating a yogi who only eats raw.

8209 **charisme** **charisma**
m
[kaʁism]
Jack a du charisme.
-Jack has charisma.

8210 **opprimer** **oppress|grind**
vb
[ɔpʁime]
Mais une démocratie ne peut-elle opprimer certains groupes de population ?
-But is it not possible for a democracy to oppress certain groups?

8211 **exécuteur** **executor**
m
[ɛgzekytœʁ]
Beaucoup de gens se disent très inquiets de la possibilité que l'OTAN endosse en quelque sorte le rôle nouveau et très dangereux d'exécuteur du droit international humanitaire.
-Many people are expressing deep concern about the possibility that somehow NATO is taking on to itself a new and very dangerous role of somehow being the enforcer of international humanitarian law.

8212 **rousseur** **redness**

	f [ʁusœʁ]	Elle a des taches de rousseur. -She has some freckles.
8213	**déloyal** adj [delwajal]	**unfair|disloyal** Le caractère déloyal de la concurrence peut être délibéré, mais aussi involontaire. -Competition may be deliberately unfair, or the unfairness may very well be involuntary.
8214	**groom** m [gʁum]	**bellhop|page** Il y a des hauts et des bas dans la vie, comme disait le groom de l'ascenseur. -There are highs and lows in life, said the elevator operator.
8215	**escroquer** vb [ɛskʁɔke]	**defraud|cheat** Mais se faire escroquer pour le plaisir que cela nous procure, c'est véritablement aller trop loin. -But to be swindled for the pleasure of doing it is really adding insult to injury.
8216	**bretzel** m [bʁɛtsɛl]	**pretzel** Mon cerveau est embrouillé façon bretzel. -My head's all tied up like a pretzel.
8217	**obligeance** f [ɔbliʒɑ̃s]	**helpfulness** Monsieur le Président, je vous remercie sincèrement pour votre obligeance et votre tolérance. -Mr President, you have my sincere thanks for your helpfulness and your tolerance.
8218	**rétrécir** vb[ʁetʁesiʁ]	**shrink** Nous nous trouvons bien plutôt face à un monde que semblent avoir rétréci les forces de la mondialisation. -We are instead confronted with a world that seems to have been reduced in size by the forces of globalization.
8219	**accroître** vb [akʁwatʁ]	**increase|enhance** S'ils font aussi des concessions, ils pourraient accroître leur influence. -If they also made concessions, they could increase their influence.
8220	**succulent** adj [sykylɑ̃]	**succulent** Je t'offre un fruit succulent ? -May I offer you a succulent fruit?
8221	**natte** f [nat]	**mat|braid** La natte de fibres est formée par électro-filage. -The fiber mat is formed by electrospinning.
8222	**babiole** f [babjɔl]	**bauble** Ils pensaient pouvoir mettre fin à des siècles de guerre en volant une babiole. -Thinking they could bring peace to centuries of war by stealing a trinket.
8223	**textile** adj; m [tɛkstil]	**textile; textile** L'industrie textile s'adaptera à un marché soumis à la libre concurrence dans les années à venir. -The textile industry will adapt to a market of free competition in the coming years.
8224	**asperge** f [aspɛʁʒ]	**asparagus** Tu aboies après la mauvaise asperge. -You're barkin' up the wrong asparagus.
8225	**linceul** m [lɛ̃sœl]	**shroud|grave clothes** C'est comme le linceul sacré de l'urine. -It's like the sacred shroud of urine.

8226 **curé** **priest**
m
[kyʁe]
Paddy a trouvé un curé pour confesser nos péchés hideux.
-Paddy Clohessy found a priest to confess our hideous sins to.

8227 **carrure** **shoulders|build**
f
[kaʁyʁ]
Thomas a une carrure athlétique.
-Thomas has an athletic build.

8228 **prochainement** **shortly**
adv
[pʁɔʃɛnmɑ̃]
L'intervenant a également prié l'ONU d'envisager d'envoyer prochainement une mission de visite à Pitcairn.
-He also wished to explore the possibility of a United Nations visiting mission to Pitcairn at an early date.

8229 **affecté** **affected**
adj
[afɛkte]
Le délai fixé pour l'achèvement de la constitution ne s'en trouverait pas affecté.
-The time frame set for the completion of the constitution would not be affected.

8230 **arithmétique** **arithmetic; arithmetic**
adj; f
[aʁitmetik]
Assez d'arithmétique pour aujourd'hui.
-I think that's enough Arithmetic for today.

8231 **buanderie** **utility room**
f
[bɥɑ̃dʁi]
Catalina nous laissera plus dormir dans la buanderie.
-There's no way Catalina's letting us sleep in the laundry room anymore.

8232 **cigogne** **stork**
f
[sigɔɲ]
Début 2006, grâce aux mêmes synergies, le Plan Cigogne II a été lancé afin de poursuivre les objectifs de développement des places d'accueil de l'enfant de 0-3 ans.
-Beginning 2006, on the basis of the same synergies, Stork Plan II was launched to pursue the objectives of developing childcare centers for children of 0-3 years of age.

8233 **éleveur** **farmer**
m
[elvœʁ]
M. Vorstenbosch, un éleveur de porcs, représentait les municipalités auprès de la Commission.
-Mr. Vorstenbosch, a hog farmer, represented municipalities on the Board.

8234 **Bolchevik** **Bolshevik**
m/f
[bɔlʃəvik]
Je pensais que vous étiez une sorte de Bolchevik fou.
-I thought you were some sort of crazy Bolshevik.

8235 **ingéniosité** **ingenuity**
f
[ɛ̃ʒenjozite]
L'ingéniosité humaine et les progrès technologiques compliquent encore ces défis.
-Human ingenuity and technological advances complicate those challenges.

8236 **rafale** **gust|flurry**
f
[ʁafal]
La première rafale d'accès peut comprendre un identifiant abrégé et/ou des données utilisateurs.
-The initial access burst may include at least one of a shortened identifier and user data.

8237 **avènement** **advent**
m
[avɛnmɑ̃]
C'est important pour l'avènement, enfin, d'une véritable Europe des citoyens.
-This is important for the advent, at long last, of a genuine citizens ' Europe.

8238 **toge** **toga**

	f [tɔʒ]	Varinia, ma toge rouge avec les glands. -Varinia, my red toga with the acorns.
8239	**thermos** m; adj [tɛʁmo]	**thermos; thermos** Ce récipient est utilisé comme bouteille thermos, comme glacière et comme réfrégirateur. -This container is utilized as a thermos jug, a cooler box and a refrigerator.
8240	**étanche** adj [etɑ̃ʃ]	**waterproof** Ce conteneur est complètement étanche. -This container is completely watertight.
8241	**inéluctable** adj [inelyktabl]	**inevitable|ineluctable** C'est la conclusion inéluctable que nous devons tirer des attaques terroristes du 11 septembre. -This is the ineluctable conclusion we must draw from the terrorist attacks of 11 September.
8242	**hâtif** adj [atif]	**hasty** J'ai déjà souligné dans ma première réponse qu'il était trop hâtif de condamner la politique structurelle. -I already emphasized in my first reply that it was too hasty to condemn the structural policy.
8243	**potassium** m[pɔtasjɔm]	**potassium** L'iodure de potassium peut également être directement administré au niveau de la prostate. -The potassium iodide also may be delivered directly to the prostate.
8244	**réglisse** f [ʁeglis]	**licorice** Mon frère vient d'attenter à ma personne en m'offrant 1,5 kilo de réglisse. Il sait bien que je vais mourir si je mange tout cela à la fois. -My brother just made an attempt on my life by offering me 1.5 kilos of licorice. He knows well that I'll die if I eat all that at once.
8245	**méduser** vb [medyze]	**daze|paralyze** Et leur réussite peut méduser même les plus aguerris. -And the success of those plans can take even the most hardened men by surprise.
8246	**antiquaire** adj; m/f [ɑ̃tikɛʁ]	**antiquarian; antiquarian** Je m'associe à un antiquaire. -I'm associated with an antique dealer.
8247	**récidiviste** m/f [ʁesidivist]	**recidivist** Un récidiviste violent, détenu à plusieurs reprises. -A violent repeat offender, repeatedly jailed.
8248	**retracer** vb [ʁətʁase]	**trace|recount** Bien que non exhaustif, il tente de retracer l'origine de certaines pratiques, de même que les actions qui ont été menées au sein de la Sous-Commission. -While it is not exhaustive, it does attempt to retrace the origins of certain practices, as well as of the actions taken by the Sub-Commission.
8249	**arrosage** m [aʁozaʒ]	**spray** D'autres municipalités ont des règlements sur l'arrosage. -Other municipalities have regulations on watering.
8250	**ressortir** vb [ʁəsɔʁtiʁ]	**stand out** Pour faire découvrir la langue internationale, on devrait écrire en faisant ressortir chaque lexie. -In order to unveil the international language, each lexical item should be written separately.
8251	**orbite**	**orbit**

f | L'ASE a mis un satellite en orbite.
[ɔʁbit] | -The ESA put a satellite into orbit.

8252 **haineux** **hateful**
adj
[ɛnø]
J'ai chaque courrier haineux archivé numériquement.
-I have every piece of hate mail digitally archived.

8253 **glauque** **glaucous**
adj
[glok]
Il s'est constitué autour de la Commission un petit monde glauque où se trafiquent toutes les influences, à mille lieues des préoccupations des citoyens.
-A sordid little world has been built up around the Commission, where influences are traded, far away from the concerns of citizens.

8254 **exalter** **exalt|extoll**
vb
[ɛgzalte]
Si les droits exaltent la liberté individuelle, les devoirs expriment la dignité de cette liberté».
-While rights exalt individual liberty, duties express the dignity of that liberty".

8255 **visqueux** **viscous|slimy**
adj[viskø]
Le fluide est présumé visqueux et incompressible. -The fluid is assumed to be viscous and incompressible.

8256 **parachutiste** **parachutist**
m/f
[paʁaʃytist]
Dupuis s'est attardé sur les parachutistes.
-After all, Mr Dupuis did mention parachutists.

8257 **convalescence** **recovery**
f
[kɔ̃valesɑ̃s]
Elle est là pour me tenir compagnie pendant que je suis en convalescence.
-She is here to keep me company while I'm still recovering.

8258 **ouvrage** **handiwork**
m
[uvʁaʒ]
Elle ne voulut pas vendre l'ouvrage.
-She didn't want to sell the book.

8259 **virtuose** **virtuoso**
m/f
[viʁtɥoz]
C'est un virtuose du violoncelle.
-He plays cello exceptionally well.

8260 **vicaire** **vicar**
m
[vikɛʁ]
Le vicaire général du diocèse s'est montré patient et compréhensif.
-The Vicar General of that diocese was patient and understanding.

8261 **relatif** **relative; relative**
adj; m
[ʁəlatif]
J'ai un dernier conseil relatif aux poignées de mains : N'oubliez pas de sourire.
-I have one final piece of advice related to handshakes: Remember to smile.

8262 **intimidation** **intimidation**
f
[ɛ̃timidasjɔ̃]
On dit que les formes insidieuses d'intimidation sont en augmentation dans les lycées.
-In junior high and high schools, they say insidious forms of bullying are on the rise.

8263 **continuité** **continuity**
f
[kɔ̃tinɥite]
Il existe une continuité, il doit exister une continuité dans tout État.
-There is continuity, there must be continuity within a state.

8264 **chirurgical** **surgical**
adj
[ʃiʁyʁʒikal]
Un service chirurgical pour les patients séropositifs y est aussi prévu.
-It has also planned to set up a surgical unit for HIV-positive patients.

8265 **ovale** **oval; oval**

	adj; m [ɔval]	Ils se rencontrent au bureau ovale maintenant. -They're meeting in the oval office right now.
8266	**enzyme** f [ɑ̃zim]	**enzyme** Ces composés interagissent avec l'enzyme bêta-sécrétase et inhibent son activité. -These compounds interact with and inhibit the activity of the enzyme beta-secretase.
8267	**vecteur** m [vɛktœʁ]	**vector** La presse est le principal vecteur d'information à l'intention du public. -The principal vector of information for the general public is the press.
8268	**végétation** f [veʒetasjɔ̃]	**vegetation** Concentrez votre activité là où la végétation est absente. -Concentrate your activities to the area where there is no vegetation.
8269	**éraflure** f [eʁaflyʁ]	**scratch|score** Vous avez une sale éraflure sur le bras. -You have a bad scratch on that arm.
8270	**contraction** f [kɔ̃tʁaksjɔ̃]	**contraction** La prochaine contraction si vous pouvez. -Well, the next contraction, if you can keep this up.
8271	**expier** vb [ɛkspje]	**atone for** Il m'a envoyé cette chance d'expier pour mes péchés. -He has sent me this chance to atone for my sins.
8272	**fouineur** m; adj [fwinœʁ]	**snoop; prying** Je ne suis pas fouineur. -I'm not prying.
8273	**lamentation** f [lamɑ̃tasjɔ̃]	**lamentation** En préparant ce règlement, nous avons organisé des audiences qui étaient en vérité une lamentation ininterrompue. -In preparing this regulation we held hearings that were, in truth, one uninterrupted lament.
8274	**immiscer** vb [imise]	**interfere** Pourquoi l'UE, en tant que telle, a -t-elle besoin de s'immiscer dans ce domaine? -Why does the EU, as such, need to muscle in on this territory?
8275	**cône** m [kon]	**cone** Je réclame le cône du silence. -Chief, I request the cone of silence.
8276	**connaisseur** m [kɔnɛsœʁ]	**connoisseur** Mais vous êtes un connaisseur, cher Falcon. -Yes, but you, my dear Falcon, are a connoisseur.
8277	**métropole** f [metʁɔpɔl]	**metropolis** Un hameau grandit jusqu'à devenir une métropole. -A small village grew into a large city.
8278	**gratifier** vb [gʁatifje]	**gratify** Nous ne devrions pas avoir à gratifier la Serbie pour qu'elle se comporte en démocratie européenne adulte. -We should not have to reward Serbia for behaving like a mature European democracy.
8279	**encombrer** vb [ɑ̃kɔ̃bʁe]	**encumber** Le point de passage autorisé des véhicules, à la 46e Rue, sera probablement très encombré.

-The vehicular crossing point at 46th Street is expected to be particularly congested.

8280 **gaine** f [gɛn] — **sheath**

La présente invention concerne également une aiguille coaxiale comprenant : une gaine ; une gaine interne qui pénètre la gaine ; et un stylet interne qui pénètre la gaine interne.
-Further, a coaxial needle comprising: a sheath; an inner sheath that penetrates the sheath; and an inner stylet that penetrates the inner sheath is disclosed.

8281 **lucidité** f [lysidite] — **lucidity**

L'intérêt supérieur de l'enfant doit être apprécié avec la plus grande lucidité.
-The best interests of the child must be weighed up with the utmost clarity.

8282 **déraisonnable** adj[deʁɛzɔnabl] — **unreasonable**

Dans les circonstances, la condition de nationalité était déraisonnable. -The citizenship requirement in these circumstances was unreasonable.

8283 **impétueux** adj [ɛ̃petɥø] — **impetuous**

Je ne peux décrire ce Traité autrement que comme un saut impétueux dans l'obscurité.
-I cannot describe this treaty as anything other than an impetuous leap in the dark.

8284 **forestier** m [fɔʁɛstje] — **forester**

Subventions et primes: Toute demande doit être déposée par un forestier agréé.
-Grants and premiums: Applications are made by an approved forester.

8285 **greffier** m [gʁefje] — **clerk|registrar**

Chambre des communes : Wayne Cole, greffier législatif; Joann Garbig, greffière à la procédure.
-House of Commons: Wayne Cole, Legislative Clerk; Joann Garbig, Procedural Clerk.

8286 **altercation** f [altɛʁkasjɔ̃] — **altercation**

Numéro trois, l'altercation Star Wars.
-Number three, the Star Wars altercation.

8287 **dérouiller** vb [deʁuje] — **stretch|whack**

Dis à ce Mafieux que je connais un truc qu'il peut dérouiller.
-Tell that Mafioso I know something he can whack.

8288 **discréditer** vb [diskʁedite] — **discredit**

À son avis, ces plaintes risquaient de discréditer Anguilla au plan international.
-In his view, that had the potential to discredit Anguilla internationally.

8289 **relief** m [ʁəljɛf] — **relief**

Ledit relief est en particulier visible à l'œil nu en lumière rasante.
-Said relief is in particular visible to the naked eye in raking light.

8290 **gâble** m [gabl] — **gable|spring**

Le ressort sollicite de façon élastique les éléments gauche et droit pour obtenir une configuration en gâble, conférant ainsi à l'auvent la forme d'un gâble.
-In another embodiment, the front support member is a left member and right member connected by a hinge and a spring.

8291 **bestial** adj [bɛstjal] — **bestial**

Monsieur le Président, celui qui qualifie de bestiales les atrocités perpétrées en Sierra Leone insulte les animaux.

-Mr President, to term these on-going brutalities in Sierra Leone as bestial is an insult to animals.

8292 **digestion** f [diʒɛstjɔ̃]
digestion
Meilleure est la cuisson d'une viande, plus rapide est sa digestion.
-The better cooked the meat is, the quicker its digestion.

8293 **ancestral** adj [ɑ̃sɛstʁal]
ancestral
Pour les premières nations, la danse constitue un élément important du patrimoine ancestral.
-To the first nations, dance is a vital component of their ancestral heritage.

8294 **enclin** adj [ɑ̃klɛ̃]
inclined
Je suis plutôt enclin à adopter une attitude cynique par rapport à la date de cet appel.
-In fact I am inclined to be rather cynical about the timing of this appeal.

8295 **cierge** m [sjɛʁʒ]
candle
Allumez un cierge, je vous prie !
-Please light a candle.

8296 **résulter** vb [ʁezylte]
result
La classification pouvant résulter des essais est également indiquée.
-The classification which may result from the testing is also indicated.

8297 **céleri** m [sɛlʁi]
celery
Troisièmement, le céleri et la moutarde ainsi que leurs produits dérivés seront ajoutés à la liste des produits allergènes.
-Third, the addition of celery and mustard and their derived products to the list of allergenic substances.

8298 **ressentiment** m [ʁəsɑ̃timɑ̃]
resentment
Le Secrétaire général a souligné que le ressentiment pourrait s'intensifier.
-The Secretary-General has underlined that the resentment might intensify.

8299 **allumeur** m [alymœʁ]
igniter
Un allumeur est ensuite excité pour émettre des étincelles dans la chambre de combustion.
-Then an igniter is excited to spark in the combustor.

8300 **commenter** vb [kɔmɑ̃te]
comment|commentate
Enfin, M. le Président, j'aimerais commenter le contenu du partenariat.
-Finally, Mr President, I would like to comment on the content of the partnership.

8301 **rangé** adj [ʁɑ̃ʒe]
tidy
Son monde était rangé, sans embûche.
-His world was tidy, uncomplicated…

8302 **gaver** vb [gave]
stuff
Si vous enfoncez un entonnoir dans la gorge d'une oie pour la gaver de maïs, il est impossible de ne lui causer ni souffrance ni dommage.
-If you stick a funnel down a goose's throat and force-feed it with maize, there is no way that you are not causing suffering or injury.

8303 **subvention** f [sybvɑ̃sjɔ̃]
grant|subsidy
Nombre de nouvelles équipes établies grâce à la subvention.
-Number of new teams established as a result of this grant.

8304 **méprise** f [mepʁiz]
mistake|misunderstanding
La troisième erreur relevait simplement d'une méprise dans l'interprétation de la description du code.
-The third error was simply a misunderstanding in the interpretation of the code description.

8305 **recruteur**
recruiter

m Le recruteur est venu vous chercher...
[ʁəkʁytœʁ] -The recruiter is here to pick you up...

8306 **rationnement** **rationing**
m Les dispositions sont en cours pour augmenter la ration alimentaire quotidienne.
[ʁasjɔnmɑ̃] -Provision is being made to increase the daily food ration.

8307 **méticuleux** **meticulous|painstaking**
adj En conséquence, des efforts méticuleux ont été déployés au cours des investigations.
[metikylø] -As a result, meticulous effort was expended in the conduct of investigations.

8308 **cloquer** **blister**
vb La peau exposée au soleil se met à cloquer.
[klɔke] -The skin blisters when it's exposed to the sun.

8309 **droitier** **right-hander; right-handed**
m; adj Jack est droitier.
[dʁwatje] -Jack is right-handed.

8310 **insécurité** **insecurity**
f L'insécurité en Afghanistan entraîne l'insécurité dans nos régions frontalières de l'ouest.
[ɛ̃sekyʁite] -Insecurity in Afghanistan causes insecurity in our Western frontier regions.

8311 **perceur** **piercer**
m Le dispositif de positionnement comprend un élément perceur qui peut percer le SS et un septum primum.
[pɛʁsœʁ] -The positioning device includes a piercing member that can pierce the SS and a septum primum.

8312 **microphone** **microphone**
m Le microphone est mort.
[mikʁɔfɔn] -The microphone is dead.

8313 **frigide** **frigid**
adj Je voulais savoir si j'étais anormale ou frigide.
[fʁiʒid] -I had to know if I was some kind of freak, or frigid.

8314 **quadrant** **quadrant**
m Le quadrant I regroupe les pays qui ont obtenu un pointage élevé dans les deux volets.
[kadʁɑ̃] -Quadrant I indicates countries that score high on both dimensions.

8315 **platiner** **platinize**
vb Platiner ce zinc en le plaçant dans un vase cylindrique et en le recouvrant avec une solution de chlorure de platine à 1 pour 20000.
[platine] -Platinize the zinc by placing it in a cylindrical flask and covering it with a 1/20000 platinum chloride solution.

8316 **renégat** **renegade; renegade**
adj; m Nous sommes chargés de ramener le renégat apache Geronimo.
[ʁənega] -We are charged with bringing in the renegade Apache, Geronimo.

8317 **occulte** **occult**
adj Les arcanes de cette science occulte ne nous intéressent pas ici.
[ɔkylt] -The mysteries of this clandestine science do not interest us here.

8318 **compère** **accomplice**
m Je vais dire oui à mon vieux compère.
[kɔ̃pɛʁ] -I'll squeeze you in, for my old compadre.

8319 **abréger** vb [abʁeʒe]
shorten
Kolby (Norvège): Je vais moi aussi abréger mon intervention.
-Kolby (Norway): I shall also shorten my statement.

8320 **éloquence** f [elɔkɑ̃s]
eloquence
Il parla avec tant d'éloquence que tout l'auditoire était en pleurs.
-He spoke so eloquently that the audience were all moved to tears.

8321 **désarroi** m [dezaʁwa]
disarray
Imaginez mon désarroi lorsque j'ai découvert qu'elle m'était attribuée.
-Imagine my dismay to discover that it was being attributed to me.

8322 **montant** m[mɔ̃tɑ̃]
amount|post
Le montant grimpera en cas de récidive. -The amount will go up in the case of recidivism.

8323 **échine** f [eʃin]
spine
Cinq mots à vous faire frissonner l'échine.
-Five words to send a chill down your spine.

8324 **anémie** f [anemi]
anemia
En prélevant des parties d'estomac canin, si les chiens développaient l'anémie pernicieuse.
-By removing parts of canine stomachs - To see if the dogs developed pernicious anaemia.

8325 **indignation** f [ɛ̃diɲasjɔ̃]
indignation
Votre indignation morale commence à me prendre la tête.
-Your moral indignation is beginning to give me a quick pain in the neck.

8326 **persuasif** adj [pɛʁsɥazif]
persuasive
Jack était très persuasif.
-Jack was very persuasive.

8327 **écorcher** vb [ekɔʁʃe]
skin
Je sais comment écorcher un lapin.
-I know how to skin a rabbit.

8328 **nageoire** f [naʒwaʁ]
fin
Cette nageoire permet au dauphin de se déplacer.
-This fin allows the dolphin to move forward.

8329 **trapèze** m [tʁapɛz]
trapeze
C'est l'attrapeur au trapèze.
-He's the catcher on the trapeze.

8330 **fret** m [fʁɛ]
freight|freight charges
Les exportateurs devraient obtenir des données plus à jour auprès d'entreprises de transport du fret.
-Exporters should obtain more up to date information from freight forwarding companies.

8331 **mobiliser** vb [mɔbilize]
mobilize|enlist
C'est un processus qui prend du temps et qui doit mobiliser tous nos efforts.
-It is a process that takes time and for which we must mobilize all our efforts.

8332 **innocenter** vb [inɔsɑ̃te]
clear|find not guilty
David Ronaldo recherchait des preuves pour innocenter Cruz.
-Well, David Ronaldo was looking for evidence to clear Cruz.

8333 **immuable** adj [imɥabl]
immuable
L'apartheid est uniquement immuable si nous l'acceptons; or nous ne devons l'accepter sous aucun prétexte.

-Apartheid is only unchangeable if we resign ourselves to it and we must therefore not do so.

8334 **pénalité** **penalty**
f
[penalite]
La pénalité réglementaire sera prévue par règlement.
-The prescribed penalty is to be set out in the regulations.

8335 **gueux** **beggar**
m
[gø]
Qu'un roi peut voyager dans les tripes d'un gueux.
-Nothing but to show you how a king may go a progress through the guts of a beggar.

8336 **adoucir** **soften**
vb
[adusiʁ]
On dit qu'une cuillère de miel de l'espace aide à adoucir la douleur.
-They say a spoonful of space honey helps ease the pain.

8337 **généreusement** **generously**
adv
[ʒeneʁøzmɑ̃]
La communauté internationale nous aide généreusement à maintenir la liberté.
-The international community has been assisting us generously in maintaining freedom.

8338 **laquais** **lackey; menial**
m; adj
[lakɛ]
Je ne suis pas un laquais du gouvernement qui suit aveuglement les ordres.
-I'm not some government lackey who blindly follows orders.

8339 **minuteur** **timer**
m
[minytœʁ]
L'énergie déplacée perturbe le minuteur.
-The energy displacement is wreaking havoc on the timer.

8340 **narration** **narration**
f
[naʁasjɔ̃]
Sa narration a été factuelle et historiquement exacte.
-His narration was factually and historically accurate.

8341 **crucifixion** **crucifixion**
f
[kʁysifiksjɔ̃]
Les victimes présumées sont passibles d'exécution par pendaison ou crucifixion.
-The alleged victims may be subject to execution by hanging or crucifixion.

8342 **cupide** **greedy**
adj
[kypid]
Tous ensemble, nous devons freiner notre mode de vie cupide et extravagant.
-Collectively, we need to restrain our avaricious and extravagant living.

8343 **piteux** **sorry**
adj
[pitø]
Le bouc émissaire a rempli sa mission, mais il se trouve dans un piteux état.
-This is the only way to stimulate growth, employment and cohesion.

8344 **rente** **annuity; income**
m; f
[ʁɑ̃t]
À ma mort, ça te fera une rente.
-Do whatever you want with it when I'm dead. It's your annuity.

8345 **insistance** **insistence**
f
[ɛ̃sistɑ̃s]
L' insistance à interdire l' entrée de l' Union européenne à ces gens doit être abordée.
-In general there is too much emphasis on turning this matter into a criminal issue.

8346 **brider** **bridle**
vb
[bʁide]
Toute tentative de brider ce vecteur est non seulement injuste, mais s'avèrera aussi inefficace.
-Trying to limit this vehicle is not only unjust, it will also prove ineffective.

8347 **courtiser** **court**

vb [kuʁtize] Certains pays font tout pour courtiser la diaspora, d'autres s'y montrent indifférents, voire hostiles.
-However, with the rapid growth of expatriate communities and new forms of ICT, it is possible to engage diasporas in an immediate and effective way.

8348 **fard** **make-up**
m[faʁ] Il faut que vous me disiez la vérité sans fard. -I need you to tell me the unvarnished truth.

8349 **Capricorne** **Capricorn**
m [kapʁikɔʁn] Mon horoscope me dit qu'un Capricorne doit m'apporter la prospérité.
-My horoscope says a Capricorn will lead me to prosperity.

8350 **efficacement** **effectively**
adv [efikasmɑ̃] Ces efforts sont efficacement soutenus avec la participation de bénévoles.
-These efforts are maintained effectively with the participation of volunteers.

8351 **camaraderie** **comeradeship**
f [kamaʁadʁi] Néanmoins, les participants ne devraient pas se contenter d'une bonne camaraderie.
-But the CD should not be complacent with only good comradeship.

8352 **négociable** **negotiable**
adj [negɔsjabl] La nouvelle directive traite les soins de santé comme un bien commercialement négociable.
-The new directive treats healthcare as a piece of commercially tradeable goods.

8353 **professionnalisme** **professionalism**
m [pʁɔfesjɔnalism] Chacun a travaillé avec dévouement, bonne volonté et force professionnalisme.
-Everyone has worked with dedication, good will and increasing professionalism.

8354 **récession** **recession**
f [ʁesesjɔ̃] La récession est une baisse temporaire des activités commerciales à une période où une telle activité généralement augmente.
-Recession is a temporary falling off of business activity during a period when such activity is generally increasing.

8355 **anthropologie** **anthropology**
f [ɑ̃tʁɔpɔlɔʒi] Tout étudiant en biologie, anatomie, anthropologie, ethnologie ou psychologie est familier de ces faits.
-Every student of biology, anatomy, anthropology, ethnology or psychology is familiar with these facts.

8356 **enregistreur** **recorder**
m [ɑ̃ʁəʒistʁœʁ] Ces trois valeurs sont affichées sur enregistreur pendant le soufflage.
-These three values are displayed on a recorder during the blowing cycle.

8357 **kleenex** **tissue**
m [klinɛks] Monsieur le Président, je fouillais dans mes poches pour trouver des Kleenex, mais je n'en ai pas.
-Speaker, I was fumbling around looking for some Kleenex and I am sorry I could not find any.

8358 **suppression** **removal**
f [sypʁesjɔ̃] Ils identifient le niveau adéquat de suppression de ces obstacles.
-They should identify the appropriate level for the removal of these obstacles.

8359 **instabilité** **instability**

f | Il faut régler ce problème d'instabilité.
[ɛ̃stabilite] | -We've got to lick this problem of instability.

8360 **peler** **peel|rind**
vb
[pəle]
Ils ne pouvaient peler des pommes de terre destinées à des blancs.
-They were not allowed to peel potatoes for the white people to eat.

8361 **plancton** **plankton**
m
[plɑ̃ktɔ̃]
Le fer dispersé à la surface des océans accroit la production de plancton.
-Iron added to the ocean surface increases the plankton production.

8362 **déroulement** **progress**
m
[deʁulmɑ̃]
Examinons certaines allégations sur le déroulement de cette guerre.
-We look at some of the allegations made about the conduct of that war.

8363 **ménopause** **menopause**
f
[menopoz]
La ménopause est la fin des menstruations.
-Menopause is the end of menstruation.

8364 **autocollant** **sticker; self-sealing**
m; adj
[otokɔlɑ̃]
Véhicule du représentant permanent, portant un autocollant spécial.
-Vehicle of the Permanent Representative, identified by a special sticker.

8365 **accouplement** **coupling**
m
[akupləmɑ̃]
Simultanément, les deux éléments d'accouplement sont désolidarisés.
-At the same time, the two coupling elements are detached from each other.

8366 **prématurément** **prematurely**
adv
[pʁematyʁemɑ̃]
Toutefois, il importe que nous ne cherchions pas à tirer prématurément des conclusions.
-However, it is important that we not seek to reach such conclusions prematurely.

8367 **syllabe** **syllable**
f
[silab]
En espéranto, l'avant-dernière syllabe est toujours accentuée.
-In Esperanto, the syllable before the last one is always stressed.

8368 **obsolète** **obsolete**
adj
[ɔpsɔlɛt]
Cette troisième option rendrait la Convention complètement superflue et obsolète.
-This third option would render the obsolete Convention superfluous.

8369 **côtier** **coastal**
adj
[kotje]
Sur les secteurs où le chenal est étroit on utilise de préférence le balisage côtier.
-On sectors where the fairway is narrow, preference shall be given to coastal marks.

8370 **mascara** **mascara**
m
[maskaʁa]
Ce dispositif permet notamment le maquillage des cils à l'aide de mascara.
-This device particularly enables eyelashes to be made up with mascara.

8371 **amygdale** **tonsil|amygdala**
f
[amigdal]
Les émotions de Penny naissent dans la partie du cerveau appelée amygdale.
-Penny's emotional responses originate in the primitive portion of brain, the amygdala.

8372 **devancer** **forestall|outstrip**
vb
[dəvɑ̃se]
Encore là, le président Milosevic a fait le minimum pour devancer les mesures prises contre lui.
-Yet again President Milosevic has done the bare minimum in an effort to forestall the action against him.

8373 **télépathique** **telepathic**

	adj	Une sorte de communication télépathique ou même plus élémentaire.
	[telepatik]	-It could be a form of telepathic communication or something more elemental.
8374	**galeux**	**mangy**
	adj	Attention, voilà le chien galeux.
	[galø]	-Watch out, here's the mangy dog.
8375	**émouvant**	**moving|touching**
	adj	Je suis personnellement profondément convaincu qu'aucune initiation véritable à la diplomatie en matière de désarmement n'est complète sans une visite émouvante à Hiroshima et Nagasaki.
	[emuvɑ̃]	-It is my deep personal conviction that no initiation into disarmament diplomacy can be complete without a soul-stirring visit to Hiroshima and Nagasaki.
8376	**déloger**	**dislodge**
	vb	Il critique indirectement le recours à la force pour déloger les terroristes de Fallouja.
	[delɔʒe]	-It indirectly criticizes the use of force to dislodge terrorists from Fallujah.
8377	**laurier**	**laurel**
	m	Vous voyez ce laurier, Ses feuilles pendent a gauche.
	[loʁje]	-See that laurel? It's leaves flows left.
8378	**gué**	**ford**
	m	Ils se trouvent comme au milieu d'un gué.
	[ge]	-It is as if they were halfway across a ford.
8379	**hypnotiser**	**hypnotize**
	vb	T'enverras tout aux oubliettes, vautré dans ton fauteuil relax, hypnotisé par la télé jusqu'à la fin de tes jours.
	[ipnɔtize]	-You'll push it into memory, then zone out in your Barcalounger, being hypnotized by daytime TV for the rest of your life.
8380	**lubie**	**whim|freak**
	f	Un dictionnaire vocal n'est déjà plus une lubie.
	[lybi]	-A talking dictionary is no longer a fantasy.
8381	**bouillotte**	**hot-water bag**
	f	C'est-à- dire... je suis là avec la bouillotte à la main.
	[bujɔt]	-I mean, I'm standing here with this hot-water bottle in my hand!
8382	**impartial**	**impartial|unbiased**
	adj	L'Union européenne doit être un acteur impartial.
	[ɛ̃paʁsjal]	-The European Union must be an impartial actor.
8383	**jacasser**	**chatter|jabber**
	vb	Les députés continuent de jacasser et de crier.
	[ʒakase]	-People keep on yapping and yelling.
8384	**leurre**	**lure**
	m	Grayson transporte les documents et Henry sert de leurre.
	[lœʁ]	-Grayson's carrying the document while Sir Henry's being used as a decoy.
8385	**immensité**	**immensity**
	f	Il ne croyait pas au vol spatial physique, mais il considérait la projection astrale à travers l'immensité comme possible.
	[imɑ̃site]	-He did not believe in physical space flight, but astral projection through the vastness he considered possible.
8386	**diagnostiquer**	**diagnose**

vb
[djagnɔstike]
La maladie de Parkinson est complexe, difficile à diagnostiquer et imprévisible.
-Parkinson's disease is complex, hard to diagnose and random.

8387 **gosier** **throat|gullet**
m
[gozje]
Elle a un gosier en or.
-She has a throat of gold.

8388 **cantique** **canticle|song**
m
[kɑ̃tik]
Commencez par le cantique des Lys.
-For the beginning I want the song of the Lilies of the Field.

8389 **écœurant** **disgusting|sickening**
adj
[ekœʁɑ̃]
N'est-ce pas écœurant ?
-Isn't it sickening?

8390 **dispensaire** **dispensary**
m
[dispɑ̃sɛʁ]
Deux autres bombes ont été découvertes dans l'école et une quatrième dans un dispensaire voisin.
-Two more bombs were also found at the school and a fourth bomb was found at a nearby community clinic.

8391 **tirade** **tirade**
f
[tiʁad]
Ce n'était pas une tirade.
-Okay, it was not a tirade.

8392 **variation** **variation|change**
f
[vaʁjasjɔ̃]
Ce genre de variation sent la manipulation...
-Because this kind of variation screams manipulation to me...

8393 **émir** **emir**
m
[emiʁ]
À l'Université des sciences islamiques Émir Abdelkader, on compte 70 % d'étudiantes.
-At the Emir Abdelkader University of Islamic Sciences, 70 per cent of students are women.

8394 **bagarreur** **brawler; feisty**
m; adj
[bagaʁœʁ]
Lorsque j'ai fait la connaissance de Sheila, elle avait un tempérament explosif, dogmatique et bagarreur et elle venait d'être nommée députée de la grande circonscription de Mont- Royal.
-When I first encountered Sheila, she was explosive, opinionated, feisty and the newly-minted member of Parliament for that great riding of Mount Royal.

8395 **subvenir** **support**
vb
[sybvəniʁ]
Titiahonjo devait subvenir seul à ses besoins.
-He also had to provide for himself and live on his own supplies.

8396 **tweed** **tweed**
m
[twi]
Il était également recouvert de la même toile de valise en tweed utilisée sur le Fender Deluxe.
-It was also covered in the same tweed suitcase cloth used on the Fender Deluxe.

8397 **sangloter** **sob**
vb
[sɑ̃glɔte]
C'est ce qui lui a permis d'assassiner ma mère et ma tante alors qu'elles sanglotaient à genoux.
-It enabled him to slaughter my Mom and my Aunt while they sobbed on their hands and knees.

8398 **aisance** **ease**
f
[ɛzɑ̃s]
Je peux lire l'espagnol avec aisance.
-I can read Spanish with ease.

8399 **baignade** **bathing**

	f[bɛɲad]	Te joindras-tu à nous pour une baignade ? -Will you join us for a swim?
8400	**piédestal**	**pedestal**
	m [pjedɛstal]	Descendre de son piédestal, traîner avec les manants. -You know, coming down from her pedestal, hang with the riffraff.
8401	**anévrisme**	**aneurism**
	m [anevʁism]	Dites-le-moi, sinon c'est l'anévrisme. -Tell me where it is, or you get an aneurysm.
8402	**conformer**	**comply with|conform**
	vb [kɔ̃fɔʁme]	Cela signifie, en substance, se conformer à ce qui se passe dans la nature. -To do that we need to model ourselves on what happens in nature.
8403	**dissimulation**	**concealment**
	f [disimylasjɔ̃]	Destruction de propriété privée, dissimulation d'arme. -Destruction of private property, concealment of a deadly weapon.
8404	**réapparaître**	**reappear**
	vb [ʁeapaʁɛtʁ]	Cette ruse a été totalement déjouée par les Nations unies, pour réapparaître maintenant au Parlement européen. -This ruse was heavily defeated in the United Nations, only to reappear now in the European Parliament.
8405	**nomade**	**nomadic; nomad**
	adj; m/f [nɔmad]	Ces tribus s'adonnaient principalement à l'élevage nomade et semi-nomade. -Such tribes were predominantly occupied with semi-nomadic and nomadic cattle-breeding.
8406	**irréparable**	**irreparable**
	adj [iʁepaʁabl]	Cette grue a été tellement endommagée qu'elle était irréparable de sorte que la réclamation correspond à la valeur comptable nette de remplacement. -The mobile crane was damaged beyond repair; thus, the claim is for depreciated replacement value.
8407	**nettoyeur**	**cleaner; cleaning**
	m; adj [netwajœʁ]	Je retourne chercher le nettoyeur vapeur. -I go back in to pick up the steam cleaner.
8408	**consortium**	**consortium**
	m [kɔ̃sɔʁsjɔm]	STI Canada coordonne les activités du consortium. -The consortium's activities are coordinated by ITS Canada.
8409	**zèbre**	**zebra**
	m [zɛbʁ]	Il est tel un zèbre au milieu des chevaux. -He's like a zebra among the horses.
8410	**imparfait**	**imperfect; imperfect**
	adj; m [ɛ̃paʁfɛ]	Néanmoins, la commission des budgets estime qu'il est imparfait. -However, the Budgets Committee opinion is that it is flawed.
8411	**rétroviseur**	**mirror**
	m [ʁetʁovizœʁ]	Le rétroviseur est toujours plus petit que le pare-brise. -The rear-view mirror is always smaller than the windshield.
8412	**niaiserie**	**silliness**
	m [njɛzʁi]	Je ne m'attendais pas à entendre pareille niaiserie. -I wasn't expecting to hear such nonsense.
8413	**latex**	**latex**
	m [latɛks]	Jack a mis une paire de gants en latex. -Jack put on a pair of latex gloves.
8414	**minibus**	**minibus**
	m[miniby]	Le minibus arrivera dans 5 minutes. -The minibus will be here in 5 minutes.

8415 **hépatite** **hepatitis**
f
[epatit]
On les utilise pour guérir des lésions, l'hépatite foudroyante ainsi que des maladies intestinales inflammatoires.
-They are used for curing wound, fulminant hepatitis and inflammatory intestinal diseases.

8416 **gonflable** **inflatable**
adj
[gɔ̃flabl]
L'article en question est une embarcation gonflable utilisée pour les sauvetages.
-This asset is a rigged inflatable boat used as a rescue craft.

8417 **apport** **contribution**
m
[apɔʁ]
À l'heure actuelle, il n'existe pas encore de politique claire concernant l'apport d'énergie décentralisée aux zones rurales.
-At this stage there is still not a clear energy policy for bringing decentralised power to rural areas.

8418 **illogique** **illogical**
adj
[ilɔʒik]
Cette pratique est illogique et rend la voie diplomatique presque sans issue.
-This practice is illogical, and makes diplomatic success practically impossible.

8419 **beuverie** **carousal|boozer**
f
[bœvʁi]
On l'a défié pour un concours de beuverie.
-He was challenged to a drinking contest.

8420 **contrebandier** **smuggler**
m
[kɔ̃tʁəbɑ̃dje]
Ton contrebandier te donnera sûrement davantage pour ça.
-Your smuggler will surely give you more for it.

8421 **quatuor** **quartet**
m
[kwatɥoʁ]
Ce quatuor est donc un orchestre.
-So that quartet's a band.

8422 **traînant** **shuffling**
adj
[tʁɛnɑ̃]
Il est arrivé en traînant les pieds.
-He came shuffling his feet.

8423 **rescapé** **survivor; surviving**
m; adj
[ʁɛskape]
Comme l'a évoqué un rescapé hongrois de l'holocauste: "Même les SS savaient que les familles tsiganes ne pouvaient pas être séparées.
-As a Hungarian Holocaust survivor recalled: 'even the SS knew that Gipsy families could not be separated.

8424 **rayonner** **beam|radiate**
vb
[ʁɛjɔne]
Que le soleil rayonne, il prie après la pluie ; qu'il pleuve, il prie après le soleil.
-When it is sunshine, he prays for rain, and when it is rain, he prays for sunshine.

8425 **jauger** **gauge**
vb
[ʒoʒe]
Nous sommes ici pour jauger, comme il se doit, les personnes désignées à la Commission ou à sa présidence.
-Once in every five years this Parliament is the Union's personnel officer.

8426 **galanterie** **gallantry**
f
[galɑ̃tʁi]
Ta galanterie laisse beaucoup à désirer.
-Your chivalry leaves a lot to be desired.

8427 **paroissien** **parishioner**
m[paʁwasjɛ̃]
Vous lui avez dit où était la cachette de votre paroissien. -You told her where your parishioner's hide-away was.

8428 **saxophone** **saxophone**

	m [saksɔfɔn]	Jack a mis une annonce pour vendre son saxophone. -Jack advertised his saxophone for sale.
8429	**froidement** adv [fʁwadmɑ̃]	**coldly** Nous venons du froid de Yalta, mais le climat en Europe devient froid et égoïste. -We are coming from the cold of Yalta, but the climate in Europe is becoming chilly and egoistic.
8430	**désirable** adj [deziʁabl]	**desirable|likeable** Nous espérons que la Présidence imposera cette limite de temps avec la souplesse désirable. -We hope that the Chair would implement such a time-limit with due flexibility.
8431	**discothèque** f [diskɔtɛk]	**disco|nightclub** Ils ne nous permettent pas d'aller à la discothèque. -They don't allow us to go to the disco.
8432	**facette** f [fasɛt]	**facet** Dans ma circonscription, Brandon-Souris, l'agriculture constitue une facette très importante de l'économie. -In my constituency of Brandon-Souris agriculture is a very important facet of the economy.
8433	**auditoire** m [oditwaʁ]	**audience** Toutes ces qualités sont encore accrues par l'appréciation et le soutien d'un auditoire. -All of these qualities are enhanced by the appreciation and support of an audience.
8434	**jongler** vb [ʒɔ̃gle]	**juggle** L'homme continue à jouer à l'apprenti sorcier, à jongler avec la sécurité alimentaire. -Humans are continuing to play the sorcerer's apprentice, juggling with food safety.
8435	**solliciter** vb [sɔlisite]	**solicit|ask** Les requérants ont alors sollicité l'autorisation de faire appel sur certains chefs. -The claimants then sought leave to appeal on some of the issues.
8436	**psyché** f [psiʃe]	**psyche** Pour survivre au traumatisme, votre psyché fracturée. -In order to survive the trauma, your psyche fractured.
8437	**nautique** adj [notik]	**nautical** Lieu: Le club nautique de l'ensemble résidentiel de la centrale, à Tiszaújváros. -Location: the premises of the Aquatic Sports Club, Tiszaújváros
8438	**chanvre** m [ʃɑ̃vʁ]	**hemp** En ce qui concerne le lin textile et le chanvre, je propose de ramener ce dernier au niveau du premier. -With flax and hemp I propose to bring hemp back into line with flax.
8439	**inquiétant** adj [ɛ̃kjetɑ̃]	**worrying; bothering** C'est inquiétant. -That's troubling.
8440	**carrosserie** f [kaʁɔsʁi]	**body** Ledit cadre support est solidarisé de manière mobile avec une structure de carrosserie du véhicule.

-The supporting frame is joined to a body structure of the vehicle in a manner that permits it to move.

8441 **colorer** vb [kɔlɔʁe]
color
Tu sais que le masque de la nuit est sur mon visage ; sans cela, tu verrais une virginale couleur colorer ma joue.
-Thou know'st the mask of night is on my face, else would a maiden blush bepaint my cheek.

8442 **arôme** m [aʁom]
aroma|flavoring
L'arôme de ce vin est supérieur à celui-ci.
-This wine is superior to that one in scent.

8443 **équitation** f [ekitasjɔ̃]
horse riding
L'équitation est un passe-temps coûteux.
-Horse riding is an expensive hobby.

8444 **renommer** vb [ʁənɔme]
rename|reappoint
Pour renommer l'imprimante sélectionnée, cliquez sur le bouton Renommer.
-To rename the selected printer, click Rename.

8445 **basique** adj [bazik]
basic
Cette directive permet l'enregistrement basique de ces remèdes traditionnels.
-This directive allows the basic registration of traditional remedies.

8446 **labourer** vb [labuʁe]
plow|till
Je suppose que je devrais labourer.
-I suppose you want me to pull the plow.

8447 **élucider** vb [elyside]
clarify
Je vous demande d'élucider cette affaire qui fait honte au Parlement européen.
-Please clarify this issue, which is bringing shame upon the European Parliament.

8448 **diaphragmer** vb [djafʁagme]
screen
La présente invention concerne également des dosages pour diaphragmer les inhibiteurs de la cytocinèse.
-There is also provided assays for screening for inhibitors of cytokinesis.

8449 **théâtral** adj [teatʁal]
theatrical
Je suis convaincue que l'écrivain théâtral se distingue par son sens de la noblesse humaine.
-I have always believed that playwrights distinguish themselves by their noble human feelings.

8450 **banquise** f [bɑ̃kiz]
pack ice
Et... Le froid a crée la banquise, et les baleines n'ont pas pu passer.
-And... the cooling created sea ice, so whales couldn't get through.

8451 **allégresse** f [alegʁɛs]
glee
Jamais nous ne goûtons de parfaite allégresse : nos plus heureux succès sont mêlés de tristesse.
-Never do we taste perfect joy: our happiest successes are mingled with sadness.

8452 **déclarant** m[deklaʁɑ̃]
declarer
Les enregistrements des naissances s'effectuent sur la bonne foi du déclarant (généralement le père). -Registration of birth is based on the declaration of the informant (usually the father).

8453 **armurier**
gunsmith|armourer

m
[aʁmyʁje]
L'homme qu'Oncle Red rencontra était plus qu'un armurier.
-The man Uncle Red had gone to see was more than a gunsmith.

8454 **engloutir** **engulf|swallow**
vb
[ɑ̃glutiʁ]
À la suite du traité de Lisbonne, certains disent à présent que le Parlement devrait engloutir une plus grande part de l'argent.
-As a consequence of the Treaty of Lisbon, people are now saying that Parliament should devour a greater proportion of the money.

8455 **tranquilliser** **calm|ease**
vb
[tʁɑ̃kilize]
Je voudrais tranquilliser les parlementaires qui ont parlé d'éventuelles sanctions.
-I would like to reassure all Members who have spoken about possible sanctions.

8456 **pendule** **pendulum**
f
[pɑ̃dyl]
Même une pendule arrêtée affiche la bonne heure deux fois par jour.
-Even a clock that is stopped shows the correct time twice a day.

8457 **déplorer** **deplore**
vb
[deplɔʁe]
Je dois toutefois déplorer quelques erreurs dans le texte imprimé.
-I have to deplore a few mistakes in the printing of the text.

8458 **nuancer** **nuance**
vb
[nyɑ̃se]
Je dois nuancer ces propos en disant que je peux seulement parler de ce que je sais.
-I must qualify that by saying that I can speak only of my own knowledge.

8459 **immobiliser** **immobilize**
vb
[imɔbilize]
Ce procede peut être utilise pour immobiliser des cellules vivantes telles que des levures.
-The method may be used to immobilize living cells such as yeast.

8460 **souder** **weld**
vb
[sude]
Des outils servant à souder et à couper le métal ont été retrouvés sur les lieux.
-Welding and metal-cutting equipment was also brought to the place of the burglary.

8461 **archange** **archangel**
m
[aʁkɑ̃ʒ]
Un archange apparaîtra pour détruire cette menace.
-An Archangel will appear to destroy that threat.

8462 **manivelle** **crank**
f
[manivɛl]
L'ensemble manivelle définit un plan généralement transversal par rapport à l'axe.
-The crank assembly defines a plane generally transverse to the axis.

8463 **ingratitude** **ingratitude**
f
[ɛ̃gʁatityd]
Le bien a pour tombeau l'ingratitude humaine.
-Good has as its grave human ingratitude.

8464 **jouissance** **enjoyment**
f[ʒwisɑ̃s]
Il ne suffisait pas de simplement démontrer une perte indéfinissable de jouissance du bien. -It was not sufficient to merely show an indefinable loss in the enjoyment of the property.

8465 **volatiliser** **volatilize**
vb
[vɔlatilize]
En outre, il ne se volatilise pas de façon appréciable.
-Chlordecone does not volatilise to any significant extent.

8466 **entraide** **mutual aid**
f
[ɑ̃tʁɛd]
Ils ont souligné l'importance de la coordination et de l'entraide.
-They stressed the importance of ensuring coordination and mutual assistance.

8467 **déboucher** **unblock|cork off**
vb
[debuʃe]
Nous espérons évidemment pouvoir déboucher sur un accord, mais ce sera difficile.
-We very much hope that we can reach agreement, but it is going to be difficult.

8468 **braille** **braille**
m
[bʁaj]
Sais-tu écrire en Braille ?
-Can you write Braille?

8469 **réformer** **reform**
vb
[ʁefɔʁme]
Pendant notre présidence, nous avons commencé à réformer le travail du Conseil.
-During our presidential term we have started to reform the work of the Council.

8470 **poltron** **coward; cowardly**
m; adj
[pɔltʁɔ̃]
Je vous avertis, je suis un peu poltron.
-I warn you, Ben, I'm a little bit of a coward.

8471 **interphone** **intercom**
m
[ɛ̃tɛʁfɔn]
Jack a appuyé sur le bouton de l'interphone.
-Jack pressed the intercom button.

8472 **cycliste** **cyclist**
m
[siklist]
Hideo tourna vivement le volant pour éviter le cycliste.
-Hideo turned the steering wheel sharply to avoid the bicyclist.

8473 **névrose** **neurosis**
f
[nevʁoz]
La maladie mentale est une psychose mais non une névrose.
-Mental disease is psychosis but not neurosis.

8474 **biscotte** **biscuit**
f
[biskɔt]
Là, face à nous est allongée une biscotte.
-Here in front of us lies a biscuit.

8475 **déséquilibre** **imbalance**
m
[dezekilibʁ]
L'amour n'est qu'un déséquilibre hormonal temporaire.
-Love is simply a temporary hormonal imbalance.

8476 **yiddish** **Yiddish; Yiddish**
adj; m
[jidiʃ]
Des cours de yiddish pour enfants sont dispensés par diverses organisations juives.
-Yiddish courses for children are common in various Jewish organisations.

8477 **cuisson** **baking**
f
[kɥisɔ̃]
Quelle cuisson pour votre steak ?
-How baked would you like your steak?

8478 **gynécologue** **gynecologist**
m/f
[ʒinekɔlɔg]
Je suis gynécologue amateur depuis longtemps.
-I've been an amateur gynecologist for years.

8479 **prévention** **prevention**
f
[pʁevɑ̃sjɔ̃]
La prévention des feux de forêt est l'affaire de tous.
-The prevention of forest fires is everyone's responsibility.

8480 **mormon** **Mormon; Mormon**
adj; m
[mɔʁmɔ̃]
No, I was at the mormon fort.
-Non, j'étais au fort mormon.

8481 **digital** **digital**
adj
[diʒital]
Je dois chercher mon projecteur digital.
-I need to look for my digital projector.

8482 **mangue** f [mɑ̃g]
mango
Cette mangue est délicieuse.
-This mango is delicious.

8483 **envoûter** vb [ɑ̃vute]
voodoo
Laissez-vous envoûter par Antidote en vous rendant dans la parfumerie de Viktor & Rolf.
-Allow Antidote to enchant you as you visit the Viktor & Rolf perfumery.

8484 **foulé** adj [fule]
trodden
Ce faisant, il a foulé aux pieds les droits du Parlement en matière budgétaire.
-By doing this, it has trodden Parliament's budgetary rights underfoot.

8485 **individuellement** adv [ɛ̃dividɥɛlmɑ̃]
individually
J'en prends acte, nous mettons donc aux voix les amendements individuellement.
-I acknowledge your objection and we shall vote on one amendment at a time.

8486 **inévitablement** adv [inevitabləmɑ̃]
inevitably
Sans cette stratégie, le club nucléaire continuera inévitablement à proliférer.
-Without such a strategy, the nuclear club will inevitably continue to proliferate.

8487 **adhérer** vb [adeʁe]
join|adhere
Lorsque nous réformons les politiques communautaires, il nous faut adhérer à des principes durables.
-When we make reforms to EU policies we have to adhere to sustainable principles.

8488 **fossoyeur** m [foswajœʁ]
gravedigger
Ce fossoyeur avait peut-être raison... les remous et le bateau qui chavire.
-Maybe that grave digger was right - the swell and the boat overturning.

8489 **maure** adj [mɔʁ]
Moorish
Pendant plus de six siècles, à part une brève interruption de 1309 à 1333, Gibraltar est resté occupé par les Maures.
-For over six centuries, with a short break from 1309 to 1333, Gibraltar remained under Moorish occupation.

8490 **teinturier** m [tɛ̃tyʁje]
dry cleaner
Lorsqu'il est revenu de chez le teinturier, mon costume était abîmé.
-My dress was ruined when it came back from the cleaner's.

8491 **sbire** m[sbiʁ]
myrmidon|henchman
Un sbire ne doit pas être aussi soupçonneux. -A henchman shouldn't be suspicious to such an extent.

8492 **chevalerie** f [ʃəvalʁi]
chivalry
L'époque de la chevalerie est révolue.
-The age of chivalry is gone.

8493 **retentir** vb [ʁətɑ̃tiʁ]
sound|resound
Vu les pressions économiques actuelles, ce signal doit maintenant retentir haut et fort si nous voulons soutenir l'accélération des réformes structurelles prévues par l'agenda de Lisbonne.
-Given current economic pressures, that signal now needs to ring out loud and clear if we are to sustain the gathering pace of structural reform under the Lisbon agenda.

8494 **ovation** f [ɔvasjɔ̃]
ovation
Quand il y avait une ovation, elle était unanime, pas de vague, pas d'approche fragmentée.

-When there was a standing ovation, it was unanimous - no wave, no fragmented approach.

8495 **hachis** **hash**
m
[aʃi]
M. Sitting Bull adore le hachis parmentier.
-Mr. Sitting Bull just loves hash.

8496 **abject** **abject**
adj
[abʒɛkt]
Il n'est que la preuve de sa soumission abjecte au Gouvernement des États-Unis.
-It is merely indicative of its abject submission to the United States Government.

8497 **chantonner** **hum**
vb
[ʃɑ̃tɔne]
Claire continue de chantonner.
-Claire continued to hum.

8498 **préoccupé** **concerned**
adj
[pʁeɔkype]
Notre Parlement se préoccupe de la défense des droits de l'homme dans le monde.
-Our Parliament is preoccupied with the defence of human rights in the world.

8499 **éplucher** **peel|clean**
vb
[eplyʃe]
Nous avons appris à éplucher des bananes parce que c'était le seul aliment que nous aurions pu manger, tout le reste étant devenu radioactif.
-We learned how to peel bananas because that was the only kind of food we would be able to eat, as everything else would be radioactive.

8500 **broyer** **grind; grinder**
vb; m
[bʁwaje]
Mais il ne sait pas broyer...
-He doesn't know about the grind...

8501 **imprudence** **imprudence|recklessness**
f
[ɛ̃pʁydɑ̃s]
L'accident est dû à son imprudence.
-The accident resulted from his carelessness.

8502 **déchiqueter** **shred**
vb
[deʃikte]
Maintenant, on aurait déchiqueté des documents sur le lait contaminé.
-Now we have allegations about shredded documents over tainted milk.

8503 **renom** **renown**
m[ʁənɔ̃]
Depuis sa création en 1993, le CIDPM est devenu une organisation internationale de renom qu coopère avec plus de 50 pays. -Since its establishment in 1993, ICMPD had grown into an international organization of renown that cooperated with over 50 States.

8504 **impertinence** **impertinence|impudence**
f
[ɛ̃pɛʁtinɑ̃s]
L'impertinence n'est pas drôle.
-There is no humor in impertinence, Pierre.

8505 **perpétuer** **perpetuate**
vb
[pɛʁpetɥe]
Le fait d'éluder cette question ne fera que perpétuer les problèmes dans ce domaine.
-Ignoring the situation would only perpetuate problems in that regard.

8506 **majuscule** **capital; capital**
adj; f
[maʒyskyl]
En allemand, les noms sont toujours écrits avec une majuscule.
-In German, nouns are always capitalised.

8507 **réfectoire** **refectory**
m
[ʁefɛktwaʁ]
Suzy, descendez au réfectoire tout de suite.
-Susy, go down to the refectory right now.

8508 **écrasant** **crushing|overwhelming;**

	adj [ekʁazɑ̃]	Il y a un consensus écrasant au sein de la communauté. -The community has an overwhelming consensus.
8509	**essor** m [esɔʁ]	**development** L'essor du tourisme et du bâtiment gagne à présent les Caïques et la Grande Turque. -The tourism and construction boom has spread to the Caicos Islands and Grand Turk.
8510	**fougue** f [fug]	**fire|spirit** Impossible de feindre une telle fougue. -You can't fake passion like that.
8511	**agréablement** adv [agʁeabləmɑ̃]	**pleasantly** Ils ont tous les dossiers, toutes les informations et vous serez agréablement surpris. -They have all the files, all the information, and you will be pleasantly surprised.
8512	**rosier** m [ʁozje]	**rosebush** C'est une épine de rosier. -It's a thorn from a rosebush.
8513	**credo** m [kʁedo]	**creed|belief** Leur credo est de semer la discorde et tuer. -Their credo is to sow discord and kill the unwary.
8514	**ébranler** vb [ebʁɑ̃le]	**shake|undermine** La confiance dans le monde politique s'est trouvée sérieusement ébranlée. -Confidence in politics suffered a severe dent.
8515	**horizontal** adj [ɔʁizɔ̃tal]	**horizontal** Quelle que soit la solution retenue, le Règlement horizontal est une bonne formule. -Whatever solution is to be pursued, the Horizontal Regulation is a good approach.
8516	**gigoter** vb [ʒigɔte]	**wriggle** Tu peux toujours gigoter, mon petit ! -You can fidget, little man.
8517	**pale** f [pal]	**blade** L'invention concerne une pale de rotor d'hélicoptère. -A rotor blade of a helicopter is presented.
8518	**aïeux** m|mpl [ajø]	**forefathers** Ces cinquante dernières années, notre famille humaine a réalisé des avancées technologiques dont nos aïeux n'auraient osé rêver. -In the past 50 years, our human family has experienced leaps of technological achievement undreamed of by our forebears.
8519	**apprivoiser** vb [apʁivwaze]	**tame** Nous devons reconnaître que nos tentatives visant à apprivoiser des dictateurs sanglants tels que Kadhafi ont échoué, et que nous n'avons pas de quoi être fiers. -We have to realise that attempts to domesticate brutal dictators like Gaddafi have failed, causing much embarrassment.
8520	**nordiste** adj [nɔʁdist]	**northern** Cette antithèse s'exprime aussi en termes d'aAfricains sudistes vis-à-vis d'es aArabes nordistes. -This antithesis is also expressed in terms of African southerners versus Arab northerners.
8521	**aliéner**	**alienate**

	vb [aljene]	A défaut, nous courons le risque de nous aliéner l'opinion publique européenne. -If it is not then we run the risk of alienating the citizens of Europe.
8522	**bavure**	**smudge|blur**
	f [bavyʁ]	L'élimination de la matière de bavure entre deux refoulements de soudage consécutifs, a lieu dans des sens alternés. -Removal of the flash material intermediate consecutive weld upsets is effected in alternate directions.
8523	**sève**	**sap**
	f [sɛv]	Veux-tu qu'ils soient vidés de leur sève par ce monstre ? -Do you want them to be robbed of their sap by this monster?
8524	**amphétamine**	**amphetamine**
	f [ɑ̃fetamin]	Trouvé de l'amphétamine dans la doublure de votre sac de voyage. -Found methamphetamine in the lining of your duffel bag.
8525	**dosage**	**dosage**
	m [dozaʒ]	Les caractéristiques d'efficacité du dosage indiquent que le dosage est précis et reproductible. -Assay performance characteristics indicate that the assay is accurate and repeatable.
8526	**uriner**	**urinate**
	vb [yʁine]	Nous étions forcées d'uriner devant tout le monde. -We were forced to urinate in front of everybody.
8527	**méthane**	**methane**
	m [metan]	Cette formation est remplie de méthane. -That sandstone formation is sure to be filled with methane.
8528	**primate**	**primate**
	m [pʁimat]	Je vous explique, la primate: -I will now explain to you, the primate:
8529	**somali**	**Somali; Somali**
	adj; m/f; mpl[sɔmali]	Il est pleinement reconnu désormais qu'il faut trouver une solution africaine au problème somali. -It has now been fully recognized that an African solution must be found to the problems of Somalia.
8530	**eunuque**	**eunuch**
	m [ønyk]	Je croyais que c'était un eunuque. -I was beginning to believe he was a eunuch.
8531	**hymen**	**hymen|marriage**
	m [imɛn]	La notion d'hymen indique la virginité. -The notion of hymen indicates virginity.
8532	**processeur**	**processor**
	m [pʁɔsesœʁ]	Chacun de ces derniers organes est couplé au processeur. -Each of the latter components are electronically coupled to the processor.
8533	**rainer**	**groove**
	vb [ʁene]	De ce fait, il n'est pas nécessaire de modifier la hauteur des matrices de rainage dans une presse à découper et à rainer. -This means that no modification need be made to the height of the creasing dies in a cutting and creasing press.
8534	**nouer**	**establish**
	vb [nue]	Un organisme autorisé ne peut nouer aucune relation avec une banque fictive. -An authorized institution may not set up agency relationships with “shell” banks.

8535 **gicler** vb [ʒikle]
spurt|spew
Deux buses sous sa antennes gicler colle.
-Two nozzles beneath its feelers squirt twin streams of glue.

8536 **activement** adv [aktivmɑ̃]
busily
Transport/interface, marchandises (entreposage actif ou passif), sécurité/sûreté.
-Transport /interface, cargoes (active or passive storage), security and safety.

8537 **inflammable** adj [ɛ̃flamabl]
flammable
Un seul degré de risque physique est donc nécessaire, inflammable/non inflammable.
-Therefore only one hazard level is required - flammable/non-flammable.

8538 **veille** f [vɛj]
eve|day before
Il a perdu la montre qu'il avait achetée la veille.
-He lost the watch which he had bought the day before.

8539 **châtier** vb [ʃatje]
chasten|smite
Notre souhait n'est pas de châtier la Russie dans la mesure où c'est un pays avec lequel nous désirons entretenir une étroite coopération.
-We have no desire to chastise Russia, as it is a country with which we wish to cooperate closely.

8540 **parfumer** vb [paʁfyme]
perfume|flavor
Le tabac à chiquer et les autres produits commercialisés sous le nom de « produits d'initiation », ou encore les produits parfumés sont particulièrement attirants pour les jeunes.
-Smokeless tobacco and other products, marketed as "starter" products, or those that are flavoured can be particularly attractive to young people.

8541 **envieux** adj[ɑ̃vjø]
green-eyed
Contrairement à ce que pensent certains envieux, il n' est pas vraiment question de corne d' abondance. -This is certainly no cornucopia, as we hear from resentful quarters.

8542 **créancier** m [kʁeɑ̃sje]
creditor
Y compris un organisme public créancier du débiteur.
-This would include a government authority that is a creditor of the debtor.

8543 **suspicion** f [syspisjɔ̃]
suspicion
Aucun discours unique ne peut effacer des années de suspicion, pas plus que je ne peux répondre, dans le temps dont je dispose, à toutes les questions complexes qui nous ont conduits à ce point.
-No single speech can eradicate years of mistrust, nor can I answer in the time that I have all the complex questions that brought us to this point.

8544 **gouvernemental** adj [guvɛʁnəmɑ̃tal]
governmental
La coopération s'exerce aux niveaux gouvernemental et non gouvernemental.
-Cooperation took place at the governmental and non-governmental level.

8545 **résidu** m [ʁezidy]
residue
Alma, fais une analyse du résidu.
-Alma, do an analysis of the residue.

8546 **communautaire** adj [kɔmynotɛʁ]
communal
Elle comporte également un élément qui favorise la participation communautaire.
-This option also features a component that cultivates a participatory community.

8547 **amiante**
asbestos

f
[amjɑ̃t]
L'isolant choisi pour ces sous-marins est l'amiante.
-The insulation of choice in these submarines was asbestos.

8548 **frontal** **frontal**
adj
[fʁɔ̃tal]
C'est une machine à laver à chargement frontal.
-This is a front-loading washing machine.

8549 **guigne** **hoodoo|bad luck**
f
[giɲ]
Je m'en soucie comme d'une guigne !
-I don't care a fig about it!

8550 **fourguer** **flog|fence**
vb
[fuʁge]
Je ne pouvais pas fourguer les diamants.
-I couldn't fence the diamonds.

8551 **bicarbonate** **bicarbonate**
m
[bikaʁbɔnat]
La présente invention concerne un procédé et un appareil permettant de préparer une solution aqueuse sensiblement claire contenant du bicarbonate de magnésium.
-A method and an apparatus for preparing a substantially clear aqueous solution containing magnesium bicarbonate are disclosed.

8552 **émaner** **emanate**
vb
[emane]
Ce mandat ne peut qu'émaner d'une nouvelle résolution du Conseil de sécurité.
-This mandate can emanate only from a new Security Council resolution.

8553 **fétiche** **fetish**
m
[fetiʃ]
Quel est votre fétiche?
-What's your fetish?

8554 **arrivage** **shipment**
m
[aʁivaʒ]
Nous suivons l'arrivage, apprenons où Sin Rostro se cachait.
-We follow this shipment, learn where Sin Rostro has been hiding.

8555 **attelage** **coupling|hitch**
m
[atlaʒ]
Ce même attelage, Prince et Pete, est retourné dans le bois avec lui.
-This same team of horses, Prince and Pete, went with him back into the bush operation.

8556 **aveuglément** **blindly**
adv
[avœglemɑ̃]
Cela ne signifie pas céder aveuglément aux pressions de la mondialisation.
-Being competitive does not mean yielding blindly to the pressures of globalisation.

8557 **acharnement** **fury|stubbornness**
m
[aʃaʁnəmɑ̃]
Je sais combien d'acharnement tu as mis sur ce travail.
-I know how much drive you have put in this work.

8558 **baroque** **baroque; baroque**
adj; m
[baʁɔk]
L'architecture est baroque d'Europe centrale avec des influences gothiques.
-Architecture is mid-European baroque with gothic influences.

8559 **gredin** **rascal**
m
[gʁədɛ̃]
Ce gredin d'inspecteur doit-tre loin maintenant.
-That scoundrel inspector must have gone quite far by now.

8560 **perturbation** **disturbance**
f
[pɛʁtyʁbasjɔ̃]
Il pense avoir découvert une perturbation paranormale.
-He seems to believe that he has discovered a paranormal disturbance.

8561 **systématique** **systematic; systematics**
adj; f
[sistematik]
Je n'appelle pas ça de la colonisation. Je l'appelle de l'exploitation systématique des matières premières.
-I don't call it colonization, I call it systematic raw materials exploitation.

8562 **abcès** **abscess**
m
[apsɛ]
Un calcul ou un abcès périphérique.
-Could be an obstructing calculus or a perinephric abscess.

8563 **entêtement** **stubbornness**
m
[ɑ̃tɛtmɑ̃]
Cela commence à friser l'entêtement.
-This is starting to look like sheer stubbornness.

8564 **hâter** **hasten|accelerate**
vb
[ate]
Le Conseil doit se hâter d'adopter le projet de résolution du Groupe arabe.
-The Council should hasten to adopt the resolution introduced by the Arab Group.

8565 **endetter** **put into debt**
vb
[ɑ̃dete]
Les prêts consentis par ces organisations ont servi à endetter les pays les plus pauvres de la Terre au point qu'ils ne peuvent plus espérer s'en sortir un jour.
-Loans from these organizations have served to put into debt the poorest countries on earth, to the point where they can never hope to escape from their debt traps.

8566 **capituler** **capitulate**
vb
[kapityle]
Une politique visant à forcer l'autre camp à capituler est vouée à la faillite.
-A policy based on forcing the other side to capitulate is a bankrupt policy.

8567 **panorama** **panorama|overview**
m
[panɔʁama]
On ne savait pratiquement rien sur le panorama.
-It is fair to say that virtually nothing was known about the panorama.

8568 **cyclope** **Cyclops**
m
[siklɔp]
Comment irez-vous à l'intérieur du cyclope ?
-How would one go about getting inside the Cyclops?

8569 **favoriser** **promote|foster**
vb
[favɔʁize]
Dans l'avenir, l'Union doit favoriser une approche de bas en haut pour sa politique de voisinage.
-In the future, the Union must favour a bottom-up approach to its Neighbourhood Policy.

8570 **pédiatre** **pediatrician**
m/f
[pedjatʁ]
J'ai finalement pu joindre son pédiatre.
-Finally, I was able to contact his pediatrician.

8571 **raffinerie** **refinery**
f
[ʁafinʁi]
Cette guerre commerciale empêche Beijing d'approuver la raffinerie.
-This trade war is preventing the refinery from being approved in Beijing.

8572 **luge** **sled**
f
[lyʒ]
Faire de la luge, c'est très simple, il suffit de se caler bien dessus et de se laisser glisser.
-Sledding is very easy. All you have to do is sit down tight and let it slide.

8573 **draper** **drape**
vb
[dʁape]
Alors il faut le draper sur ton épaule.
-That's why you drape it over your shoulder.

8574 **presbytère** **presbytery|rectory**
m
[pʁɛsbitɛʁ]
Retrouve-moi au presbytère dans une heure.
-Just meet me in the Rectory in an hour.

8575 **confessionnal** **confessional**
m
[kɔ̃fesjɔnal]
J'espérais le faire dans le confessionnal.
-I was hoping to do it under the confessional.

8576 **pleurnichard** **crybaby; whingeing**

	m; adj	Pourquoi l'Europe doit-elle jouer l'enfant pleurnichard à Bâle ?
	[plœʁniʃaʁ]	-Why does Europe have to be the cry-baby of Basel?
8577	**toxine**	**toxin**
	f	Il s'agit bien sûr d'une toxine très dangereuse et nous en sommes conscients.
	[tɔksin]	-It is, of course, a very dangerous toxin and we are aware of that.
8578	**chrome**	**chrome**
	m	L'interconnecteur est constitué d'un alliage métallique contenant du chrome.
	[kʁom]	-The interconnect is made of a metal alloy containing chromium.
8579	**container**	**bowl**
	m	Comment transformer un container maritime en abri de jardin.
	[kɔ̃tɛnɛʁ]	-How to turn a shipping container into a backyard garden shed.
8580	**sono**	**sound system**
	f	Blake, faut que tu détruises sa sono.
	[sɔno]	-Blake, you need to destroy his sound system.
8581	**paon**	**peacock**
	m	Elle devient vaniteuse comme un paon.
	[pɑ̃]	-She's getting as vain as a peacock.
8582	**ailier**	**wing**
	m	Je suis supposé être ton ailier.
	[elje]	-I'm supposed to be your wingman.
8583	**sculpter**	**sculpt|carve**
	vb	Par manque de temps, je sculpte mes biscoteaux au bureau !
	[skylte]	-I have little time to get to the gym, so I have to sculpt my guns at the office.
8584	**grosseur**	**size|thickness**
	f	Ce serait bien si nous pouvions maintenir le troupeau à une grosseur raisonnable.
	[gʁosœʁ]	-That is wise if we can get the herd down to a manageable size.
8585	**crissement**	**screech**
	m	A chaque fois qu'il tournait, j'imitais le crissement des pneus.
	[kʁismɑ̃]	-Every time he would turn the corner, I would make the sound of tires squealing.
8586	**silo**	**silo**
	m	L'analogie avec le silo est probablement la plus pertinente pour illustrer le contexte actuel.
	[silo]	-The silo analogy probably most accurately portrays the current environment.
8587	**abonner**	**subscribe**
	vb	Vous pouvez vous abonner en communiquant avec la Glenn Gould Foundation.
	[abɔne]	-Subscribe through the Glenn Gould Foundation.
8588	**mégot**	**butt|cigarette end**
	m	Il y avait également trouvé un mégot de cigarette et des restes de repas, notamment des os, preuves manifestes que ces cellules avaient été utilisées récemment.
	[mego]	-A cigarette butt and some bones with the remains of cooked meat on them were also present in the cells, which had obviously been used recently.
8589	**falsifier**	**falsify; falsifier**
	vb; m	Holloway a fait falsifier sa déposition à Eve.
	[falsifje]	-Holloway made Eve falsify her statements.
8590	**pruneau**	**prune**

m
[pʁyno]
Chalets et clapotis au pays du pruneau.
-Chalets and gentle lapping waves in the land of the prune.

8591 **sommation** **summons**
f
[sɔmasjɔ̃]
Les résultats de cette sommation figurent au tableau 2.
-The results of this summation are shown in Table 2.

8592 **euthanasie** **euthanasia**
f
[øtanazi]
La déclaration équivaut à une demande concrète d'euthanasie.
-The declaration has the same status as a concrete request for euthanasia.

8593 **hypnotique** **hypnotic; hypnotic**
adj; m
[ipnɔtik]
Vous voilà dans un léger état hypnotique.
-You are now in a light hypnotic state.

8594 **précipice** **drop**
m
[pʁesipis]
Aussi est-il particulièrement tragique de le voir aller tout droit vers le précipice.
-That is why it is so incredibly tragic to see it heading straight for the abyss.

8595 **euphorie** **euphoria**
f[øfɔʁi]
C'était une période d'euphorie et la tendance était même de confondre liberté et licence. -There was a period of euphoria and even a tendency to confuse liberty with licence.

8596 **rigoureux** **rigorous**
adj
[ʁiguʁø]
Elles sont nommées au terme d'un processus rigoureux, que le gouvernement appuie.
-They are appointed after a rigorous process, which the government stands behind.

8597 **demeure** **residence|abode**
f
[dəmœʁ]
Et les mécréants sauront bientôt à qui appartient la bonne demeure finale.
-So the unbelievers will know whose is the ultimate, everlasting abode.

8598 **plouf** **plonk|splash**
m
[pluf]
Les enfants aiment faire un plouf dans l'eau lorsqu'ils glissent sur un toboggan à eau.
-Children enjoy making a splash in the water as they come off a waterslide.

8599 **blason** **blazon|shield**
m
[blazɔ̃]
Le Triglav est aussi le symbole national, qui figure sur le blason et le drapeau du pays.
-Triglav is also a national symbol, featured on the national coat of arms and the flag.

8600 **importun** **unwelcome; intruder**
adj; m
[ɛ̃pɔʁtɛ̃]
On me traite avec un léger dédain... comme un chien errant ou un hôte importun.
-Mostly, I'm treated with a kind of a mild neglect... as if I were a stray dog or an unwelcome guest.

8601 **électrode** **electrode**
f
[elɛktʁɔd]
Les ions lithium passent d'une électrode à l'autre en fonction de l'état de charge de l'accu.
-Lithium ions move from one electrode to the other depending on the state of charge (SOC) of the cell.

8602 **croupe** **rump|croup**
f
[kʁup]
Je pensais que tu ferais un rôti de croupe.
-I figured you'd go with the rump roast.

8603 **cambrousse** **outback**

f [kɑ̃bʁus] La cambrousse, c'est déjà perdu.
-It's all over in the boonies.

8604 **matador** **matador**
m [matadɔʁ] Le taureau est épuisé avant même... que le matador n'entre dans l'arène.
-The bull is tired before the matador...... ever steps into the ring.

8605 **lèpre** **leprosy**
f [lɛpʁ] La lèpre est facilement traitable par antibiotiques.
-Leprosy is easily treated with antibiotics.

8606 **athlétique** **athletic**
adj [atletik] L'excellente compétition athlétique sera accompagnée d'activités sociales et d'animation.
-There will be entertainment and social activities to go with the excellent athletic competition.

8607 **tibia** **tibia**
m[tibja] Okay, entrée dans tibia gauche. -Okay, IO going in to the left tibia.

8608 **indolore** **painless**
adj [ɛ̃dɔlɔʁ] La réforme dans ce domaine ne sera pas indolore, mais une possibilité s'offre à nous que nous ne pouvons pas laisser passer.
-Reform in this area will not be without pain, but we are presented with an opportunity we cannot afford to miss.

8609 **éternuer** **sneeze**
vb [etɛʁnɥe] Et selon les données les plus récentes, l'Amérique ne se contente plus d'éternuer, elle a une mauvaise grippe ».
-And according to recent data, America is not just sneezing, it has a bad case of the flu."

8610 **ténébreux** **gloomy**
adj [tenebʁø] La ténacité de l'homme ténébreux porte chance.
-The perseverance of a gloomy man brings good fortune.

8611 **parabole** **parable**
f [paʁabɔl] Une parabole sur un groupe d'ennemis qui sèment des mauvaises graines pour gâcher les récoltes.
-There's a parable about a group of enemies who plant bad seeds amongst the good ones to ruin the crops.

8612 **tortiller** **twirl|twist round**
vb [tɔʁtije] Si tu achetais la bonne taille de corset, je n'aurais pas à me tortiller.
-If you bought me the proper-sized corset, I wouldn't have to squirm.

8613 **boîtier** **housing**
m [bwatje] Un disque amortisseur est fixé élastiquement au boîtier.
-A shock absorbing disc is resiliently attached to the switch housing.

8614 **pistache** **pistachio**
f [pistaʃ] Tu sais combien j'aime la pistache.
-You know how I love pistachio.

8615 **passionnel** **passionate**
adj [pasjɔnɛl] Ceux qui ont assisté à ce débat ont participé à un véritable débat passionnel.
-Those who were present witnessed a truly passionate debate.

8616 **avarice** **greed|stinginess**
f [avaʁis] Une histoire de trahison et d'avarice.
-A story of betrayal and greed.

8617 **vieillissement** **aging**
m [vjejismɑ̃] Personne n'échappe au vieillissement.
-No one can escape growing old.

8618 **courroie** **belt**
f
[kuʁwa]
Deux rouleaux différents commandés par deux moteurs séparés entraînent la courroie.
-Two different rollers drive the belt, and are controlled by two separate motors.

8619 **lobby** **lobby**
m
[lɔbi]
Ce lobby de consommateurs doit être écouté.
-The consumer lobby on this issue really needs to be listened to.

8620 **surchauffer** **overheat**
vb
[syʁʃofe]
Les freins correctement réglés risquent beaucoup moins de surchauffer.
-Correctly adjusted brakes are much less likely to overheat.

8621 **enrouler** **wrap**
vb[ɑ̃ʁule]
«réservoir entièrement bobiné»: réservoir dans lequel le filament est enroulé autour de la chemise circonférentiellement et longitudinalement; -"Fully wrap": Over-wrap with the filaments wound around the liner both in the circumferential and longitudinal directions of the container.

8622 **souveraineté** **sovereignty**
f
[suvʁɛnte]
Personne n'a enclenché la souveraineté.
-No one has put in motion the process leading to sovereignty.

8623 **logistique** **logistics; logistical**
f; adj
[lɔʒistik]
Il faudrait déterminer la logistique de cette option.
-The logistics of this option would have to be determined.

8624 **céramique** **ceramic; ceramics**
adj; f
[seʁamik]
Parmi les secteurs concernés figurent notamment l'industrie du papier et celle de la céramique.
-Examples of this are the paper industry and the ceramics industry.

8625 **disqualifier** **disqualify**
vb
[diskalifje]
And, malheureusement, nous allons devoir disqualifier nos étudiants de la compétition pour la bourse scolaire.
-And, unfortunately, we will disqualify your students from the scholarship competition.

8626 **ricain** **Yank**
adj
[ʁikɛ̃]
Ça aurait pu être un ricain.
-Could have been a Yank's.

8627 **foreuse** **drill**
f
[fɔʁøz]
Si seulement ils pouvaient couper la foreuse...
-Hold on, if they can just shut down the drill...

8628 **gnome** **gnome**
m
[gnom]
Je ne suis pas meilleure qu'un gnome.
-I'm no better than a gnome.

8629 **carnivore** **carnivorous**
adj
[kaʁnivɔʁ]
Alors que les fabricants n'ont pas hésité à rendre les ruminants carnivores, on connaît toujours la faim dans le monde.
-At a time when manufacturers have had no misgivings about turning ruminants into carnivores, there is still hunger in the world.

8630 **kebab** **kebab**
m
[kəbab]
Pour la kebab Caprese : Couper les tomates en deux et les assaisonner avec sel, poivre et huile d’olive vierge extra.
-For the Caprese kebab: Cut the cherry tomatoes in half and season with salt, pepper and extra virgin olive oil.

8631 **infrastructure** **infrastructure**

	f [ɛ̃fʁastʁyktyʁ]	Formant une infrastructure d'informations, le réel impact de l'autoroute de l'information est une attente du développement de la nouvelle économie due au passage d'une industrie de matériel informatique tangible à une industrie de logiciels intelligents. -Forming an information infrastructure, the real impact of the information highway is an expectation of new economic development due to a shift from a tangible hardware-industry to brain-oriented software-industry.
8632	**télex**	**telex**
	m [telɛks]	Je serai joignable par télex et par téléphone. -I shall be reachable by telex and telephone.
8633	**berline**	**sedan|tramcar**
	f[bɛʁlin]	Attendez une seconde, une autre berline bleue suit ce camion. -Wait a second, another blue sedan following that truck.
8634	**hospitalier**	**hospital**
	adj [ɔspitalje]	Nous saluons le peuple vaillant, hospitalier et généreux de Tanzanie. -We salute the gallant, hospitable and generous people of Tanzania.
8635	**minimiser**	**minimize|play down**
	vb [minimize]	Involontairement, on peut exagérer - ou en fait minimiser - l'ampleur des problèmes. -Unintentionally, people can exaggerate — or indeed understate — the extent of problems.
8636	**subsister**	**subsist|remain**
	vb [sybziste]	Le Compte ne peut pas subsister grâce aux excédents provenant d'autres comptes - qui sont inexistants. -The Development Account could not subsist on non-existent surpluses from other accounts, in other words on nothing.
8637	**graisser**	**grease**
	vb [gʁese]	Et t'es le seul flic à qui je dois graisser la patte ? -How do I know you're the last cop I'm gonna have to grease?
8638	**fève**	**bean**
	f [fɛv]	Détruire toute la récolte de café colombien... jusqu'à la dernière fève. -Destroy the entire Colombian coffee crop... right down to the last bean.
8639	**sauveteur**	**rescuer|wrecker**
	m [sovtœʁ]	Sous cet angle, le devoir envers le sauveteur est clairement indépendant...». -Thus viewed, the duty to the rescuer is clearly independent... .
8640	**malice**	**malice|mischief**
	f [malis]	Nous préférons être cyniques spontanément, sans malice. -We prefer our cynicism to be spontaneous, without malice.
8641	**longitude**	**longitude**
	f [lɔ̃ʒityd]	Nous avons été directement au sud en courant le long du 30ème degré de longitude. -We've been running due south along the 30th degree of longitude.
8642	**vénérable**	**venerable**
	adj [veneʁabl]	Mme Blandine Jourdain atteindra l'âge vénérable de 100 ans. -Blandine Jourdain will reach the venerable age of 100.
8643	**impudence**	**impudence**
	f [ɛ̃pydɑ̃s]	Quelle impudence ! -What impudence!
8644	**débaucher**	**poach|harass**
	vb [deboʃe]	C'est comme si j'essayais de débaucher ton assistante. -I know it seems like I'm trying to poach your assistant.

8645 **cruellement** adv [kʁyɛlmɑ̃]
cruelly
Ils sont cruellement exploités comme enfants soldats et comme manoeuvres.
-They are cruelly exploited as child soldiers or labourers.

8646 **solstice** m [sɔlstis]
solstice
Le festival se termine au solstice d'hiver pour une raison.
-There's a reason the Glacier Spirits Festival ens on the winter solstice.

8647 **périphérie** f[peʁifeʁi]
periphery
Après 15 heures de combats intenses, les Taliban ont gagné la périphérie de Taloqan. -After 15 hours of fierce fighting, the Taliban reached the outskirts of Taloqan.

8648 **prompt** adj [pʁɔ̃pt]
prompt
Il a par ailleurs été proposé que ce recours soit également «prompt».
-It was also suggested that the remedy should be "prompt".

8649 **raisonnablement** adv [ʁɛzɔnabləmɑ̃]
reasonably
Dès lors, je crois que le délai de 2015 ne saurait raisonnablement être raccourci.
-As a result, I believe that it would not be reasonably to bring forward the 2015 deadline.

8650 **maussade** adj [mosad]
sulky|surly
Les Européens doivent être préparés à surmonter toute réaction maussade à ces sentiments.
-We in Europe must be prepared to rise above any peevish reactions to those sentiments.

8651 **exceller** vb [ɛksele]
excel
Ces jeux m'ont donné la chance d'exceller dans la vie.
-The Special Olympics have given me the chance to excel in life.

8652 **surhumain** adj [syʁymɛ̃]
superhuman
C'est ce que le gouvernement américain doit faire, même si cela implique apparemment un effort surhumain.
-That is what the US administration must do, even if it seemingly involves a superhuman effort.

8653 **fervent** adj; m [fɛʁvɑ̃]
fervent; enthusiast
Toute sa vie durant, il a été un fervent avocat de l'intégration régionale des Caraïbes.
-Throughout his life, he was an ardent advocate of Caribbean regional integration.

8654 **duvet** m [dyvɛ]
duvet
Attention au duvet, s'il vous plaît.
-Be careful with the duvet, please.

8655 **épier** vb [epje]
spy
Peut-être que quelqu'un d'USR en profitait pour l'épier.
-Maybe...... somebody at USR was using those systems to spy on him.

8656 **modeler** vb [mɔdle]
shape|model
Nous pouvons modeler votre vision à tout ce que notre imagination peut concevoir.
-We can shape your vision to anything our imagination can conceive.

8657 **fermeté** f [fɛʁməte]
firmness
Une telle fermeté aujourd'hui serait un atout pour le maintien de la paix demain.
-Using this degree of firmness now would help to maintain peace in the future.

8658 **postérieur** **posterior; posterior**
adj; m
[pɔsteʁjœʁ]
Chaque bride souple traverse une boucle fixée au support postérieur.
-Each flexible strap passes through a loop attached to the posterior support.

8659 **braver** **brave**
vb[bʁave]
Seuls les entraîneurs capables de braver la tempête... sont dignes de lui. -Only the trainers capable of braving the storm...... are worthy in my master's eyes.

8660 **plaidoirie** **pleading**
f
[plɛdwaʁi]
La plaidoirie relative à la requête en annulation portait essentiellement sur les principes de droit applicables.
-The argument on the motion to set aside centred upon applicable legal principles.

8661 **contradictoire** **contradictory**
adj
[kɔ̃tʁadiktwaʁ]
Cela semble assez contradictoire.
-This comes across as being extremely self-contradictory.

8662 **véridique** **truthful**
adj
[veʁidik]
Le contrôle de la publicité est essentiel afin de la garder saine et véridique.
-Advertising control is vital if we are to keep it sound and truthful.

8663 **parader** **show**
vb
[paʁade]
Un défilé de fanfares a lieu la veille et l'avant-veille du mercredi des cendres.
-A parade of bands takes place on the Monday and Tuesday immediately preceding Ash Wednesday.

8664 **étroitement** **closely**
adv
[etʁwatmɑ̃]
Le trou doit être d'un diamètre tel que la sonde soit étroitement enserrée.
-The diameter of the hole should be as close fit as possible to the proble.

8665 **brouette** **wheelbarrow**
f
[bʁuɛt]
Hier, ma brouette a été volée.
-Yesterday, my wheelbarrow was stolen.

8666 **électrocuter** **electrocute**
vb
[elɛktʁɔkyte]
Je trouve cela extraordinaire parce qu'il m'empêchera peut-être de m'électrocuter un jour.
-That is wonderful because he will probably save me from electrocuting myself somewhere down the road.

8667 **galoper** **gallop**
vb
[galɔpe]
Le premier cheval à galoper sur le sol canadien a été débarqué à Québec, le 25 juin 1647.
-The first horse to gallop on Canadian soil was unloaded in Quebec on June 25, 1647.

8668 **meubler** **furnish**
vb
[mœble]
La maison - le cadre financier - doit se tenir debout avant que nous puissions meubler les différentes pièces.
-We all know that the whole house, the financial framework, must be standing before we can furnish the rooms.

8669 **rémission** **remission**
f
[ʁemisjɔ̃]
Les patients atteints de leucémie myéloïde aigüe en rémission présentent des quantités normales d'ADNmt dans leurs cellules.
-AML patients in remission have normal amounts of mtDNA in their cells.

8670 **fredonner** **hum**
vb
[fʁədɔne]
Jack entendit quelqu'un fredonner sa chanson préférée.
-Jack heard someone humming his favorite tune.

8671 **aversion** **aversion**

f[avɛʁsjɔ̃] Une aversion particulière pour les langues et cultures slaves peut être observée. -A particular aversion to the Slavonic languages and cultures can be observed.

8672 **grincer** **squeak|grind**
vb
[gʁɛ̃se]
C'est censé être de l'ecstasy propre, mais ça me faisait grincer des dents.
-Supposed to be like a clean ecstasy, but it made me grind my teeth.

8673 **volcanique** **volcanic**
adj
[vɔlkanik]
C'est un cône volcanique massif, qui est, heureusement, endormi la plupart du temps.
-It is volcanic, a massive cone that, fortunately, remains dormant most of the time.

8674 **arrondir** **round**
vb
[aʁɔ̃diʁ]
Note : Veuillez arrondir tous les montants de revenu et de paiement au dollar le plus proche.
-Note: Please round all income and award amounts to the nearest dollar.

8675 **jarre** **jar**
f
[ʒaʁ]
J'aurais dû voir ça venir quand vous avez mentionné la jarre.
-I should've seen this coming when you mentioned the jar.

8676 **déstabiliser** **shake**
vb
[destabilize]
Mon ami, M. Telkämper, me déstabilise toujours au niveau politique, Monsieur le Président.
-My friend Mr Telkämper always unsettles me politically, Mr President.

8677 **calmar** **squid**
m
[kalmaʁ]
Un calmar a 10 bras.
-A squid has ten arms.

8678 **déconnecter** **disconnect**
vb
[dekɔnɛkte]
Je vais le déconnecter de l'imprimante.
-Don't worry. I'll disconnect him from the printer.

8679 **obscénité** **obscenity**
f
[ɔpsenite]
L'obscénité menace clairement les avantages de l'Internet.
-Obscenity is clearly endangering the benefits of the Internet.

8680 **photocopie** **photocopy**
f
[fɔtɔkɔpi]
Remplissez le formulaire avec photocopie et donnez-les-moi lundi.
-Just fill in the receipt forms, photocopy it and then file them on Monday.

8681 **blanchiment** **whitening**
m
[blɑ̃ʃimɑ̃]
Je suis autant mouillé que vous dans le blanchiment de cet argent.
-I'd be as indictable as you for laundering that money.

8682 **frisé** **curly**
adj
[fʁize]
Si je laisse pousser trop longtemps il devient tout frisé.
-If I let it grow too long it gets all curly.

8683 **pyromane** **pyromaniac**
m/f
[piʁɔman]
Même signature et un pyromane différent.
-Same signature; it's a different pyromaniac

8684 **frappeur** **striker**
m
[fʁapœʁ]
Je crois qu'il devrait y avoir un amendement constitutionnel... bannissant l'Astroturf et le frappeur désigné.
-I believe there ought be a constitutional amendment... outlawing Astroturf and the designated hitter.

8685 **utilisateur** **user**

m[ytilizatœʁ] Vérifie que ton nom d'utilisateur et ton mot de passe sont écrits correctement. -Check that your username and password are written correctly.

8686 **baiseur** **fucker**
m Ferme-la et crève, baiseur de truies.
[bɛzœʁ] -Mump off and die, you pig fucker.

8687 **internement** **detention**
m Quatorze seraient décédées pendant leur internement.
[ɛ̃tɛʁnəmɑ̃] -Allegedly, a total of 14 detainees have died while in detention.

8688 **exceptionnellement** **exceptionally**
adv La Zambie se trouve dans une situation géopolitique exceptionnellement difficile.
[ɛksɛpsjɔnɛlmɑ̃] -Zambia is placed in an exceptionally difficult position geopolitically.

8689 **polluer** **pollute|taint**
vb Il s'agit d'un droit abstrait de polluer l'atmosphère, attribué administrativement.
[pɔlɥe] -They represent an administratively allocated abstract right to pollute the atmosphere.

8690 **couver** **smolder|brood**
vb Beaucoup de conflits couvaient depuis longtemps.
[kuve] -Many situations have been brewing for a long time.

8691 **harpon** **harpoon**
m Très bien, Enfin un peu de harpon dans le bowling.
[aʁpɔ̃] -All right, finally a little harpoon in the bowling alley.

8692 **dévisager** **stare at**
vb Il est impoli de dévisager les autres.
[devizaʒe] -It's not polite to stare at others.

8693 **lampadaire** **floor lamp**
m Je vais m'asseoir sur le banc là-bas, près du lampadaire.
[lɑ̃padɛʁ] -I'm going to sit on the bench over there next to the street lamp.

8694 **agrandissement** **enlargement**
m Un des projets comprenait l'agrandissement d'un site de mytiliculture dans la baie de Lamèque.
[aɡʁɑ̃dismɑ̃] -One project involved expansion of a mussel site in Lamèque Bay.

8695 **déchirure** **tear|tearing**
f L'accident laissa une longue et profonde déchirure sur le côté de l'avion.
[deʃiʁyʁ] -The accident left a long, deep gash in the side of the airplane.

8696 **raviver** **revive|rekindle**
vb Par conséquent, nous devons raviver leur intérêt pour le processus politique.
[ʁavive] -Therefore, we must revive their interest in the political process.

8697 **rhumatisme** **rheumatism**
m Un Européen sur cinq est en traitement permanent pour le rhumatisme ou l'arthrite.
[ʁymatism] -One in five Europeans are in permanent therapy for rheumatism or arthritis.

8698 **baveux** **runny**
adj Il veut les œufs baveux, pas...
[bavø] -And he wants them eggs runny, not...

8699 **cécité** **blindness**
f[sesite] Mais je semble être condamné à la cécité -But I seem to have been doomed to blindness.

8700 **inconvenant** **improper**
adj
[ɛ̃kɔ̃vənɑ̃]
Elle sait qu'il serait inconvenant que je commente un rapport qui n'a pas encore été déposé.
-She knows that it would be improper for me to comment on a report that has yet to be tabled.

8701 **standardiste** **operator**
m/f
[stɑ̃daʁdist]
La standardiste m'a passé le Canada.
-The operator put me through to Canada.

8702 **brillamment** **brilliantly**
adv
[bʁijamɑ̃]
Monsieur le Président, le rapporteur a très brillamment réalisé un exercice budgétaire complexe.
-Mr President, the rapporteur has handled a complicated budgetary exercise quite brilliantly.

8703 **vermouth** **vermouth**
m
[vɛʁmut]
Du fermet, un mélange de bière et vermouth.
-Fermet, a mixture of beer and vermouth.

8704 **ambulant** **traveling; traveler**
adj; m
[ɑ̃bylɑ̃]
Un marchand ambulant s'est installé au pub.
-Some travelling salesman's set up at the pub for the afternoon.

8705 **entendement** **understanding**
m
[ɑ̃tɑ̃dmɑ̃]
Son idée dépasse mon entendement.
-His idea is beyond the reach of my understanding.

8706 **chenil** **kennel**
m
[ʃənil]
Mais tu aimais vraiment ces chiens au chenil.
-No, but you really cared about those dogs at the kennel.

8707 **absinthe** **absinthe**
f
[apsɛ̃t]
L'antidote parfait contre l'absinthe.
-It's the perfect antidote to that absinthe.

8708 **enfantillage** **childishness**
m
[ɑ̃fɑ̃tijaʒ]
L'esquive, la dissimulation, l'enfantillage.
-The ducking, the hiding, the childishness.

8709 **tignasse** **wig**
f
[tiɲas]
Ils ont toujours une belle tignasse.
-They always have a beautiful head of hair.

8710 **invisibilité** **invisibility**
f
[ɛ̃vizibilite]
Il est, à cet égard, important de souligner l'invisibilité des travailleuses rurales.
-In this respect, it is important to emphasize the invisibility of rural workingwomen.

8711 **chapelier** **milliner**
m
[ʃapəlje]
Un, appelle un grand chapelier.
-Next, call any first-class hatter.

8712 **rafler** **grab**
vb
[ʁafle]
Comme auparavant, des entreprises nationales peuvent rafler des subventions sans aucun contrôle et nuire à des régions.
-National undertakings can still go on grabbing up aid unchecked and thereby damage regions.

8713 **maboul** **crazy|nuts**
adj[mabul]
Les filles, il est devenu maboul. -He's gone crazy, girls.

8714 **barde** **bard**

m [baʁd] La Gaelic Society d'Écosse, An Comunn Gàidhealach, a désigné Lewis MacKinnon nouveau barde écossais.
-An Comunn Gàidhealach, the Gaelic Society of Scotland, has crowned Lewis MacKinnon the newest Scottish bard.

8715 **irrespectueux** **disrespectful**
adj [iʁɛspɛktɥø] Il est totalement irrespectueux de leur part de ne pas les prendre en considération.
-It is very disrespectful of them not to take this into account.

8716 **désertion** **desertion**
f [dezɛʁsjɔ̃] Ce nouveau Code prévoira les peines minimales et maximales en cas de désertion.
-The new Military Code will regulate the minimum and maximum sanctions for desertion.

8717 **rénover** **renovate|restore**
vb [ʁenɔve] On constate un besoin croissant de rénover le parc de logements de l'État.
-There is a growing need to refurbish the States-owned housing stock.

8718 **courageusement** **courageously**
adv [kuʁaʒøzmɑ̃] Elle défend toujours courageusement les valeurs auxquelles elle croit.
-She has been absolutely fearless in representing the values in which she believes.

8719 **commère** **tattletale**
f [kɔmɛʁ] C'est une vraie commère.
-She's a real gossip.

8720 **finaliste** **finalist**
m/f [finalist] Notre neuvième finaliste, Miss Planète Méthane... Halatina Smogmeyer.
-Our ninth finalist, Miss Methane Planet... Halatina Smogmeyer.

8721 **rythme** **pace|rhythm**
m [ʁitm] Si tu continues à ce rythme, tu échoueras sûrement.
-If you go on at that rate, you will surely fail.

8722 **jeunot** **youngster**
m [ʒœno] J'en ai assez de passer pour un jeunot.
-I'm tired of passing for a youngster.

8723 **sauvegarder** **safeguard**
vb [sovgaʁde] Au contraire, c'est un moyen de sauvegarder l'aide globale actuelle au secteur.
-On the contrary, it is a way of safeguarding the current overall aid to the sector.

8724 **importation** **import**
f [ɛ̃pɔʁtasjɔ̃] Le marché du riz japonais est fermé à l'importation.
-Japan's rice market is closed to imports.

8725 **relaxant** **relaxing**
adj [ʁəlaksɑ̃] Dans certains cas, des enfants de 9 ans à peine sont soumis à des électrochocs sans bénéficier de relaxants musculaires ou d'une anesthésie.
-In some cases children as young as nine are subjected to electroconvulsive treatment (ECT) without the use of muscle relaxants or anaesthesia.

8726 **engraisser** **fatten|grow fat**
vb[ɑ̃gʁese] Elle ne mange pas de gâteaux, afin de ne pas engraisser. -She does not eat cake, so as not to put on any more weight.

8727 **intraveineux** **intravenous**
adj [ɛ̃tʁavɛnø] Je tiens un sac contenant 1 000 cc de soluté intraveineux.
-I held up an intravenous bag with 1,000 cc's of IV fluid in it.

8728 **arbitraire** **arbitrary**
adj
[aʁbitʁɛʁ]
C'est la deuxième fois cette année que cette session est annulée de façon arbitraire.
-This is the second time this year that this session has been arbitrarily cancelled.

8729 **pépite** **nugget**
f
[pepit]
Je voulais garder cette pépite pour le procès.
-I wanted to keep that nugget for trial.

8730 **opus** **opus**
m
[ɔpys]
Pierre les appelait ses opus, de 1 à 5.
-Pierre called them his Opus 1 through Opus 5.

8731 **épitaphe** **epitaph**
f
[epitaf]
J'imagine que ce sera mon épitaphe.
-I suppose that will become my epitaph.

8732 **bicoque** **shanty|shack**
f
[bikɔk]
Garde la bicoque pendant que je suis parti.
-Hold down the shack while I'm gone.

8733 **incendiaire** **incendiary; arsonist**
adj; m/f
[ɛ̃sɑ̃djɛʁ]
Ce que le maire prétend est infondé et incendiaire.
-What the mayor is claiming is spurious and inflammatory.

8734 **rachat** **redemption|buying back**
m
[ʁaʃa]
En outre, le ministère a reporté à plusieurs reprises le rachat de différentes émissions.
-Additionally, the Ministry allowed delays in the redemption of individual issues several times.

8735 **bricoleur** **handyman**
m
[bʁikɔlœʁ]
Je ne pense pas que ce type était un bricoleur.
-I do not think that guy was a handyman.

8736 **albatros** **albatross**
m
[albatʁos]
On a plongé pour un albatros quadrimoteur.
-Looks as if we dunked for a four-motored albatross.

8737 **magnétisme** **magnetism**
m
[maɲetism]
Un courant électrique peut générer du magnétisme.
-An electric current can generate magnetism.

8738 **bricolage** **do-it-yourself**
m
[bʁikɔlaʒ]
En conséquence, les secteurs résidentiels et du bricolage ont été relégués au second plan à cet égard.
-The home improvement/DIY and residential sectors have therefore taken more of a back row seat.

8739 **fresque** **fresco**
f
[fʁɛsk]
Il a vendu une fresque aujourd'hui pour un demi-million de dollars.
-He sold a mural today for a half-million bucks.

8740 **litière** **litter**
f[litjɛʁ]
Afin de réduire les émissions de NH3, la litière humide doit être évitée autant que possible. -To minimize NH3 emission, it is important to keep the litter as dry as possible.

8741 **commerce** **trade|business**
m
[kɔmɛʁs]
Jack a fait une école de commerce.
-Jack went to business school.

8742 **rasta** **rasta**

m Mortimer Planno était un chef spirituel rasta que Bob a côtoyé.
[ʁasta] -Mortimer Planno was a Rasta spiritual leader who taught Bob.

8743 **apesanteur** **weightlessness**
f La sensation d'apesanteur les rassure.
[apəzɑ̃tœʁ] -They're comforted by the feeling of weightlessness...

8744 **corner** **corner; honk**
m; vb C'est Joaquinzinho, le numéro trois, qui frappera le corner.
[kɔʁne] -Joaquinzinho, number 3, will take a corner kick.

8745 **configuration** **configuration**
f La configuration des bureaux extérieurs a été rationalisée et normalisée.
[kɔ̃figyʁasjɔ̃] -The configuration of the field offices has been streamlined and standardized.

8746 **ancienneté** **seniority**
f L'ancienneté des fonctionnaires est un indicateur de l'expérience à l'Organisation.
[ɑ̃sjɛnte] -Length of service is an indicator of acquired experience by the Organization.

8747 **variole** **smallpox**
f L'année de ses 15 ans, la variole a été officiellement déclarée vaincue.
[vaʁjɔl] -In the year that that child turned 15, smallpox had been officially eradicated.

8748 **discipliner** **discipline**
vb Corporal punishment is commonly practised to discipline children.
[disipline] -On recourt communément aux châtiments corporels pour discipliner les enfants.

8749 **vaseline** **petroleum jelly**
f On a peut-être utilisé une sorte de vaseline.
[vazlin] -Maybe some kind of petroleum jelly was used.

8750 **tuile** **tile**
f L'invention concerne une tuile utilisant du charbon actif, qui agit comme un excellent absorbant de formaldéhyde.
[tɥil] -A tile using an activated carbon, which is excellent as a formaldehyde absorbent, and a preparation process thereof are disclosed.

8751 **fraude** **fraud**
f Elle est coupable de fraude.
[fʁod] -She is guilty of fraud.

8752 **inspirant** **inspiring**
adj Le comité pense que la charte proposée pourrait être un document inspirant qui prendrait une valeur morale dans les pays du Commonwealth.
[ɛ̃spiʁɑ̃] -The Committee believes that the proposed Charter can be an inspirational document that has moral standing in Commonwealth countries.

8753 **broder** **embroider**
vb[bʁɔde] Pourquoi omet-on de se demander s'il est seulement possible de continuer à broder sur le modèle existant ? -Why has no attention been paid to the question whether it might be possible to simply elaborate on the existing model?

8754 **indiscrétion** **indiscretion**
f Il a commis une autre indiscrétion, et il devrait démissionner.
[ɛ̃diskʁesjɔ̃] -He committed another indiscretion and he should resign.

8755 **décemment** **decently**
adv Il était à la limite de tout ce que l'on peut décemment demander à un être de supporter.
[desamɑ̃]

-They had reached the limit of what one can decently ask someone to put up with.

8756 **liquidation** **liquidation**
f
[likidasjɔ̃]
Ils ont une liquidation.
-They're having a going-out-of-business sale.

8757 **piazza** **piazza**
f
[pjadza]
Et je l'ai laissé seul sur cette piazza.
-And I left him all alone in that piazza.

8758 **abondant** **abundant; affluent**
adj; m
[abɔ̃dɑ̃]
Le charbon demeure le combustible fossile le plus abondant et le plus sûr au monde.
-Coal remains the world's most abundant, safe and secure fossil fuel.

8759 **illisible** **illegible**
adj
[ilizibl]
Son écriture est illisible.
-His handwriting is illegible.

8760 **convocation** **convocation**
f
[kɔ̃vɔkasjɔ̃]
Nous appuyons la convocation du Conseil de sécurité en séance publique aujourd'hui.
-We support the Security Council in convening this public debate today.

8761 **humainement** **humanly**
adv
[ymɛnmɑ̃]
La situation actuelle est absolument intenable, humainement insupportable et moralement inacceptable.
-The current situation is absolutcly untenable, humanly unbearable and morally unacceptable.

8762 **inébranlable** **unwavering|steadfast**
adj
[inebʁɑ̃labl]
Hank doit apprécier votre dévotion inébranlable.
-I'm sure Hank appreciates your unwavering devotion.

8763 **chevelu** **haired|hairy**
adj
[ʃəvly]
Je suis coincé à l'arrière avec un péruvien chevelu et mordeur.
-I am jammed in the backseat with a hairy Peruvian biter.

8764 **condescendant** **patronizing**
adj
[kɔ̃desɑ̃dɑ̃]
Je ne sais pas, elle a un ton vraiment condescendant quand elle parle, tu ne trouves pas ? Parfois, ça m'agace.
-I don't know, she really has a condescending way of talking, don't you think? Sometimes it gets to me.

8765 **arménien** **Armenian; Armenian**
adj; m
[aʁmenjɛ̃]
Un enfant adopté par un Arménien a également droit à la nationalité arménienne.
-A child adopted by an Armenian citizen is also entitled to Armenian citizenship.

8766 **traînée** **trail|drag**
f
[tʁene]
Avantages : diminution de la traînée résiduelle après freinage.
-The advantage of the present invention is a decrease in the residual drag after braking.

8767 **impolitesse** **rudeness**
f
[ɛ̃pɔlitɛs]
Je m'excuse de mon impolitesse.
-I apologize for my rudeness.

8768 **soupe** **soup**
f
[sup]
Leur idée, c'est que tout le monde mange de la soupe et que la soupe transcende les frontières.
-Their idea was that soup is a common food amongst people and that soup transcends boundaries.

8769 **illustrer** **illustrate**
vb
[ilystʁe]
Un exemple concret peut illustrer le processus de création d'une contravention.
-A practical example can illustrate the process of establishing a contravention.

8770 **idylle** **idyll**
f
[idil]
-Votre idylle victorienne ne vous plaît plus ?
-Aren't you enjoying your Victorian idyll any longer?

8771 **siroter** **sip**
vb
[siʁɔte]
Des petits truands qui s'assoient dans un café, sirotant du thé dans des petits verres, des morceaux de sucre entre les dents, gérant leur propre business en se la pétant...
-Mobster thugs sitting in cafes, sipping tea in little glasses, sugar cubes between their teeth, wheelin ' and dealin ' and schemin '.

8772 **capuche** **hoodie**
f
[kapyʃ]
Elle a emprunté son chandail à capuche.
-She borrowed his hoodie.

8773 **captif** **captive; captive**
adj; m
[kaptif]
Nous appelons à la libération imminente de tout 227 prisonniers politiques vous avez retenu captif.
-We call for the imminent release of all 227 political prisoners you've held captive.

8774 **contemporain** **contemporary|coeval; contemporary**
adj; m
[kɔ̃tɑ̃pɔʁɛ̃]
Quelques aspects internationaux du droit international contemporain, Tbilisi, 1982
-Some International Aspects of Contemporary International Law, Tbilisi, 1982.

8775 **altérer** **alter**
vb
[alteʁe]
J'ai dû altérer le plan.
-I had to change the plan.

8776 **dégradant** **degrading**
adj
[degʁadɑ̃]
Sortir à moitié nu est dégradant.
-To go out half-naked is shameful.

8777 **speech** **speech**
m
[spitʃ]
C'était le speech de demain.
-I actually just started my speech for tomorrow.

8778 **douanier** **customs officer**
m[dwanje]
La destruction est effectuée sous contrôle douanier. -The destruction shall be carried out under customs control.

8779 **académique** **academic**
adj
[akademik]
Facteur académique, au profit des étudiants ayant de hauts niveaux de formation.
-Academic factor, for the benefit of students with advanced levels of training.

8780 **tolérant** **tolerant|forgiving**
adj
[tɔleʁɑ̃]
L'Europe de l'intégration ne peut tolérer le nationalisme.
-This integrated Europe must not accept nationalism.

8781 **spéculer** **speculate**
vb
[spekyle]
Il n'est donc pas pertinent de spéculer sur un report éventuel de leur adhésion.
-As such, it is not relevant to speculate about deferring their accession.

8782 **satisfaisant** **satisfactory**

	adj [satisfəzɑ̃]	Le feu spécial d'avertissement est considéré comme satisfaisant si le résultat d'essai est favorable. -The special warning lamp shall be considered as acceptable if the test has passed.
8783	**gravier** m [gʁavje]	**gravel** En échange de sa protection, il reçoit des sacs de gravier riche en diamants. -In exchange for protection, the Commander receives sacks of diamond-rich gravel.
8784	**indéniable** adj [ɛ̃denjabl]	**undeniable** Le processus de mondialisation suscite un sentiment indéniable de malaise. -The process of globalization is tainted by an undeniable sense of unease.
8785	**gibet** m [ʒibɛ]	**gallows** Vos enfants, cher comte, mourront au gibet. -Your children, My Lord, shall die on the gallows.
8786	**sobriété** f [sɔbʁijete]	**sobriety** Je demande en échange ta sobriété. -All I ask in return is your sobriety.
8787	**rosaire** m [ʁozɛʁ]	**rosary** Elle avait un rosaire de perles et un crucifix en or... -She had a rosary of pearls and a golden crucifix...
8788	**pénombre** f [penɔ̃bʁ]	**penumbra** Cette fois, sans la protection de la pénombre. -This time without the cover of darkness.
8789	**remorquer** vb [ʁəmɔʁke]	**tow** Véhicule routier pour le transport de marchandises conçu pour être remorqué par un véhicule routier automobile. -Goods road vehicle designed to be towed by a road motor vehicle.
8790	**attendrir** vb [atɑ̃dʁiʁ]	**tenderize|pound** Dans la même poêle, attendrir l'ail et déglacer avec le vinaigre. -In same skillet, soften the garlic and deglaze with the vinegar.
8791	**délinquance** f [delɛ̃kɑ̃s]	**delinquency** La croissance de la délinquance juvénile est un problème grave. -The augmentation of juvenile delinquency is a serious problem.
8792	**volupté** f[vɔlypte]	**sensuousness** Pensez à la volupté de me rendre obéissante. -Think of the sensuousness of making me obey.
8793	**gigot** m [ʒigo]	**leg** Je pourrais faire un gigot les yeux fermés. -I could do a leg of lamb in my sleep.
8794	**postuler** vb [pɔstyle]	**apply|postulate** Il encourage les membres des minorités ethniques à postuler en plus grand nombre. -He is encouraging greater numbers of ethnic minority practitioners to apply.
8795	**problématique** adj [pʁɔblematik]	**problematic** Monsieur le Président du Conseil, la rencontre sera indubitablement marquée par cette double problématique. -There is no doubt, Mr President-in-Office, that the meeting will be dominated by these two fundamental questions.
8796	**trognon**	**core**

m | Un morceau du trognon se coince entre ses dents.
[tʁɔɲɔ̃] | -He gets a piece of the core stuck between his teeth.

8797 **asphalte** **asphalt**
m
[asfalt]
La présente invention porte sur l'utilisation d'additifs chimiques organiques pour la préparation de mélanges d'asphalte tièdes.
-The present invention relates to use of organic chemical additives for the preparation of warm asphalt mixtures.

8798 **déminage** **sweeping**
m
[deminaʒ]
Ces pays devraient également soutenir les opérations de déminage.
-These countries should also extend assistance in the mine clearance operations.

8799 **capuchon** **cap|hood**
m
[kapyʃɔ̃]
Le capuchon fileté est relié au porte-joint.
-The threaded cap is connected to the seal holder.

8800 **calice** **chalice**
m
[kalis]
Un calice, symbolique de la fontaine.
-A chalice, symbolic of a fountain.

8801 **inné** **innate|inborn**
adj
[ine]
Ce n'est pas quelque chose d'inné, c'est une chose qui doit s'acquérir.
-It is not something with which we are born, but something that we have to earn.

8802 **marquant** **outstanding|remarkable**
adj
[maʁkɑ̃]
C'est un univers de changement, et souvenons-nous que les décennies les plus marquantes de l'histoire européenne n'ont jamais été pleinement comprises sur le moment même.
-This is a world of change, and we should remind ourselves that the most epoch-making decades in European history have never been fully understood as they have happened.

8803 **forer** **drill|sink**
vb
[fɔʁe]
L'appareil de forage Challenger aurait ensuite été déplacé pour forer d'autres puits d'évaluation tels que le SLK-3.
-Thereafter, the Challenger rig would have moved on to drill other appraisal wells, such as SLK-3.

8804 **grincement** **grinding|squeak**
m[gʁɛ̃smɑ̃]
Et je fais un test de grincement du lave-vaisselle. -Then I give 'em the squeak test and into the dishwasher they go.

8805 **théologie** **theology**
f
[teɔlɔʒi]
Voilà ma contribution à toute cette théologie.
-That's my only contribution to all this theology.

8806 **séchoir** **dryer**
m
[seʃwaʁ]
Mettons nos affaires dans le séchoir.
-We could throw our clothes in the dryer.

8807 **pulsation** **pulsation**
f
[pylsasjɔ̃]
La pulsation cyclique comprend un écoulement oscillant du circuit fluide.
-The cyclic pulsation further comprises an oscillating flow of the fluid stream.

8808 **vidanger** **drain**
vb
[vidɑ̃ʒe]
Il faut vidanger l'eau et détruire l'enceinte de confinement.
-We've got to remove the waterjacket and destroy the containment shell.

8809 **malfaiteur** **malefactor|wrongdoer**
m
[malfɛtœʁ]
Mon oncle n'est pas malfaiteur.
-My uncle's not a criminal...

8810 **obstination** f [ɔpstinasjɔ̃]
obstinacy
Une vieille obstination humaine, je suppose.
-Plain, old, human stubbornness, I guess.

8811 **ducat** m [dyka]
ducat
Apparemment, c'est un ancien ducat de Valachie.
-Apparently, it's an antique Wallachian ducat.

8812 **tonique** adj; f [tɔnik]
tonic; tonic
Oui, j'ai un tonique qui pourrait aider.
-Yes, I have a tonic that might help.

8813 **intrigant** adj; m [ɛ̃tʁigɑ̃]
intriguing; intriguer
Je le trouve intrigant.
-I find him intriguing.

8814 **garniture** f [gaʁnityʁ]
topping|filling
Quelle est ta garniture de pizza préférée ?
-What's your favorite pizza topping?

8815 **soupçonneux** adj [supsɔnø]
suspicious
Il ne fait aucun doute que nos électeurs se montrent plutôt soupçonneux à notre égard dans ce Parlement.
-There is no doubt that we in this Chamber are regarded with a fair amount of suspicion by our constituents.

8816 **dresseur** m [dʁesœʁ]
trainer
Le dresseur serait tout simplement l'auteur principal.
-The trainer simply becomes the main perpetrator.

8817 **lavement** m [lavmɑ̃]
enema|washing
Il avait dû faire son lavement au cappuccino.
-Must have had his cappucino enema.

8818 **fondant** m; adj [fɔ̃dɑ̃]
fondant; melting
Notre responsabilité consiste à exprimer une opinion sur ces états financiers consolidés en nous fondant sur nos vérifications.
-Our responsibility is to express an opinion on these consolidated financial statements based on our audits.

8819 **catégorique** adj[kategɔʁik]
categorical
Une interdiction absolue paraissait par trop catégorique pour être justifiée. -An absolute prohibition seemed far too categorical to be justified.

8820 **interposer** vb [ɛ̃tɛʁpoze]
interpose
Dans les deux opérations, les Nations Unies s'interposent entre deux parties à un conflit.
-In both operations, the United Nations is interposed between parties to a conflict.

8821 **sommeiller** vb [sɔmeje]
sleep|doze
Car je dois sommeiller, pour ainsi dire.
-For I must slumber, so to say.

8822 **boudoir** m [budwaʁ]
boudoir
Merci pour la confidentialité du boudoir.
-So much for the sanctity of the boudoir.

8823 **entraver** vb [ɑ̃tʁave]
impede|hamper
Il m'arrive parfois de rire de certaines descriptions courantes du Parlement, et d'ailleurs de la Commission, présentés comme des institutions qui entravent la progression de l'Union européenne.
-I am sometimes amused by popular descriptions of Parliament, and indeed

of the Commission, as being institutions which clog the progress of the European Union.

8824 **coquet** **pretty|stylish**
adj
[kɔkɛ]
Plus masculin, mais pas coquet.
-More manly, yes, but not pretty.

8825 **californien** **Californian**
adj
[kalifɔʁnjɛ̃]
Je commencerai par la salade aux têtes californienne, puis un shake-shake.
-I'll start with the tossed Californian bud salad, then a shake-shake.

8826 **lubrique** **lewd|lustful**
adj
[lybʁik]
Pour un enfant, l'abus, qu'il soit le fait d'un adulte lubrique ou de l'internet, devient un poids psychologique qui peut le briser pour toute sa vie.
-For a child, abuse, whether it is at the hand of a lecherous adult or the Internet, becomes a psychological millstone that blights the child for life.

8827 **stimuler** **stimulate**
vb
[stimyle]
Les réductions d'impôts sont souvent utilisées comme outil fiscal principal pour stimuler l'économie.
-Tax cuts are often used as a major fiscal tool to stimulate the economy.

8828 **ébullition** **boiling**
f
[ebylisjɔ̃]
Détermination du point d'ébullition/point d'ébullition initial.
-Determination of the boiling point / initial boiling point.

8829 **glas** **knell**
m
[gla]
L'UEM sonne le glas de la souveraineté, de la liberté, de l'indépendance de nos nations.
-EMU sounds the death knell for the sovereignty, freedom and independence of our nations.

8830 **raffinement** **refinement|sophistication**
m
[ʁafinmɑ̃]
La simplicité est le comble du raffinement.
-Simplicity is the ultimate sophistication.

8831 **normalité** **normality**
f[nɔʁmalite]
Une situation extrêmement anormale ne devrait pas donner lieu à un sentiment de normalité. -A sense of normalcy should not be created in an extremely abnormal situation.

8832 **caille** **quail**
f
[kaj]
Disons juste que j'avais une soudaine envie de caille au Madison Six.
-Let's just say that I had a sudden craving for the quail at Madison Six.

8833 **difforme** **misshapen**
adj
[difɔʁm]
Mais quand l'enfant est né, il était tout difforme.
-But when the child was born, it was deformed.

8834 **pluvieux** **rainy|wet**
adj
[plyvjø]
À ce moment, il se produit en général 2 à 3 brefs épisodes de pics pluvieux.
-At this time, usually 2-3 short rain peaks take place.

8835 **agilité** **agility**
f
[aʒilite]
Tu as une étonnante... agilité.
-You have an amazing... agility.

8836 **sophistiqué** **sophisticated**
adj
[sɔfistike]
Les résumés peuvent être recherchés au moyen d'un système de recherche sophistiqué.
-The abstracts can be searched through a sophisticated search system.

8837 **utopie** **Utopia**
f
[ytɔpi]
Pour transformer cette terre en utopie.
-And help us make this land our utopia.

8838	**délicieusement** adv [delisjøzmɑ̃]	**deliciously** Bien sûr, il y a des exceptions à la règle, comme le discours d'adieu délicieusement spirituel que le sénateur Murray a prononcé lorsque le sénateur MacEachen nous a quittés. -Of course there are exceptions, like the deliciously witty goodbye speech by Senator Murray when Senator MacEachen was leaving us.
8839	**réglage** m [ʁeglaʒ]	**setting** Le réglage du régulateur peut être exécuté manuellement ou électro-mécaniquement. -Adjustment of the regulator may be accomplished manually or by power means.
8840	**pragmatique** adj [pʁagmatik]	**pragmatic** Pareille hiérarchie informelle illustre l'aspect pragmatique du raisonnement juridique qui établit une distinction entre les cas «simples» et les cas «difficiles». -Such informal hierarchy is an aspect of the pragmatics of legal reasoning that makes a difference between "easy" and "hard" cases.
8841	**interlocuteur** m [ɛ̃tɛʁlɔkytœʁ]	**interlocutor** Le Procureur général du Liban demeure l'interlocuteur principal de la Commission. -The Prosecutor General of Lebanon remains the main interlocutor of the Commission.
8842	**aria** f [aʁja]	**aria** Il y a une aria dans le deuxième acte du Boulevardier. -There's an aria in the second act of The Boulevardier.
8843	**treuil** m[tʁœj]	**winch|hoist** Ce navire est pourvu d'un treuil pour lever l'encre. -This ship is outfitted with a windlass to heave up the anchor.
8844	**appartenance** f [apaʁtənɑ̃s]	**membership** Cela permet une gestion efficace de l'appartenance des groupes qui reçoivent les divers services. -This permits efficient management of the membership of the groups that receive the various services.
8845	**cime** f [sim]	**top|crown** La cime est recouverte de neige. -The top is covered with snow.
8846	**chaînon** m [ʃɛnɔ̃]	**link** L'intégration de nos systèmes de prévisions météorologiques est un exemple remarquable d'un nouveau chaînon important. -Integrating our weather prediction systems is an outstanding example of an important new link.
8847	**dépravation** f [depʁavasjɔ̃]	**depravity** Mesdames et messieurs, la dépravation hante cette université. -Ladies and gentlemen, depravity is haunting this university.
8848	**douzième** num [duzjɛm]	**twelfth** Hadjidakis, au nom de la Grèce, a participé à une partie de la douzième réunion. -Hadjidakis, on behalf of Greece, attended part of the twelfth meeting.
8849	**régent** m [ʁeʒɑ̃]	**regent** Je vous nomme temporairement régent pendant mon absence. -I'm naming you temporary regent while I'm gone.
8850	**lauréat**	**laureate; laureate**

adj; m
[loʁea]
Yitzhak Rabin a été le lauréat du prix Nobel de la paix en 1994.
-Itzhak Rabin was the Nobel Peace Prize laureate for the year 1994.

8851 **déséquilibrer** **unbalance**
vb
[dezekilibʁe]
Certaines données montrent que l'immigration pourrait avoir une influence sur le marché du travail intérieur et le déséquilibrer.
-Evidence shows that migrants might affect and bring unbalance to the internal labour market.

8852 **aride** **arid**
adj
[aʁid]
Pays aride, la Namibie importe près de la moitié des produits alimentaires dont il a besoin.
-Namibia, an arid country, imported close to half its domestic food requirements.

8853 **éblouir** **dazzle**
vb
[ebluiʁ]
À mon sens, il n'est pas convenable de nous laisser éblouir par l'illusion technologique.
-I do not think it is appropriate to let ourselves be dazzled by technological wizardry.

8854 **régulateur** **regulator; control**
m; adj
[ʁegylatœʁ]
L'oxyde nitrique (NO) constitue un important régulateur de croissance dans un organisme en développement intact.
-Nitric oxide (NO) is an important growth regulator in an intact developing organism.

8855 **arbalète** **crossbow**
f[aʁbalɛt]
Une arbalète géante... pour protéger vos hommes. -A giant crossbow... to protect the men from harm.

8856 **vénéneux** **poisonous**
adj
[venenø]
Je n'ai pas mangé de champignons vénéneux !
-I have not eaten any poisonous mushrooms!

8857 **disciplinaire** **disciplinary**
adj
[disiplinɛʁ]
Une procédure disciplinaire pour actes répréhensibles répétés a été engagée.
-Disciplinary proceedings for repeated instances of misconduct were initiated.

8858 **verrue** **wart**
f
[veʁy]
La verrue devrait disparaître dans un délai de 1 mois.
-The wart should disappear within 1 month.

8859 **réchaud** **stove**
m
[ʁeʃo]
Les efforts impliquant les réfugiés des communautés locales pour produire certains articles (par exemple combustibles de cuisine, farine, couvertures et réchaud).
-Efforts involving both refugees and local communities in producing certain items (e.g. cooking oil, flour, blankets, stoves).

8860 **teigne** **ringworm**
f
[tɛɲ]
C'est comme ça qu'on attrape la teigne.
-That's how you get ringworm.

8861 **secouriste** **rescuer|paramedic**
m/f
[səkuʁist]
Il a eu un accident et une secouriste a répondu.
-He was in an accident, and a paramedic picked it up.

8862 **visualiser** **visualize**
vb
[vizɥalize]
Dans un univers très très lointain, où chaque vision devient réalité, un nouveau essaya de visualiser un objet en quatre dimensions, pour visualiser en définitive un objet comportant une infinité de dimensions qui plongea soudain notre existence entière dans le chaos, en finissant ainsi avec

l'univers tel que nous le connaissons.
-In a far, far away universe where whatever is visualized becomes real, a noob tried to visualize a four dimensional object only to end up visualizing an object with an infinite number of dimensions that sent our entire existence into disarray thereby ending the universe as we know it.

8863 **négociant** m [negɔsjɑ̃]
merchant
Sir William Lucas, autrefois négociant à Meryton, possédait une jolie fortune. Ayant exercé honorablement l'office de maire, il avait obtenu du roi le titre de chevalier.
-Sir William Lucas had been formerly in trade in Meryton, where he had made a tolerable fortune, and risen to the honour of knighthood by an address to the king during his mayoralty.

8864 **expiration** f [ɛkspiʁasjɔ̃]
expiry
Une liste des dates d'expiration pour chaque dérogation spécifique enregistrée.
-A list of the expiry dates for each registered specific exemption.

8865 **thérapeutique** adj; f [teʁapøtik]
therapeutic; therapeutics
La marijuana thérapeutique est légale dans cet État.
-Medical marijuana is legal in this state.

8866 **rebond** m[ʁəbɔ̃]
rebound
Il y a eu un certain rebond, mais les marchés restent frileux et hautement volatiles. -There has been some rebound, but markets remain at a low ebb and are highly volatile.

8867 **interstellaire** adj [ɛ̃tɛʁstelɛʁ]
interstellar
Pour la première fois, l'humanité commencera à explorer le milieu interstellaire local.
-For the first time, humankind will begin to explore the local interstellar medium.

8868 **bâillon** m [bajɔ̃]
gag
Dès qu'il se heurte à une difficulté, c'est la motion de bâillon.
-Anytime it runs into a problem, gag orders are used.,

8869 **rembobiner** vb [ʁɑ̃bɔbine]
rewind
On a juste à rembobiner la cassette et la combiner avec votre mémoire.
-We just need to rewind the tape and fiddle with your memory.

8870 **dysfonctionnement** m [disfɔ̃ksjɔnmɑ̃]
dysfunction
Oubliez la nature du dysfonctionnement hépatique.
-Forget about the specific nature of the liver dysfunction.

8871 **saoudien** adj [saudjɛ̃]
Saudi
Le Rapporteur spécial a adressé trois communications au Gouvernement saoudien.
-The Special Rapporteur sent three communications to the Saudi Arabian Government.

8872 **gourdin** m [guʁdɛ̃]
club|mace
Attention au type avec le gourdin.
-Watch that fellow with the club.

8873 **pluriel** adj; m [plyʁjɛl]
plural; plural
S'il renvoie aux mots « présents articles », il devrait porter la marque du pluriel.
-If the phrase refers to "présents articles", it should be recast in the plural.

8874 **circonscription** f [siʁkɔ̃skʁipsjɔ̃]
district|riding
La circonscription s'appelle Bonavista-Trinity-Conception depuis longtemps.

-The name of the riding of Bonavista-Trinity-Conception has been around for a long time.

8875	**canalisation**	**piping**
	f [kanalizasjɔ̃]	Le raccord de filtration à trois voies est disposé sur la canalisation d'extraction d'air. -The filtration three-way connector is provided on the air extraction pipe.
8876	**faction**	**faction**
	f [faksjɔ̃]	Il existe une autre faction qui veut empêcher le lancement. -There's a new faction that wants to prevent your launch.
8877	**goupille**	**pin**
	f [gupij]	La goupille de verrouillage comprend également une partie tige comprenant l'extrémité distale. -The locking pin further comprises a shaft portion having the distal end.
8878	**hémorroïde**	**hemorrhoid**
	f [emɔʁɔid]	La dernière fois, j'ai saigné comme une hémorroïde. -Last time, I was bleeding like a hemorrhoid.
8879	**perspicacité**	**insight**
	f[pɛʁspikasite]	Niemöller offre une forme de perspicacité. -Now, Niemöller is offering a certain kind of insight.
8880	**dérangeant**	**unpalatable**
	adj [deʁɑ̃ʒɑ̃]	Le nombre de travailleurs humanitaires qui sont tués est tout aussi dérangeant. -Equally disturbing is the number of humanitarian personnel being killed.
8881	**perçant**	**piercing|shrill**
	adj [pɛʁsɑ̃]	Des hommes considérant les femmes de leur regard perçant et menaçant. -Men with piercing eyes scowling at women.
8882	**neurologue**	**neurologist**
	m/f [nøʁɔlɔg]	Un examen par un neurologue doit être envisagé. -Consultation with a neurologist should be considered as clinically indicated.
8883	**gaiement**	**gladly**
	adv [gemɑ̃]	Comme dans le passé, il semble qu'on s'attende à ce que des pays comme le Royaume-Uni continuent gaiement à financer cette folie. -As in the past, the expectation seems to be that countries like the United Kingdom will happily continue to bankroll this runaway madness.
8884	**glouton**	**gluttonous; glutton**
	adj; m [glutɔ̃]	Comme un glouton aime son repas. -Like a glutton loves his lunch.
8885	**poterie**	**pottery**
	f [pɔtʁi]	Ça veut dire que si demain tu es morte, tout ce que j'aurai de toi, c'est un pot de vinaigrette et un saladier. -So, if you die tomorrow all that I get from you is a jar of vinaigrette and a salad bowl.
8886	**froideur**	**coldness|ice**
	f [fʁwadœʁ]	Bowis vient de prononcer un discours dans lequel il est parvenu à mettre des visages sur la froideur des chiffres de la Cour des comptes. -Just now, Mr Bowis made a touching speech in which he managed to put faces, human faces, to the dry coldness of these numbers from the Court of Auditors.
8887	**fiacre**	**carriage**
	m [fjakʁ]	Laissons le fiacre ici, et marchons. -We'd best leave the cab here and walk.

8888 **accumuler** **accumulate**
vb
[akymyle]
Elle accorde cinq ans pour accumuler ces trois années de résidence réelle.
-Now it allows one five years to accumulate these three years of actual residence.

8889 **lamenter** **lament**
vb
[lamɑ̃te]
Nous devons donc nous lamenter sur les lacunes que présente cette mesure législative.
-We therefore have to lament what is missing from the bill.

8890 **panoplie** **range|toolbox**
f
[panɔpli]
Le juge peut imposer une panoplie d'amendes.
-The judge may give a range of fines.

8891 **mousser** **foam|froth**
vb
[muse]
L'enduit d'étanchéité moussant est capable de mousser pour sceller un espace.
-The foaming sealant is able to foam in order to seal a space.

8892 **pitre** **clown**
m[pitʁ]
Je le prenais pour un dépensier et un pitre. -I thought he was only a wastrel and a clown.

8893 **étouffant** **stifling**
adj
[etufɑ̃]
On ne trouvera pas une solution en étouffant ce débat, mais en mettant en œuvre ces résolutions.
-The solution lies not in stifling this debate, but in implementing these resolutions.

8894 **notoriété** **notoriety**
f
[nɔtɔʁjete]
Vous ne voulez que la notoriété.
-Well it looks as if you'll have to settle for notoriety.

8895 **ratisser** **rake|comb**
vb
[ʁatise]
Le LFAS produit un son basse fréquence de 1000 hertz et de 250 décibels de moyenne qui ratisse les fonds marins à des centaines de kilomètres de distance.
-The LFAS equipment produces low frequency noise at 1 000 hertz and an average of 250 decibels to comb the seabed from hundreds of kilometres away.

8896 **flâner** **stroll|loiter**
vb
[flane]
Elle aime flâner en ville.
-She likes strolling around town.

8897 **caricature** **caricature**
f
[kaʁikatyʁ]
Toutefois, lorsqu'on perd ses assises traditionnelles, il est dangereux de devenir une caricature de soi-même.
-However when one is taken and shaken from its traditional foundations the danger is that it will shift to a caricature of itself.

8898 **basilic** **basil**
m
[bazilik]
J'aime ajouter du basilic pour relever ma sauce spaghetti.
-I like to add basil to season my spaghetti sauce.

8899 **confiant** **confident**
adj
[kɔ̃fjɑ̃]
Ne sois pas trop confiant.
-Don't be too confident.

8900 **intolérance** **intolerance**
f
[ɛ̃tɔleʁɑ̃s]
Elle a probablement été elle-même victime d'intolérance.
-Yes, she has probably been a victim of intolerance.

8901 **crinière** **mane**

f
[kʁinjɛʁ]
Ma crinière doit être coiffée parfaitement en permanence.
-My mane needs to be perfectly coiffed at all times.

8902 **mécène** **sponsor**
m
[mesɛn]
L'UE n'est pas non plus le mécène naïf disposé à payer les dégâts causés par le sale travail réalisé par les Américains.
-Neither is the EU a naïve Maecenas, who pays up once the United States has done the dirty work.

8903 **soustraire** **subtract|remove**
vb
[sustʁɛʁ]
Outre l'addition, vous pouvez également soustraire, multiplier ou diviser les valeurs.
-Besides addition, you can also subtract, multiply or divide values.

8904 **femmelette** **wimp|sissy**
adj
[fɛmlɛt]
C'est vraiment une femmelette, ce type.
-He's a sissy, you know, that young one.

8905 **collation** **collation|snack**
f[kɔlasjɔ̃]
Pouvez-vous me préparer une collation ? -Can you make me a snack?

8906 **métaphysique** **metaphysical; metaphysics**
adj; f
[metafizik]
Je pose là une sérieuse question métaphysique.
-I'm trying to pose a serious metaphysical question here.

8907 **militer** **militate**
vb
[milite]
Car deux éléments peuvent militer contre l'adoption d'un texte qui nous est aujourd'hui proposé.
-The fact is that there are two factors that can militate against the adoption of the text before us today.

8908 **cellophane** **cellophane**
m
[selɔfan]
Malheureusement pour lui, le cellophane a été découvert relativement trop tôt.
-Sadly for him, cellophane it was discovered rather too early.

8909 **psaume** **psalm**
m
[psom]
Chaque semaine l'aumônier récite le psaume 23.
-It seems like every week, the chaplain preaches on psalm 23.

8910 **scrutin** **ballot|polling**
m
[skʁytɛ̃]
Il est trop tard pour voter maintenant. Les bureaux de scrutin sont fermés.
-It's too late to vote now. The polls are closed!

8911 **exactitude** **accuracy**
f
[ɛgzaktityd]
Fiabilité/exactitude: Le degré d'exactitude de l'indicateur proprement dit doit être acceptable.
-Reliability/accuracy: The level of accuracy of the indicator itself should be acceptable.

8912 **catcheur** **wrestler**
m
[katʃœʁ]
Forme un catcheur spécialisé dans la tricherie.
-Just train me a wrestler who specializes in cheating.

8913 **magouiller** **fiddle**
vb
[maguje]
C'est l'une des petites compensations d'être chef, de pouvoir magouiller ce genre de choses.
-It's one of management's little consolation prizes being able to fiddle such things.

8914 **canarder** **snipe**
vb
[kanaʁde]
I will read to honourable senators from one section of it, which should put to rest forever the canard that Senator Stanbury has raised before us.
-Je vais lire, à l'intention des honorables sénateurs, un article du document

qui devrait prouver, une fois pour toutes, que l'affirmation du sénateur Stanbury n'est qu'un bobard.

8915 **aryen**
adj
[aʁjɛ̃]
Aryan
La culture prédominante de type indo-aryen idéalise la femme et l'exclut de la vie publique.
-The predominant Indo-Aryan culture in the country idealizes women's seclusion from public life.

8916 **sabbatique**
adj
[sabatik]
sabbatical
Programme d'études avec congé sabbatique et cours d'été réunis.
-Figures include Sabbatical Programme and summer workshops.

8917 **tourelle**
f[tuʁɛl]
turret
Un ensemble magasin à tourelle permet une alimentation continue en articles. -A turret magazine assembly which provides a constant supply of articles.

8918 **perdrix**
f
[pɛʁdʁi]
partridge
Elle a bondi si haut des fourrés que je l'ai prise pour une perdrix.
-She came out of some bushes and jumped so high... that I thought it was a partridge.

8919 **rajeunir**
vb
[ʁaʒœniʁ]
rejuvenate
Il estime que cette situation offre l'occasion de rajeunir l'organisation.
-In the view of the Committee, this affords an opportunity to rejuvenate the organization.

8920 **récapituler**
vb
[ʁekapityle]
summarize|recapitulate
Je vais maintenant récapituler les points saillants du projet de loi C-53.
-I would now like to recap the key elements of Bill C-53.

8921 **naïveté**
f
[naivte]
naivete
Sa naïveté m'a beaucoup étonné.
-I was quite astounded at his naivety.

8922 **concepteur**
m
[kɔ̃sɛptœʁ]
designer
Il est clair que le concepteur devait avoir la tour de Babel de Breughel en tête.
-The designer clearly must have had Breughel' s Tower of Babel in mind.

8923 **spiritualité**
f
[spiʁitɥalite]
spirituality
Et ton visage manque de spiritualité.
-And there's not enough spirituality on your face.

8924 **cardlgan**
m
[kaʁdigɑ̃]
cardigan
Ne sont-ils pas un peu grumeleux, avec des lunettes et un cardigan?
-Aren't they usually a little lumpy, with glasses and a cardigan sweater?

8925 **inconscience**
f
[ɛ̃kɔ̃sjɑ̃s]
unconsciousness
Vous ne pourrez plus plaider l'inconscience.
-You won't be able to plead unconsciousness again.

8926 **obsessionnel**
adj
[ɔpsesjɔnɛl]
obsessive
Le contrôle obsessionnel des frontières dans ces circonstances ne résoudra pas le problème.
-Obsessive policing of the borders under these circumstances will not solve the problem.

8927 **volley**
m
[vɔlɛ]
volleyball
Aimes-tu jouer au volley ?
-Do you like playing volleyball?

8928 **écaille**
scale

	f	Il a perdu une écaille sous l'aile gauche.
	[ekaj]	-He loosened a scale under the left wing.
8929	**calotte**	**cap|dome**
	f	La fonte de la calotte glaciaire arctique a de nombreuses graves conséquences.
	[kalɔt]	-However, the melting of the Arctic ice cap has numerous, drastic consequences.
8930	**essaim**	**swarm**
	m	Un essaim de frelons attaqua les enfants.
	[esɛ̃]	-A swarm of hornets attacked the children.
8931	**malabar**	**bruiser**
	m[malabaʁ]	Comment le pleurnicheur qu'on a ramené de l'hôpital est devenu ce malabar ? -How did that little peewee we brought back From the hospital turn into this bruiser?
8932	**kaki**	**khaki; khaki**
	adj; m	Portez-la au bureau avec le kaki Signature.
	[kaki]	-Wear it with the Signature Khaki to the office.
8933	**projectile**	**projectile**
	m	Le projectile doit frapper la paroi latérale sous un angle d'environ 45°.
	[pʁɔʒɛktil]	-The projectile shall impact the sidewall at an approximate angle of 45°.
8934	**compresseur**	**compressor**
	m	L'efficacité du compresseur est néanmoins limitée.
	[kɔ̃pʁesœʁ]	-The efficiency of the compressor is limited, however.
8935	**échauffement**	**heating**
	m	Les amis, OK, faisons nos exercices d'échauffement.
	[eʃofmɑ̃]	-Fellas, okay, let's do our warm-up exercises.
8936	**rayonnant**	**radiant|shining**
	adj	Ils nous détestent car nous montrons un exemple rayonnant de ségrégation réussie.
	[ʁɛjɔnɑ̃]	-They hate us because we present a shining example... of successful segregation.
8937	**dissection**	**dissection**
	f	Après dissection, j'observe deux événements distincts.
	[disɛksjɔ̃]	-Based on my dissection, I've detected two separate events.
8938	**caïman**	**caiman**
	m	Cela pourrait être un caïman. Ou un iguane des terres.
	[kaimɑ̃]	-Could be a Cayman or a land iguana.
8939	**dégrader**	**degrade|deteriorate**
	vb	l'α-HBCDD semble se dégrader plus lentement que les isomères β et γ.
	[degʁade]	-α-HBCDD seems to be subject to a slower degradation than β- and γ-HBCDD.
8940	**ménagerie**	**menagerie**
	f	Des coquillages et des câbles torsadés ainsi qu'une ménagerie d'animaux réels et fabuleux munis d'une queue de poisson accentuent également le thème marin.
	[menaʒʁi]	-Motifs of shells and twisted rope, as well as a menagerie of real and fictitious sea creatures with fish tails also emphasize the maritime theme.
8941	**équivoquer**	**equivocate**
	vb	D'un autre côté, l'objectif du pragmatisme critique est d'accomplir le travail et non d'équivoquer ou de temporiser.
	[ekivɔke]	

-At the same time, however, critical pragmatism is concerned to get the job done, not to equivocate or temporize.

8942 **susciter** vb [sysite]
create|arouse
Susciter des attentes que nous ne pourrons jamais satisfaire n'a pas de sens selon moi.
-I do not think it makes sense to arouse expectations that we can never satisfy.

8943 **phonographe** m[fɔnɔɡʁaf]
phonograph
Il ressemblait au phonographe mais comptait quelques améliorations importantes. -It was much like the phonograph, but with a few significant improvements.

8944 **surestimer** vb [syʁɛstime]
overestimate
Je pense qu'il est difficile de surestimer l'importance des marchés de capitaux.
-It is difficult to overestimate the importance of these capital markets.

8945 **fonderie** f [fɔ̃dʁi]
foundry
Celles-ci sont particulièrement utiles dans la préparation de coulées en sable utilisées pour produire des pièces de fonderie.
-The binder compositions are particularly useful for preparing sand castings used for making foundry parts.

8946 **cardiologue** m/f [kaʁdjɔlɔɡ]
cardiologist
En tant qu'ancien cardiologue, je pense avoir une assez bonne connaissance du sujet.
-As a former cardiologist, I feel I have a fair amount of knowledge on the subject.

8947 **défavoriser** vb [defavɔʁize]
disadvantage
Les entreprises actives dans le commerce international, notamment, seraient défavorisées.
-Those companies that carry out cross-border trade, in particular, would be put at a disadvantage.

8948 **bagatelle** f [bagatɛl]
trifle
Hélas, c'est une bagatelle ! Je serais honteux de vous donner cela.
-Good sir, alas, it is a trifle, I would not shame myself to give you this.

8949 **incruster** vb [ɛ̃kʁyste]
inlay|insert
Les groupes dominants, qui peuvent s'incruster dans les institutions publiques et privées, définissent les paramètres de l'adhésion sociale.
-Dominant groups, which can be embedded in public and private institutions, define the parameters of social membership.

8950 **ressasser** vb [ʁəsase]
turn over
Ce qui importe le plus, c'est de ne pas ressasser ces vieilles controverses.
-What matters most is not to rake over these old controversies.

8951 **replonger** vb [ʁəplɔ̃ʒe]
relapse
C'est la seule façon de les empêcher de replonger dans un conflit violent.
-It is the only way to prevent them from sliding back into violent conflict.

8952 **négligeable** adj [negliʒabl]
negligible
L'ampleur du trafic d'armes légères est loin d'être négligeable.
-The levels of illicit trafficking in small arms are not negligible.

8953 **indirectement** adv [ɛ̃diʁɛktəmɑ̃]
indirectly
Cette question a indirectement trouvé une réponse.
-This question has indirectly met an answer.

8954 **loyalement**
loyally

adv [lwajalmɑ̃] Je réitère encore une fois mon souhait de travailler loyalement, concrètement et dans le meilleur esprit, avec nos amis tchèques.
-Once again I reiterate my wish to work loyally, constructively and in the best spirit, with our Czech friends.

8955 **tétanos** **tetanus**
m[tetanos] L'injection du tétanos fit plus mal que la morsure du chien. -The tetanus shot hurt more than the dog bite.

8956 **soupirant** **suitor**
m [supiʁɑ̃] Ce n'était pas un beau parleur, comme le soupirant classique.
-He wasn't the smooth talker in terms of what your normal suitor would have been.

8957 **resservir** **serve again**
vb [ʁəsɛʁviʁ] Je vais vous resservir du vin.
-I'm going to top up some wine.

8958 **vagabondage** **vagrancy**
m [vagabɔ̃daʒ] L'emploi rémunéré est la meilleure solution au problème du vagabondage et de la mendicité.
-Gainful employment was the best solution to the problem of vagrancy and begging.

8959 **avantageux** **advantageous**
adj [avɑ̃taʒø] Ce programme avantageux pour les céréaliculteurs est entré en vigueur cet été.
-This program kicked in for the benefit of grain producers earlier this summer.

8960 **longer** **follow**
vb [lɔ̃ʒe] Continuer tout droit sur le boulevard du Gave, longer l'esplanade du Paradis.
-Continue quite straight ahead on the boulevard du Gave, follow the esplanade du Paradis.

8961 **aristocratie** **aristocracy**
f [aʁistɔkʁasi] Et il s'agit le plus souvent de membres de l'aristocratie ou d'une famille royale.
-And these are usually members of the aristocracy or royalty.

8962 **lionne** **lioness**
f [ljɔn] Ça signifie "Quelle jeune lionne".
-She says that you are a young lioness.

8963 **désinfecter** **disinfect**
vb [dezɛ̃fɛkte] Elle enseigne à ces communautés comment traiter et désinfecter l'eau pour protéger les enfants comme les adultes des maladies d'origine hydrique.
-Antenna also provides lessons on how to treat and disinfect drinking water to save children and adults from water-borne diseases.

8964 **trésorerie** **treasury**
f [tʁezɔʁʁi] Malgré les excédents de trésorerie réalisés ces dernières années, ces comptes affichent une dette actuarielle très préoccupante.
-In spite of their cash surpluses in recent years these accounts have had very serious actuarial liabilities.

8965 **nuisible** **harmful|injurious**
adj [nɥizibl] Mais si nous échouons, nous nous trouverons plongés dans une concurrence âpre et nuisible.
-But if we fail, we will be plunged into damaging and acrimonious competition.

8966 **alarmant** **alarming**

	adj [alaʁmɑ̃]	Vous conviendrez que ce chiffre est alarmant et mérite une attention particulière. -You will agree that this statistic is alarming and deserves particular attention.
8967	**angélique** adj [ɑ̃ʒelik]	**angelic** Notre fils est un monstre angélique. -I think he's an angelic monster, our son.
8968	**dorsal** adj [dɔʁsal]	**dorsal** J'an ai fait l'expérience dans le Limousin avec le projet DORSAL. -I had experience of this in the Limousin with the DORSAL project.
8969	**fraternel** adj [fʁatɛʁnɛl]	**fraternal** Nous parlons tous d'un monde fraternel, solidaire. -We all talk about a world of brotherly love and solidarity.
8970	**rapatrier** vb [ʁapatʁije]	**repatriate** Elle a travaillé sans relâche pour protéger, maintenir et rapatrier les réfugiés. -It has worked strenuously to protect, maintain and repatriate refugees.
8971	**manille** m [manij]	**shackle** L'ensemble comprend une poutre et une manille. -The assembly includes a beam and a shackle.
8972	**moqueur** m; adj [mɔkœʁ]	**mocker; derisive** Le mot de passe est "moqueur" en russe. -The password is "mockingbird." In Russian.
8973	**flamenco** m [flamɛŋko]	**flamenco** Assistez à un spectacle de flamenco pendant que vous jouissez de votre dîner. -Watch a flamenco show while you enjoy dinner.
8974	**irrigation** f [iʁigasjɔ̃]	**irrigation** Ils mettent une sonde d'irrigation. -They're putting in an irrigation catheter.
8975	**similitude** f [similityd]	**similitude** Nous contrôlons la similitude visuelle des marques figuratives existantes. -We check existing device marks on visual similarity to your mark.
8976	**dureté** f [dyʁte]	**hardness|toughness** La dureté Shore est mesurée sur des échantillons du sujet d'essai lui-même. -The shore hardness measurement is made on samples of the test subject itself.
8977	**regrouper** vb [ʁəgʁupe]	**regroup|gather** Le fait de regrouper plusieurs projets en un seul est positif sous plusieurs aspects. -In many respects, it is a good idea to group the various programmes together.
8978	**articulation** f [aʁtikylasjɔ̃]	**joint|speech** Le système de commande peut également moduler un équilibre d'articulation. -The controller may also modulate a joint equilibrium.
8979	**chope** f [ʃɔp]	**mug** Ne fais rien que tu ne veuilles pas qu'on te chope en train de faire en mourant. -Don't do anything you wouldn't want somebody to catch you doing if you died while doing it.

8980	**astrologie**	**astrology**
	f	L'astrologie est une science fascinante.
	[astʁɔlɔʒi]	-Believe me, astrology's a fascinating science.
8981	**paître**	**graze|feed**
	vb	Au milieu de la Manche, il n'est pas possible de laisser paître les animaux dans un pré.
	[pɛtʁ]	-There is no possibility of taking an animal out to graze in the middle of the Channel.
8982	**inflexible**	**inflexible|unyielding**
	adj	La junte au pouvoir demeure inflexible; pourtant, le désir de liberté du peuple ne fait aucun doute.
	[ɛ̃flɛksibl]	-The ruling junta remains unyielding, yet the people's desire for freedom is unmistakable.
8983	**armoiries**	**arms**
	msf	Les armoiries sont l'autre symbole souvent utilisé.
	[aʁmwaʁi]	-The other symbol often used is the coat of arms.
8984	**crescendo**	**crescendo**
	m	Nous savons aussi que depuis trois ans, il y a un «crescendo» d'activités et d'initiatives visant à relancer les négociations.
	[kʁeʃɛ̃do]	-We also know that for the past three years there has been a crescendo in activities and initiatives aimed at relaunching negotiations.
8985	**motte**	**sod|clump**
	f	Dis donc, tu devrais remettre une petite motte sur le green.
	[mɔt]	-By the way, you're gonna need a little sod on the fairway there.
8986	**fantaisiste**	**fanciful; joker**
	adj; m/f	C'est cette maison fantaisiste au dessus de la colline Farrel.
	[fɑ̃tezist]	-It's that big fancy thing on the top of the hill Farrel.
8987	**persévérer**	**persevere**
	vb	Là où l'unité nous a permis de remporter de premiers succès, il faut persévérer.
	[pɛʁseveʁe]	-Where unity has enabled us to achieve initial success, we must persevere.
8988	**confédération**	**confederation**
	f	Votre homologue, représentant notre confédération.
	[kɔ̃fedeʁasjɔ̃]	-Let me introduce your counterpart from our confederation.
8989	**recensement**	**census|count**
	m	Les dernières données de recensement montrent que la population totale du pays dépasse légèrement les sept millions d'habitants.
	[ʁəsɑ̃smɑ̃]	-Latest census data shows that the total population of the country is slightly above 7 million people.
8990	**varicelle**	**varicella**
	f	Oreillons, varicelle, pneumonie et plusieurs attaques de grippe.
	[vaʁisɛl]	-Measles, chicken pox, pneumonia... and several bouts of influenza.
8991	**rance**	**rancid**
	adj	Je me fichais de l'odeur rance du frigo tiède.
	[ʁɑ̃s]	-I didn't even mind the warm, stale refrigerator.
8992	**suzerain**	**suzerain**
	m	Je ne puis donc vous reconnaître pour suzerain.
	[syzʁɛ̃]	-Thus I cannot give you fealty... nor own you as my liege.
8993	**balafrer**	**slash|scar**
	vb	Il est donc arrivé à se balafrer avec de l'argent de façon permanente.
	[balafʁe]	-So he somehow managed to permanently scar himself with silver.

8994 **névrosé** **neurotic**
adj[nevʁoze]
Eh bien, la nouvelle névrose obsessionnelle voit du CO_2 et des gaz de serre partout. -And now the latest neurotic obsession is seeing CO_2 and greenhouse gases everywhere.

8995 **fouillis** **mess**
m
[fuji]
Les programmes de support à la recherche et au développement sont dans un fouillis monumental.
-Research and development support programs are in a real mess.

8996 **paprika** **paprika**
m
[papʁika]
Ajoutez une petite cuillère de paprika.
-Add one teaspoon of paprika.

8997 **minutieux** **thorough**
adj
[minysjø]
La Commission a pris cette décision à l'issue d'une analyse minutieuse et d'une discussion interne en profondeur.
-The Commission has taken this decision after a thorough examination and in-depth internal debate.

8998 **rangement** **arrangement**
m
[ʁɑ̃ʒmɑ̃]
Le déploiement et le rangement de la rampe peuvent être effectués manuellement ou électriquement.
-Deployment and stowage of the ramp may be either manual or power-operated.

8999 **paranormal** **paranormal**
adj
[paʁanɔʁmal]
Tout est plutôt paranormal ici.
-Yes, everything's nice and paranormal here.

9000 **milligramme** **milligram**
m
[miligʁam]
Laisser refroidir au dessiccateur et peser à au moins un milligramme près.
-Let cool in a desiccator and weigh to the nearest milligram or better.

9001 **filière** **die|sector**
f
[filjɛʁ]
La filière peut comporter plusieurs passages pour l'application de couches multiples.
-The die can include several passageways for coating multiple layers.

9002 **gencive** **gum**
f
[ʒɑ̃siv]
Coincez-la entre votre gencive et votre joue.
-Just tuck it between your gum and cheek.

9003 **filleul** **godson**
m
[fijœl]
Elle fera une excellente épouse pour mon filleul.
-She'll make an excellent bride for my godson.

9004 **exportation** **export**
f
[ɛkspɔʁtasjɔ̃]
Les ventes de la société augmentèrent grâce à une forte demande à l'exportation, mais les profits ne suivirent pas en raison d'une compétition féroce.
-Sales at the company zoomed thanks to brisk export demand, but profit did not keep up because of intense competition.

9005 **aéroporté** **airborne**
adj
[aeʁɔpɔʁte]
La MONUG a vu un bataillon aéroporté russe se diriger vers la zone de conflit ce matin.
-UNOMIG observed a Russian airborne battalion move towards the zone of conflict this morning.

9006 **aphrodisiaque** **aphrodisiac; aphrodisiac**
adj; m[afʁɔdizjak]
Savez-vous que c'est aphrodisiaque ? -Did you know oysters are an aphrodisiac?

9007 **safran** **saffron**

m | Le safran, votre ingrédient secret...
[safʁɑ̃] | -Saffron... Your secret ingredient, of course.

9008 **recycler** | **recycle**
vb | Peut-on recycler ceci ?
[ʁəsikle] | -Can we recycle this?

9009 **racer** | **racer**
m | Francine fantasme sur le street racer que vous avez vu hier.
[ʁase] | -Francine is fantasizing... about the street racer you saw last night.

9010 **verseau** | **Aquarius**
m | On est dans l'ére du verseau.
[vɛʁso] | -It's the Age of Aquarius.

9011 **variable** | **variable; variable**
adj; f | La variable chimique Brix est une variable qui a une influence sur l'appréciation globale.
[vaʁjabl] | -The Brix chemical variable is a variable that influences overall evaluation.

9012 **pancréas** | **pancreas**
m | Chez les femmes, les cancers les plus fréquents étaient celui du sein (24 %), du colon (9 %) et du pancréas (8 %).
[pɑ̃kʁeas] | -In women the commonest killers were cancer of the breast (24%), the colon (9%), and the pancreas (8%).

9013 **hypothermie** | **hypothermia**
f | Le risque de mortalité, chez ce type de nourrissons, est élevé, par asphyxie, hypothermie et infection.
[ipɔtɛʁmi] | -The risk of mortality in LBW babies is high due to asphyxia, hypothermia and infection.

9014 **impérialisme** | **imperialism**
m | D'autres voient les droits de la personne et les activités humanitaires comme une forme d'impérialisme.
[ɛ̃peʁjalism] | -Others see our human rights and humanitarianism activities as a form of imperialism.

9015 **anthrax** | **anthrax**
m | L'anthrax peut revenir plus résistante.
[ɑ̃tʁaks] | -The anthrax could relapse and be more resistant.

9016 **latte** | **lath|latte**
f | Le voisinage s'est embourgeoisé. Désormais, ça grouille de bobos qui sucent des latte écrémés au Starbucks. Ils s'agglutinent autour du café et du WiFi gratuit comme des abeilles autour d'un pot de miel.
[lat] | -The neighborhood has been gentrified. Now it's teeming with pretend hipsters slurping skinny lattes at Starbucks. They gather round coffee and free Wi-Fi like bees round a honeypot.

9017 **affliction** | **affliction**
f | Mais nous ne devons pas baisser les bras devant cette terrible affliction.
[afliksjɔ̃] | -However, we must not give up the fight against this terrible affliction.

9018 **proclamation** | **proclamation**
f | Sans oublier de facto habeas corpus émancipation proclamation.
[pʁɔklamasjɔ̃] | -I am full of de facto habeas corpus Emancipation Proclamation.

9019 **démarche** | **step|gait**
f[demaʁʃ] | Jack a insisté qu'il n'avait pas bu, mais son élocution et sa démarche instable le trahissait. -Jack insisted he hadn't been drinking, but his slurred speech and unsteady gait gave him away.

9020 **crédule** | **credulous**

adj
[kʁedyl]
Je ne suis pas crédule.
-I am not credulous.

9021 **séjourner**
vb
[seʒuʁne]
stay
Nous devrons séjourner ici quelques mois.
-We shall have to stay here for several months.

9022 **infortune**
f
[ɛ̃fɔʁtyn]
misfortune
Je suis d'opinion qu'elle est seule responsable de son infortune.
-In my opinion, he was solely responsible for his misfortune.

9023 **restituer**
vb
[ʁɛstitɥe]
return|restore
Lady Catherine a ordre de restituer les joyaux officiels.
-A command that Lady Katherine return her official jewels.

9024 **inaugurer**
vb
[inogyʁe]
inaugurate
Il est grand temps de clore la période de réflexion et d'inaugurer la période de l'action.
-It is high time to end the reflection period and inaugurate a period of action.

9025 **étendard**
m
[etɑ̃daʁ]
standard
L'étendard français dans la poussière.
-French standard's in the dirt.

9026 **indésirable**
adj
[ɛ̃deziʁabl]
undesirable
La privatisation de ces services électriques est indésirable et risquée.
-Privatisation of these mains services is undesirable and risky.

9027 **paravent**
m
[paʁavɑ̃]
screen
Mais la subsidiarité doit servir à faire quelque chose, et non de paravent.
-Subsidiarity must serve some purpose, however, and not act as a screen.

9028 **chrétienté**
f
[kʁetjɛ̃te]
Christendom
C'est le cri de toute la chrétienté des Amériques, de l'Asie, de tous.
-It is the cry of all Christendom: of the Americas, of Africa, of Asia, of everyone.

9029 **causette**
f
[kozɛt]
rap|chat
Je ferai la causette à Saïd.
-I'll have a chat with Said.

9030 **ébauche**
f
[eboʃ]
draft
L'ébauche de ce projet de loi contient la disposition suivante : [Traduction]
-A provision of the draft version of the proposed legislation states the following.

9031 **mobilisation**
f
[mɔbilizasjɔ̃]
mobilization
Toutefois, des signes de mobilisation politique apparaissent dans certains camps.
-However, there are indications of increased political mobilization in some camps.

9032 **éloquent**
adj[elɔkɑ̃]
eloquent
C'est assez éloquent, et je crois que c'est la partie la plus intéressante du jugement. -It is most eloquent, and to my mind the most interesting part of the decision.

9033 **imperfection**
f
[ɛ̃pɛʁfɛksjɔ̃]
imperfection
Il devrait y avoir une petite imperfection.
-It should have the slightest imperfection in it.

9034 **catalyseur**
m
[katalizœʁ]
catalyst
Ce catalyseur est très actif à basse température.
-The catalyst has a high activity at low temperatures.

9035 **empocher** **pocket**
vb
[ɑ̃pɔʃe]
Car il n'est pas ici question d'empocher de l'argent; il est question de valeurs éthiques et morales.
-For this is not a question of pocketing money; it is a question of ethics and moral values.

9036 **parieur** **gambler**
m
[paʁjœʁ]
Un parieur et un contrebandier lié au trafic de stupéfiants.
-A gambler and a bootlegger with ties to the narcotics trade.

9037 **cartable** **satchel**
m
[kaʁtabl]
Mais ne salissez pas votre cartable.
-But don't make a mess of your satchel.

9038 **florin** **florin**
m
[flɔʁɛ̃]
Pour un florin d'argent, j'ai libéré mon grand-père du Purgatoire.
-For a silver florin, I freed my grandfather from Purgatory.

9039 **rapt** **abduction|kidnapping**
m
[ʁapt]
Tu es à l'origine du rapt de Kayden Fuller.
-You are behind the abduction of Kayden Fuller.

9040 **justification** **justification**
f
[ʒystifikasjɔ̃]
Sans autre justification que la sécurité intérieure.
-Without any other justification than the one of homeland security.

9041 **palissade** **palisade**
f
[palisad]
La foule devint incontrôlable et força la palissade.
-The crowd got out of control and broke through the fence.

9042 **puiser** **draw**
vb
[pɥize]
Il espère puiser dans cette expérience pour renforcer l'action de la Commission.
-It hoped to draw on that experience to strengthen the Commission's work.

9043 **collet** **collar|neck**
m
[kɔlɛ]
Ton collet est taché.
-Your collar has a stain on it.

9044 **poseur** **poseur; phony**
m; adj
[pozœʁ]
Ça veut dire, comme un poseur.
-It means, like, a poser.

9045 **aplatir** **flatten**
vb
[aplatiʁ]
Comme elle est si légère, un collier réel serait lui aplatir.
-As she's so slight, a real necklace would flatten her.

9046 **exclusion** **exclusion**
f
[ɛksklyzjɔ̃]
Il adore l'argent à l'exclusion de toute autre chose.
-He worships money to exclusion of everything else.

9047 **tourneur** **turner**
m
[tuʁnœʁ]
Je suis un bon tourneur de page, si vous voulez que je vous aide.
-I'm a pretty good page turner... if you ever need any help.

9048 **dérisoire** **derisory|paltry**
adj
[deʁizwaʁ]
Le budget prévu de 167 millions d'écus pour cinq ans est tellement dérisoire.
-The forecast budget of ECU 167 million for five years is derisory.

9049 **bourbier** **quagmire|slough**
m
[buʁbje]
C'était comme ramper dans un bourbier
-It was like crawling through a quagmire.

9050 **penseur** **thinker**

	m [pɑ̃sœʁ]	Les idées de Freud sur le comportement humain l'ont amené à être honoré en tant que profond penseur. -Freud's insights into human behavior led to him being honored as a profound thinker.
9051	**bosquet** m [bɔskɛ]	**grove** Les mineurs vont déplacer la dépouille de mon mari du bosquet. -Miners are fetching my husband's body from the grove.
9052	**rêvasser** vb [ʁevase]	**daydream** Je perds beaucoup de temps à rêvasser. -I waste a lot of time daydreaming.
9053	**sarcophage** m [saʁkɔfaʒ]	**sarcophagus** Une nouvelle chape sera coulée au-dessus du sarcophage existant. -A new construction will be built on top of the sarcophagus.
9054	**anticorps** m [ɑ̃tikɔʁ]	**antibody** Un enfant ayant reçu les anticorps est à Bundang. -A child who is said to have received the antibody is in Bundang.
9055	**nationaliste** adj; m/f [nasjɔnalist]	**nationalist; nationalist** Je suis contre tout discours nationaliste. -I am not in favour of nationalist speeches.
9056	**accrochage** m [akʁɔʃaʒ]	**hanging|coupling** Lorsque la sonde intérieure est retirée, l'attache entre les éléments d'accrochage se défait. -When the inner probe is removed, the attachement between the hooking elements becomes loose.
9057	**microfilm** m [mikʁɔfilm]	**microfilm** Quelques volumes sont accessibles sur microfilm. -Some of the volumes are available on microfilm.
9058	**révélateur** m; adj [ʁevelatœʁ]	**developer; revealing** L'invention concerne un racloir de nettoyage pour retirer les résidus de révélateur sur un élément photosensible. -Disclosed in the present invention is a cleaning scraper, for removing developer remaining on a light-sensitive element.
9059	**gril** m [gʁil]	**grill** Dacia, nous allons démarrer le gril. -Dacia, let's start up the grill.
9060	**abstraction** f[apstʁaksjɔ̃]	**abstraction** Il en résulte une imagerie hybride alternant entre abstraction et représentation. -The result is a hybrid of imagery that flips between abstraction and representation...
9061	**biopsie** f [bjɔpsi]	**biopsy** Faisons une biopsie intestinale pour confirmer. -We just need to do an intestinal biopsy to confirm.
9062	**photocopier** vb [fɔtokɔpje]	**photocopy** Le Secrétariat ne sera pas en mesure de photocopier les déclarations des délégations. -The Secretariat will not be in a position to photocopy statements on behalf of delegations.
9063	**management** m [manadʒmɛnt]	**management** Management of safety should be integrated with the overall management of the mission.

-La gestion de la sûreté devrait s'inscrire dans la gestion générale de la mission.

9064 **castrer** **castrate**
vb
[kastʁe]
Ce ne sont pas les porcs, mais cette politique agricole, qu'il faudrait castrer.
-It is not pigs, but an agricultural policy like this that should be castrated.

9065 **proton** **proton**
m
[pʁɔtɔ̃]
Le dernier proton devrait pourrir maintenant.
-The last proton should be decaying about now.

9066 **prélude** **prelude**
m
[pʁelyd]
C'est une sorte de prélude à ce qui se produira après l'adhésion complète.
-This is intended as a kind of prelude to what will happen after full membership.

9067 **animosité** **animosity**
f
[animozite]
Cette situation causait une animosité accrue entre la victime et l'accusé.
-As a result, there was increasing animosity between the victim and the accused.

9068 **concessionnaire** **dealer**
m
[kɔ̃sesjɔnɛʁ]
Ce concessionnaire automobile a la réputation de vendre des guitares.
-That car dealership has a reputation for selling lemons.

9069 **jante** **rim**
f
[ʒɑ̃t]
Cette jante a des entailles triangulaires.
-I've got triangular indentations on this rim.

9070 **syndical** **union|labor**
adj
[sɛ̃dikal]
C'était l'avocat du conseil syndical.
-So that was our union's legal counsel.

9071 **friser** **curl**
vb
[fʁize]
Mais ils m'ont demandé de me faire friser les cheveux.
-But then they wanted me to curl my hair.

9072 **sensualité** **sensuality**
f
[sɑ̃sɥalite]
Je vais vous révéler l'intimité et la sensualité joyeuses.
-I will reveal you intimacy and sensuality merry.

9073 **halo** **halo**
m
[alo]
L'explaination habituel est qu'il y a un grand halo de matière foncée.
-The usual explaination is that there is a large halo of dark matter.

9074 **perdition** **perdition**
f[pɛʁdisjɔ̃]
Ignorez notre exemple aujourd'hui et vous serez sur la voie de la perdition. -Ignore our example now, and you are on your way to perdition.

9075 **opter** **opt**
vb
[ɔpte]
Toute personne a la liberté d'opter pour la forme d'éducation de son choix.
-Everyone has the liberty to opt for the form of education they desire.

9076 **tendu** **tense|tight**
adj
[tɑ̃dy]
Ces dernières semaines ont été caractérisées par un répit, un calme tendu.
-They were characterised by a tense calmness.

9077 **convulser** **convulse**
vb
[kɔ̃vylse]
En cas d'ingestion, si la victime est consciente et ne convulse pas, il faut administrer 1 ou 2 verres d'eau pour diluer le produit chimique.
-In the case of ingestion, if the victim is conscious and not convulsing, give 1 or 2 glasses of water to dilute the chemical.

9078 **vérole** **pox**
f
[veʁɔl]
Celui-ci permet de créer une poussée de vérole avec de grosses cloques.
-This one says it can create a pox of redness raw and blisters bubbling.

9079 **frissonner** **shiver|tremble**
vb
[fʁisɔne]
Ça m'a plutôt fait frissonner.
-I was sort of thrilled by it.

9080 **correspondant** **corresponding; correspondent**
adj; m
[kɔʁɛspɔ̃dɑ̃]
La simple réflexion montrera que la doctrine de la rédemption est fondée sur une simple idée pécuniaire correspondant à celle d'une dette qu'un autre personne pourrait payer.
-This single reflection will show that the doctrine of redemption is founded on a mere pecuniary idea corresponding to that of a debt which another person might pay.

9081 **chenapan** **scoundrel**
m
[ʃənapɑ̃]
Tu m'as surpris, petit chenapan.
-You surprised me, you little rascal.

9082 **chatouilleux** **ticklish**
adj
[ʃatujø]
Notre groupe se montre très chatouilleux sur un élargissement général des interdictions de circuler le week-end.
-A general expansion of weekend driving bans is a very sensitive issue in our group.

9083 **discernement** **discernment**
m
[disɛʁnəmɑ̃]
C'est du discernement.
-That's hindsight.

9084 **éparpiller** **scatter**
vb
[epaʁpije]
Primo, nous devrions éviter de trop nous éparpiller.
-Firstly, we should avoid spreading ourselves too thinly.

9085 **roussir** **scorch|brown**
vb
[ʁusiʁ]
Pourquoi tu fais toujours roussir les restes?
-Why do you always scorch the leftovers?

9086 **pore** **pore**
f
[pɔʁ]
Cette initiative repose - ce qui transpire de chaque pore du texte - sur une position exceptionnelle, une position que l'Union européenne observe depuis un certain temps.
-This initiative is based - and the text exudes this from every pore - on a position which is exceptional, a position that the European Union has held for some time.

9087 **arnaquer** **rip off**
vb
[aʁnake]
Il n'est pas normal que de plus en plus de citoyens se fassent arnaquer.
-It is unacceptable that more and more citizens are being scammed.

9088 **canicule** **heat wave**
f
[kanikyl]
Il n'y a rien de tel qu'une bière fraîche un jour de canicule !
-There is nothing like cold beer on a hot day.

9089 **sprint** **sprint**
m
[spʁɛ̃]
Verizon, sprint, AT&T téléphones.
-Verizon, sprint, AT&T wireless.

9090 **atténuant** **attenuating**
adj
[atenɥɑ̃]
Il existe également d'autres dispositions relatives aux circonstances atténuantes, etc.
-There are also further provisions covering extenuating circumstances, etc.

9091 **exécrable** **execrable**
adj
[ɛgzekʁabl]
Je souhaite tout d'abord déplorer et condamner énergiquement la pratique de la mutilation génitale des femmes, tant en Egypte que partout où l'on veut mettre fin à cette pratique exécrable.

-Firstly, I wish vigorously to deplore and condemn the practice of sexual mutilation of women, both in Egypt and anywhere else that this execrable practice takes place.

9092	**bourde**	**howler|blunder**
	f [buʁd]	La plus grande réussite scientifique de ma vie est basée sur une bourde. -The greatest scientific achievement of my life is based on a blunder.
9093	**risible**	**ludicrous**
	adj [ʁizibl]	Tout cela serait risible, Madame le Président, si toute cette affaire de drogue n'était parfaitement tragique. -All this would be ludicrous, Madam President, if this whole drugs business were not totally tragic.
9094	**fana**	**addict|fanatic**
	m/f [fana]	Ça dépend si le juge est un fana d'autos. -Depends if the judge is a car freak.
9095	**infester**	**infest|be infested**
	vb [ɛ̃fɛste]	Les cellules non ventilées étaient infestées de punaises et de moustiques. -The cells were unventilated and were infested with bed bugs and mosquitoes.
9096	**consciencieux**	**conscientious**
	adj [kɔ̃sjɑ̃sjø]	En donnant cette approbation, il nous faudra être très prudents et consciencieux. -We will need to be very careful and conscientious in giving that approval.
9097	**fourreau**	**sheath**
	m [fuʁo]	L'épée se coince dans le fourreau de cuir. -The sword gets stuck in the leather sheath.
9098	**impresario**	**impresario**
	m [ɛ̃pʁəzaʁjo]	Eric Murphy, mon producteur et impresario. -This is my producer and manager, Eric Murphy.
9099	**canin**	**canine**
	adj[kanɛ̃]	Il serait plus rentable pour l'Organisation de mettre en place sa propre unité canine. -It would be more cost-effective for the Organization to establish its own canine unit.
9100	**photographique**	**photographic**
	adj [fɔtɔɡʁafik]	Je me suis procuré un nouvel appareil photographique. -I got a new camera.
9101	**opportuniste**	**opportunistic; opportunist**
	adj; m/f [ɔpɔʁtynist]	C'est véritablement une décision opportuniste qui ne nous fait pas progresser. -This really is an opportunist decision which does not help us to progress.
9102	**empêchement**	**impediment**
	m [ɑ̃pɛʃmɑ̃]	Il n'existe aucun empêchement en la matière. -There is no impediment in this respect.
9103	**ténacité**	**tenacity**
	f [tenasite]	Cet anniversaire symbolise la ténacité de l'institution et les principes qu'elle incarne. -This anniversary symbolizes the tenacity of this institution and the principles it represents.
9104	**inédit**	**novel**
	adj [inedi]	Ce que vous suggérez est inédit. -What you're suggesting is unprecedented.
9105	**néon**	**neon**

m
[neɔ̃]
Ce procédé permet de produire des diamants attrayants vert jaunâtre, jaune verdâtre et jaune vert néon.
-Attractive yellowish-green, greenish-yellow and neon yellow-green diamonds can be made by this method.

9106 **monarque** **monarch**
m
[mɔnaʁk]
Peut-être est-elle le monarque qui sera couronné.
-Maybe she's the monarch who will be crowned.

9107 **régénération** **regeneration**
f
[ʁeʒeneʁasjɔ̃]
La régénération du cortex prendra du temps.
-I've started him on a cortical regeneration but it'll take some time.

9108 **citadin** **city dweller; city dwelling**
m; adj
[sitadɛ̃]
Voilà que je perdais ma virginité avec un citadin.
-I had actually lost my virginity to a townie.

9109 **spiritisme** **spiritism**
m
[spiʁitism]
J'irai pas à une séance de spiritisme.
-I'm not going to a séance.

9110 **démêler** **untangle|tease**
vb
[demele]
Il est très difficile de démêler ces réseaux et connexions complexes.
-It is very difficult to disentangle these complex networks and connections.

9111 **décerner** **award**
vb
[desɛʁne]
Les États-Unis le reconnaissent et veulent décerner des médailles à des membres de nos forces.
-The United States recognizes this and wants to award medals to our service personnel.

9112 **chignon** **bun|catfight**
m[ʃiɲɔ̃]
Les filles se crêpèrent le chignon. -The girls had a catfight.

9113 **cathédrale** **cathedral**
f
[katedʁal]
Pour autant que je sache, la cathédrale date du Moyen-Âge.
-To the best of my knowledge, the cathedral dates back to the Middle Ages.

9114 **pivert** **woodpecker**
m
[pivɛʁ]
Chut, ou j'envoie un pivert te becqueter.
-Quiet, or I'll throw a woodpecker on you.

9115 **éventuel** **prospective**
adj
[evɑ̃tɥɛl]
Le passif éventuel sera automatiquement renouvelé tous les cinq ans.
-This contingent liability would automatically be renewed every five years.

9116 **bénédicité** **benediction**
f
[benedisite]
Aimerais-tu dire le bénédicité, Eric ?
-Would you like to say Grace, Eric?

9117 **embarcadère** **jetty; wharf**
f; m
[ɑ̃baʁkadɛʁ]
Amarre le bateau dans l'embarcadère.
-Moor the ship at the pier.

9118 **malter** **malt**
vb
[malte]
Écoute, j'ai trouvé des cigarettes, du lait malté, et un tas d'autres choses aussi.
-Look, I got some cigarettes, and some malted milk tablets... and a lot of other junk, too.

9119 **exhibition** **display**
f
[ɛgzibisjɔ̃]
Cette triste exhibition fit arriver l'impossible...
-This sad display made the impossible happen...

9120 **brasse** **fathom**

	f [bʁas]	Il nageait le crawl au lieu de la brasse. -Instead of doing the crawl he was swimming breaststroke.
9121	**almanach** m [almana]	**almanac** Source : sites Web des municipalités et Almanach national de 2005. -Source: Websites of the municipalities and the 2005 National Almanac.
9122	**vertèbre** f [vɛʁtɛbʁ]	**vertebra** La vertèbre doit appuyer sur un nerf. -The vertebra must be pressing on the nerve ending.
9123	**pétrifier** vb [petʁifje]	**petrify|stone** Sans remarquer que l'on commençait à se pétrifier. -We didn't notice we were beginning to petrify.
9124	**idéalisme** m [idealism]	**idealism** Quelque part tu dois admirer son idéalisme. -On some level you have to admire his idealism.
9125	**luciole** f [lysjɔl]	**firefly** La présente invention concerne des colorants fluorescents qui sont fondés sur une structure du type luciférine de luciole. -The present invention provides fluorescent dyes that are based on firefly luciferin structure.
9126	**naissant** adj[nɛsɑ̃]	**nascent** Les membres savent que les experts civils dispenseront un appui crucial à l'Administration est-timoraise naissante. -As members know, the civilian experts would provide crucial support to the emergent East Timorese Administration.
9127	**jésuite** m; adj [ʒezɥit]	**Jesuit; Jesuit** Selon sa biographie, il a obtenu son diplôme d'une école jésuite de Bagdad. -According to his biography, he graduated from a Jesuit school in Baghdad.
9128	**spacieux** adj [spasjø]	**spacious** Ces locaux doivent être spacieux, propres, désinfectés et entretenus. -Such facilities should be spacious, clean, disinfected and maintained.
9129	**urbanisme** m [yʁbanism]	**town planning** 300-2 du code de l'urbanisme (concertation pour les actions ou opérations d'aménagement). -300-2 of the Town Planning Code (consultation on town planning action and operations).
9130	**troyen** adj [tʁwajɛ̃]	**Trojan** Que les Padouans réclament aujourd'hui le sol troyen, dès lors qu'Antênor était autrefois troyen! -Let the Paduans now reclaim Trojan soil, since Antenor was once Trojan!
9131	**neutron** m [nøtʁɔ̃]	**neutron** Ces méthodes sont notamment la spectrométrie gamma à haute ou à faible résolution et la spectrométrie neutron à corrélation temporelle. -These have included low and high resolution gamma ray spectroscopy and time-correlated neutron spectroscopy.
9132	**mégatonne** f [megatɔn]	**megaton** Une mégatonne équivaut à un million de tonnes. -A megatonne is shorthand for one million tonnes.
9133	**génital** adj [ʒenital]	**genital** Le nombre d'infections virales (herpès génital et condylomes acuminés) a en revanche diminué. -The number of viral infections (genital herpes and warts) has decreased.

9134 **anaconda** **anaconda**
m
[anakɔ̃da]
C'était un anaconda ou un python.
-It was an anaconda or a python.

9135 **papal** **papal**
adj
[papal]
It seems I am not papal legate after all.
-Il me semble que je ne sois pas un légat papal après tout.

9136 **appâter** **bait**
vb
[apate]
Ce qui mérite d'être fait mérite d'être bien fait, même appâter un démon.
-Anything worth doing is worth doing well, even being demon bait.

9137 **précaire** **precarious**
adj
[pʁekɛʁ]
La situation reste toutefois précaire et la vigilance reste dès lors de mise.
-However, the situation remains precarious, and vigilance is still warranted.

9138 **Mongolie** **Mongolia**
f
[mɔ̃gɔli]
Onze types de médicaments psychotropes sont actuellement recensés en Mongolie.
-11 brands of psychotropic drugs are currently registered in Mongolia.

9139 **sinus** **sinus**
m[sinys]
C'est parce qu'il a des problèmes de sinus. -We named him that ' cause he's got this sinus condition.

9140 **foudroyer** **blast**
vb
[fudʁwaje]
Lancer une boule de feu pour foudroyer son tortionnaire ?
-Unleash a thunderbolt to strike down his tormentor?

9141 **dévastateur** **devastating**
adj
[devastatœʁ]
Le budget est plutôt dévastateur pour la province de Terre-neuve et du Labrador.
-Instead, the budget is devastating to the province of Newfoundland and Labrador.

9142 **embolie** **embolism**
f
[ɑ̃bɔli]
Désolé, mais vous faites une embolie schizophrénique.
-I'm sorry to tell you this, but you've suffered a schizoid embolism.

9143 **tricherie** **cheating**
f
[tʁiʃʁi]
Lewis va avoir des démêlés pour tricherie.
-Lewis is about to get in trouble with the school for cheating.

9144 **chaux** **lime|whitewash**
f
[ʃo]
Certains traitements (p. ex., à la chaux) pourraient être nécessaires.
-Some treatment (e.g., with limestone) may be required.

9145 **stature** **stature**
f
[statyʁ]
Sa petite stature le fait se sentir peu sûr de lui.
-His short stature makes him feel insecure.

9146 **prologue** **prologue**
m
[pʁɔlɔg]
Dans le Prologue de son Évangile, Jean résume en une seule phrase toute la profondeur du mystère de l'Incarnation.
-John, in the Prologue of his Gospel, captures in one phrase all the depth of the mystery of the Incarnation.

9147 **mutiler** **mutilate|maim**
vb
[mytile]
L'exposition à l'amiante peut mutiler et tuer, et les travailleurs qui y sont exposés doivent être protégés.
-Exposure to asbestos can maim and kill and asbestos workers have to be protected.

9148 **affliger** **afflict**

	vb	Les problèmes de santé ne sont pas les seuls à affliger les pays pauvres.
	[afliʒe]	-It is not only health problems that afflict poor countries.
9149	**frigidaire**	**fridge**
	m	Jack a regardé dans le frigidaire.
	[fʁiʒidɛʁ]	-Jack looked in the refrigerator.
9150	**étau**	**vice|stranglehold**
	m	Les États ont desserré l'étau imposé à l'économie et ont autorisé une plus grande libéralisation.
	[eto]	-Governments have relaxed their stranglehold on the economy and allowed greater liberalization.
9151	**ramassage**	**collection|gathering**
	m	Le sac ou le contenant est positionné de cette manière pour le ramassage.
	[ʁamasaʒ]	-The bag or container is positioned in its way for collection.
9152	**tordu**	**twisted; crackpot**
	adj; m[tɔʁdy]	Cela révèle, de la part du gouvernement, un sens complètement tordu des priorités. -It shows a completely contorted sense of priorities on the part of the government.
9153	**dévergondé**	**wanton**
	adj	Allez embrasser l'autre, la chanteuse, pauvre dévergondé.
	[devɛʁgɔ̃de]	-Go kiss your neighbour, the singer, you rake.
9154	**tambourin**	**tambourine**
	m	Je n'ai que le tambourin.
	[tɑ̃buʁɛ̃]	-All I've got is a tambourine.
9155	**frêle**	**frail**
	adj	En tout cas, le deuxième pilier «développement rural» n'est pas encore un pilier: c'est un arbuste encore bien frêle.
	[fʁɛl]	-Or at least the second pillar, namely rural development, is not so much a pillar as a frail little tree.
9156	**généalogique**	**genealogical**
	adj	L'identité généalogique (faasinomaga) d'un enfant samoan est un élément déterminant de sa vie quotidienne.
	[ʒenealɔʒik]	-The Fa'asinomaga (genealogical identity) of a Samoan child is a fundamental part of every child's life.
9157	**latéral**	**lateral**
	adj	On détermine le déplacement latéral par intégration de la vitesse latérale recalée au zéro.
	[lateʁal]	-Determine lateral displacement by integrating zeroed lateral velocity.
9158	**baryton**	**baritone**
	m	Arnold fait auditionner un nouveau baryton.
	[baʁitɔ̃]	-Mr. Arnold is trying out a new baritone.
9159	**mitrailler**	**volley**
	vb	S'il ne s'agit que de bombarder et de mitrailler quelques régions pour montrer que nous avons fait quelque chose, je ne sais pas quel genre d'engagement nous pouvons faire.
	[mitʁaje]	-If it is just to bomb and strafe a few regions to make our point, I am not sure what commitment we can make.
9160	**mésaventure**	**misadventure**
	f	Cette mésaventure offensive conduit le Groupe sur un terrain dangereux.
	[mezavɑ̃tyʁ]	-This offensive misadventure leads the Panel into dangerous waters.
9161	**inexcusable**	**inexcusable**

adj
[inɛkskyzabl]
Et le fait de ne pas décourager ces actes est tout bonnement inexcusable.
-And failure to discourage this is quite simply inexcusable.

9162 **distinct** **separate**
adj
[distɛ̃]
Il existe donc à l'intérieur du droit administratif un domaine distinct que l'on appelle " droit carcéral ".
-Thus there is a discrete area of administrative law known as "prison law."

9163 **vestibule** **vestibule**
m
[vɛstibyl]
Elle m'attendait dans le vestibule.
-She was waiting for me in the vestibule.

9164 **significatif** **significant**
adj
[siɲifikatif]
Ce sujet me semble vraiment important et significatif.
-I think this is a really important and significant matter.

9165 **réincarner** **reincarnate**
vb[ʁeɛ̃kaʁne]
Il va se réincarner plus tôt, c'est tout. -It just means he'll be reincarnated sooner, that's all.

9166 **jurisprudence** **jurisprudence**
f
[ʒyʁispʁydɑ̃s]
À cet égard, la jurisprudence constitutionnelle s'est considérablement enrichie.
-A wealth of constitutional jurisprudence has been produced in this area.

9167 **fourmilière** **anthill**
f
[fuʁmiljɛʁ]
Non, je préférerais être... ligotée sur une fourmilière.
-No, I'd rather be strapped down on an anthill.

9168 **battant** **clapper|fighter; swinging**
m; adj
[batɑ̃]
Il est étonnant de constater que les Iraniens, auxquels les Arabes ont imposé l'Islam en les battant militairement, sont devenus ses plus zélés adeptes au point d'opprimer ceux du Zoroastrisme, qui est pourtant la religion de leurs propres pères. Une sorte de syndrome de Stockholm à l'échelle nationale.
-It is astonishing to witness that the Iranians, onto whom the Arabs imposed Islam through military defeat, have become its most zealous followers to the point of oppressing those of Zoroastrianism, though it is the religion of their own fathers. A kind of Stockholm syndrome on the national scale.

9169 **subversif** **subversive**
adj
[sybvɛʁsif]
Quatre condamnés ont été transférés dans d'autres établissements pénitentiaires de la Republika Srpska, en raison de leur comportement subversif avant et durant la grève.
-Four convicts were transferred to other institutions of correction in the The Republika Srpska, due to their destructive behaviour before and during the strike.

9170 **suppliant** **begging; suppliant**
adj; m
[syplijɑ̃]
C'est un geste suppliant suggérant de la culpabilité.
-It's a supplicant gesture, suggesting a guilty conscience.

9171 **maladresse** **clumsiness**
f
[maladʁɛs]
Excusez ma maladresse.
-Excuse my clumsiness.

9172 **teneur** **content**
f
[tənœʁ]
Teneur en eau. La teneur en eau de 10% pour l'ensemble fruit/coque a été adoptée.
-Moisture content: A moisture content of 10% for the whole nut was agreed.

9173 **immuniser** **immunize**

vb
[imynize]
Un programme élargi de vaccination a été mis en place pour immuniser les enfants contre les maladies infantiles infectieuses graves.
-An expanded programme on immunization has been introduced in order to immunize children against serious childhood infections.

9174 **immaculé** **immaculate**
adj
[imakyle]
Notre Dame dit Elle voulait la consécration de la Russie à Son Coeur immaculé.
-(...) Our Lady said She wanted the consecration of Russia to Her Immaculate Heart.

9175 **rabattre** **tilt|turn down**
vb
[ʁabatʁ]
Fixer la plaque et rabattre à 90 degrés l'extrémité libre du ruban.
-Fix the plate and fold back the free end of the tape at 90 deg.

9176 **résonance** **resonance**
f
[ʁezɔnɑ̃s]
Ils tirent des charges à résonance quantique.
-They're firing some kind of quantum resonance charges, Captain.

9177 **laquer** **lacquer**
vb
[lake]
Une seule couche de la composition selon l'invention permet de former une couche passivante et de laquer, et assure une protection contre la rouille.
-The inventive metal protective lacquer composition provides a wash primer, protection against rust and a lacquer in a single coat...

9178 **pastille** **pellet|chip**
f
[pastij]
Le substrat de transistor à film mince comprend en outre une pastille de test.
-The thin-film transistor substrate further comprises a test pad.

9179 **tintement** **ringing**
m
[tɛ̃tmɑ̃]
Sa voix envoûtante et le tintement de ses grelots font partout sensation.
-Her mesmerising voice and the tinkling of her dancing bells are a sensation all over.

9180 **soyeux** **silky|silk**
adj
[swajø]
Regarde-toi et ton adorable cou soyeux.
-Look at you and your lovely silky neck.

9181 **esthéticien** **beautician**
m
[ɛstetisjɛ̃]
Mon esthéticien est l'épouse de Guido, le beau conducteur d'autobus.
-My beautician is the bride of Guido, the pretty bus driver.

9182 **corniche** **cornice|ledge**
f
[kɔʁniʃ]
Je veux saisir cette conversation sur la corniche.
-I want to catch that conversation out on that ledge.

9183 **extirper** **remove**
vb
[ɛkstiʁpe]
Nous appuyons l'action internationale visant à extirper la menace terroriste en Iraq.
-We support international action to eradicate the terrorist threat in Iraq.

9184 **fusilier** **rifleman**
m
[fyzilje]
Et que serait la motivation de ce fusilier ?
-And what is the motivation of this rifleman?

9185 **rixe** **brawl**
f
[ʁiks]
Il a été acquitté du meurtre en 1999 mais reconnu coupable d'avoir déclenché une rixe et condamné à quatre ans d'emprisonnement.
-He was acquitted of murder in 1999 but convicted of brawling and sentenced to four years in prison.

9186 **réélire** **re-elect**
vb
[ʁeeliʁ]
Le Groupe de travail devra (ré)élire son président et ses vice-présidents.
-The Working Party is expected to (re)elect its Chairman and Vice-Chairmen.

9187 **hiéroglyphe** m [jeʁɔglif]
hieroglyph
L'hiéroglyphe qui signifiait «scribe» dépeignait son matériel.
-The hieroglyph meaning "scribe" depicted his tool-set.

9188 **reluquer** vb [ʁəlyke]
ogle
On peux aller reluquer les pauvres gens de East Riverside.
-We can go ogle the poor people of East Riverside.

9189 **réfuter** vb[ʁefyte]
refute|disprove
Ce Parlement doit être capable de débattre, de réfuter, de ratifier et de rectifier. -It has to be a Parliament capable of debate, rebuttal, ratification and rectification.

9190 **bercer** vb [bɛʁse]
rock
Comme ce sont les femmes qui bercent les enfants, elles ont bien évidemment un rôle essentiel à jouer pour que la bonne volonté et la paix règnent dans le monde.
-As the hands that rock the cradle, women of course have a pivotal role in assuring good will and peace in the world.

9191 **récipient** m [ʁesipjɑ̃]
container
Soit un récipient spécial autre qu'un récipient cylindrique normal.
-A special container: other containers than standard cylindrical containers.

9192 **excessivement** adv [ɛksesivmɑ̃]
excessively
Il était excessivement long et répétitif, mais il aborde un sujet important.
-It was excessively long and duplicative, but it deals with an important subject.

9193 **gisement** m [ʒizmɑ̃]
deposit
Cette dernière propriété avait un gisement de sable d'environ 2,300,000 verges cubes.
-That property had a sand deposit of approximately 2,300,000 cubic yards.

9194 **baratiner** vb [baʁatine]
sweet talk
Henry Stafford n'est pas un jeune homme disposé à se laisser baratiner.
-Henry Stafford is not some young maiden disposed to sweet-talk.

9195 **calcium** m [kalsjɔm]
calcium
Le calcium peut quitter vos cellules.
-The calcium can be drawn out of your cells.

9196 **frénésie** f [fʁenezi]
frenzy
Après avoir gagné à la loterie, elle se lança dans une frénésie d'achats.
-After winning the lottery she went on a shopping frenzy.

9197 **échiquier** m [eʃikje]
chessboard
Promets-moi que tu renverseras l'échiquier.
-Promise me you, will often turn the chessboard.

9198 **mono-** pfx [mɔno-]
mono-
Les compositions durcissables par rayonnement comprennent des acrylates mono- ou multifonctionnels, une amine et la résine photosensible mentionnée ci-dessus.
-The radiation curable compositions include mono or multi-functional acrylates, an amine and the above-mentioned photoactive resin.

9199 **rondelle** f [ʁɔ̃dɛl]
washer
La tige dotée des doigts porte une rondelle.
-A washer is mounted on the rod within the fingers.

9200 **plaignant** m [plɛɲɑ̃]
plaintiff
Le plaignant est natif du Nouveau-Brunswick.
-The Complainant is a native of New Brunswick.

9201 **citoyenneté** **citizenship**
f
[sitwajɛnte]
Abandonner la citoyenneté française et quitter l'armée.
-You wish to surrender your French citizenship and resign from the army.

9202 **référer** **refer**
vb[ʁefeʁe]
Ces 50 dernières années, nous avons élaboré ensemble des documents auxquels nous pouvons nous référer. -We have drawn up documents together in the last 50 years that we can refer to.

9203 **mensuel** **monthly**
adj
[mɑ̃sɥɛl]
Les enseignants du secondaire ont un salaire mensuel de départ de 1 633 quetzales.
-Middle-level teaching posts carry a starting salary of 1,683 quetzales for 30 periods.

9204 **aborigène** **aboriginal; aborigine**
adj; m/f
[abɔʁiʒɛn]
C'est un État construit sur une base triangulaire - aborigène, francophone et anglophone.
-A state that is built upon a triangular foundation - aboriginal, francophone and anglophone.

9205 **athlétisme** **athletics**
m
[atletism]
La rencontre d'athlétisme a été reportée d'une semaine.
-The athletic meet was put off until next week.

9206 **ségrégation** **segregation**
f
[segʁegasjɔ̃]
Elle ne dit pas que la ségrégation et la ségrégation éducative constituent une discrimination.
-This directive does not say that segregation and educational segregation are discrimination.

9207 **pornographique** **pornographic**
adj
[pɔʁnɔgʁafik]
Que soit pénalisée la possession du matériel pornographique à destination des enfants.
-Let the possession of pornographic material intended for children be criminalized.

9208 **empathie** **empathy**
f
[ɑ̃pati]
Donc... Celui ci est capable d'empathie.
-So... one that's capable of empathy.

9209 **compulsif** **compulsive**
adj
[kɔ̃pylsif]
Le ministre se montre encore une fois un prédateur compulsif.
-The President of the Treasury Board is once again a compulsive fund raider.

9210 **catégoriquement** **categorically**
adv
[kategɔʁikmɑ̃]
Pour le moment, la Commission refuse catégoriquement d'adopter un tel amendement.
-At this moment, the Commission has set its face against accepting this amendment.

9211 **androïde** **android; android**
adj; m
[ɑ̃dʁɔid]
Si quelque chose est un androïde, alors c'est aussi un robot.
-If something's an android, it's also a robot.

9212 **percussion** **percussion**
f
[pɛʁkysjɔ̃]
Un instrument de musique à percussion se compose de plus de trois sections allongées, monobloc et essentiellement linéaires.
-A musical percussion instrument consists of more than three integrally formed, substantially linear, elongate sections.

9213 **ajustement** **adjustment**

m
[aʒystəmɑ̃]

Les puissants syndicats européens résistent à l'ajustement.
-The strong unions in Europe are making the adjustment difficult on labour.

9214 **régression**
f
[ʁegʁesjɔ̃]

regression
Tes modèles de régression sont légendaires.
-Your regression models are the stuff of legend.

9215 **sédition**
f
[sedisjɔ̃]

sedition|rebellion
En 1810, il a été arrêté pour sédition et emprisonné sans procès.
-In 1810, he was arrested for sedition and held without trial.

9216 **guépard**
m
[gepaʁ]

cheetah
Regardez, il est assis sur la branche comme un guépard.
-See, he is sitting on the branch like a cheetah.

9217 **hameau**
m
[amo]

hamlet
Un charmant petit hameau, et tu étais enceinte.
-A sweet little village, and you were pregnant.

9218 **nitrater**
vb
[nitʁate]

nitrate
Le réacteur tubulaire convient particulièrement pour nitrater des composés organiques avec formation de faibles niveaux de produits imparfaitement nitratés et de faibles niveaux nitrophénoliques.
-The tubular reactor is particularly suitable for nitrating organic compounds while forming low levels of improperly nitrated by-products and low levels of nitrophenolics.

9219 **bouille**
f
[buj]

mug|face
T'aurais vu sa petite bouille à la porte.
-You should have seen his little face at the gates.

9220 **attelle**
f
[atɛl]

brace|splint
Je vais mettre une attelle provisoire.
-I'll put a temporary splint on it.

9221 **pronostic**
m
[pʁɔnɔstik]

prognosis
Le pronostic ici me semble excellent.
-I feel that the prognosis here is excellent.

9222 **soviet**
m
[sɔvjɛt]

Soviet
Les citoyens soviétiques n'étaient pas supposés être en faveur de l'Union soviétique.
-Soviet citizens were not supposed to be for the Soviet Union.

9223 **ajourner**
vb
[aʒuʁne]

adjourn|postpone
Nous ne pouvons toujours attendre la dernière minute, manquer de temps et ajourner.
-We cannot always wait until the last minute, run out of time, and put it off.

9224 **pelage**
m
[pəlaʒ]

coat|fur
La présente invention concerne des emballages scellés thermorétractés en film thermoplastique transparent souple s'ouvrant facilement par pelage.
-The present disclosure is concerned with heat shrunk sealed packages of flexible transparent thermoplastic film that easily opened by peeling.

9225 **continuation**
f
[kɔ̃tinɥasjɔ̃]

continuation
Il y a, selon nous, des arguments solides en faveur de la continuation d'un programme de coopération visant l'amélioration des conditions de vie de la population.
-In our view, there is a strong argument for the continuance of a cooperation programme which aims at the improvement of the living conditions of the population.

9226 **habitation**

home|habitation

f[abitasjɔ̃] | Les villages javanais traditionnels partageaient leur ressources les plus essentielles entre les terres d'habitation et celles pour la riziculture. -Traditional Javanese villages partitioned their most essential resource into house land and rice land.

9227 **rafraîchissement** **refreshment**
m
[ʁafʁeʃismɑ̃]
On peut ainsi éviter tout essai de rafraîchissement excessif.
-Any excessive refresh test can be prevented.

9228 **lest** **ballast**
m
[lɛst]
Un bloc-piles attaché sert de lest stabilisateur.
-An attached battery pack functions as a stabilizing ballast.

9229 **beigne** **donut**
f
[bɛɲ]
On dirait une vieille édentée qui aspire la gelée d'un beigne.
-You look like some old, toothless woman sucking the jelly out of a donut.

9230 **silencieusement** **silently**
adv
[silɑ̃sjøzmɑ̃]
Silencieusement mais très rapidement, le monde dérive vers une autre crise dangereuse qui est la pénurie d'eau.
-Silently but very quickly, the world is drifting towards another dangerous crisis: water scarcity.

9231 **sciure** **sawdust**
f
[sjyʁ]
NE PAS absorber à l'aide de sciure ou d'autres matières absorbantes combustibles.
-Do NOT absorb in saw-dust or other combustible absorbents.

9232 **romanesque** **dreamy|fictional**
adj
[ʁɔmanɛsk]
C'est une expérience si romanesque.
-It's such a romantic experiment.

9233 **palourde** **clam**
f
[paluʁd]
On dirait une palourde géante mangeuse d'hommes.
-You know, it looks like a giant man-eating clam.

9234 **tsarine** **tsarina**
f
[tsaʁin]
Je viens prendre congé de la tsarine.
-I come to take leave of the tsarina.

9235 **croquet** **croquet**
m
[kʁɔkɛ]
Pour faire la quatrième au croquet.
-We need her to make a four at croquet.

9236 **royauté** **royalty**
f
[ʁwajote]
C'est presque la royauté à Philadelphie.
-That's as close to royalty as Philadelphia gets.

9237 **toboggan** **slide**
m
[tɔbɔgɑ̃]
Tu devrais garder le toboggan allume.
-You should keep your slide on all the time.

9238 **clipper** **clip**
vb
[klipe]
Rendez-vous à Lisbonne où vous prendrez le clipper transatlantique pour New York.
-Fly to Lisbon, then take the transatlantic clipper to New York.

9239 **acrobatie** **acrobatics**
f
[akʁɔbasi]
Dorénavant, nous appellerons cela de l'acrobatie administrative.
-From now on we shall call these things 'administrative acrobatics '.

9240 **dérision** **derision|mockery**
f[deʁizjɔ̃]
J'espère que notre proposition ne sera pas, comme à l'accoutumée, tournée en dérision. -I hope this proposal of ours will not be received with the usual derision.

9241 **vraisemblable** adj [vʁɛsɑ̃blabl] **similar**
L'effet suspensif n'est accordé en la matière que si le recourant rend ce dommage vraisemblable.
-A stay of judgement is granted only if the claimant makes such damage appear credible.

9242 **modération** f [mɔdeʁasjɔ̃] **moderation**
Modération en toute chose.
-Moderation in all things.

9243 **salopette** f [salɔpɛt] **overalls**
J'allais juste repasser cette vieille salopette.
-I was just going to press this old dungarees.

9244 **gravitation** f [gʁavitasjɔ̃] **gravitation**
Certains secteurs soutenaient la création dans l'espace de structures géantes pour le logement, dotées de gravitation artificielle.
-Certain industries advocated creating megastructures in space for habitation with artificial gravity.

9245 **taxer** vb [takse] **tax**
C'est lui qui est capable de taxer à des fins d'investissement.
-The government can tax for investment purposes.

9246 **chaufferie** f [ʃofʁi] **boiler room**
Danner le surveille dans la chaufferie.
-Danner's watching him in the boiler room.

9247 **mathématicien** m [matematisjɛ̃] **mathematician**
Elle a été présentée par la Suède et inventée par un mathématicien britannique.
-It was presented by Sweden, and invented by a British mathematician.

9248 **attribut** m; adj [atʁiby] **attribute; predicate**
La capacité à produire des paroles nouvelles est un attribut de tout langage naturel.
-The capacity to produce novel utterances is an attribute of every natural language.

9249 **chaste** adj [ʃast] **chaste**
Un vrai chrétien doit rester chaste jusqu'au mariage.
-I thought a true Christian remained chaste until marriage.

9250 **insecticide** m; adj [ɛ̃sɛktisid] **insecticide; insecticidal**
L'insecticide microbien Bacillus thuringiensis est recommandé contre ces chenilles.
-The microbial insecticide, Bacillus thuringiensis, is recommended for control of caterpillars.

9251 **tremplin** m [tʁɑ̃plɛ̃] **springboard**
Pensez-y comme un tremplin pour accomplir votre destin.
-Think of it as a springboard for fulfilling your destiny.

9252 **râper** vb [ʁape] **grate**
Râper l'échantillon jusqu'à obtention de fragments ne dépassant pas 3 mm.
-Grate the test sample until the size of the particles obtained is no greater than 3 mm.

9253 **procréer** vb[pʁɔkʁee] **procreate**
Leur mariage a-t-il une valeur moindre parce qu'elles ne peuvent procréer ?
-Is their marriage any less valid because they cannot procreate?

9254 **craquement** **crack**

m
[kʁakmɑ̃]
Je pense que mon craquement de nuque empire.
-I think my neck crack's getting worse.

9255 **provincial** **provincial; provincial**
adj; m
[pʁɔvɛ̃sjal]
J'ai été moi-même un fonctionnaire provincial permanent.
-In my personal example, I was a permanent provincial public employee.

9256 **ignare** **ignoramus; clueless**
m/f; adj
[iɲaʁ]
Tu es vraiment ignare, non ?
-You really don't have a clue, do you?

9257 **bulgare** **Bulgarian; Bulgarian**
adj; m
[bylgaʁ]
Est-ce que tu parles bulgare ?
-Do you speak Bulgarian?

9258 **cloaque** **cesspool**
m
[klɔak]
Ce motel est le cloaque des One-Niners.
-That motel is a One-Niner cesspool.

9259 **friction** **friction**
f
[fʁiksjɔ̃]
Les pneus s'usent à cause de la friction entre le caoutchouc et la route.
-Tires wear down because of friction between the rubber and the road surface.

9260 **cliquetis** **clatter|rattle**
m
[klikti]
Nous guettons la voix de la conciliation à Chypre, c'est le cliquetis des armes que nous entendons.
-We expect words of reconciliation on Cyprus; instead all we hear is the clang of arms.

9261 **traction** **traction**
f
[tʁaksjɔ̃]
Une légère traction devrait nous amener aux aisselles.
-Some gentle traction can help us get to the axilla.

9262 **trempette** **dip**
f
[tʁɑ̃pɛt]
Mes choses préférées sont la bière et la trempette des haricots.
-Well, my favorite things are beer and bean dip.

9263 **impérialiste** **imperialist; imperialist**
adj; m/f
[ɛ̃peʁjalist]
L'attitude impérialiste du gouvernement fédéral échappe à toute logique.
-The federal government's imperialist attitude is beyond all understanding.

9264 **éjaculation** **ejaculation**
f
[eʒakylasjɔ̃]
En règle générale, dans la syariah, le signe de la puberté est l'éjaculation de sperme, pour l'homme, et la première menstruation, pour la femme.
-Generally, under the Syariah law, the sign of puberty for a male is ejaculation of sperm and for a female is the first menses she experiences.

9265 **instinctivement** **instinctively**
adv
[ɛ̃stɛ̃ktivmɑ̃]
En outre, la population autrichienne rejette instinctivement ce maïs génétiquement modifié.
-In addition, the people of Austria instinctively reject the idea of genetically modified maize.

9266 **orbe** **orb**
m
[ɔʁb]
Trouver l'enfant à l'orbe.
-We must find the boy with the orb.

9267 **moelleux** **soft; mellowness**
adj; m[mwalø]
Mon oreiller est si moelleux ! -My pillow is so soft!

9268 **globalement** **overall**
adv
[glɔbalmɑ̃]
Globalement, la conteneurisation continue de progresser dans le transport maritime.
-Globally, containerization is continuing to increase for maritime cargo.

9269 **atmosphérique** **atmospheric**
adj
[atmɔsfeʁik]
Le risque de pollution atmosphérique transfrontière est particulièrement grave.
-The risk of transboundary atmospheric pollution was particularly serious.

9270 **constipé** **constipated**
adj
[kɔ̃stipe]
Je ne suis plus constipé.
-I'm no longer constipated.

9271 **dignitaire** **dignitary; genual**
m; adj
[diɲitɛʁ]
Je ne suis pas vraiment un dignitaire.
-You know, I'm not really a dignitary.

9272 **refoulé** **discharged|repressed**
adj
[ʁəfule]
Ainsi du gaz peut être refoulé vers la cuve en passant par le dispositif de carbonatation.
-Thus gas can be discharged via the carbonating device to the vessel.

9273 **réprimer** **repress**
vb
[ʁepʁime]
Souvent, le Gouvernement a recours aux forces de police pour réprimer les grèves.
-The Government often mobilizes the police force to crack down on strikes.

9274 **réjouissant** **cheerful**
adj
[ʁeʒwisɑ̃]
Le Dieu qui se repose le septième jour en se réjouissant de sa création est celui-là même qui montre sa gloire en libérant ses fils de l'oppression du pharaon.
-The God who rests on the seventh day, rejoicing in his creation, is the same God who reveals his glory in liberating his children from Pharaoh's oppression.

9275 **mante** **mantis**
f
[mɑ̃t]
Certains d'entre eux auraient pu être causés par la mante.
-Some may have been caused by the Mantis.

9276 **mécontentement** **discontent**
m
[mekɔ̃tɑ̃tmɑ̃]
Sans cette réforme, le mécontentement lié à la mondialisation ne fera que grandir.
-Without this reform, the discontent associated with globalization will only deepen.

9277 **volage** **flighty**
adj
[vɔlaʒ]
La Floride est une maitresse volage.
-Florida. You are a fickle mistress.

9278 **imprenable** **impregnable**
adj
[ɛ̃pʁənabl]
La seule défense imprenable, c'est la compréhension entre les hommes. »
-The only impregnable line is that of human understanding."

9279 **affluent** **tributary**
m[aflyɑ̃]
Le projet de développement est situé près d'un petit affluent de la rivière Virginia. -The proposed development is located near a small tributary of the Virginia River.

9280 **positivement** **positively**
adv
[pozitivmɑ̃]
De nombreux États ont répondu positivement et communiqué des renseignements.
-Many States have responded positively and provided information.

9281 **désinvolte** **casual**
adj
[dezɛ̃vɔlt]
De plus, je pense que nous traitons la protection des mineurs d'une façon très désinvolte aujourd'hui.

-I also think that we tend to be extremely casual in the way we deal with the protection of minors these days.

9282 **platonique** **platonic**
adj
[platɔnik]
C'est une relation strictement platonique.
-No, we have a strictly platonic relationship.

9283 **rancunier** **spiteful**
adj
[ʁɑ̃kynje]
Votre régénération vous a rendu rancunier, Docteur.
-Your regeneration has made you vindictive, Doctor.

9284 **trappeur** **trapper**
m
[tʁapœʁ]
Alors laissez un vieux trappeur vous montrer comment tendre un bon piège.
-So let an old trapper show you how to set a proper trap.

9285 **harpie** **harpy; harpy**
f; adj
[aʁpi]
Pour beaucoup, il s'agit d'espèces rares, menacées et en voie d'extinction, comme l'aigle harpie, le jaguar ou encore le tapir.
-Many of these species, such as the harpy eagle, the jaguar and the tapir, are considered rare and endangered species at risk of extinction.

9286 **faiblir** **weaken**
vb
[fɛbliʁ]
Nous sommes préoccupés par le cycle de violence qui sévit dans la région, visiblement sans faiblir, et dont pâtissent les civils.
-We are concerned that the cycle of violence in the region does not seem to be abating and is causing misery to ordinary civilians.

9287 **pommier** **apple**
m
[pɔmje]
C'est Malus domestica, autrement dit un pommier commun.
-That's M. Domestica, otherwise known as the common apple.

9288 **cabanon** **shed**
m
[kabanɔ̃]
Dans une arrière-cour ou un cabanon.
-Like in a yard or somebody's shed.

9289 **dysenterie** **dysentery**
f
[disɑ̃tʁi]
Le médecin dit que ça peut donner une dysenterie.
-The doctor said she might get dysentery.

9290 **géologue** **geologist**
m/f
[ʒeɔlɔg]
Jack est géologue.
-Jack is a geologist.

9291 **pedigree** **pedigree; pedigree**
adj; m
[pedigʁe]
Monte-Carlo est un hongre hanovrien de six ans avec un pedigree de champion.
-Monte Carlo is a six-year-old Hanoverian gelding with a championship pedigree.

9292 **droiture** **righteousness**
f
[dʁwatyʁ]
Son amour du bien et sa droiture sont inconstestables.
-His indomitable spirit for good and righteousness is unquestionable.

9293 **acquittement** **acquittal**
m
[akitmɑ̃]
Si cette condition n'était pas remplie, l'auteur aurait droit à l'acquittement.
-If this burden was not met, the author would therefore be entitled to an acquittal.

9294 **chiqué** **sham|airs**
adj
[ʃike]
Mais, c'est tout de l'astuce et du chiqué.
-But that's all his craft and artfulness.

9295 **crémaillère** **rack**

f
[kʁemajɛʁ]

Un second capteur détecte une position de l'engrenage de mesure de crémaillère.
-A second sensor senses a position of the rack measurement gear.

9296 **progressiste** **progressive; progressive**
adj; m/f
[pʁɔgʁesist]
Nous lutterons alors pour un programme de Stockholm progressiste et pour une législation progressiste.
-We will then fight for a progressive Stockholm Programme and progressive legislation.

9297 **élocution** **speech**
f
[elɔkysjɔ̃]
Elle est intelligente et a une grande facilité d'élocution.
-She's bright and articulate.

9298 **diction** **diction**
f
[diksjɔ̃]
Je suis sûr qu'il va remporter le concours de diction.
-I am sure of his winning the speech contest.

9299 **frange** **fringe**
f
[fʁɑ̃ʒ]
La présente invention permet d'atténuer le problème de frange sombre des antériorités.
-The present invention can improve the dark fringe problem in the prior art.

9300 **laïus** **speech|spiel**
m
[lajy]
Je peux remballer mon petit laïus.
-Well, I guess I can throw away that little speech.

9301 **marginal** **marginal; dropout**
adj; m
[maʁʒinal]
Depuis quelques décennies la culture est présentée comme un accessoire marginal quelconque de la société, a-t-il affirmé en 1999.
-In 1999 he made the point that culture has been presented over the last few decades as if somehow it were a marginal adjunct to society.

9302 **couturier** **fashion designer**
m
[kutyʁje]
C'est rangé par ordre de ton et de couturier.
-It's all perfectly organized by color and designer.

9303 **steppe** **steppe**
f
[stɛp]
Le pire, cétait de trouver de leau dans la steppe.
-The worst was the water on the way, along the steppe.

9304 **corser** **lace**
vb[kɔʁse]
Pour corser le tout, un État membre au moins nous demande de trouver 65 millions d'euros supplémentaires, ce qui complique les choses puisque nous savons que la position du Conseil est déjà arrêtée. -To make it worse, at least one Member State is asking us to find the extra EUR 65 million, which complicates matters when we know what the Council's position is already.

9305 **austère** **austere**
adj
[ostɛʁ]
Grâce au programme austère que le gouvernement fédéral a présenté ?
-Was it with the austere program this Liberal government put forward?

9306 **pivot** **pivot; pivotal**
m; adj
[pivo]
Les pièces de pivot peuvent être des segments de roulements à billes.
-The pivot pads may be segments of ball bearings.

9307 **émigrer** **emigrate**
vb
[emigʁe]
Les Béliziens continuent d'émigrer dans l'espoir d'améliorer leur situation socioéconomique.
-Belizeans continue to emigrate in search of social and economic opportunities.

9308 **suie** **soot**

f

[sɥi]

Son visage était couvert de suie.

-His face was sooty.

9309 **prémonition** **premonition**

f

[pʁemɔnisjɔ̃]

J'ai eu une prémonition que ça arriverait.

-I had a premonition that this would happen.

9310 **devis** **quotation**

m

[dəvi]

Définir clairement les travaux requis et obtenir un devis.

-Clearly define the work required and obtain an estimate of the cost of completing the work.

9311 **approvisionner** **provision|store**

vb

[apʁɔvizjɔne]

Dans bien des cas ces pays dépendent dans une large mesure de ces bassins pour s'approvisionner en eau douce.

-Many of these countries are heavily reliant upon these rivers for the provision of freshwater.

9312 **mondialement** **worldwide**

adv

[mɔ̃djalmɑ̃]

L'activité de la pêche doit être basée mondialement sur le principe de durabilité.

-The fisheries activity needs to be oriented globally on the basis of sustainability.

9313 **grief** **grievance**

m

[ɡʁijɛf]

Il n'y a ni cause, ni grief, ni revendication qui puissent justifier ces actes.

-There is no cause, grievance or claim that can justify those actions.

9314 **accabler** **overwhelm**

vb

[akable]

C'est le coeur même de la région de l'ANASE qui est touché, et nous sommes particulièrement accablés par la lâcheté de cette attaque.

-That struck at the heart of the ASEAN region, and we are particularly overwhelmed by that cowardly attack.

9315 **perfectionner** **improve**

vb

[pɛʁfɛksjɔne]

Un apprentissage, une vie à perfectionner.

-A moment to learn, a lifetime to perfect.

9316 **oxyde** **oxide**

m[ɔksid]

Cet oxyde comprend un oxyde de vanadium (V), un oxyde d'un métal alcalino-terreux et un oxyde d'un métal alcalin. -This oxide is comprises an oxide of vanadium (V), an oxide of an alkaline earth metal and an oxide of an alkali metal.

9317 **éditorial** **editorial; editorial**

adj; m

[editɔʁjal]

Avez-vous lu l'éditorial du journal de ce matin ?

-Have you read the leading article in today's paper?

9318 **affectif** **affective**

adj

[afɛktif]

Le développement affectif des enfants et des jeunes retient aussi l'attention.

-The emotional development of children and youth also receives attention.

9319 **planification** **planning**

f

[planifikasjɔ̃]

Comment cette planification s'intègre-t-elle dans leur planification générale ?

-How is such HR planning integrated with their substantive planning?

9320 **diadème** **tiara**

m

[djadɛm]

Tu ne portes pas le diadème.

-You're not wearing the tiara.

9321 **déconcertant** **disconcerting**

adj

[dekɔ̃sɛʁtɑ̃]

C'est déconcertant.

-It's disconcerting.

9322 **rot** m [ʁo]

burp

Si je pouvais lâcher un rot, je devrais pouvoir avaler un bout de gâteau.
-If I can just rally a burp here, I might be able to squeeze in a piece of zebra cake.

9323 **sparadrap** m [spaʁadʁap]

plaster|band-aid

C'est comme arracher un sparadrap.
-It's just like pulling off a Band-Aid.

9324 **intérieurement** adv [ɛ̃teʁjœʁmɑ̃]

internally

Intérieurement, il faut que la loi et l'ordre règnent; extérieurement il faut assurer la défense.
-They need to have law and order internally and there is a need for defence externally.

9325 **astrologue** m/f [astʁɔlɔg]

astrologer

Dans dix ans, elle sera une astrologue célèbre.
-Ten years from now, she's going to be a famous astrologer.

9326 **poirier** m [pwaʁje]

pear tree|handstand

Pouvez-vous faire le poirier ?
-Can you stand on your hands?

9327 **labrador** m [labʁadɔʁ]

Labrador dog

Les analyses montrent qu'elles proviennent d'un labrador.
-Further analysis showed they were from a Labrador Retriever.

9328 **ravitailler** vb [ʁavitaje]

supply

Pour nous ravitailler en essence, nous nous servions... directement dans les pipelines.
-For gas we used the leakage from the valves of the pipelines...... we found along the way.

9329 **cravacher** vb [kʁavaʃe]

whip

C'est vrai qu'il y en a qui aiment cravacher les filles?
-Is it true that some like to whip you?

9330 **pilleur** m; adj[pijœʁ]

looter; deceitful

C'est un pilleur de fonds. -He is a fund looter.

9331 **recouvrement** m [ʁəkuvʁəmɑ̃]

recovery|collection

Elle est connue pour provoquer un recouvrement quasi instantané.
-In many cases, it has been known to effect an almost instantaneous recovery.

9332 **boomerang** m [bumʁɑ̃g]

boomerang

Ces problèmes sont inévitables et reviennent comme un boomerang.
-These problems are unavoidable, and come back like a boomerang.

9333 **blablabla** m [blablabla]

blah

C'est à cause de la "blablabla droits de l'homme".
-It's because of the "human rights blablabla".

9334 **druide** m [dʁɥid]

druid

Exécuter le druide enverra un message clair.
-Executing the Druid will send out a clear message.

9335 **lobotomie** f [lɔbɔtɔmi]

lobotomy

Vous êtes en retard pour votre lobotomie.
-Look, Derek, you're clearly late for your lobotomy.

9336 **spoon** m [spɔ̃]

spoon

Leave to cool, mix the aubergines with the ricotta and stir well with a spoon.

-Laisser refroidir et mélanger les aubergines à la ricotta, puis bien travailler l'appareil avec une cuillère.

9337 **strudel** **strudel**
m
[stʁydɛl]
A nice piece of strudel, Mrs. Fremont?
-Un peu de strudel, Mme Fremont ?

9338 **oubliette** **oubliette**
f
[ublijɛt]
Je parie pour une oubliette satanique.
-I'm betting Satanic dungeon.

9339 **brouillage** **interference**
m
[bʁujaʒ]
Cela peut entraîner un brouillage entre des communications des première et seconde classes de dispositifs CPL.
-This can result in interference between communications of the first and the second classes of PLC devices.

9340 **immunitaire** **immune**
adj
[imynitɛʁ]
Ils cherchaient à amener le système immunitaire de la souris à provoquer une autostérilisation.
-It was an attempt to provoke the immune system of the mice to sterilise themselves.

9341 **thoracique** **thoracic**
adj
[tɔʁasik]
Entre la septième vertèbre cervicale et la première vertèbre thoracique
-Between the 7th cervical and 1st thoracic vertebrae.

9342 **nationalisme** **nationalism**
m
[nasjɔnalism]
Le nationalisme est intrinsèquement lié à l'identité individuelle.
-Nationalism, after all, is intrinsically bound up with individual identity.

9343 **écologique** **ecological**
adj
[ekɔlɔʒik]
Vous ne portez pas un projet de conversion écologique et sociale de l'Europe.
-You do not have a project for transforming Europe environmentally and socially.

9344 **scotcher** **tape**
vb
[skɔtʃe]
Alors tu as besoin de scotcher un revêtement de sécurité autour du détonateur.
-Then you'll need to tape a secure casing around the detonator.

9345 **prieuré** **priory**
m
[pʁijœʁe]
Les revenus du prieuré viennent de ce pont.
-The priory's income comes from this bridge.

9346 **Bengale** **Bengal; Bengal**
m; adj
[bɛ̃gal]
Et en Inde, des tigres du Bengale.
-In India, I'm sure there are Bengal tigers.

9347 **sauvagerie** **savagery**
f
[sovaʒʁi]
Nous voyons aujourd'hui des tempêtes se déchaîner avec une sauvagerie sans précédent.
-Today, we are seeing those storms hit with a savagery unknown in recent times.

9348 **amasser** **amass|pile**
vb
[amase]
Celui qui ne cherche à amasser des trésors que sur la terre ne peut « s'enrichir en vue de Dieu ».
-Whoever is concerned to accumulate treasure only on earth is not rich in the sight of God.

9349 **comestible** **edible**
adj
[kɔmɛstibl]
Ce champignon n´est pas comestible.
-This mushroom is not good to eat.

9350 **dédommagement** m [dedɔmaʒmɑ̃] **compensation**
Convention européenne relative au dédommagement des victimes d'infractions violentes.
-European Convention on the Compensation of Victims of Violent Crimes.

9351 **passade** adj [pasad] **fancy**
De ce fait, ce qui aux yeux de certains n'est qu'une simple passade peut, en réalité, être enraciné beaucoup plus profondément.
-As a result, what appears to some to be a mere development fad may, in fact, be more deeply rooted.

9352 **roseau** m [ʁozo] **reed**
La dissuasion est un roseau trop faible pour qu'on puisse s'y appuyer pour affronter ce genre d'acteurs qui, en fait, ne sont pas sensible à cette méthode.
-Deterrence is a weak reed on which to lean in confronting these kinds of actors, who fundamentally will not be deterred.

9353 **rectum** m [ʁɛktɔm] **rectum**
Pour info, je garde votre sabre laser dans mon rectum.
-Just so you know, the compartment I keep your lightsaber in is my rectum.

9354 **inquisiteur** m; adj [ɛ̃kizitœʁ] **inquisitor; inquisitive**
Je vous vois, Monsieur le Commissaire, non pas comme le grand inquisiteur.
-I do not regard you as the grand inquisitor, Commissioner.

9355 **prolongé** adj [pʁɔlɔ̃ʒe] **extended**
Le processus de règlement se prolonge indéfiniment et n'a toujours pas abouti, le référendum ayant été repoussé d'année en année.
-The long-drawn-out settlement process had still not concluded; the referendum had been postponed year after year.

9356 **persécuter** vb [pɛʁsekyte] **persecute**
J'espère que vous ne vous sentirez pas persécuté comme Carlos.
-I hope this business doesn't victimise you the way it did Carlos.

9357 **menaçant** adj [mənasɑ̃] **threatening|menacing**
La session s’est ouverte alors que le spectre de la guerre en Irak se faisait de plus en plus menaçant.
-The beginning of the session was overshadowed by the looming war in Iraq.

9358 **ériger** vb [eʁiʒe] **erect**
Si j'ai choisi de prendre la parole, c'est parce qu'il a été proposé d'ériger un mur.
-A proposal was made to erect a wall, which is why I have chosen to speak.

9359 **servitude** f [sɛʁvityd] **servitude**
L'arracher à cette vie de servitude.
-I'll take him away from this dismal life of servitude.

9360 **gréviste** m/f; adj [gʁevist] **striker; striking**
En cas de grève illégale, l'employeur peut mettre un terme à la relation de travail avec le gréviste.
-In case of an illegal strike, the employer may terminate the working relationship with the striker.

9361 **précipité** adj [pʁesipite] **rushed**
Je trouve cette solution nettement préférable à celle d'un débat précipité.
-I consider this far better than such a rushed debate.

9362 **atténuer** **mitigate|ease**

vb
[atenɥe]
Mais les problèmes qu'on a cherché à atténuer ou à régler sont toujours là.
-However, the problems they sought to attenuate or resolve persist.

9363 **barmaid** **barmaid**
f
[baʁmɛ]
Une barmaid de Fresno, elle doit être prête à réagir au quart de tour.
-She's a Fresno bartender, and they got to be ready to throw down at the drop of a hat.

9364 **royalement** **royally**
adv
[ʁwajalmɑ̃]
Tous sont d'accord pour dire que la Reine-Mère était une femme royalement remarquable.
-They all agree that the Queen-Mum was a royally remarkable woman.

9365 **décompresser** **decompress**
vb
[dekɔ̃pʁese]
Je viens souvent ici pour décompresser.
-I come here a lot when I need to decompress.

9366 **brocoli** **broccoli**
m
[bʁɔkɔli]
Et le brocoli était super aussi.
-And the broccoli was really nice as well.

9367 **illettré** **illiterate**
adj
[iletʁe]
Ce sont des illettrés, ou des gens dont l'éducation est manifestement déficitaire.
-They are illiterate, or obviously poorly educated.

9368 **pépée** **chick|babe**
f
[pepe]
Sapristi, en voilà une jolie pépée!
-By thunder, here's a pretty dame.

9369 **paradisiaque** **heavenly**
adj[paʁadizjak]
Replanter nos oliveraies, permettre à nos pêcheurs d'exercer leur métier, accueillir plongeurs et touristes dans un site paradisiaque, tel est l'avenir que nous voulons bâtir avec nos voisins. -The vision of restored olive groves, fishermen's boats, snorkels and a tourist paradise is the future we want to shape with our neighbours.

9370 **amputation** **amputation**
f
[ɑ̃pytasjɔ̃]
La mutilation la plus courante a été l'amputation de la main ou de l'avant-bras.
-The most commonly performed amputation was that of the hand or forearm.

9371 **monotonie** **monotony**
f
[mɔnɔtɔni]
La monotonie de ces rapport annuels n'a d'égal que leur optimisme sans limite.
-The monotony of these annual reports is equalled only by their limitless optimism.

9372 **hachoir** **chopper**
m
[aʃwaʁ]
Les pilotes du hachoir ont vu seulement vous et Garai.
-The chopper pilots only saw you and Garai.

9373 **pathologique** **pathological**
adj
[patɔlɔʒik]
La propension pathologique au jeu constitue une forme d'addiction.
-Pathological inclination to gamble is attributed to habitual and inclination disorders.

9374 **déportation** **deportation**
f
[depɔʁtasjɔ̃]
La déportation du peuple acadien a eu lieu de 1755 à 1763.
-The deportation of the Acadian people took place between 1755 and 1763.

9375 **toupie** **top**
f
[tupi]
La toupie tourbillonna encore et encore.
-The top went around and around.

9376 **crème** adj; f [kʁɛm]
cream; cream
Un café crème est un plaisir peu onéreux.
-Coffee with cream is not a very expensive pleasure.

9377 **chenal** m [ʃənal]
channel
Ces structures ont été construites afin d'aider à réduire le taux de sédimentation dans le chenal maritime.
-These structures were built to help reduce the rate of sedimentation in the shipping channel.

9378 **toxicomane** m/f [tɔksikɔman]
addict
Il devient rapidement alcoolique et toxicomane.
-He is soon to become an alcoholic and drug addict.

9379 **freinage** m [fʁɛnaʒ]
braking
Cette bague forme une chambre annulaire de récupération servant à retenir le matériau de frottement pendant le freinage.
-This ring forms an annular collecting chamber for catching the friction material during braking.

9380 **flexible** adj [flɛksibl]
flexible
Par "flexible", un conduit flexible pour l'écoulement du gaz naturel.
-"Flexible fuel lines" mean a flexible tubing or hose through which natural gas flow.

9381 **braise** f[bʁɛz]
embers
Tu as une braise sur ton pied. -You've got an ember on your instep.

9382 **isolé** adj; m [izɔle]
isolated|insulated; isolated person
Plus tu seras têtu, plus tu seras isolé.
-The more stubborn you are, the more isolated you become.

9383 **visuellement** adv [vizɥɛlmɑ̃]
visually
Il doit être possible de reconnaître visuellement si l'appareil est en service.
-It must be visually possible to check whether the apparatus is in operation.

9384 **minutieusement** adv [minysjøzmɑ̃]
thoroughly
À nouveau, je demande à la Commission de surveiller minutieusement cet aspect.
-Again, this is something I would like to ask the Commission to monitor carefully.

9385 **douve** f [duv]
stave|moat
Creuse la douve avant que le monstre n'arrive.
-Dig the moat before the monster comes.

9386 **rancœur** f [ʁɑ̃kœʁ]
rancor
La contribution de la présence africaine à tout ceci s'est faite sans orgueil ni rancœur.
-The contribution of the African Presence to all this is without hubris or rancour.

9387 **blindage** m [blɛ̃daʒ]
shield
L'invention concerne un blindage magnétique.
-A magnetic shield is presented.

9388 **manipulateur** m [manipylatœʁ]
manipulator
Plusieurs modules ont un manipulateur commun.
-Several modules are disposed within the operation zone of one common manipulator.

9389 **ralliement** m [ʁalimɑ̃]
rally
C'est, en quelque sorte, devenu un sujet de ralliement pour les écologistes.
-This has somehow become a rallying issue for environmentalists.

9390 **angulaire** **angular**
adj
[ɑ̃gylɛʁ]
Notre gouvernement a fait du Nord une pierre angulaire de son programme.
-Our Government has made Canada's North a cornerstone of its agenda.

9391 **épopée** **epic**
f
[epɔpe]
C'est l'épopée de Dunkerque.
-This is the epic of Dunkirk.

9392 **tumulte** **tumult**
m
[tymylt]
Il pourra se marier, fonder une famille avoir un poste lucratif loin du tumulte du Knick.
-He can get married, have a family and an excellent, lucrative practice away from the tumult of The Knick.

9393 **notice** **notice**
f
[nɔtis]
Les seules vraies choses qui t'ont values ta burn notice.
-The very things that earned you your burn notice.

9394 **rebrousser** **turn back**
vb[ʁəbʁuse]
Rebrousser chemin reviendrait à déclencher un effondrement qui nous toucherait tous. -Any attempt to turn back the clock would result in a collapse that would affect every one of us.

9395 **nitroglycérine** **nitroglycerine**
f
[nitʁɔgliseʁin]
No ONU 3064 NITROGLYCÉRINE EN SOLUTION ALCOOLIQUE, avec plus de 1 % mais pas plus de 5 % de nitroglycérine
-UN No. 3064 NITROGLYCERIN SOLUTION IN ALCOHOL with more than 1% but not more than 5% nitroglycerin

9396 **piéton** **pedestrian; pedestrian**
m; adj
[pjetɔ̃]
Au moment du choc avec le piéton, le capot du moteur se soulève automatiquement.
-At the moment the pedestrian is hit, the engine cover automatically rises.

9397 **distinctement** **distinctly|audibly**
adv
[distɛ̃ktəmɑ̃]
À ce propos, il faut préciser ce point bien plus distinctement qu'il ne l'a été au sein du système des Nations unies.
-Incidentally, this must be made a great deal clearer than it has been within the UN system.

9398 **malhonnêteté** **dishonesty**
f
[malɔnɛtte]
Je suppose que la malhonnêteté... engendre forcément la malhonnêteté.
-I suppose a certain amount of dishonesty... is bound to beget a certain amount of dishonesty.

9399 **urticaire** **urticaria|hives**
f
[yʁtikɛʁ]
Elle fait de l'urticaire lorsqu'elle mange des œufs.
-She gets hives when she eats eggs.

9400 **marteau-piqueur** **jackhammer**
m
[maʁtopikœʁ]
On en a pour une heure avec le marteau-piqueur.
-It'll take an hour with the pneumatic drill.

9401 **transparence** **transparency**
f
[tʁɑ̃spaʁɑ̃s]
Mon gouvernement s'est engagé à créer un niveau sans précédent d'ouverture dans la conduite de l'État. Nous travaillerons ensemble pour assurer la confiance du public et établir un système de transparence, de participation du public et de collaboration.
-My Administration is committed to creating an unprecedented level of openness in Government. We will work together to ensure the public trust and establish a system of transparency, public participation, and collaboration.

9402 **parlementaire** **parliamentary; parliamentarian**

adj; m/f
[paʁləmɑ̃tɛʁ]

Nous devons évoquer le souvenir de Pierre Elliot Trudeau à titre de parlementaire.
-It was as a parliamentarian that we should remember Pierre Elliott Trudeau.

9403 **persil** **parsley**
m
[pɛʁsi]
Peut-être irons-nous dans le jardin voir son persil.
-Maybe we'll go in the garden, and she'll show me her parsley.

9404 **stratège** **strategist**
m
[stʁatɛʒ]
Le plus briLLant stratège poLitique du parti.
-Meet the most brilliant political strategist in the party.

9405 **golfeur** **golfer**
m
[gɔlfœʁ]
Êtes-vous bon golfeur ?
-Are you a good golfer?

9406 **gourmet** **gourmet**
m
[guʁmɛ]
L'activité a été incorporée dans l'unité Produits «gourmet» et spécialités du groupe.
-The business was integrated into the Group's Gourmet & Specialties business unit.

9407 **incinérateur** **incinerator**
m
[ɛ̃sineʁatœʁ]
Attachez-le et jetez-le dans l'incinérateur.
-Tie him up and toss him in the incinerator.

9408 **vésicule** **vesicle**
f
[vezikyl]
L'invention concerne également des procédés d'utilisation de la vésicule en vue de délivrer des biomolécules.
-Methods of using the vesicle for delivery of biomolecules are also provided.

9409 **impossibilité** **impossibility**
f
[ɛ̃pɔsibilite]
Il fut dans l'impossibilité de se joindre à la discussion.
-He was not able to join in the discussion.

9410 **embargo** **embargo**
m
[ɑ̃baʁgo]
Un embargo ferait tort à notre cause.
-An embargo, it would be so harmful to our cause.

9411 **propagation** **spread**
f
[pʁɔpagasjɔ̃]
Ce mécanisme préviendrait également leur propagation.
-This mechanism will also prevent the spread of such weaponry.

9412 **sismique** **seismic**
adj
[sismik]
Application notamment à la prospection sismique d'un milieu.
-It is particularly useful in the seismic prospection of a site.

9413 **polio** **polio**
f
[pɔljo]
L'invention concerne également un nouveau peptide support à polyépitope comprenant l'épitope PV1 provenant du virus polio.
-The specification also provides a new polyepitope carrier peptidecomprising the PV1 epitope from polio virus.

9414 **conditionnement** **packaging**
m
[kɔ̃disjɔnmɑ̃]
Matériaux de conditionnement et/ou d'isolation.
-The invention relates to packaging and/or insulation materials.

9415 **crânien** **cranial**
adj
[kʁanjɛ̃]
Le 7e nerf crânien est près de la fracture.
-The seventh cranial nerve is near the site of the fracture.

9416 **circoncision** **circumcision**

	f [siʁkɔ̃sizjɔ̃]	Le Ministre a ajouté que la circoncision féminine était un «problème d'éducation». -The Minister added that female circumcision is a "problem of education".
9417	**judaïsme** m [ʒydaism]	**Judaism** Chrétienté, islam et judaïsme sont réunis en Bosnie-Herzégovine. -Christianity, Islam and Judaism are all found in Bosnia and Herzegovina.
9418	**criquet** m [kʁikɛ]	**locust** L'Afrique de l'Ouest doit actuellement faire face à une crise croissante due au criquet pèlerin qui provoque d'importants dégâts aux cultures. -West Africa is currently facing a worsening locust crisis, which is causing significant crop damage.
9419	**tragiquement** adv[tʁaʒikmɑ̃]	**tragically** Ils ont été tragiquement privés de capacités essentielles au développement humain. -They have been tragically deprived of the basic capacities for human development.
9420	**tisser** vb [tise]	**weave** Il est nécessaire de tisser au niveau mondial une toile antiterroriste homogène. -It was necessary to weave a seamless global counter-terrorism web.
9421	**mixture** f [mikstyʁ]	**mixture** Cette mixture devrait répliquer le composé que vous recherchez. -And we think this mixture should replicate the compound you're looking for.
9422	**artefact** m [aʁtefakt]	**artifact** Elle ne connaît même pas son artefact. -She doesn't even know what the artifact is.
9423	**orifice** m [ɔʁifis]	**orifice** Un orifice externe communique avec le plénum. -An external port is provided for communication with the plenum.
9424	**clandestinement** adv [klɑ̃dɛstinmɑ̃]	**clandestinely** Lors de ma seconde visite, j'ai pu rencontrer Aung San Suu Kyi clandestinement. -On the second occasion I was able to meet with Aung San Suu Kyi clandestinely.
9425	**provocateur** adj; m [pʁɔvɔkatœʁ]	**challenging; agitator** Et je peux vous rassurer: les provocateurs intelligents s'en sortent généralement bien. -I can assure you: intelligent agitators invariably do well in the end.
9426	**illustration** f [ilystʁasjɔ̃]	**illustration** Une illustration peut éclaircir le propos. -An illustration may make the point clear.
9427	**débusquer** vb [debyske]	**flush** Autre objectif fondamental de ces clubs: démasquer et débusquer toutes les petites «arnaques» que ne manquera pas de générer l'arrivée de l'euro. -Another main aim of such clubs is to unmask and flush out all the little 'swindles' that the arrival of the euro will certainly entail.
9428	**benêt** m [bənɛ]	**dullard** Chère Zerline, nous voilà enfin débarrassés de ce benêt. -At last we are free, dear Zerlina, of that bore.
9429	**converser** vb [kɔ̃vɛʁse]	**converse** Une cliente a même dit de son avocat « qu'il voulait converser avec mon mari et apprendre à le connaître » (Étude de cas no 7, client 1, entrevue

initiale, unité 35).
-One client commented her lawyer "wanted to chat up my husband and bond with him."

9430 **seigle** **rye**
m
[sɛgl]
Monsieur le Commissaire, le seigle possède un statut très particulier en Finlande.
-Commissioner, in Finland rye is very special.

9431 **forcené** **madman|gunner; fanatical**
m; adj
[fɔʁsəne]
Un commentaire sur le forcené.
-Ma'am, any comments about the gunman?

9432 **massue** **mace**
f
[masy]
Peut-être un tomahawk ou une massue cérémonielle de votre pays.
-Perhaps a tomahawk or ritual club from your own country.

9433 **captivant** **captivating**
adj
[kaptivɑ̃]
En d'autres termes, les multitudes qui se sont rassemblées ce soir pour écouter ce débat captivant sur les émissions de gaz polluants par les engins mobiles non routiers peuvent être satisfaites.
-In other words the multitudes of people who have gathered here tonight to listen to this riveting debate on gaseous pollutants emitted by non-road mobile machinery can be satisfied.

9434 **fortuné** **wealthy**
adj
[fɔʁtyne]
Cette règle vaut même si le père est fortuné.
-This will not be affected even if the father is wealthy and rich.

9435 **mousseux** **sparkling|foamy**
adj
[musø]
Les vins mousseux sont les véritables stars du marché, dans le sillage de leur cousin noble français, le champagne.
-These are the stars of the market, following in the footsteps of their noble cousin, French champagne.

9436 **fêtard** **roisterer|rounder**
m
[fetaʁ]
Viens par là, le grand fêtard.
-Over here, you big party animal.

9437 **saindoux** **lard**
m
[sɛ̃du]
Du porridge froid gorgé de saindoux.
-Some nice ice-cold oatmeal smothered with lard.

9438 **accoster** **land|dock**
vb
[akɔste]
Les gens devaient attendre la marée haute pour pouvoir accoster.
-People have to wait for high tide to dock.

9439 **traquenard** **trap|booby trap**
m
[tʁaknaʁ]
Je crois que ce traquenard était destiné à votre équipier.
-We believe that trap was meant for your partner.

9440 **bienséance** **propriety**
f
[bjɛ̃seɑ̃s]
« La liberté pousse l'homme à dépasser les limites de la bienséance et à porter atteinte à la dignité de sa condition.
-"Liberty causeth man to overstep the bounds of propriety, and to infringe on the dignity of his station.

9441 **inertie** **inertia**
f
[inɛʁsi]
Ils meurent d'inertie face aux difficultés.
-They die through inertia in the face of challenge.

9442 **appareiller** **pair**
vb
[apaʁeje]
De nombreux navires, comme tout le monde le sait dans ce Parlement, ne peuvent plus être appareillés.

-Many vessels, as everyone in this Chamber knows, can no longer afford to put to sea.

9443 **privation** **deprivation**
f La privation de soins médicaux serait courante.
[pʁivasjɔ̃] -The denial of medical care to prisoners was alleged to be prevalent.

9444 **rugissement** **roaring**
m Avez-vous entendu le rugissement des lions ?
[ʁyʒismɑ̃] -Did you hear the roar of the lions?

9445 **autochtone** **native; native**
m/f; adj[ɔtɔktɔn] Personne, ni autochtone ni non-autochtone, n'en retirera quelque avantage que ce soit. -This benefits nobody, native or non-native.

9446 **insouciance** **recklessness**
f Pris ensemble, ces éléments constituent de l'insouciance criminelle.
[ɛ̃susjɑ̃s] -Together they add up to criminal recklessness.

9447 **aisselle** **armpit**
f Les veines sont noires jusqu'à l'aisselle.
[ɛsɛl] -Them veins is blackening' all the way up to his armpit.

9448 **anciennement** **formerly**
adv Ce droit ancien a résisté à l'épreuve du temps et existe encore aujourd'hui.
[ɑ̃sjɛnmɑ̃] -This ancient right has stood the test of time and is very much alive today.

9449 **caveau** **vault**
m Votre Henri gît dans le caveau.
[kavo] -Your Henry's lies in the vault, you know.

9450 **gringalet** **weakling**
m Hier à la même heure, j'étais un gringalet pathétique.
[gʁɛ̃galɛ] -At this time yesterday, I was a pathetic weakling.

9451 **mousquet** **musket**
m C'est un mousquet ?
[muskɛ] -Is that a freaking musket?

9452 **canaliser** **channel**
vb Ce traité avait pour objectif de canaliser l'agression allemande vers l'est.
[kanalize] -That treaty was designed to channel German aggression eastward.

9453 **dorloter** **pamper|mother**
vb Il doit être dorloté.
[dɔʁlɔte] -He must be pampered.

9454 **turquoise** **turquoise; turquoise**
f; adj La couleur turquoise évoque la couleur de l'eau claire, c'est un bleu clair et pâle.
[tyʁkwaz] -The turquoise colour evokes the colour of clear water, it's a light and pale blue.

9455 **carboniser** **carbonize|char**
vb Leurs corps carbonisés auraient ultérieurement été découverts au milieu d'une place de marché à Dera Bugti.
[kaʁbɔnize] -Their charred bodies were later found in the centre of a market place in Dera Bugti.

9456 **brouter** **graze|chatter**
vb Qui peut contrôler le temps que passent les vaches à brouter dans les prés?
[bʁute] -Who can check the time that cows spend grazing in pastures?

9457 **flore** **flora**
f Ils veulent protéger la flore et la faune de notre pays.
[flɔʁ] -They want to protect flora and fauna.

9458	**beurré** adj [bœʁe]	**plastered|buttered** Ce matin, j'ai mangé du pain beurré. -I ate bread and butter this morning.
9459	**longévité** f [lɔ̃ʒevite]	**longevity** Nous ne connaissons pas la longévité des pesticides. -We do not know the longevity of the pesticides that are being used.
9460	**épi** m[epi]	**ear|cob** Elles laissent des trous d'entrée sur l'extérieur de l'épi. -Larvae leave entry holes on the exterior of ear.
9461	**langer** vb [lɑ̃ʒe]	**swaddle** Tu pourrais même langer ton propre beau-frère. -You can burp and change your own brother-in-law.
9462	**dissolution** f [disɔlysjɔ̃]	**dissolution** Nous ne voulons pas provoquer la dissolution de collectivités entières. -We do not want to preside over the dissolution of entire communities in the country.
9463	**divaguer** vb [divage]	**ramble|rave** Ainsi serait -on certain de ne pas divaguer et de rester fortement ancré sur les démocraties nationales. -In this way we would be sure of not wandering off track and we would remain firmly anchored to the national democracies.
9464	**intégral** adj [ɛ̃tegʁal]	**integral** Le satellite Intégral a été lancé avec succès le 17 octobre 2002 par une fusée Proton. -An Integral satellite was successfully launched on 17 October 2002 by a proton rocket.
9465	**dédicacer** vb [dedikase]	**autograph** Pourriez-vous dédicacer ce livre, s'il vous plaît ? -Would you please autograph this book?
9466	**bribe** f [bʁib]	**scrap** Un signal porteur HF est modulé conformément à la valeur de la bribe composite. -An RF carrier is modulated in accordance with the value of the composite chip.
9467	**sonde** f [sɔ̃d]	**probe** La sonde lambda déconne de nouveau. -The lambda sensor is on the fritz again.
9468	**apathie** f [apati]	**apathy** Toutefois, il y a peut-être une raison à cette inaction et à cette apparente apathie. -However, perhaps there is a reason for the inaction and apparent apathy.
9469	**magnésium** m [maɲezjɔm]	**magnesium** "332 Le nitrate de magnésium hexahydraté n'est pas soumis aux prescriptions du ADN. -“332 Magnesium nitrate hexahydrate is not subject to the requirements of ADN.
9470	**revêtement** m [ʁəvɛtmɑ̃]	**coating|lining** Le revêtement arrière est optiquement transparent et électroconducteur. -The back side coating is optically transparent and is electrically conductive.
9471	**pectoral**	**pectoral; pectoral**

adj; m
[pɛktɔʁal]
Un "filet" est obtenu en séparant le muscle pectoral interne de la poitrine et du sternum.
-A "tenderloin" is produced by separating the inner pectoral muscle from the breast and the sternum.

9472 **dépannage** **help|fixing**
m[depanaʒ]
Ce système peut être utilisé pour effectuer un dépannage à distance avec l'appui d'experts distants du service clientèle. -The system can be used for performing remote troubleshooting with the support of distant customer service experts.

9473 **narcissisme** **narcissism**
m
[naʁsisism]
M. Gruner souffre certainement de narcissisme clinique.
-Mr. Gruner suffers from what must surely be clinical narcissism.

9474 **pédiatrie** **pediatrics**
f
[pedjatʁi]
Titre Professeur Emeritus, départements de la pédiatrie et de la pathologie, université de McMaster.
-Title Professor Emeritus, Departments of Pediatrics and Pathology, McMaster University.

9475 **dîmer** **tithe**
vb
[dime]
Je suppose que le député a déjà entendu dire que l'on devrait verser le dixième de ses revenus au titre de la dîme.
-I am assuming the hon. member has heard of the term tithing or one-tenth.

9476 **suffoquer** **suffocate**
vb
[syfɔke]
et nourriture à faire suffoquer, et châtiment douloureux.
-And food that chokes, and a painful punishment.

9477 **squash** **squash**
m
[skaʃ]
1986-1987 Honorary Treasurer of Lusaka Club (Squash Section).
-Trésorier honoraire du club de Lusaka (section squash), 1986-1987

9478 **actionner** **activate**
vb
[aksjɔne]
Ce dispositif ne doit pas pouvoir être actionné par inadvertance.
-It shall be impossible to activate these devices accidentally.

9479 **conservation** **preservation**
f
[kɔ̃sɛʁvasjɔ̃]
Aucun colorant, agent de conservation ou arôme artificiel.
-No artificial colours, preservatives or flavours.

9480 **palpitation** **palpitation|flutter**
f
[palpitasjɔ̃]
Mais j'ai regardé tes résultats, et il y a une légère palpitation lors de ta réponse à cette question.
-But then I looked at your results, and there is a slight flutter in your answer to that question.

9481 **orchestre** **orchestra**
m
[ɔʁkɛstʁ]
L'orchestre joue.
-The orchestra is playing.

9482 **malmener** **bully|manhandle**
vb
[malməne]
Récemment, deux membres internationaux ont également été malmenés et arrêtés.
-Recently two international staff members were also manhandled and arrested.

9483 **brindille** **twig**
f
[bʁɛ̃dij]
Mes sous-vêtements sont coincés sur une brindille.
-Well, my drawers, they're cotched up here on a twig.

9484 **invétérer** **ingrain**

vb
[ɛ̃veteʁe]
Il est joueur invétéré depuis 20 ans.
-He's been a compulsive gambler for 20 years.

9485 **argenté** adj[aʁʒɑ̃te]
silver
Les quantités de merlu argenté que Cuba est autorisé à prendre en 1999 sont faibles. -Foreign participation by Cuba this year, 1999, in the silver hake fishery is low.

9486 **pickpocket** m/f [pikpɔkɛ]
pickpocket
Un pickpocket est aussi un champion de l'entreprise privée.
-A pickpocket is also a champion of private enterprise.

9487 **instaurer** vb [ɛ̃stɔʁe]
establish|instigate
Elles contribuent à instaurer une dynamique de changement qui dure toute l'année.
-These events help to instigate the momentum for change that lasts throughout the year.

9488 **abattage** m [abataʒ]
slaughter|felling
Il la suit immédiatement, comme un bœuf à l'abattage.
-He immediately follows her, like an ox to the slaughter.

9489 **moucheron** m [muʃʁɔ̃]
gnat
Je serai toujours là, tel un moucheron.
-I'll always be buzzing around like a gnat.

9490 **zigzag** m [zigzag]
zigzag
Je les ai cousues machine avec un point zigzag.
-I have machine sewn with a zigzag.

9491 **chiffonner** vb [ʃifɔne]
crumple|ruffle
Mais je voulais pas me chiffonner... et te faire danser avec un débraillé.
-But I didn't want to ruffle myself up, and have you dance with a sloppy guy.

9492 **intendance** f [ɛ̃tɑ̃dɑ̃s]
stewardship
Nous reconnaissons que beaucoup de volontaires souscrivent pleinement à l'intendance comme moyen de protéger les espèces dans leur habitat essentiel.
-We agree, support and recognize that many volunteers and voluntary measures have fully endorsed the stewardship as a means of providing protection for species in their critical habitat.

9493 **marchandage** m [maʁʃɑ̃daʒ]
bargaining
Holkeri a dit à juste titre que ce type de marchandage était inacceptable.
-Holkeri quite rightly said that bargaining over that is not acceptable.

9494 **lourdaud** adj; m [luʁdo]
clumsy|heavy; oaf
C'est un lourdaud.
-He's a slowpoke.

9495 **dédain** m [dedɛ̃]
disdain
Ne le considérez pas avec dédain juste parce qu'il est pauvre.
-Don't look down on him just because he's poor.

9496 **culbuter** vb [kylbyte]
tumble
Le tambour tourne autour d'un axe horizontal pour faire culbuter les particules.
-The drum is rotated about a horizontal axis to tumble the particles.

9497 **fiel** m [fjɛl]
gall
Sang et fiel d'un chien noir.
-Blood and gall of a black dog.

9498 **gravure**
engraving|print

	f[gʁavyʁ]	Je ne vois aucune gravure cependant. -I don't see any etching, though.
9499	**photogénique**	**photogenic**
	adj [fɔtoʒenik]	Je n'ai jamais été photogénique. -I am not photogenic at the best of times.
9500	**haltère**	**dumbbell**
	m [altɛʁ]	Parce que si non, j'aimerais lui presser mon haltère. -Because if not, I wouldn't mind bench pressing her with my dumbbell.
9501	**tutu**	**tutu**
	m [tyty]	Et aujourd'hui c'est le jour ballerine et tutu. -And today it is ballerina tutu day.
9502	**farfelu**	**wacky; crazy**
	m; adj [faʁfəly]	Je sais que ça semble farfelu, mais je vous dit... -Now, I know that it sounds wacky, but I'm telling you...
9503	**boniment**	**pitch**
	m [bɔnimɑ̃]	Mais nous voulions préparer le moment où il raconte son boniment. -But what we were trying to do was build towards a moment where he was... really making his pitch.
9504	**chandelier**	**candlestick**
	m [ʃɑ̃dəlje]	Kyle a frappé Duke avec un chandelier dans la cave. -Kyle hit the Duke with a candlestick in the crypt.
9505	**louable**	**commendable|rentable**
	adj [lwabl]	C'est un objectif apparemment louable, mais impossible à atteindre. -This is an apparently laudable objective, but one that is impossible to achieve.
9506	**roupiller**	**saw wood**
	vb [ʁupije]	Les enregistrer, ça me donne envie de roupiller. -Their tapes always put me to sleep.
9507	**dormeur**	**sleeper**
	m [dɔʁmœʁ]	La conscience du dormeur est stockée dans la mémoire qui entretient son corps. -A sleeper's consciousness is stored in the same memory that maintains their body.
9508	**interurbain**	**interurban**
	adj [ɛ̃tɛʁyʁbɛ̃]	Oui, il y a eu un appel interurbain. -Yes, there was a long-distance call.
9509	**nullité**	**nullity|nonentity**
	f [nylite]	L'appelante a contesté, dans une action en nullité, la validité des art. -By an action in nullity, appellant challenged the validity of ss.
9510	**débordant**	**boundless**
	adj [debɔʁdɑ̃]	La société coréenne est comme une large et harmonieuse famille, débordant de moralité honorable. -His society was like a large, harmonious family, overflowing with honourable morality.
9511	**camoufler**	**camouflage**
	vb [kamufle]	Ou finira-t-il par être un programme qui vise simplement à camoufler le chômage ? -Or will it end up being a programme that is simply aimed at covering up unemployment?
9512	**sauce**	**sauce**

f[sos] | Faire cuire les pâtes dans beaucoup d'eau chaude salée, égoutter et mélanger à la sauce. -Cook the Caserecce in plenty boiling salted water, drain and mix into the sauce.

9513 **revirement** **turn-around**
m
[ʁəviʁmɑ̃]
Quel revirement remarquable dans une période relativement courte.
-What an outstanding turnaround in a very short period of time.

9514 **moustachu** **moustached**
adj
[mustaʃy]
Si nous pouvions donner ça au gentleman moustachu.
-If we could just get that over to the mustachioed gentleman.

9515 **magnanime** **magnanimous**
adj
[maɲanim]
L'élargissement concrétise la vision magnanime et ouverte du projet européen original.
-Enlargement specifically embodies the magnanimous and open vision of the original European project.

9516 **cornemuse** **bagpipe**
f
[kɔʁnəmyz]
Cette scène avec la cornemuse, c'était trop drôle, mec.
-That bagpipe scene, that was the funniest shit, man.

9517 **diagramme** **diagram**
m
[djagʁam]
Laisse-moi l'expliquer à l'aide d'un diagramme.
-Let me explain it with a diagram.

9518 **aviron** **rowing|oar**
m
[aviʁɔ̃]
Le rameur met la faute sur son aviron.
-The rower blames his oar.

9519 **dompteur** **tamer**
m
[dɔ̃ptœʁ]
C'est un dompteur de lions.
-He is one of us, a lion tamer.

9520 **rustique** **rustic|country**
adj
[ʁystik]
Je t'ai dit que c'était rustique.
-I told you that it was rustic.

9521 **opossum** **opossum**
m
[ɔpɔsɔm]
Voilà pourquoi j'entraîne un opossum.
-That's why I'm training a possum.

9522 **spontanéité** **spontaneity**
f
[spɔ̃taneite]
Que ses rencontres avec la Madone se caractérisent par maximum de spontanéité.
-That his meetings with the Our Lady are characterized by maximum spontaneity.

9523 **jérémiade** **complaint**
f
[ʒeʁemjad]
Une jérémiade à propos d'une amourette que tu connais depuis 6 semaines.
-Have a moan about some bird you've known for six weeks.

9524 **pygmée** **Pygmy; pygmy**
f; adj
[pigme]
Les projets en cours promeuvent la langue et la culture pygmée, y compris la « Formation audiovisuelle du peuple de la forêt ».
-Ongoing projects promote Pigmy language and culture, including "Audiovisual Training for the Forest People".

9525 **fragilité** **fragility**
f[fʁaʒilite]
Cependant, la fragilité de telles alliances laisse présager un avenir hésitant et incertain. -However, the fragility of such alliances portends a shaky and uncertain future.

9526 **éboulement** **landslide**

	m [ebulmɑ̃]	Jack est coincé dans un éboulement. -Jack's trapped in a cave-in.
9527	**fuselage** m [fyzlaʒ]	**fuselage** The aircraft also had the numbers 26563 on its fuselage. -L'aéronef portait aussi les chiffres 26563 inscrits sur son fuselage.
9528	**ramoneur** m [ʁamɔnœʁ]	**chimney sweep** Comme un petit ramoneur du 19eme siècle. -Like a little 19th century chimney sweep.
9529	**dégel** m [deʒɛl]	**thaw** Toute la paperasserie sera ainsi réglée à temps pour le dégel printanier. -That way, you'll have all the paperwork taken care of in time for the spring thaw.
9530	**imaginatif** adj [imaʒinatif]	**imaginative** C'est pour cela que le langage imaginatif de ces visions est un langage symbolique. -For this reason, the figurative language of the visions is symbolic.
9531	**panthéon** m [pɑ̃teɔ̃]	**pantheon** J'ai rencontré sir Edmund au tournoi de golf du Panthéon des sports canadiens en 1980. -I first met Sir Edmund at the Sports Hall of Fame Golf Tournament in 1980.
9532	**agriculteur** m [agʁikyltœʁ]	**farmer** L'agriculteur possède un grand domaine. -The farmer has a large amount of land.
9533	**palper** vb [palpe]	**feel** On se contente de graber des boutiques... pour palper que des miettes. -We go around shop crasting and the like...... coming out with a pitiful rookerfull of money each.
9534	**vernissage** m [vɛʁnisaʒ]	**varnishing|opening** Je crois que tout était vendu au moment du vernissage. -I think everything was sold at the opening.
9535	**receleur** m [ʁəslœʁ]	**fence** Alec ira voir un receleur à Amsterdam. -Alec is going to Amsterdam next week to see a fence.
9536	**fonctionnel** adj [fɔ̃ksjɔnɛl]	**functional** Il ne semble pas encore fonctionnel. -It does not appear to be yet functional.
9537	**vioque** adj [vjɔk]	**wrinkly** Remets donc tes chaussures de vioque. -Put your old man shoes back on.
9538	**transplantation** f [tʁɑ̃splɑ̃tasjɔ̃]	**transplantation** Le chirurgien m'a convaincu de subir une opération de transplantation. -The surgeon persuaded me to undergo an organ transplant operation.
9539	**hydromel** m[idʁɔmɛl]	**mead** Encore, Jarucha aime bien l'hydromel. -Pour me some. Jarucha likes her mead.
9540	**interaction** f [ɛ̃tɛʁaksjɔ̃]	**interaction** On renforcera l'interaction avec les collectivités et les organisations de base. -Interaction with municipalities and grassroots organizations will be strengthened.
9541	**chromosome**	**chromosome**

m
[kʁomozom]

Les vecteurs d'élimination servent à supprimer certaines régions désignées d'un chromosome.
-The knockout vectors are used to delete designated regions of one chromosome.

9542 **diminution** f [diminysjɔ̃]
decrease
Toute diminution du coefficient traduit un engorgement du filtre.
-A decrease in the coefficient of performance indicates that the air filter is clogged.

9543 **incinération** f [ɛ̃sineʁasjɔ̃]
incineration
La peur est normale durant l'incinération.
-It is normal to experience fear during your incineration.

9544 **charognard** m [ʃaʁɔɲaʁ]
scavenger
Ensuite, les morsures et des griffures sur Purl pourraient être dûes à un charognard.
-Then the bites and scratches on Purl could be scavenger activity.

9545 **équité** f [ekite]
equity
Il n'y a qu'une loi pour tous, à savoir cette loi qui gouverne toutes les lois, la loi de notre Créateur, la loi de l'humanité, de la justice et de l'équité - la loi de la nature et des nations.
-There is but one law for all, namely, that law which governs all law, the law of our Creator, the law of humanity, justice, equity — the law of nature, and of nations.

9546 **scintiller** vb [sɛ̃tije]
twinkle|sparkle
Le soir, regardez les lumières scintiller dans les Ponts Jumeaux.
-At night, watch the lights twinkle in Twin Bridges.

9547 **millet** m [mijɛ]
millet
Plantation simultanée de graines de sorgho ou de millet et de jeunes arbres.
-Simultaneous planting of sorghum or millet seeds and saplings.

9548 **gondoler** vb [gɔ̃dɔle]
warp
C'est comme si le clavier allait se gondoler...
-Somehow the keys are starting to look distorted.

9549 **shaker** m [ʃake]
shaker
Le shaker comprend un ou plusieurs canaux remplis de matériau de percussion.
-The shaker comprises one or more channels filled with a striker material.

9550 **insipide** adj [ɛ̃sipid]
tasteless
Nous avons constaté qu'une citoyenneté théorique ou insipide, un vague sentiment d'appartenance affaiblissent l'Europe.
-We have seen that theoretical or bland citizenship, some vague feeling of belonging, makes Europe weaker.

9551 **obliquer** vb[ɔblike]
skew
Il avait alors vu l'auteur de l'autre côté du camion et l'avait vu, en compagnie de celui qui avait tiré, se mettre à poursuivre le garde puis obliquer vers la décharge. -He had then seen the author on the other side of the truck and that the author and the gunman had pursued the guard for some distance and then ran back towards the dump.

9552 **saturer** vb [satyʁe]
saturate
On sature du papier avec du sang que l'on laisse complètement sécher.
-The blood is allowed to saturate paper and then dry completely.

9553 **courber** vb [kuʁbe]
bend
Un point d' inflexion est le point où la trajectoire d' une courbe change brusquement de direction en formant un angle.

-At a corner point, the curve abruptly changes direction, thus forming a corner.

9554 **liane** **liana**
f
[ljan]
Coupez la liane le moment venu.
-When you see them in position, cut the vine.

9555 **gracieusement** **graciously|free of charge**
adv
[gʁasjøzmɑ̃]
De surcroît, des traitements antirétroviraux sont mis gracieusement à la disposition de toutes les personnes séropositives.
-In addition, antiretroviral treatment was available free of charge to all persons diagnosed with HIV/AIDS.

9556 **rétrograder** **demote|downgrade**
vb
[ʁetʁɔgʁade]
Par contre, envisager de bannir, par définition ou pour tout autre motif, les dons rémunérés revient à rétrograder.
-However, to even consider, by definition or otherwise, banning all products that come from remunerated donors is a retrograde step.

9557 **empailler** **stuff**
vb
[ɑ̃paje]
Ce serait pas plus simple de le faire empailler ?
-Wouldn't it be simpler if you had him stuffed?

9558 **solidement** **firmly**
adv
[sɔlidmɑ̃]
Les cannelures doivent être solidement collées aux feuilles de couverture.
-The fluting of corrugated fibreboard shall be firmly glued to the facings.

9559 **progressif** **progressive**
adj
[pʁɔgʁesif]
Nous voulons un démantèlement progressif des bureaux d'assistance technique.
-We want to see the gradual dismantling of the Technical Assistance Offices.

9560 **symétrie** **symmetry**
f
[simetʁi]
La symétrie établie entre droits et responsabilités garantit cette durabilité.
-The symmetry between rights and responsibilities ensures sustainability.

9561 **vacant** **vacant**
adj
[vakɑ̃]
Un poste vacant sera pourvu en 2001 et plusieurs questions restées en suspens seront alors traitées.
-Several pending issues will be attended to once a vacant post is filled in 2001.

9562 **nouba** **party**
f
[nuba]
Elle adore faire la nouba.
-She loves to party.

9563 **désintéresser** **pay off**
vb[dezɛ̃teʁese]
Cela n'a pas de sens d'imposer des conditions strictes au point de désintéresser tous les opérateurs de réseau. -There is no point in imposing conditions so stringent that all the network operators lose interest.

9564 **agrément** **approval**
m
[agʁemɑ̃]
Dans le dispositif proposé, cet agrément est indispensable.
-In the proposed scheme of things, such approval is indispensable.

9565 **consolider** **consolidate**
vb
[kɔ̃sɔlide]
Je pense que, sous cet angle, nous devrions consolider ce débat avec un vote du Parlement.
-I think that in this light we should consolidate this debate with a House vote.

9566 **assoupir** **dull**

	vb [asupiʁ]	Voilà pourquoi, Monsieur le Président, les peuples ne peuvent se permettre de s' assoupir. -That is why the people cannot afford to rest on their laurels.
9567	**réanimer** vb [ʁeanime]	**resuscitate** Le médecin, soucieux de le sauver, commence par le réanimer et à lui faire reprendre conscience. -The physician, anxious to save the patient's life, tries, as a first step, to resuscitate the patient and make him regain consciousness.
9568	**épineux** adj [epinø]	**thorny|tricky** Il s'agit malheureusement de l'un des problèmes les plus épineux au Kosovo. -Unfortunately, this continues to be one of the most complex problems in Kosovo.
9569	**asservir** vb [asɛʁviʁ]	**enslave** Nous n'allons pas nous laisser asservir par l'OTAN ni d'autres puissances étrangères. -We shall not allow ourselves to become enslaved to NATO or any other foreign power.
9570	**mocassin** m [mɔkasɛ̃]	**moccasin** Il est aussi méchant qu'un mocassin mais Sonny était la famille. -He is mean as a moccasin, but Sonny was kinfolk.
9571	**bouledogue** m [buldɔg]	**bulldog** Un cordonnier aveugle qui mâche un bouledogue. -A blind cobbler chewing on a bulldog.
9572	**digestif** adj [diʒɛstif]	**digestive** La fibrose kystique est une maladie héréditaire des appareils respiratoire et digestif. -Cystic fibrosis is a genetic disease affecting the respiratory and digestive systems.
9573	**espadon** m [ɛspadɔ̃]	**swordfish** Par ailleurs, la pêche à l'espadon s'intensifie dans l'océan Indien. -There is also intensification of fisheries targeting swordfish in the Indian Ocean.
9574	**adhésion** f [adezjɔ̃]	**membership** Les citoyens croates attendent beaucoup de cette adhésion. -The people of Croatia have great expectations of this membership.
9575	**siéger** vb[sjeʒe]	**sit** Le comité demande la permission de siéger cet après-midi et demain après-midi. -The committee is asking for leave to sit this afternoon and tomorrow afternoon.
9576	**pupitre** m [pypitʁ]	**desk** Promouvoir la Convention et parvenir à l'adhésion universelle demeure une priorité. -Promoting and achieving universal adherence to the Convention remain priorities.
9577	**ronflement** m [ʁɔ̃fləmɑ̃]	**snoring|roar** Et ton ronflement est si rythmé. -Plus, your snoring is so rhythmic.
9578	**déclenchement** m [deklɑ̃ʃmɑ̃]	**release** Le récepteur de diffusion reconnaît le type d'informations de déclenchement. -The broadcast receiver recognizes the type of the trigger information.

9579 **sermonner** **lecture|sermonize**
vb
[sɛʁmɔne]
L'honorable David Tkachuk : Honorables sénateurs, jeudi dernier, pendant la période des questions, le sénateur Mitchell a sermonné le leader du gouvernement au Sénat.
-David Tkachuk: Honourable senators, last Thursday during Question Period, Senator Mitchell admonished our Leader of the Government in the Senate.

9580 **plastic** **plastic explosive**
m
[plastik]
On injecte le premier matériau de plastic souple dans un moule.
-The flexible plastic material first injected into the mold.

9581 **discutable** **questionable|debatable**
adj
[diskytabl]
Secundo, la répartition des compétences entre les gouvernements nationaux et l'administration européenne par ligne d'action est discutable.
-Secondly, the distribution of powers between national authorities and the European authority according to line of action is arguable.

9582 **diagnostique** **diagnostic**
adj
[djagnɔstik]
Le Mexique a établi et publié en 2004 un Rapport diagnostique national sur le lindane.
-Mexico developed and published in 2004 a National Diagnostic Report on Lindane.

9583 **comptine** **nursery rhyme**
f
[kɔ̃tin]
On dirait une vieille comptine terrienne.
-It's like an Old Earth nursery rhyme sort of thing.

9584 **assimiler** **assimilate|absorb**
vb
[asimile]
Les tentatives pour assimiler et américaniser la population de Vieques doivent toutes cesser.
-Attempts to assimilate and Americanize the people of Vieques must cease.

9585 **embryon** **embryo**
m
[ɑ̃bʁijɔ̃]
Plus 50.000$ pour chaque embryon viable.
-On delivery, $50,000 more for each viable embryo.

9586 **entasser** **pile|pile up**
vb
[ɑ̃tase]
Les factures continuent à s'entasser.
-The bills keep piling up.

9587 **décomposer** **decompose**
vb[dekɔ̃poze]
Certains peuvent se décomposer en produisant une explosion, surtout sous confinement. -Some organic peroxides may decompose explosively, particularly if confined.

9588 **surgeler** **quick-freeze**
vb
[syʁʒəle]
Cette chambre est celle où nous entreposons le venin... pour le surgeler en cristaux... comme du café.
-This room here is where we store venom... and dry freeze it into crystals... just like coffee.

9589 **respirateur** **respirator**
m
[ʁɛspiʁatœʁ]
Gardez le respirateur jusqu'au dernier moment.
-All right, but save yourself the respirator till the last moment.

9590 **tournesol** **sunflower**
m
[tuʁnəsɔl]
Ces végétaux sont de préférence du colza et du tournesol.
-Preferred plants are rapeseed and sunflower plants.

9591 **imaginable** **imaginable**
adj
[imaʒinabl]
Il est tout à fait imaginable que d'autres groupes soient visés à l'avenir.
-It is quite conceivable that other groups of workers will be up for consideration.

9592 **écrémer** **skim|separate**
vb
[ekʁeme]
Ce projet de loi dit aux banques étrangères que les portes du Canada leur sont toutes grandes ouvertes et qu'elles peuvent venir écrémer notre marché.
-We are saying we are now open for business for foreign banks to come in and cream off the top of the market.

9593 **spoutnik** **sputnik**
m
[sputnik]
Spoutnik fut lancé le quatre octobre dix-neuf-cent-cinquante-sept.
-Sputnik was launched on October 4, 1957.

9594 **mobylette** **moped**
f
[mɔbilɛt]
Mon travail consistait à livrer des pizzas en mobylette.
-My work was to deliver pizza by motorcycle.

9595 **unifier** **unify|standardize**
vb
[ynifje]
Afin d'unifier la nomenclature des publications de la Commission des OPA au sens de l'art.
-In order to unify the nomenclature of the publications of the TOB in terms of Art.

9596 **triton** **triton|merman**
m
[tʁitɔ̃]
C'est comme tenir la main d'un triton.
-It's like holding hands with a merman.

9597 **stéréotype** **stereotype**
m
[steʁeɔtip]
Le rapport tout entier réaffirme le stéréotype de la femme au foyer.
-The stereotype of the woman as homemaker was reaffirmed throughout the report.

9598 **ciboire** **ciborium**
m
[sibwaʁ]
À Gilba Superiore, dans l'église St Sisto est sauvegardé un ciboire en pierre du 1590.
-In the district Gilba Superiore, in the church of Saint Sixtus, a ciborium made of stone from 1590 is conserved.

9599 **anorexique** **anorexic; anorexic**
adj; m/f[anɔʁɛksik]
Elle est anorexique. -She's anorexic.

9600 **hindi** **Hindi**
m
[indi]
She's the richest Hindi I know.
-C'est l'Hindoue la plus riche que je connaisse.

9601 **linguistique** **linguistic; linguistics**
adj; f
[lɛ̃gɥistik]
Les préjugés contre le Québec existent à cause de son intransigeance linguistique.
-The prejudices against Québec exist due to its linguistic intransigence.

9602 **erroné** **wrong|erroneous**
adj
[eʁɔne]
C'est absolument et totalement faux, erroné et trompeur.
-This is simply, completely, totally inaccurate, false, wrong and misleading.

9603 **idyllique** **idyllic**
adj
[idilik]
Ce tableau idyllique ne nous fait pas oublier que beaucoup reste à faire.
-This idyllic picture does not obscure the fact that much remains to be done.

9604 **hypothétique** **hypothetical**
adj
[ipɔtetik]
Elle renferme une question hypothétique dont le libellé est clairement hypothétique.
-It deals with a hypothetical question which is clearly stated in hypothetical terms.

9605 **catacombe** **catacomb**

f | Tu ne veux pas pourrir dans cette catacombe, non ?
[katakɔ̃b] | -You don't want to rot in this catacomb, do you?

9606 **lyrique** | **lyrical; lyric**
adj; f | Mais il a finalement plus d'affinités avec le groupe dit d'abstraction lyrique.
[liʁik] | -In the end, however, he found that he had more of an affinity with what was known as the Lyrical Abstraction group.

9607 **fiévreux** | **feverish|hectic**
adj | Le Conseil de sécurité et son travail suscitaient alors beaucoup d'intérêt fiévreux, mais nous y avons à peine accordé d'attention.
[fjevʁø] | -There was a lot of interest and excitement about the Security Council and its performance a few months ago, but we have barely taken note of it.

9608 **suave** | **sweet**
adj | Commit De Suave (CDS) (Comité d'information), composé d'ONG travaillant dans le domaine de l'environnement dans la région méditerranéenne.
[sɥav] | -Commit De Suave (CDS) (Information Committee), which consists of seven non-governmental organizations working in the field of environment in the Mediterranean region.

9609 **brouillon** | **draft; untidy**
m; adj | Merci de rédiger un brouillon de l'idée proposée.
[bʁujɔ̃] | -Please compose a draft of the proposal idea.

9610 **repassage** | **ironing**
m | L'élément de repassage préféré comporte une bande continue en acier inoxydable.
[ʁəpasaʒ] | -A preferred ironing element comprises a continuous stainless steel belt.

9611 **lacune** | **gap**
f | Cette lacune sera comblée par les radios communautaires.
[lakyn] | -This gap will be filled up by community ratio operations.

9612 **nette** | **clear|frank**
adj | Le rapport Giannakou représente une nette amélioration sur plusieurs points.
[nɛt] | -The Giannakou report represents a clear improvement on a number of points.

9613 **objectivité** | **objectivity**
f | Vous avez perdu toute objectivité concernant cette mission.
[ɔbʒɛktivite] | -You lost your objectivity as it related to this assignment.

9614 **rajah** | **rajah**
m | Son mari était un rajah extrêmement influent.
[ʁaʒa] | -Her husband was a rajah and very influential.

9615 **souillon** | **slut|slob**
m | Ça vient sûrement de ta souillon de sœur.
[sujɔ̃] | -I probably got it from your dirty little sister.

9616 **répartir** | **allocate|divide**
vb | Le temps n'est pas venu de répartir les responsabilités ou d'accuser qui que ce soit.
[ʁepaʁtiʁ] | -Now is not the time to apportion blame or to point fingers.

9617 **débiter** | **debit|cut**
vb | Vous autorisez eBay à débiter les frais de vente de votre compte.
[debite] | -You authorize eBay to debit your account for selling fees.

9618 **tandem** | **tandem**

	m	C'est une tâche à laquelle il faut s'atteler en tandem avec les institutions.
	[tɑ̃dɛm]	-This is a task that must be tackled in tandem with the institutions.
9619	**chroniqueur**	**chronicler|journalist**
	m	Il est présentement chroniqueur à la radio de Radio-Canada sur les affaires municipales à Ottawa.
	[kʁɔnikœʁ]	-He is currently a regular radio columnist on municipal affairs in Ottawa for Radio-Canada.
9620	**animalerie**	**pet shop**
	f	Trent et moi possédions une animalerie.
	[animalʁi]	-Well, Trent and I owned a pet store.
9621	**aliénation**	**alienation**
	f	Elle conduit à un sentiment d'aliénation, de désillusion et d'impuissance.
	[aljenasjɔ̃]	-It leads to alienation, a sense of disenfranchisement, and feelings of powerlessness.
9622	**extorquer**	**extort|exact**
	vb	Le recours à la torture et aux mauvais traitements pour extorquer des aveux est largement répandu.
	[ɛkstɔʁke]	-The use of torture and ill-treatment to extract confessions is widely reported.
9623	**ahurir**	**astound**
	vb	Je suis, à vrai dire, quelque peu ahuri.
	[ayʁiʁ]	-I feel a little astounded.
9624	**remake**	**remake**
	m	On dirait que tu joues dans un remake albanais du Cosby show.
	[ʁəmak]	-You look like you're starring in an Albanian remake of the Cosby show.
9625	**totem**	**totem**
	m	C'est un totem de guérison.
	[tɔtɛm]	-It is a totem of healing.
9626	**enclume**	**anvil**
	f	Il nage comme une enclume.
	[ɑ̃klym]	-He swims like an anvil.
9627	**frusques**	**thread**
	msf	C'est celui qui boxe, avec les belles frusques.
	[fʁysk]	-That's him there, fighting in those fancy threads.
9628	**bique**	**nanny-goat**
	f	Alors vieille bique, veux-tu me dire mon...
	[bik]	-Now, you old goat, why don't you tell me my...
9629	**panser**	**dress**
	vb	Le reste de ce qu'il propose consiste à panser les plaies causées par ce choix.
	[pɑ̃se]	-The remainder of his proposals serve to dress the wounds that this option will cause.
9630	**gifle**	**slap|cuff**
	f	Voilà le compliment et bientôt la gifle.
	[ʒifl]	-There's the compliment, here comes the slap.
9631	**pointilleux**	**punctilious**
	adj	Les interventions pointilleuses du législateur dans les divers moyens ne servent qu'à épuiser les organisations en question.
	[pwɛ̃tijø]	-The legislator's pernickety interference in the ways and means only serves to exhaust the organisations in question.
9632	**tutoyer**	**tutoyer**

vb
[tytwaje]
Excuse-moi, j'aimerais te tutoyer.
-Excuse me, but I want to speak to you informally.

9633 **cancan** **cancan|dirt**
m
[kɑ̃kɑ̃]
Un french cancan, avec Gwen Verdon.
-The cancan, danced by Gwen Verdon and company.

9634 **plant** **plant|seedling**
m
[plɑ̃]
Consigner le nombre de criocères adultes et de larves trouvés sur chaque plant.
-Record the number of beetles and larvae found per plant.

9635 **arête** **arete**
f
[aʁɛt]
J'ai une arête coincée dans ma gorge.
-I got a fish bone stuck in my throat.

9636 **chloroforme** **chloroform**
m
[klɔʁɔfɔʁm]
L'odeur du chloroforme m'endort.
-The smell of that chloroform's putting me to sleep.

9637 **ardu** **difficult|arduous**
adj
[aʁdy]
C'est pourquoi, à mes yeux, aussi ardu et épineux que soit ce cycle, nous ne devons surtout pas abandonner, et nous n'abandonnerons pas.
-That is why, in my view, however taxing and however vexing this round is, we certainly should not give up, and nor will we.

9638 **cireur** **polisher**
m
[siʁœʁ]
Le cireur! Vous m'entendez?
-Shine man, you can't hear me?

9639 **bouillonner** **bubble|boil**
vb
[bujɔne]
Chaque bulle se met à bouillonner.
-Every bubble starts to bubble.

9640 **palette** **palette|paddle**
f[palɛt]
Je vais chercher la palette derrière. -I'll bring the pallet from the back.

9641 **oppresseur** **oppressor**
m
[ɔpʁesœʁ]
Ma première action alors que j'étais un oppresseur colonial a été d'abolir la peine capitale à Hong Kong !
-The first act that I carried out when I was a colonial oppressor was to abolish capital punishment in Hong Kong!

9642 **hennissement** **neigh**
m
[enismɑ̃]
Vous pensiez que Méchant Cheval n'a pas travaillé sur son hennissement.
-Did you think Bad Horse didn't work on his neigh?

9643 **utilisable** **usable|serviceable**
adj
[ytilizabl]
Vous devrez ensuite paramétrer chaque commande utilisable.
-Then you will have to setup every usable command.

9644 **tantinet** **mite**
m
[tɑ̃tinɛ]
Oui, un tantinet.
-Yes, a little bit.

9645 **médiéval** **medieval**
adj
[medjeval]
Je serais comme un bélier médiéval.
-I'd be like a medieval battering ram.

9646 **finlandais** **Finnish**
adj
[fɛ̃lɑ̃dɛ]
Les Finlandais participent activement à la coopération internationale pour le déminage.
-The Finns are involved in international cooperation with regard to mine clearance.

9647 **brisant** **breaking; breaker**

adj; m
[bʁizɑ̃]
Se décomposant, s'étouffant, se brisant sous son propre poids.
-Convulsing. Choking. Breaking under its own weight.

9648 **sursaut** **start|spurt**
m
[syʁso]
Nous l'appelons à un sursaut de courage.
-We call on it for a burst of courage.

9649 **inopportun** **inappropriate**
adj
[inɔpɔʁtɛ̃]
Je trouve également inopportun de citer deux dirigeants de partis d'extrêmedroite.
-I also find it inappropriate to cite the leaders of the two parties of the far right.

9650 **surexciter** **overexcite**
vb
[syʁɛksite]
Les circuits peuvent surexciter la structure de commande afin d'induire l'état souhaité de formation de canal.
-The circuits may overdrive the control structure to induce the desired state of channel information.

9651 **dragueur** **dredger|player**
m
[dʁagœʁ]
Ce dragueur a eu ce qu'il méritait.
-That player got what he deserved.

9652 **rétention** **retention**
f
[ʁetɑ̃sjɔ̃]
Cette période de rétention doit être prévue par règlement.
-The period of the retention is to be prescribed by regulation.

9653 **salarié** **salaried; wage earner**
adj; m
[salaʁje]
L'homme responsable est un salarié rival dans la société de Mr Morolto.
-The man responsible is a rival employee in Mr. Morolto's company.

9654 **dansant** **dancing**
adj[dɑ̃sɑ̃]
Les jeunes veulent voyager et danser, mais les personnes âgées aussi veulent voyager et danser. -Young people want to travel and dance, but old people also want to travel and dance.

9655 **contagion** **contagion**
f
[kɔ̃taʒjɔ̃]
Charlotte devrait pouvoir créer un vaccin contre la contagion.
-Charlotte might be able to create a vaccine against the contagion.

9656 **toscan** **Tuscan**
adj
[tɔskɑ̃]
Il a exprimé la gratitude du LWG au Gouvernement toscan et à l'Electronic Commerce Platform Netherlands (ECP.NL), qui ont financé la participation du secrétariat.
-He expressed the gratitude of the LWG to the Government of Tuscany and to the Electronic Commerce Platform Netherlands (ECP.NL) for financing the participation of the secretariat.

9657 **vestimentaire** **dress|clothing**
adj
[vɛstimɑ̃tɛʁ]
Il n'y a pas de code vestimentaire.
-There is no dress code.

9658 **ambigu** **ambiguous**
adj
[ɑ̃bigy]
Nous sommes tous soucieux des perspectives nées de ce phénomène complexe et ambigu.
-We are all concerned about the prospects of this complex and ambiguous phenomenon.

9659 **inflammation** **inflammation**
f
[ɛ̃flamasjɔ̃]
Mon médecin a dit que cette inflammation de la gorge est une infection à streptocoques.
-My doctor said that this sore throat is a streptococcal infection.

9660 **pédagogique** **educational|pedagogical**

	adj [pedagɔʒik]	Le programme comporte à la fois la formation pédagogique et celle des praticiens. -The programme includes both training of trainers and training of practitioners.
9661	**alliage**	**alloy|mixture**
	m [aljaʒ]	Cet alliage est particulièrement adapté comme matériau de machines automatiques. -The inventive alloy is particularly useful as a material for automatic devices.
9662	**obtempérer**	**obey**
	vb [ɔptɑ̃peʁe]	Comme il refusait d'obtempérer, le personnel a utilisé l'aérosol et l'a menotté. -As he refused to comply, the spray was used and he was placed in handcuffs.
9663	**relativité**	**relativity**
	f [ʁəlativite]	Einstein décrivit l'intrication quantique comme une « effrayante action à distance ». Avant la théorie générale de la relativité d'Einstein, la théorie de la gravitation de Newton aurait pu être qualifiée de même . -Einstein described quantum entanglement as "spooky action at a distance." So, before Einstein's own Theory of General Relativity, might Newton's theory of gravitation have been described.
9664	**communément**	**commonly**
	adv[kɔmynemɑ̃]	On recourt communément aux châtiments corporels pour discipliner les enfants. -Corporal punishment is commonly practised to discipline children.
9665	**glucose**	**glucose**
	m [glykoz]	On décrit également des capsules contenant des cellules sensibles au glucose et des électrodes destinées à détecter l'activité électrique. -Capsules containing glucose sensitive cells and electrodes for detecting electrical activity are also disclosed.
9666	**rotule**	**patella**
	f [ʁɔtyl]	Le segment à rotule est relié pivotant à l'élastomère. -The ball segment is rotatably coupled to the elastomer.
9667	**campeur**	**camper**
	m [kɑ̃pœʁ]	Je veux ce campeur déchiré, recherches de cavité complètes tout autour. -I want that camper torn apart, full cavity searches all around.
9668	**futuriste**	**futuristic; futurist**
	adj; m/f [fytyʁist]	Je ne voudrais pas conclure par une note trop futuriste. -I do not wish to end on too futuristic a note.
9669	**iranien**	**Iranian; Iranian**
	adj; m [iʁanjɛ̃]	Le programme nucléaire iranien vient de faire l'objet d'une attaque par un logiciel malveillant. -The Iranian nuclear program has just been attacked by malware.
9670	**hurleur**	**howler|squealer**
	m [yʁlœʁ]	Il y a un noueau type de hurleur. -We've got a new kind of screamer.
9671	**fausser**	**distort|skew**
	vb [fose]	Je vous en citerai deux exemples: Les appareils servant à fausser les cartes de crédit, on peut se les procurer librement sur le marché sans qu'aucune licence ne soit requise. -The equipments one needs to counterfeit credit cards can be obtained freely on the open market without a licence.
9672	**activiste**	**activist; smart**

m/f; adj
[aktivist]

Simone Reyes, activiste en droit des animaux.
-Simone Reyes, animal rights activist, as well, that works with Russell Si.

9673 **stoppeur** **stopper**
m
[stɔpœʁ]
Le stoppeur est revetu de preference avec un lubrifiant au silicone.
-The stopper is preferably coated with a ilicone lubricant.

9674 **syntaxe** **syntax**
f
[sɛ̃taks]
La syntaxe à employer dépend du système de base de données que vous utilisez.
-The syntax used depends on the database system you are using.

9675 **malveillance** **malice|malignancy**
f
[malvɛjɑ̃s]
Les références aux résolutions du Conseil de sécurité et aux projets de résolution de la Troisième Commission témoignent d'une politisation et une malveillance délibérées.
-Making references to the Security Council and to draft resolutions of the Third Committee indicated politicization and deliberate ill will.

9676 **notable** **notable|worthy; worthy**
adj; m
[nɔtabl]
Notre siècle a vu un accroissement notable de la somme des connaissances.
-Our century has seen a notable increase of knowledge.

9677 **agitateur** **agitator**
m
[aʒitatœʁ]
On peut prévoir un agitateur mécanique du liquide.
-A mechanical agitator of the liquid may also be included.

9678 **profaner** **defile**
vb
[pʁɔfane]
C'était une armée partant profaner Bethlehem, la ville de notre Seigneur.
-But an army had it for better handle to desecrate the birth place of our lord!

9679 **incorporer** **mix|weave**
vb
[ɛ̃kɔʁpɔʁe]
Un SDV peut être combiné avec d'autres systèmes du véhicule ou y être incorporé.
-A VDS may be combined with other vehicle systems or may be integrated into them.

9680 **glissade** **slip|slide**
f
[glisad]
Je viens de nous imaginer dans une glissade d'eau.
-I just got a flash of us together on a water slide.

9681 **plaisantin** **joker; bantering**
m; adj
[plɛzɑ̃tɛ̃]
Alors, quel est le plaisantin?
-All right, who was the joker?

9682 **huis** **door**
m
[ɥi]
Le procès se tient à huis clos.
-The trial is not open to the public.

9683 **arriviste** **pushy; go-getter**
adj; m/f
[aʁivist]
Elle n'a pas l'air d'une arriviste.
-She doesn't look that pushy.

9684 **boutonneux** **spotty**
adj
[butɔnø]
C'est un informaticien boutonneux.
-He's a pimply computer nerd.

9685 **recel** **concealment**
f
[ʁəsɛl]
Le recel lié à l'enrichissement illicite est également incriminé.
-The concealment of such illicit enrichment is also made a crime.

9686 **affranchir** **enfranchise|frank**
vb
[afʁɑ̃ʃiʁ]
Ce dialogue doit enfin savoir s'affranchir de toute intervention politique.
-Lastly, this dialogue should be free from all political involvement.

9687 **cribler** **sift|riddle**
vb
[kʁible]
Le réacteur parallèle est utilisé pour synthétiser et/ou cribler plusieurs composés ou matières en même temps.
-The parallel reactor is used to synthesize and/or screen multiple compounds or materials at the same time.

9688 **pichet** **pitcher**
m
[piʃɛ]
On a tout le pichet ici.
-We have the whole pitcher right here.

9689 **abnégation** **denial|self-sacrifice**
f
[abnegasjɔ̃]
Dans le même temps la CNUCED pratique une sorte d'abnégation en termes d'impact.
-Meanwhile, UNCTAD has chosen an approach of self-sacrifice with respect to impact.

9690 **estomper** **blur**
vb[ɛstɔ̃pe]
Le Conseil estime qu'il sera dommageable de tendre à mélanger et à estomper les responsabilités. -The Council is against anything that would tend to confuse or blur the different responsibilities.

9691 **poireau** **leek**
m
[pwaʁo]
Cette invention concerne des plantes de poireau à stérilité mâle dominante codées dans le noyau.
-The present invention is directed to nuclear encoded dominant male sterile leek plants.

9692 **bamboula** **negro; tamboula**
m; f
[bɑ̃bula]
Dieu sait quelle merde vit dans le cul d'un bamboula des dunes.
-Lord knows what vermin live in the butt of a dune coon.

9693 **prononciation** **pronunciation**
f
[pʁɔnɔ̃sjasjɔ̃]
Ne soyez pas intimidé. Votre prononciation est plus ou moins correcte.
-Do not be shy. Your pronunciation is more or less correct.

9694 **marmonner** **mumble**
vb
[maʁmɔne]
Vous voyez, vous n'avez rien d'autre à marmonner que "paix".
-You see, you are incapable of doing anything except mumbling 'peace'.

9695 **désarmement** **disarmament**
m
[dezaʁməmɑ̃]
L'Union européenne devrait profiter de cette nouvelle opportunité de désarmement.
-The European Union ought to take advantage of this new opportunity for disarmament.

9696 **exclamation** **exclamation**
f
[ɛksklamasjɔ̃]
Cette phrase se termine par un point d'exclamation !
-This sentence ends with an exclamation mark!

9697 **vaillance** **valour**
f
[vajɑ̃s]
Ces récits témoignent d'une vaillance et d'une persévérance hors du commun.
-These stories bear witness to their extraordinary valour and perseverance.

9698 **satyre** **Satyr**
m
[satiʁ]
Voilà pourquoi il lui faut un satyre.
-That's why he needs a satyr.

9699 **énigmatique** **enigmatic**
adj
[enigmatik]
C'est un processus tellement archaïque et énigmatique qu'il défie toute logique et toute raison.
-Its design is so archaic and cryptic that it defies logic and reason.

9700 **fifre** **fife**

m
[fifʁ]

Les marionnettes, en plus de parler, exécutent des pas de danse au son d'un violon, d'un tambour et exceptionnellement d'un fifre.
-In addition to speaking, the puppets did little dances accompanied by a violin, a drum, and occasionally a fife.

9701 **timonier**
m
[timɔnje]
helmsman
Le timonier est affecté à la veille.
-The helmsman is assigned to watch duty.

9702 **transpiration**
f
[tʁɑ̃spiʁasjɔ̃]
transpiration
Pour le dire clairement : l'odeur de ta transpiration est abominable.
-To put it bluntly, your sweat smells awful.

9703 **bougeotte**
f[buʒɔt]
wanderlust
Au bout d'un moment, j'attrape la bougeotte. -After a while, I get itchy feet.

9704 **dégagement**
m
[degaʒmɑ̃]
clearance|disengagement
Le dégagement du dioxyde de carbone cause ces bulles.
-The release of carbon dioxide gas is what causes the bubbling of it.

9705 **panne**
f
[pan]
breakdown
À l'avenir, cette responsabilité n'incombera aux usagers qu'en cas de panne du système.
-In future, users would have this responsibility only in case of a system breakdown.

9706 **pétunia**
m
[petynja]
petunia
J'ai dû les récurer avec de l'essence de pétunia.
-I had to scrub them with essence of petunia.

9707 **surmener**
vb
[syʁməne]
overwork
C' est presque devenu une tradition de surmener les médecins et les infirmiers, mais un personnel fatigué, stressé, est bien plus exposé aux risques.
-It is almost a tradition to overwork doctors and nurses, but tired, stressed staff are far more prone to dangers.

9708 **sangle**
f
[sɑ̃gl]
strap
Un récepteur portatif comprend une antenne sous forme de sangle.
-A portable receiver which has a strap antenna.

9709 **saphir**
m
[safiʁ]
sapphire
On peut former le substrat dans un cristal à saphir.
-The substrate may be formed of a sapphire crystal.

9710 **substitution**
f
[sypstitysjɔ̃]
substitution
Attention: cette substitution arrivera seulement et exclusivement une fois.
-Pay attention: this substitution will occur only and exclusively one time.

9711 **extraordinairement**
adv
[ɛkstʁaɔʁdinɛʁmɑ̃]
extraordinarily
Je reconnais aussi que la situation est extraordinairement délicate et triste.
-I also acknowledge that this is an extraordinarily difficult and sad situation.

9712 **réélection**
f
[ʁeelɛksjɔ̃]
re-election
Je remercie les gens des quatre coins du Canada qui ont appuyé généreusement ma réélection.
-I want to thank people from across the country who have generously supported my re-election.

9713 **ortie**
f
[ɔʁti]
nettle
Cette composition peut en outre contenir d'autres composants, tels que la grande ortie et Boswellia serrata.

-The composition may further contain other components including stinging nettle, and Boswellia serrata.

9714 **harmonieux** **harmonious**
adj
[aʁmɔnjø]
Sans cela le développement harmonieux du monde contemporain est impossible.
-Without this, the harmonious development of the modern world is impossible.

9715 **retouche** **retouch**
f[ʁətuʃ]
Le Studio Fahrenheit propose en outre des services photographiques, l'élaboration d'images et la retouche numérique. -Other services offered by Studio Fahrenheit include photography, image processing and digital retouching.

9716 **frénétique** **frantic**
adj
[fʁenetik]
J'étais frénétique, comme tous les autres.
-I was frantic, like everyone else.

9717 **courbette** **bowing**
f
[kuʁbɛt]
J'aurais bien fait une courbette mais mon carquois est plutôt tendu.
-I'd bow but this quiver's rather tight.

9718 **tendon** **tendon**
m
[tɑ̃dɔ̃]
J'ai été capable de relâcher le tendon.
-I was able to do the tendon release.

9719 **profiteur** **profiteer**
m
[pʁɔfitœʁ]
Que j'étais un profiteur de guerre.
-He knew that I was a war profiteer.

9720 **infusion** **infusion**
f
[ɛ̃fyzjɔ̃]
Cette approche est appelée infusion.
-This approach is called infusion.

9721 **réceptif** **receptive**
adj
[ʁesɛptif]
Le RUF se montre généralement réceptif à la question de la Commission.
-In general, RUF appears receptive to the Truth and Reconciliation Commission.

9722 **jugulaire** **jugular; chinstrap**
adj; f
[ʒygylɛʁ]
La balle est passée à trois mm de la jugulaire.
-The bullet missed your jugular by about three millimetres.

9723 **éponge** **sponge**
f
[epɔ̃ʒ]
Je vais chercher une éponge pour nettoyer.
-OK, OK. I'll get a sponge and start cleaning up.

9724 **braconnier** **poacher**
m
[bʁakɔnje]
Menée par un célèbre braconnier connu sous le nom de Morgan, les attaquants ont incendié les locaux et détruits le matériel.
-Led by the notorious elephant poacher known as Morgan, the attackers torched buildings and destroyed equipment.

9725 **juron** **oath|profanity**
m
[ʒyʁɔ̃]
Et dissipez-vous comme un juron bohémien, Je vous dit...
-And banished like a gypsy's cuss, I say to thee...

9726 **garagiste** **mechanic**
m/f
[gaʁaʒist]
La mamie se faisait arnaquer par son garagiste.
-That old woman was being scammed by her mechanic.

9727 **pieuter** **sleep**
vb
[pjœte]
Je sortais d'une sale affaire et j'allais me pieuter.
-I had just finished a tough case. I was ready to hit the sack.

9728 **marmelade**
f
[maʁməlad]
marmelade
J'aime manger de la marmelade.
-I like eating marmalade.

9729 **surveillant**
m[syʁvɛjɑ̃]
supervisor
Son professeur l'a envoyé au bureau du surveillant général pour avoir été en retard trop de fois. -His teacher sent him to the principal's office for being tardy too many times.

9730 **marxiste**
m/f
[maʁksist]
Marxist
Je suis un marxiste tendance Groucho.
-I'm a Marxist of the Groucho tendency.

9731 **corniaud**
m; m
[kɔʁnjo]
mutt; analogy
Je pleurais d'avoir perdu ce pauvre corniaud blanc.
-I was crying over losing that big, white mutt.

9732 **virtuellement**
adv
[viʁtɥɛlmɑ̃]
virtually
Il s'agit du type de fouille le plus indiscret et, virtuellement, le plus dégradant.
-This is the most intrusive and potentially most degrading form of search.

9733 **individualité**
f
[ɛ̃dividɥalite]
individuality
Un zombi a plus d'individualité.
-I mean, I've seen zombies with more individuality.

9734 **indisponible**
adj
[ɛ̃dispɔnibl]
unavailable
La restitution, malgré sa primauté sur le plan des principes juridiques, est souvent indisponible ou inadaptée.
-Restitution, despite its primacy as a matter of legal principle, is frequently unavailable or inadequate.

9735 **chimiothérapie**
f
[ʃimjɔteʁapi]
chemotherapy
Chimiothérapie et radiothérapie remboursées à 100 %.
-Chemotherapy, radiotherapy reimbursed at 100 per cent.

9736 **multinational**
adj
[myltinasjɔnal]
multinational
Ma deuxième remarque concerne la durée du mandat de la force multinationale.
-My second point pertains to the duration of the mandate of the multinational force.

9737 **démanteler**
vb
[demɑ̃tle]
dismantle
Il est indispensable de maîtriser et de démanteler ces sources de financement.
-It is essential to take control of and dismantle such sources of financing.

9738 **galon**
m
[galɔ̃]
braid|stripe
Un galon or souligne la naissance du cou deux galons or parallèles encerclent le poignet.
-A gold stripe emphasizes the start of the neck, two parallel gold stripes encircle the waist.

9739 **sympathisant**
m
[sɛ̃patizɑ̃]
sympathizer
Gouvernement tourne autour et l'appelle un sympathisant communiste.
-Government turns around and calls him a Communist sympathizer.

9740 **tanguer**
vb
[tɑ̃ge]
pitch|sway
J'ai vraiment essayé de ne pas faire tanguer le bateau.
-I've tried really hard not to rock the boat.

9741 **assortiment**
assortment

	m [asɔʁtimɑ̃]	Nos partenaires turcs ont sous les yeux un assortiment de mauvais exemples. -Our Turkish partners are confronted with an assortment of bad examples.
9742	**superbement**	**magnificently**
	adv [sypɛʁbəmɑ̃]	Ils sont superbement écrits, M. Cafferty. -They're beautifully written, Mr. Cafferty.
9743	**galipette**	**somersault**
	f [galipɛt]	La vérité se résume à quatre restos chinois et une galipette. -The truth is, it came down to 4 Chinese meals and a roll in the hay.
9744	**joute**	**joust**
	f [ʒut]	M. Modeste a gagnè la joute d'hier. -Mr. Modesty won the joust last night.
9745	**essouffler**	**make breathless**
	vb [esufle]	Ce n'est donc pas le moment de s'essouffler ou de baisser les bras. -This, therefore, is not the time to run out of steam or to throw in the towel.
9746	**pommette**	**cheekbone**
	f [pɔmɛt]	L'examen physique révèle des hématomes sur le cuir chevelu, sur la pommette gauche, sur les lèvres supérieure et inférieure et dans la région nasale au niveau de la narine gauche. -On physical examination he displays haematoma on the scalp, haematomas on the left cheekbone, on the upper and lower lips and in the nasal region at the left ala.
9747	**snobisme**	**snobbery**
	m [snɔbism]	Ton snobisme t'empêche de voir les gens en bien. -Your snobbery stops you seeing anything good about anybody.
9748	**rejeton**	**offshoot|kid**
	m [ʁʒətɔ̃]	En amenant son rejeton chez nous. -Yet you bring her offspring into our home.
9749	**plomber**	**seal**
	vb [plɔ̃be]	L'Administration peut neutraliser ces dispositifs en les faisant plomber. -The Administration may put these devices out of action by sealing.
9750	**succursale**	**branch**
	f [sykyʁsal]	Envoie la photo à chaque succursale. -Eric, we need to get the photograph to every branch.
9751	**gribouillis**	**scrawl**
	m [gʁibuji]	Daniel, je pense que c'est beaucoup de foie pour un gribouillis dans un carnet. -Daniel, I feel like that's a lot of faith to put in a scribble in a notebook.
9752	**statuette**	**small statue**
	f [statɥɛt]	Une statuette de bronze représentant un homme du Sud-Est asiatique jouant d'un instrument de musique. -One bronze statuette of a south-east Asian man playing a musical instrument.
9753	**exode**	**exodus**
	m [ɛgzɔd]	Les derniers chiffres de l'exode massif de la population kosovare sont terrifiants. -The latest figures on the massive exodus of the Kosovar population are terrifying.
9754	**broncher**	**stumble**

	vb[bʁɔ̃ʃe]	Il est absolument inconcevable et inacceptable que des parlementaires laissent faire pareille chose sans broncher. -It is absolutely unconscionable and unacceptable for parliamentarians to stand by and let this happen.
9755	**inhibition**	**inhibition**
	f [inibisjɔ̃]	L'inhibition peut être constatée de plusieurs manières. -The inhibition may be evidenced in a number of ways.
9756	**têtard**	**tadpole**
	m [tetaʁ]	Une comète est comme un têtard. -A comet looks like a tadpole.
9757	**perfidie**	**perfidy**
	f [pɛʁfidi]	Eh bien, leur perfidie rend cela pratiquement impossible. -Well, their perfidy makes that course all but impossible.
9758	**accolade**	**hug|accolade**
	f [akɔlad]	Vous n'êtes pas obligés de leur donner l'accolade. -You do not have to hug them.
9759	**abordable**	**affordable**
	adj [abɔʁdabl]	Avant tout, la contraception doit être abordable et socialement acceptable. -Above all, contraception must be affordable and socially acceptable.
9760	**remorqueur**	**tug**
	m [ʁəmɔʁkœʁ]	Les remorqueurs sont opérés par un capitaine remorqueur. -The tugs are operated by a tug master.
9761	**contour**	**contour|outline**
	m [kɔ̃tuʁ]	Le symbole Contour vous permet d' activer et désactiver les contours de l' objet actuel. -Click Contour to activate or deactivate the object's contour line.
9762	**dépeindre**	**depict**
	vb [depɛ̃dʁ]	Doit-il descendre si bas et dépeindre les étudiants protestataires comme des bourreaux ? -Must he stoop so low and depict protesting students as violent?
9763	**gargouiller**	**gurgle**
	vb [gaʁguje]	Nous ferions mieux de rester ici à écouter mon estomac gargouiller. -Beats sitting around here listening to my stomach growl.
9764	**ébriété**	**intoxication**
	f [ebʁijete]	Appliquez-vous à votre ébriété et elle sera moins pitoyable. -Try harder with your drunkenness and you won't be so terrible at it.
9765	**liège**	**cork**
	m [ljɛʒ]	Qu'il retourne humer la bonne odeur du liège. -He should go back to the office and smell some more cork.
9766	**discerner**	**discern|detect**
	vb [disɛʁne]	On a quand même du mal à discerner le niveau de contribution du CCR. -However, it is difficult to discern the level of the RCF contribution.
9767	**apaisant**	**soothing**
	adj [apɛzɑ̃]	Sur ce point, le paragraphe 12 de la résolution est particulièrement apaisant et donc inacceptable. -Paragraph 12 of the resolution, therefore, is particularly appeasing in this respect and unacceptable.
9768	**gérant**	**manager; managing**
	m; adj [ʒeʁɑ̃]	Je veux parler à votre gérant. -I want to talk to your manager.
9769	**contrecarrer**	**thwart|oppose**

	vb [kɔ̃tʁəkaʁe]	Les gouvernements ne doivent pas penser qu'ils sont les seuls à pouvoir contrecarrer l'accord. -The governments should not think that the deal can be thwarted only from their end.
9770	**attester** vb [atɛste]	**certify|attest** Des millions de personnes dans le monde peuvent l'attester. -Millions of people in the world can testify to this.
9771	**sursauter** vb [syʁsote]	**jump up** L'adjectif va faire sursauter M. Lamy!... -The adjective is one that will make Mr Lamy jump with fright!
9772	**compresser** vb [kɔ̃pʁese]	**compress** S'il y a lieu de compresser le fichier, le programme à utiliser pour ce faire est WinZip. -Should it be necessary to compress the file, the Winzip program should be used.
9773	**adorateur** m; adj [adɔʁatœʁ]	**adorer; worshipful** Comme sa mère, Al-Drifa devint un fervent adorateur de Neutra. -Like his mother, Al-Drifa became a fervent worshipper of Neutra.
9774	**blême** adj [blɛm]	**pale** Il devint blême de peur. -He turned pale with fright.
9775	**calepin** m [kalpɛ̃]	**notebook** Il a sorti un calepin. -He took a notebook out.
9776	**soudure** f [sudyʁ]	**welding** Réaliser une belle soudure n'est pas à la portée de tout le monde ! -Achieving a nice weld bead is not within everyone's reach!
9777	**arbitrage** m; adj [aʁbitʁaʒ]	**arbitrage; arbitral** Tout différend syndical-patronal sera ensuite réglé par arbitrage des propositions finales. -Then, any outstanding settlement differences would be settled by final offer arbitration.
9778	**conjonction** f [kɔ̃ʒɔ̃ksjɔ̃]	**conjunction** Ces tendances se poursuivront en conjonction avec la mondialisation. -Those trends will continue in conjunction with globalization.
9779	**potiron** m [pɔtiʁɔ̃]	**pumpkin** Marshall, voici votre lait potiron. -Marshall, here's your pumpkin latte.
9780	**arsenic** adj; m [aʁsənik]	**arsenic; arsenic** Arsenic (black or metallic); arsenic (white or arsenic anhydride, also alled arsenic trioxide) 31. -Arsenic noir ou métallique, arsenic blanc (anhydride arsénieux ou trioxyde d'arsenic)
9781	**cagibi** m [kaʒibi]	**storage room|cupboard** Jenna t'attend dans le cagibi. -Jenna's waiting for you in the broom cupboard.
9782	**calcaire** m; adj [kalkɛʁ]	**limestone; calcareous** La roche est composée de calcaire et de cormalite. -The rocks are composed of limestone and cormalite.
9783	**grillon**	**cricket**

m
[gʁijɔ̃]
Je serai aussi silencieux qu'un grillon.
-I'll be as quiet as a cricket.

9784 **thaïlandais**
adj; mpl
[tailɑ̃dɛ]
Thai
Le droit thaïlandais dit clairement que les enfants reçoivent la nationalité thaïlandaise.
-Thai law clearly stated that the children were granted Thai citizenship.

9785 **expiation**
f
[ɛkspjasjɔ̃]
atonement
L'expiation représente depuis lors une composante décisive de l'identité allemande.
-Atonement has been a defining element of German identity ever since.

9786 **thriller**
m
[tʁije]
thriller
Cela ressemble à un scénario de thriller, mais ce n'est pas un film, c'est la réalité, et cela fait partie de la vie quotidienne au Guatemala.
-This really sounds like a thriller screenplay, but it is not just a movie, it is life, and part of the pattern of everyday life in Guatemala.

9787 **septique**
adj
[sɛptik]
septic
La plupart des foyers urbains disposent de toilettes, avec fosse septique ou chasse d'eau.
-Most urban households have access to toilet facilities, either septic systems, or pour flush.

9788 **ricaner**
vb
[ʁikane]
sneer
Il y a une citation du hansard qui la fait rire et ricaner lorqu'on l'interroge à la Chambre.
-There is a quote in Hansard which she laughs and sneers at when she is questioned in the House.

9789 **aménagement**
m
[amenaʒmɑ̃]
planning
Toute demande de concession aquacole doit être accompagnée d'un plan d'aménagement quinquennal.
-A five-year development plan must be submitted together with the application for a concession.

9790 **conque**
f
[kɔ̃k]
conch
La conque compte ici et partout dans l'île.
-The conch counts here and all over the island.

9791 **ombilical**
adj
[ɔ̃bilikal]
umbilical
Êtes-vous disposée à couper le cordon ombilical entre le sport et l'activité professionnelle ?
-Are you willing to cut the umbilical cord between sport and professional activity?

9792 **psychédélique**
adj
[psiʃedelik]
psychedelic
La boisson psychédélique qui te fais vomir constamment ?
-Is that the psychedelic drink that makes you constantly vomit?

9793 **cellulite**
f
[selylit]
cellulite
Il est déjà plein de cellulite.
-He's already got a bunch of cellulite.

9794 **godemiché**
m
[gɔdmiʃe]
dildo
Alors utilise un godemiché, Vanessa.
-Yeah, well, use a dildo, Vanessa.

9795 **survêtement**
m[syʁvɛtmɑ̃]
track suit
Très bien, mais je porte ces pantalons de survêtement. -Fine, but I'm wearing these sweatpants.

9796 **pubien**
pubic

adj [pybjɛ̃] Je suis très fier de ma crinière pubienne, merci.
-I'm very proud of my mane of pubic hair, so thank you.

9797 **walkman** **walkman**
m [walkmɑ̃] Mon walkman et l'argent d'Osvaldo ont disparu.
-My walkman and Osvaldo's money are missing!

9798 **apartheid** **apartheid**
f [apaʁtɛd] Héritée de l'apartheid, cette situation demeure largement inchangée.
-This situation, a consequence of the apartheid system, remains largely unchanged.

9799 **aberration** **aberration**
f [abeʁasjɔ̃] Ce semble être une aberration génétique.
-Whatever it is, it appears to be a genetic aberration.

9800 **malnutrition** **malnutrition**
f [malnytʁisjɔ̃] La malnutrition semble augmenter dans les PMA.
-Malnutrition in the least developed countries seems to be increasing.

9801 **hypertension** **hypertension**
f [ipɛʁtɑ̃sjɔ̃] J'ai de l'hypertension.
-I have high blood pressure.

9802 **posthume** **posthumous**
adj [pɔstym] C'est une glorification posthume de l'idéologie communiste qui n'est pas à mon goût.
-This is a posthumous glorification of the communist ideology which is not to my taste.

9803 **chuchotement** **whisper**
m [ʃyʃɔtmɑ̃] Vous deux devriez vraiment bosser votre chuchotement.
-You two really have to work on your whispering.

9804 **ensanglanter** **cover in blood**
vb [ɑ̃sɑ̃glɑ̃te] Évitons d'ensanglanter votre jolie cape blanche.
-We don't want to get blood all over your pretty white cloak.

9805 **munir** **provide|fit**
vb [myniʁ] Les délégations sont priées de bien vouloir se munir de leur exemplaire des documents.
-Delegates are kindly requested to bring their copies of documents to the meeting.

9806 **illicite** **illicit**
adj [ilisit] Garder des animaux sauvages comme animaux domestiques est illicite.
-It's not legal to keep wild animals as pets.

9807 **télégraphier** **telegraph**
vb [telegʁafje] Je vais télégraphier à mon collègue que vous arrivez.
-I'll telegraph to my colleague that you're going to arrive.

9808 **réjouissance** **rejoicing**
f [ʁeʒwisɑ̃s] Nous pouvions nous permettre une brève période de réjouissance.
-We may allow ourselves a brief period of rejoicing.

9809 **fringant** **frisky**
adj[fʁɛ̃gɑ̃] Le sénateur Doyle, un vieil ami, se demandait pourquoi j'étais moins fringant ces temps-ci. -Senator Doyle, an old friend, has worried why I have been less frisky in the recent past.

9810 **dessécher** **dry out**
vb [deseʃe] Je ne pourrai jamais me dessécher !
-I don't think I'll ever dry out.

9811 **invulnérable** **invulnerable**

adj
[ɛ̃vylneʁabl]
La plus puissante des nations n'est pas invulnérable.
-Even the strongest nation of all is not invulnerable.

9812 **paillasse** **pallet**
f
[pajas]
Elle ne reconnaît cependant pas la paillasse.
-She did not, however, recognize the straw mattress.

9813 **cuivre** **copper**
m
[kɥivʁ]
Donnez-lui ça en échange du cuivre.
-You can give him these for the copper.

9814 **dramaturge** **dramatist**
m/f
[dʁamatyʁʒ]
Je pense à cette excellente représentation de l'hypocrisie qu'a donnée le célèbre dramaturge français Molière, dans son .
-I am put in mind of that excellent account of hypocrisy provided by the famous French dramatist Molière in his play .

9815 **indiscutable** **indisputable**
adj
[ɛ̃diskytabl]
Le lien entre changement climatique et catastrophes naturelles est indiscutable.
-The nexus of climate change and natural disasters is indisputable.

9816 **abasourdir** **stun|dumbfound**
vb
[abazuʁdiʁ]
Les Canadiens sont abasourdis par ce terrible événement.
-Canadians have been shocked and numbed by this awful event.

9817 **retiré** **withdrawn|retired**
adj
[ʁətiʁe]
Cette invitation s'adresse également aux États qui ont retiré leurs déclarations.
-That invitation applies also to States that have withdrawn their declarations.

9818 **laudanum** **laudanum**
m
[lodanɔm]
C'est le laudanum qui parle.
-It's just the laudanum speaking.

9819 **frémir** **tremble|shudder**
vb
[fʁemiʁ]
Comment ne pas frémir en pensant à nos jeunes, aux jeunes femmes, aux jeunes mères?
-How is it possible not to shudder when thinking of our young people, our young women and our young mothers?

9820 **clopinettes** **peanuts**
fpl
[klɔpinɛt]
Monsieur le Président, nous ne parlons pas ici de clopinettes.
-Mr President, we are not talking about peanuts here.

9821 **butée** **toe**
f
[byte]
La butée empêche tout avancement distal supplémentaire du filtre.
-Further distal advancement of the filter is prohibited by the stop.

9822 **chiffe** **spineless individual**
f
[ʃif]
Sois gentil avec lui et il deviendra comme une chiffe.
-All right, be nice to him, and then he'll fall apart in small pieces.

9823 **pompette** **tipsy**
adj
[pɔ̃pɛt]
Je pense que je suis pompette.
-My God, I think I'm tipsy.

9824 **incontestable** **indisputable**
adj
[ɛ̃kɔ̃tɛstabl]
Nous estimons qu'il s'agit là d'une déclaration de fait, qui est incontestable.
-We find this to be a simple statement of fact and unarguable.

9825 **centième** **hundredth**
num
[sɑ̃tjɛm]
Du côté des recettes prévisibles, on évoque quelques gains économiques plutôt abstraits qui atteindront peut-être un centième ou un millième du

produit national brut.
-On the positive side we have some abstract economic gains which perhaps amount to a hundredth or a thousandth of a per cent of the gross domestic product.

9826 **façonner** **shape|fashion**
vb
[fasɔne]
Nous espérons que toutes les parties saisiront cette occasion pour, ensemble, façonner un avenir meilleur.
-We hope that all parties will seize this opportunity to fashion a better future together.

9827 **condescendance** **condescension**
f
[kɔ̃desɑ̃dɑ̃s]
La tolérance n'est ni concession, ni condescendance, ni complaisance.
-Tolerance is not concession, condescension or indulgence.

9828 **képi** **cap**
m
[kepi]
L'emblème du lion sur notre képi.
-There is a lion's emblem on our cap.

9829 **électrocution** **electrocution**
f
[elɛktʁɔkysjɔ̃]
Grissom a enquêté sur une électrocution à l'abattoir de poulet Mannleigh.
-Grissom investigated an electrocution at the Mannleigh chicken plant.

9830 **menuiserie** **carpentry**
f
[mənɥizʁi]
Nous fabriquons la menuiserie depuis 1997.
-We began to manufacture building carpentry in 1997.

9831 **broutille** **trifle**
f
[bʁutij]
Tu ne dois pas te hérisser à propos d'une telle broutille.
-You don't have to go getting so hairy about such a small thing.

9832 **espiègle** **playful|impish; imp**
adj; m/f
[ɛspjɛgl]
Le garçon arborait un petit sourire espiègle.
-The boy had a mischievous smirk on his face.

9833 **assaillir** **assail**
vb
[asajiʁ]
À l'examen de ces questions, on est assailli par l'énorme complexité de leur trouver une solution.
-As we tackle those issues, we are assailed by the enormous complexity of finding solutions to them.

9834 **indubitablement** **undoubtedly**
adv
[ɛ̃dybitabləmɑ̃]
Et lorsqu'ils reviendront ils continueront indubitablement de lutter contre l'extrémisme en Europe.
-And when they get home they will doubtless continue the fight against extremism in Europe.

9835 **voyance** **clairvoyance**
f
[vwajɑ̃s]
Un chien extra-terrestre pince-sans-rire avec des dons de voyance.
-Extraterrestrial, wisecracking dog with psychic abilities.

9836 **agrafe** **clip**
f[agʁaf]
Cette agrafe élastique peut mieux amortir les vibrations et réduire et/ou supprimer la résonance. -The spring clip can better dampen vibrations and reduce and/or eliminate resonance.

9837 **litige** **litigation**
m
[litiʒ]
Monsieur le Président, ce litige commercial avec les États-Unis est très regrettable.
-Mr. Speaker, the U.S. trade litigation is very unfortunate.

9838 **subtilité** **subtlety**
f
[syptilite]
Le fait qu'elle choisisse de s'appeler «leader adjoint suppléant» est une question de forme et une subtilité, et non une question de fond.

-The fact that he chose to call himself "interim deputy leader" is a matter of form and a nicety; it does not go to the substance.

9839 **percepteur** m; adj [pɛʁsɛptœʁ] **collector; percipient**
Le bandit était le percepteur des impôts.
-The bandit was the tax collector.

9840 **sciemment** adv [sjamɑ̃] **knowingly**
La confidentialité des renseignements personnels ne sera jamais compromise sciemment.
-Personal privacy will not, should not, and will never be privatized knowingly.

9841 **amirauté** f [amiʁote] **admiralty**
L'amirauté a déjà nommé John Fryer capitaine.
-The Admiralty's already assigned a Mr John Fryer as Master of the ship.

9842 **bistouri** m [bistuʁi] **scalpel**
Je voulais m'assurer que l'incision a été faite par un bistouri pour cerveau.
-Well, dear, I just wanted to be sure that the incision was made by a brain scalpel.

9843 **caillot** m [kajo] **clot**
Un caillot peut empêcher le saignement.
-It's got to be a clot keeping her from bleeding out.

9844 **embouchure** f [ɑ̃buʃyʁ] **mouth|outlet**
L'embouchure de la rivière Rouge n'a pas été draguée depuis 1999.
-The mouth of the Red River has not been dredged since 1999.

9845 **suffisance** f [syfizɑ̃s] **sufficiency**
Utiliser les intervalles de suffisance seulement à titre de référence.
-Only use sufficiency ranges as a reference and a guideline.

9846 **zeste** m [zɛst] **zest**
Paul had a zest for life and a zest for living.
-Paul avait un enthousiasme pour la vie et une véritable joie de vivre.

9847 **persan** adj; m [pɛʁsɑ̃] **Persian; Persian**
«J'arrive à me raser sans regarder dans un miroir !» «C'est bien, mais ne reste pas au-dessus de mon tapis persan, tu vas l'ensanglanter !»
-"I can shave without looking in a mirror!" "That's good, but do not stand over my Persian carpet. You're bloody!"

9848 **bourgeon** m [buʁʒɔ̃] **bud**
Le bourgeon d'une nouvelle relation naissant à travers le froid glacial.
-The bud of a new relationship popping through the frosty ground.

9849 **diphtérie** f[difteʁi] **diphtheria**
La diphtérie et la coqueluche tuaient nos jeunes. -Diphtheria and whooping cough caused death among our young.

9850 **inexact** adj [inɛgzakt] **incorrect|inexact**
Troisièmement, le projet est simplement inexact et contient des contre-vérités.
-Thirdly, the draft was simply inaccurate and misrepresented the true situation.

9851 **intentionnel** adj [ɛ̃tɑ̃sjɔnɛl] **intentional**
«Element of intent» est plus précis que «References to intent» (référence à l'intention).
-"Elements of intent" was more specific than "References to intent".

9852 **gond** **hinge**

	m	Au moment où ce gond saute, tu me cales cette porte.
	[gɔ̃]	-The moment that hinge pops, you wedge that door open.
9853	**broderie**	**embroidery**
	f	La Tapisserie de Bayeux est en fait une broderie.
	[bʁɔdʁi]	-The Bayeux Tapestry is actually an embroidery.
9854	**insomniaque**	**insomniac**
	m/f	De plus, notre insomniaque local cherchait quelque chose à faire.
	[ɛ̃sɔmnjak]	-Besides, our resident insomniac was looking for something to do.
9855	**prolongement**	**extension|prolongation**
	m	Les deux mandats permettent un prolongement éventuel.
	[pʁɔlɔ̃ʒmɑ̃]	-For both sets of terms, there is a possibility of extension.
9856	**anesthésique**	**anesthetic**
	adj	Sur le plan pharmacologique, consommé à hautes doses, il a des effets sédatifs et anesthésiques.
	[anɛstezik]	-Pharmacologically, it produces sedative and anaesthetic effects at high doses.
9857	**déboussoler**	**confuse**
	vb	Le public est aujourd'hui déboussolé par ce festival des droits de l'homme.
	[debusɔle]	-The public are now bamboozled by this human rights fest.
9858	**belette**	**weasel**
	f	Une demeure propice pour une sale belette volante.
	[bəlɛt]	-Quite an auspicious dwelling for a filthy, flying weasel.
9859	**guetteur**	**watchman|look-out**
	m	Le guetteur voit un navire pirate naviguant vers eux.
	[gɛtœʁ]	-The lookout sees a pirate ship sailing their way.
9860	**poncho**	**poncho**
	m	Les disparitions d'abeilles dans le sud de l'Allemagne, par exemple, ont été clairement associées à l'utilisation du pesticide Poncho Pro.
	[pɔ̃ʃo]	-For example, bee losses observed in southern Germany have been clearly attributed to poisoning by the pesticide Poncho Pro.
9861	**décimer**	**decimate**
	vb	Le VIH/sida menace de décimer une grande partie de notre population active.
	[desime]	-HIV/AIDS threatens to decimate large numbers of our productive population.
9862	**maléfice**	**devilry**
	m	C'est la dernière nuit du maléfice et...
	[malefis]	-It's the final night of the curse and.
9863	**itinérant**	**itinerant; itinerant**
	adj; m	Les codes de transporteur itinérant (ITN) ne sont pas acceptables.
	[itineʁɑ̃]	-Itinerant (ITN) carrier codes are not acceptable.
9864	**imbiber**	**soak**
	vb	Je vais imbiber le matelas en dessous de vous.
	[ɛ̃bibe]	-I'm going to soak the mattress under your body.
9865	**kayak**	**kayak**
	m	Il nagea vers mon kayak et murmura mon nom.
	[kajak]	-It swam up to my kayak and whispered my name.
9866	**engrenage**	**gearing**
	m	Un arbre d'entraînement est accouplé fonctionnellement audit engrenage.
	[ɑ̃gʁənaʒ]	-A drive shaft is operatively coupled to the at least one gear.
9867	**allaiter**	**breast-feed|nurse**

vb
[alete]

La volonté des femmes qui tiennent à allaiter leur enfant devra être respectée.
-The plan states that mothers who strongly intend to breastfeed their children shall be respected.

9868 **déformation** — **deformation|distortion**
f
[defɔʁmasjɔ̃]
Ces implants résistent à la déformation latérale.
-Spinal implants are also provided that are resistant to lateral deformation.

9869 **anéantissement** — **annihilation**
m
[aneɑ̃tismɑ̃]
Il existe également une perte plus profonde : l'anéantissement de l'espoir d'un avenir meilleur.
-There is also a more profound loss: the destruction of hope for a better future.

9870 **libanais** — **Lebanese**
adj; mpl
[libanɛ]
Il faut être avec les Libanais, et il faut être avec les démocrates libanais.
-We must support the Lebanese people and we must support the Lebanese democrats.

9871 **pubis** — **pubis**
m
[pybis]
C'est la robe noire du pubis.
-It's like the little black dress of pubic hair.

9872 **intergalactique** — **intergalactic**
adj
[ɛ̃tɛʁgalaktik]
Cette base est un vaisseau intergalactique.
-This base is an intergalactic vessel.

9873 **migration** — **migration**
f
[migʁasjɔ̃]
L'Afrique est un continent de migration.
-Africa is a continent of migration.

9874 **supérette** — **minimarket**
f
[sypeʁɛt]
Alors voici le parking de la supérette.
-So here's the convenience store parking lot.

9875 **subterfuge** — **subterfuge**
m
[syptɛʁfyʒ]
Par conséquent, la Cour de justice essaie d'éviter un artifice qui permettrait le recours à ce subterfuge.
-The Court of Justice is therefore trying to prevent any contrivance by means of which this subterfuge could be employed.

9876 **traditionnellement** — **traditionally**
adv[tʁadisjɔnɛlmɑ̃]
Traditionnellement, le taux de participation aux élections est de quelque 95 %. -Historically, as much as 95 per cent of the electorate have participated in elections.

9877 **engouement** — **infatuation**
m
[ɑ̃gumɑ̃]
Ton engouement est basé sur une attirance physique.
-Your infatuation is based on a physical attraction.

9878 **pesticide** — **pesticide; pesticidal**
m; adj
[pɛstisid]
Le Canada n'a jamais homologué le mirex en tant que pesticide agricole.
-Mirex was never registered for use as an agricultural pesticide in Canada.

9879 **multiplication** — **multiplication**
f
[myltiplikasjɔ̃]
La multiplication de la discrimination ne contribuera pas à cette stabilisation régionale.
-The multiplication of discrimination will not help in such regional stabilization.

9880 **verso** — **back|reverse**
m
[vɛʁso]
Remplissez ceci et lisez le verso.
-Fill this out and read what's on the back.

9881 **faubourg** **suburb**
m
[fobuʁ]
Un mois auparavant, le faubourg Saint-Roch avait été victime d'une catastrophe similaire.
-A month before, the suburb of Saint-Roch had suffered a similar fate.

9882 **cordial** **cordial; cordial**
adj; m
[kɔʁdjal]
Ça sonne vraiment cordial et adulte.
-This feels very, like, cordial and grown-up.

9883 **induire** **induce**
vb
[ɛ̃dɥiʁ]
Ce serait s'aveugler que de croire que la monnaie unique à elle seule pourrait induire une réforme politique.
-It would be naive to think that the single currency could on its own induce political reform.

9884 **libéré** **released**
adj
[libeʁe]
L'adolescent sera complètement libéré à l'âge de 21 ans.
-The adolescent shall be freed compulsorily at the age of 21 years.

9885 **moquerie** **mockery**
f
[mɔkʁi]
Croustilleux de croire que je te courtise par moquerie.
-It's piquant to think I am courting you out of mockery.

9886 **gémissant** **moaning|groaning**
adj
[ʒemisɑ̃]
Le capitaine s'écroule en gémissant et meurt.
-The captain falls to the ground, groaning, and dies.

9887 **cueillette** **picking**
f
[kœjɛt]
Ce mécanisme de cueillette de renseignements est essentiel aux enquêtes portant sur des pratiques marchandes complexes, dont les complots commerciaux sophistiqués.
-This information gathering mechanism is essential to the investigation of complex market behaviour including sophisticated trade combinations.

9888 **incriminer** **incriminate**
vb
[ɛ̃kʁimine]
Un témoin peut refuser de faire toute déclaration qui risquerait de l'incriminer.
-A witness may object to making any statement that might tend to incriminate him or her.

9889 **ébruiter** **spread**
vb
[ebʁɥite]
Le projet de résolution qui a été ébruité ne ressemble à rien de plus qu'un plan en vue d'une invasion non contestée.
-Leaked drafts resemble nothing so much as a plan for unopposed invasion.

9890 **perpétrer** **perpetrate**
vb
[pɛʁpetʁe]
Les terroristes ont réagi en profitant de ces ouvertures pour perpétrer d'autres attaques.
-Terrorists have responded by taking advantage of those openings in order to perpetrate further attacks.

9891 **poudrier** **powder compact**
m
[pudʁije]
J'appelle au sujet de mon poudrier.
-I am calling about my compact.

9892 **esquisser** **sketch|outline**
vb
[ɛskise]
On peut donc désormais esquisser les contours dans lesquels un compromis va devoir être trouvé.
-We can now sketch the outlines within which a compromise will have to be reached.

9893 **fanfaron** **braggart; boastful**
m; adj
[fɑ̃faʁɔ̃]
Le Puck dont je suis tombée amoureuse était un fanfaron.
-The Puck I fell in love with had swagger.

9894 **teint** adj; m [tɛ̃]

dyed; color

Jill dormait; elle était encore vêtue de sa robe blanche déchirée, et ses longs cheveux noirs qui flottaient en désordre sur ses épaules, faisaient ressortir la pâleur de son teint.
-Jill was sleeping; she was still wearing her torn white dress, and her long black hair, resting in a dishevelled manner upon her shoulders, contrasted strongly with the paleness of her face.

9895 **tricycle** m [tʁisikl]

tricycle

Le tricycle peut être plié selon plusieurs niveaux de compacité.
-The tricycle is collapsible to several levels of compactness.

9896 **plumard** m [plymaʁ]

sack

T'assureras jamais comme lui au plumard.
-And I assure you that you may not be never like him in the sack.

9897 **réglementation** f [ʁɛgləmɑ̃tasjɔ̃]

regulation

En l'absence d'une telle réglementation, la réglementation du pays exportateur doit s'appliquer.
-If no such regulation exists the regulation of the exporting country shall be used.

9898 **colonisation** f [kɔlɔnizasjɔ̃]

colonization

Je n'appelle pas ça de la colonisation. Je l'appelle de l'exploitation systématique des matières premières.
-I don't call it colonization, I call it systematic raw materials exploitation.

9899 **déporté** m; adj [depɔʁte]

deportee; deported

Il allait être arrêté et déporté.
-He was going to be arrested and deported.

9900 **crible** m [kʁibl]

screen|riddle

Le procédé peut être utilisé en tant que crible à haut débit.
-The method may be used as a high throughput screen.

9901 **révolutionner** vb[ʁevɔlysjɔne]

revolutionize

Il y a urgence à révolutionner l'OMC pour que la démocratie s'y installe. -There is an urgent need to revolutionise the WTO so that democracy may be established there.

9902 **abolir** vb [abɔliʁ]

abolish|lift

Ce sont les mêmes libéraux qui, en 1993, allaient abolir la TPS.
-These are the same Liberals who in 1993 were going to abolish the GST.

9903 **mélodramatique** adj [melɔdʁamatik]

melodramatic

Ne soyez pas si mélodramatique.
-Don't be so melodramatic.

9904 **vingtième** adj [vɛ̃tjɛm]

twentieth|twentieth

Cela s'inscrit naturellement dans la préparation de notre vingtième programme-cadre.
-This figures naturally in the preparation of our twentieth framework programme.

9905 **aigre** adj [ɛgʁ]

sour

Monsieur le Président, Monsieur le Commissaire, je débute en exprimant la sensation aigre-douce que ce débat suscite en moi.
-Mr President, Commissioner, I would like to begin by saying that my feelings about this debate are bittersweet.

9906 **invaincu** adj [ɛ̃vɛ̃ky]

unbeaten

On a beaucoup parlé de la grippe aviaire récemment; de plus, le SIDA reste toujours invaincu, pour ne rien dire d'anciennes maladies transmissibles, telles que la tuberculose.

-Bird flu has been a conspicuous topic of discussion recently, and AIDS is still unbeaten, to say nothing of older communicable diseases such as tuberculosis.

9907 **bidet** **bidet**
m
[bidɛ]
I just fixed Charlie's bidet upstairs.
-Je viens de réparer le bidet de Charlie à l'étage.

9908 **vacciner** **vaccinate|inject**
vb
[vaksine]
Byrne aurait pu prendre l'initiative de vacciner les animaux des jardins zoologiques.
-Mr Byrne should have taken the initiative to vaccinate animals in zoos.

9909 **altruiste** **altruistic; altruist**
adj; m/f
[altʁyist]
Il était... désintéressé... altruiste.
-He was, you know, selfless, altruistic.

9910 **délaisser** **abandon|neglect**
vb
[delese]
Or, nous devons préserver cet équilibre et ne le délaisser ne aucun cas.
-So we should maintain this balance here and certainly not abandon it.

9911 **immoralité** **immorality**
f
[imɔʁalite]
Même les inventions modernes de la science cultivent l'immoralité.
-Even the modern inventions of science... are used to cultivate immorality.

9912 **rami** **rummy**
m
[ʁami]
Je ne sais pas, moi, un rami, une belote...
-I don't know rummy, or any other card game...

9913 **enthousiasmer** **enthuse**
vb
[ɑ̃tuzjasme]
Paul avait un enthousiasme pour la vie et une véritable joie de vivre.
-Paul had a zest for life and a zest for living.

9914 **asthmatique** **asthmatic; asthmatic**
adj; m/f[asmatik]
J'allais toujours à la montagne, je suis asthmatique. -I always went to the mountain because I'm asthmatic.

9915 **calculateur** **calculating**
adj
[kalkylatœʁ]
Nous critiquons le gouvernement parce qu'il agit en calculateur et en manipulateur à l'égard des finances publiques.
-We are criticizing the government because it has been calculating and manipulative with the public's finances.

9916 **angoissant** **scary**
adj
[ɑ̃gwasɑ̃]
C'est donc un processus à la fois long, angoissant et pénible, où la consultation ne tient pas une grande place.
-So I have something that is long, agonizing and painful but with not a lot of consultation.

9917 **bru** **daughter-in-law**
f
[bʁy]
Rita est la bru de Dan.
-Rita is Dan's daughter-in-law.

9918 **mors** **bit**
m
[mɔʁ]
Vitesse du mors mobile pendant l'étirement de la maille.
-Speed of the movable jaw during the stretching of the mesh.

9919 **bâti** **built; bed**
adj; m
[bati]
Jack s'est bâti un nom.
-Jack built up a good name for himself.

9920 **feuillage** **foliage**
m
[fœjaʒ]
À la campagne, les couleurs du ciel et du feuillage sont entièrement différentes de celles qu'on voit en ville.

-In the country, the colors of the sky and of the foliage are entirely different from those seen in the city.

9921 **décommander** vb [dekɔmɑ̃de]
cancel
Dites Guruji de décommander le séjour et devenu mon associé.
-Tell Guruji to cancel the stay and become my partner.

9922 **appréhension** f [apʁeɑ̃sjɔ̃]
apprehension
Son appréhension gêne considérablement son progrès.
-His apprehension greatly hinders his progress.

9923 **jarretelle** f [ʒaʁtɛl]
garter
C'est vous le chanceux qui avez attrapé la jarretelle de Bev.
-I saw you were the lucky one who caught Bev's garter.

9924 **abolition** f [abɔlisjɔ̃]
abolition
L'abolition des symboles, l'abolition du droit de décider de la vie appartient à chaque pays.
-The abolition of symbols, the abolition of the right to decide on life belongs to each state.

9925 **relaxation** f [ʁəlaksasjɔ̃]
relaxation
La présente invention a pour objet général la relaxation musculaire.
-The present invention relates generally to muscle relaxation.

9926 **éreinter** vb [eʁɛ̃te]
hammer|exhaust
Attends. Quel châssis, elle doit t'éreinter.
-That frame of hers - she must be wearing you out.

9927 **monticule** m [mɔ̃tikyl]
mound
Ernie Bonham des Yanks est sur le monticule.
-On the mound for the New York Yanks was Ernie Bonham.

9928 **sternum** m[stɛʁnɔm]
sternum
C'est le groupe de muscles qui se situe sur le sternum et une partie des côtes. -Consist of the group of muscles that lies on the sternum and part of the ribs.

9929 **flambeur** m [flɑ̃bœʁ]
high-roller
Un peu jeune pour un flambeur.
-That's kind of young for a high roller.

9930 **imitateur** m; adj [imitatœʁ]
imitator; mimic
Je forme une entreprise qui n'eut jamais d'exemple et dont l'exécution n'aura point d'imitateur.
-I have entered on an enterprise which is without precedent, and will have no imitator.

9931 **quiétude** f [kjetyd]
quietude
La longue quiétude cachait les prodromes d'une explosion.
-The lengthy peace hid the early signs of an explosion.

9932 **cerne** m [sɛʁn]
circle
Le même ingrédient que le cerne autour de ta baignoire après un bain.
-Same ingredient as the ring around your tub after a bath.

9933 **génisse** f [ʒenis]
young cow
Et il lui dit: Prends une génisse de trois ans, et une chèvre de trois ans, et un bélier de trois ans, et une tourterelle, et un jeune pigeon.
-And he said: Take a young cow of three years old, and a she-goat of three years old, and a sheep of three years old, and a dove and a young pigeon.

9934 **prude** m/f; adj [pʁyd]
prude; prudish
Pour moi, Christina était très prude.
-As far as I knew, Christina was a prude.

9935 **palmarès** **prize list**
m
[palmaʁɛs]
Mets leur palmarès sous leurs noms.
-Put them under the name record.

9936 **perversité** **perversity**
f
[pɛʁvɛʁsite]
L'homme est une malformation, une perversité de la nature.
-Man is a malformation, a perversity of nature.

9937 **préconiser** **advocate**
vb
[pʁekɔnize]
Le Conseil continuera de préconiser la création de ces capacités.
-The Council will continue to advocate for the creation of such capability.

9938 **détergent** **detergent; cleanser**
adj; m
[detɛʁʒɑ̃]
Le détergent aqueux liquide s'écoule du doseur.
-The liquid aqueous detergent flows out of the dispensing device.

9939 **négation** **negation**
f
[negasjɔ̃]
La dépendance par rapport à une structure linguistique monolithique revient à une négation de facto de notre marginalité géographique septentrionale.
-Dependence on a monolithic linguistic structure involves a de facto denial of our geographical marginality in the North.

9940 **œillet** **eyelet**
m
[œjɛ]
Un œillet raccorde la couche conductrice au bouton-pression.
-An eyelet interconnects the conductive layer with the press stud.

9941 **nécrologie** **obituary**
f[nekʁɔlɔʒi]
Elle prépare votre nécrologie depuis longtemps. -I think she's been after your obituary for a while, now.

9942 **quiche** **quiche**
f
[kiʃ]
École régionale d'art « Ovidio Rodas Corzo » à Chichicastenango, El Quiché : 4 femmes.
-The Ovidio Rodas Corzo Regional Art School in Chichicastenango, Quiché, with four women.

9943 **disponibilité** **availability**
f
[dispɔnibilite]
Évolution et disponibilité de l'information biologique aviaire.
-The Changing State of Avian Biological Information and its Availability.

9944 **ukrainien** **Ukrainian; Ukrainian**
adj; m|mpl
[ykʁɛnjɛ̃]
Je suis Ukrainien.
-I'm Ukrainian.

9945 **urinoir** **urinal**
m
[yʁinwaʁ]
Les eaux usées du lavabo sont utilisées pour rincer l'urinoir.
-Therein, the waste water from the hand washing facility is used for flushing the urinal.

9946 **émancipation** **emancipation**
f
[emɑ̃sipasjɔ̃]
Les stéréotypes font massivement obstacle à l'émancipation des filles.
-Stereotyped images are a major barrier to the empowerment of adolescent girls.

9947 **lotissement** **allotment|project**
m
[lɔtismɑ̃]
Ce projet de lotissement fut soumis à la municipalité.
-This subdivision plan was submitted to the municipality.

9948 **magma** **magma**
m
[magma]
Le magma sous Praxis est lié a plusieurs volcans en sommeil sur trois de vos continents.
-The magma below Praxis is linked to several dormant volcanoes on three of your continents.

9949 **tabard** **tabard**

m
[tabaʁ]
Au moins le tabard doré drapé autour de son torse lui apportait-il un peu de chaleur.
-At least the golden tabard draped over his torso brought some scant warmth.

9950 **duveteux**
adj
[dyvtø]
fluffy
La nuit, il enfile un costume de lapin duveteux.
-At night, he puts on a furry bunny outfit.

9951 **oblong**
adj
[ɔblɔ̃]
oblong
Le corps oblong de la sonde est de préférence creux et souple.
-The probe's elongated body is preferably hollow, and flexible.

9952 **prolétaire**
m/f; adj
[pʁɔletɛʁ]
proletarian; prolete
Mais cet enfant est une prolétaire.
-But this child is a proletarian.

9953 **surcharger**
vb
[syʁʃaʁʒe]
overload|overburden
Je dois pouvoir surcharger son relai.
-I might be able to overload the relay.

9954 **pélican**
m[pelikɑ̃]
pelican
Elle participe à des procès en cour huit jours par mois à Sandy Bay, Pelican Narrows, Big River et Montreal Lake. -This Cree Circuit Court Party attends court eight days a month at Sandy Bay, Pelican Narrows, Big River First Nation and Montreal Lake.

9955 **convoitise**
f
[kɔ̃vwatiz]
greed|desire
Il n'apportera que meurtres et convoitise.
-It'll bring us nothing but murder and greed.

9956 **obligatoirement**
adv
[ɔbligatwaʁmɑ̃]
inevitably
Cela signifie que le conducteur doit obligatoirement être responsable de sa conduite.
-This means that the driver should be inevitably responsible for his/her driving.

9957 **enivrer**
vb
[ɑ̃nivʁe]
intoxicate|get drunk
Un fonctionnaire s'est enivré en public et a harcelé une fonctionnaire.
-A staff member became publicly intoxicated and harassed a female staff member.

9958 **calife**
m
[kalif]
caliph
Le calife va chercher son épouse.
-The Caliph is on his way to fetch his bride.

9959 **terrasser**
vb
[teʁase]
crush
Je résisterai pour te laisser me terrasser et... me menotter.
-Resist arrest just so you can wrestle me down...... and cuff me.

9960 **treizième**
num
[tʁɛzjɛm]
thirteenth
Les treizième, quatorzième et quinzième vagues de privatisation ont été lancées.
-The thirteenth, fourteenth and fifteenth waves were initiated.

9961 **fourni**
adj
[fuʁni]
provided
Un État Membre a également fourni un expert associé.
-An associate expert has also been provided by one Member State.

9962 **trombe**
f
[tʁɔ̃b]
whirlwind
Il partit en trombe.
-He went off in a hurry.

9963 **plénitude**
fullness

f | Le mariage est sanctifié dans la plénitude des concessions.
[plenityd] | -Marriage is sanctified in the fullness of the claims between man and woman.

9964 **vantard** — **boastful; braggart**
adj; m
[vɑ̃taʁ]
Je pensais que vous étiez juste un vantard vieux et riche.
-I thought you were just a rich, old blowhard.

9965 **aubergine** — **eggplant**
f
[obɛʁʒin]
J'aurais entendu l'aubergine crier.
-No, chef. I'd have heard the eggplant scream.

9966 **physiologique** — **physiological**
adj
[fizjɔlɔʒik]
Dans ce bilan de santé, nous voulons parler non seulement du côté physiologique, mais également de l'état d'âme de la société européenne.
-And in this check-up, we wish to consider not only the physical state of European society, but also its state of mind, the state of its soul.

9967 **ébattre** — **frolic**
vb[ebatʁ]
Si nous n'édifions pas une défense européenne crédible, l'Europe restera ce roquet autorisé à s'ébattre à côté du bulldog américain. -Without the development of credible European defence, Europe remains a yapping puppy that is allowed to frolic alongside the American bulldog.

9968 **nécessiteux** — **needy; needy person**
adj; m/f
[nesesitø]
La ville pourvut les nécessiteux de couvertures.
-The city supplied the needy with blankets.

9969 **habilement** — **skilfully|cleverly**
adv
[abilmɑ̃]
Il dit que j'ai tenté habilement de prendre mes distances par rapport aux événements.
-He speaks about my skilfully trying to distance myself from events.

9970 **perforer** — **perforate**
vb
[pɛʁfɔʁe]
Le revêtement extérieur doit être perforé de façon à éviter la formation de bulles.
-The cover has to be intentionally perforated to avoid the forming of bubbles.

9971 **nymphe** — **nymph**
f
[nɛ̃f]
Dans l'histoire, c'est une nymphe aquatique.
-A narf, the bedtime story says, is a sea nymph.

9972 **linotte** — **linnet**
f
[linɔt]
Tu semblais brune et douce, comme une linotte.
-You seemed all brown and soft, just like a linnet.

9973 **périmer** — **expire**
vb
[peʁime]
Certaines autorisations de dépenses vont se périmer.
-Some spending authorities in the Estimates are expected to lapse.

9974 **admirablement** — **admirably**
adv
[admiʁabləmɑ̃]
Je pense que la démocratie est représentée admirablement ici par ses élus.
-I believe that democracy is borne here admirably by its elected representatives.

9975 **impayable** — **priceless**
adj
[ɛ̃pɛjabl]
La tête que tu as fait, c'était impayable.
-The look on your face was priceless.

9976 **intégralité** — **entirety**
f
[ɛ̃tegʁalite]
Les recommandations doivent donc être adoptées dans leur intégralité.
-Accordingly, this set of recommendations should be adopted in its entirety.

9977 **concocter** **concoct**
vb
[kɔ̃kɔkte]
Ils se contentaient de s'éloigner juste assez pour qu'on ne les entende pas concocter leurs plans.
-They just went out of earshot to concoct what was going on.

9978 **communier** **communicate**
vb
[kɔmynje]
Je vous supplie de nous aider à communier avec Charlotte.
-I beseech you to help us communicate with Charlotte Cross.

9979 **torero** **bullfighter**
m
[tɔʁʁo]
On reconnaît un grand torero dès son entrée dans l'arène.
-You'd know a great bullfighter the moment he stepped into the ring.

9980 **médiateur** **mediator**
m[medjatœʁ]
Le médiateur coopère étroitement avec la Maison internationale à Reykjavík. -The ombudsman worked in close cooperation with the International House in Reykjavík.

9981 **érafler** **scratch|scuff**
vb
[eʁafle]
Une balle tirée par la police zambienne a éraflé le sommet de mon crâne.
-A bullet fired by the Zambian police grazed the top of my head.

9982 **exténuer** **exhaust**
vb
[ɛkstenɥe]
Vers le soir, Jean était totalement exténué et se demanda à nouveau : « Pourquoi Jésus n'est-Il pas venu m'aider aujourd'hui ?
-By the evening John was totally exhausted and again wondered, "Why didn't Jesus come and help me today?

9983 **débiner** **run down**
vb
[debine]
Je pourrai débiner tout le quartier avant qu'on me le fasse.
-That way I can bad-mouth the rest of the block before they do it to me.

9984 **favoritisme** **favoritism**
m
[favɔʁitism]
Je crois qu'ils parlent de favoritisme éhonté.
-I think what they are talking about is corrupt patronage.

9985 **destinataire** **recipient|addressee**
m
[dɛstinatɛʁ]
Définit l'adresse e-mail du destinataire.
-Sets the internet email address of the recipient.

9986 **charnel** **carnal**
adj
[ʃaʁnɛl]
Accès charnel ou acte sexuel sur une personne mise dans l'incapacité de résister.
-Carnal penetration or sexual act perpetrated against a person who is unable to resist.

9987 **évaporer** **evaporate**
vb
[evapɔʁe]
Utilisé à des températures normales, il peut s'évaporer jusqu'à des niveaux dangereux.
-Under normal temperatures their use causes them to evaporate to dangerous levels.

9988 **bouleversant** **upsetting**
adj
[bulvɛʁsɑ̃]
La date du 11 septembre 2001 a été une épreuve bouleversante, qui a changé l'histoire et l'Amérique.
-The date of 11 September 2001 was a shattering ordeal. It changed history and it changed America.

9989 **clameur** **clamor|shouting**
f
[klamœʁ]
Ce n'est que clameur et confusion.
-It's all just clamour and confusion.

9990 **tarentule** **tarantula**

f
[taʁɑ̃tyl]
Je vous préviens, j'ai une tarentule.
-Just so you guys know, I have a tarantula.

9991 **affolement** **panic**
m
[afɔlmɑ̃]
Nous ne voulons pas d'affolement.
-We don't want a panic.

9992 **cloître** **cloister|enclosure**
m
[klwatʁ]
Rendez-vous au cloître de Las Minillas.
-Meet me at the cloister of Las Minillas.

9993 **rattrapage** **picking up**
m[ʁatʁapaʒ]
J'ai un rattrapage en anglais la semaine prochaine. -I have to resit an English exam next week.

9994 **hydravion** **seaplane**
m
[idʁavjɔ̃]
Louer un hydravion pour aller en Norvège coûte plus cher que je croyais, ma puce.
-Okay, it costs more to hire a seaplane... to fly us to Norway than I had suspected, sweet pea.

9995 **navrant** **heartbreaking**
adj
[navʁɑ̃]
Je reconnais que les demandeurs d'asile expulsés se retrouvent souvent dans une situation navrante.
-I recognise that deported asylum seekers often find themselves in a distressing position.

9996 **constructif** **constructive**
adj
[kɔ̃stʁyktif]
Deuxièmement, l'engagement constructif des puissances administrantes est essentiel.
-Secondly, the constructive engagement of the administering Powers was essential.

9997 **briseur** **breaker**
m
[bʁizœʁ]
Je suis briseur de couple professionnel.
-I am a professional couple breaker.

9998 **replacer** **replace**
vb
[ʁəplase]
The principle of parity and cooperation should replace such an approach.
-Le principe de parité et de coopération devrait remplacer cette approche.

9999 **dièse** **sharp; sharp**
adj; m
[djɛz]
Si bémol ce soir, fa dièse demain.
-B flat tonight, F sharp tomorrow.

10000 **aveuglement** **blindness**
m
[avœgləmɑ̃]
Cet aveuglement les amène à nier les conséquences prévisibles d'une telle adhésion.
-Their blindness leads them to deny the foreseeable consequences of its accession.

10001 **illégalité** **illegality**
f
[ilegalite]
Un mot sur l'illégalité pour conclure.
-I should like to finish off with a comment on illegality.

10002 **réorganiser** **reorganize|reorder**
vb
[ʁeɔʁganize]
vi) Réorganiser les entreprises en vue d'en améliorer la gestion et l'exploitation;
-Reorganize companies to achieve improved managerial and operational efficiency.

10003 **pirouetter** **pirouette**
vb
[piʁwete]
Lors du sommet de Thessalonique, il ne doit pas y avoir de pirouette autour d'une formule alambiquée destinée à tromper.

-At Thessaloniki we should not see this pirouetting around a convoluted formula designed to deceive.

10004 **dominateur** adj; m [dɔminatœʁ]
domineering; ruler
Mon identité était sous le joug de cet homme brillant et dominateur.
-I was tired of submerging my identity to a brilliant, dominating man.

10005 **camomille** f [kamɔmij]
chamomile
Une eau pétillante, un thé à la camomille.
-One sparkling water, One chamomile tea.

10006 **obtus** adj [ɔpty]
obtuse|thick
Tous les députés devraient le savoir ici, mais ils sont obtus.
-All members of the House should know this, but they are obtuse.

10007 **betterave** f [bɛtʁav]
beet
Je veux notamment parler du problème très sensible de la betterave sucrière.
-I refer in particular to the concern about the very sensitive sugar beet issue.

10008 **aveuglant** adj [avœglɑ̃]
blinding
C'est maintenant d'une évidence aveuglante. Cela fait huit ans qu'elle aurait dû l'être.
-The need for a revision to the Works Council Directive is now glaringly obvious: it was due for revision eight years ago.

10009 **cancéreux** adj [kɑ̃seʁø]
cancerous
L'année dernière, un cancéreux est mort après avoir reçu une transfusion de sang infecté par ce virus.
-Last year, a cancer patient died after receiving a blood transfusion infected with West Nile.

10010 **distancer** vb [distɑ̃se]
distance|outrun
Vous croyez qu'on peut le distancer ?
-Do you think we can outrun it?

10011 **vinaigrette** f [vinɛgʁɛt]
vinaigrette
Verser 50 ml de vinaigrette italienne sur les pommes de terre; mélanger délicatement et réfrigérer.
-Pour 50 mL of the Italian dressing over potatoes; mix gently and refrigerate.

10012 **arachide** f [aʁaʃid]
peanut
Un agriculteur d'arachide La Géorgie a été le leader du monde libre.
-A Georgia peanut farmer was leader of the free world...

10013 **dividende** m [dividɑ̃d]
dividend
Autrement dit, nous avons besoin du dividende de l'élimination du déficit.
-In other words, we need a deficit elimination dividend.

10014 **arrivant** adj; m [aʁivɑ̃]
incoming; arrival
Les pompiers ont découvert en arrivant la maison bien en feu.
-The fire brigade arrived to find the house well alight.

10015 **poulpe** m [pulp]
octopus
Paul le poulpe avait raison.
-Octopus Paul was right.

10016 **banalité** f [banalite]
banality|ordinariness
Tel est le danger de votre stratégie: la banalité qui en découlera.
-That is the danger of your strategy: the banality that will result from it.

10017 **risotto** m [ʁizɔto]
risotto
J'attends peut-être le bon risotto.
-Maybe I'm just waiting for the right risotto.

10018 **carême** **fast**
m
[kaʁɛm]
Tu crois qu'il y a un lien entre la crème et le Carême ?
-Do you think there's any connection between lentils and Lent?

10019 **strangulation** **strangulation**
f[stʁɑ̃gylasjɔ̃]
Un des rares guerriers à échapper à la strangulation est Ambiorix. -One of the few warriors who escaped death by strangulation, was Ambiorix.

10020 **insuffisance** **insufficiency**
f
[ɛ̃syfizɑ̃s]
Il souffre d'une insuffisance rénale.
-He is suffering from kidney failure.

10021 **décadent** **decadent; decadent**
adj; m
[dekadɑ̃]
Tellement sombre, gothique, atrocement décadent.
-It's so dark and Gothic and... disgustingly decadent.

10022 **cabriolet** **convertible**
m
[kabʁijɔlɛ]
Tu sais que je veux un cabriolet.
-You know I want a convertible.

10023 **fétide** **fetid|rank**
adj
[fetid]
D'une manière générale, l'entretien des cellules des établissements pénitentiaires pour les mineurs laisse à désirer; elles sont humides, sombres et l'odeur y est fétide.
-In general, cells in juvenile correctional institutions are not properly maintained, and are damp, dark and fetid.

10024 **pater** **pater**
m
[patɛʁ]
Il, je déteste décevoir ce cher vieux pater, Mais il est clair que cette ville n'existe pas.
-Ll, I hate to disappoint dear old pater, but clearly this city can't exist.

10025 **prolongation** **extension|prolongation**
f
[pʁɔlɔ̃gasjɔ̃]
Aucune prolongation supplémentaire de la détention n'est autorisée.
-No further extension of the duration of the detention is permitted.

Adjectives

Rank	French-PoS	Translation
7502	**répugnant**-*adj*	repugnant
7503	**synthétique**-*adj; m*	synthetic; synthetic
7506	**traumatique**-*adj*	traumatic
7507	**énervant**-*adj*	annoying
7509	**trompeur**-*adj; m*	misleading; deceiver
7537	**grognon**-*adj; m*	grumpy; grumbler
7551	**savoureux**-*adj*	tasty| savory
7555	**résistant**-*adj*	resistant
7556	**lunatique**-*adj*	lunatic
7563	**supportable**-*adj*	bearable| tolerable
7568	**indécent**-*adj*	indecent| improper
7571	**solennel**-*adj*	solemn
7572	**ballot**-*m; adj*	bundle; clownish
7585	**préventif**-*adj*	preventive
7586	**nébuleux**-*adj*	nebulous
7587	**venimeux**-*adj*	venomous
7588	**insaisissable**-*adj*	elusive
7593	**électromagnétique**-*adj*	electromagnetic
7602	**déplorable**-*adj*	deplorable
7609	**unanime**-*adj*	unanimous
7610	**pénitentiaire**-*adj*	penitentiary
7611	**mufle**-*m; adj*	oaf; caddish
7615	**alchimie**-*f; adj*	alchemy; alchemic
7616	**anarchiste**-*adj; m/f*	anarchist; anarchist
7617	**alphabétique**-*adj*	alphabetical| alphabet
7619	**paumé**-*adj*	lost| godforsaken
7628	**incomplet**-*adj*	incomplete
7629	**intérim**-*adj*	interim
7638	**ponctuel**-*adj*	punctual
7641	**frivole**-*adj*	frivolous
7642	**circulaire**-*adj; f*	circular; circular
7643	**centenaire**-*adj; m/f*	centenary; centenary
7652	**invraisemblable**-*adj*	unlikely| incredible
7655	**alto**-*adj; m*	alto; alto
7657	**gothique**-*adj; m*	Gothic; Gothic
7663	**titulaire**-*m/f; adj*	holder; titular
7664	**hebdomadaire**-*adj; m*	weekly; weekly
7668	**épileptique**-*adj; m/f*	epileptic; epileptic person
7672	**protestant**-*adj; m*	Protestant; Protestant
7675	**intérimaire**-*adj; m/f*	interim; deputy
7676	**tranquillisant**-*m; adj*	tranquilizer; tranquilizing
7678	**malchanceux**-*adj*	unlucky| unfortunate
7684	**inapte**-*adj*	unfit
7685	**doré**-*adj*	golden| coated
7691	**éprouvant**-*adj*	testing
7693	**colosse**-*m; adj*	colossus; colossal
7694	**narcotique**-*adj; m*	narcotic; narcotic
7699	**vertical**-*adj*	vertical
7701	**éphémère**-*adj; m*	ephemeral; ephemeral
7707	**lucratif**-*adj*	lucrative
7716	**tamisé**-*adj*	screened| sifted
7719	**exigeant**-*adj*	demanding| exacting
7726	**enfantin**-*adj*	infantile
7730	**resplendissant**-*adj*	resplendent
7733	**abstrait**-*adj; m*	abstract; abstract
7736	**profane**-*adj; m/f*	profane; layman
7739	**colonial**-*adj*	colonial
7747	**déroutant**-*adj*	disconcerting
7750	**artériel**-*adj*	arterial
7752	**schizophrène**-*adj*	schizophrenic
7758	**irakien**-*adj*	Iraqi
7763	**hardi**-*adj*	bold| daring
7771	**juvénile**-*adj*	juvenile
7773	**pavé**-*adj; m*	paved; pavement
7775	**désireux**-*adj*	eager
7779	**bis**-*m; adv; adj*	bis; twice; repeat
7780	**myope**-*adj; m/f*	short-sighted; myope
7787	**bénéficiaire**-*m/f; adj*	beneficiary; profitable
7804	**vigoureux**-*adj*	vigorous
7808	**fautif**-*adj; m*	incorrect| culprit
7812	**accidentel**-*adj*	accidental| incidental
7813	**prélèvement**-*m; adj*	sample; compensatory
7825	**éducatif**-*adj*	educative
7829	**instantané**-*adj; m*	instant; snapshot
7838	**mortuaire**-*adj*	mortuary
7852	**mixte**-*adj*	mixed
7860	**épique**-*adj*	epic
7868	**opposant**-*adj; m*	opponent; oppositionist
7869	**poussiéreux**-*adj*	dusty
7873	**ethnique**-*adj*	ethnic
7874	**islamique**-*adj*	Islamic
7881	**insatiable**-*adj*	insatiable

7883	**niais**-*m; adj*	simpleton; simple
7886	**extravagant**-*adj*	extravagant
7887	**dominant**-*adj*	dominant
7894	**pat**-*adj; m*	stalemate; stalemate
7900	**incorrect**-*adj*	incorrect
7902	**aigri**-*adj*	embittered
7903	**originel**-*adj*	original
7906	**réglementaire**-*adj*	regulation
7907	**présomptueux**-*adj*	presumptuous
7908	**osseux**-*adj*	bony| angular
7914	**administratif**-*adj; m*	administrative; executive
7919	**distingué**-*adj*	distinguished
7921	**panoramique**-*adj*	panoramic
7922	**hindou**-*adj; m*	Hindu; Hindu
7923	**féministe**-*adj; m/f*	feminist; feminist
7926	**lavette**-*f; adj*	mop; wet
7931	**chaotique**-*adj*	chaotic
7933	**serviable**-*adj*	helpful
7937	**gaga**-*adj*	gaga
7949	**étiré**-*adj*	spread| stretch
7950	**tangible**-*adj*	tangible
7951	**appétissant**-*adj*	appetizing
7955	**exterminateur**-*m; adj*	exterminator; exterminating
7960	**anal**-*adj*	anal
7962	**sensuel**-*adj*	sensual
7968	**incompris**-*adj*	misunderstood
7972	**colossal**-*adj*	colossal| huge
7981	**pillard**-*m; adj*	plunderer; predatory
7982	**perpétuel**-*adj*	perpetual
7985	**hygiénique**-*adj*	hygienic
8019	**nuageux**-*adj*	cloudy| misty
8020	**parisien**-*adj*	Parisian
8021	**solidaire**-*adj*	solidary
8025	**normand**-*adj*	Norman
8032	**philosophique**-*adj*	philosophical
8034	**roumain**-*adj; m*	Romanian; Romanian
8037	**mythique**-*adj*	mythical
8038	**spartiate**-*adj*	Spartan
8045	**inaudible**-*adj*	inaudible
8055	**boueux**-*adj; m*	muddy; bin man
8056	**satanique**-*adj*	satanic| ghoulish
8060	**autrichien**-*adj*	Austrian
8067	**préhistorique**-*adj*	prehistoric
8068	**botanique**-*adj; f*	botanical; botany
8070	**morose**-*adj*	morose
8071	**inefficace**-*adj*	ineffective| inefficient
8073	**tabou**-*adj; m*	taboo; taboo
8076	**pompeux**-*adj*	pompous
8080	**désinfectant**-*adj; m*	disinfectant; disinfectant
8087	**irrationnel**-*adj; m*	irrational; irrational
8091	**narcissique**-*adj*	narcissistic
8094	**divisionnaire**-*adj*	divisional
8096	**vandale**-*adj; m/f*	vandal; vandal
8118	**recteur**-*m; adj*	rector; rectorial
8119	**irréfutable**-*adj*	irrefutable
8124	**sexiste**-*adj*	sexist
8126	**furtif**-*adj*	furtive| slinking
8130	**majestueux**-*adj*	majestic| stately
8133	**manquant**-*adj*	missing
8134	**rapace**-*adj; m*	rapacious; predator
8137	**croustillant**-*adj; m*	crispy; crispness
8141	**claustrophobe**-*adj*	claustrophobic
8144	**posé**-*adj*	laid
8148	**alternatif**-*adj*	alternative
8153	**fictif**-*adj*	fictional
8155	**symphonique**-*adj*	symphonic
8156	**phénoménal**-*adj*	phenomenal
8158	**balourd**-*m; adj*	oaf; awkward
8161	**veilleur**-*m; adj*	watchman; watchful
8164	**révolu**-*adj*	gone
8173	**irréversible**-*adj*	irreversible
8177	**réputé**-*adj*	renowned| reputed
8181	**bigleux**-*adj*	cross-eyed| four-eyed
8184	**moite**-*adj*	moist
8186	**abruti**-*m; adj*	jerk; stupid
8188	**néfaste**-*adj*	harmful
8201	**indescriptible**-*adj*	indescribable
8203	**énergique**-*adj*	energetic
8213	**déloyal**-*adj*	unfair| disloyal
8220	**succulent**-*adj*	succulent
8223	**textile**-*adj; m*	textile; textile
8229	**affecté**-*adj*	affected
8230	**arithmétique**-*adj; f*	arithmetic; arithmetic
8239	**thermos**-*m; adj*	thermos; thermos
8240	**étanche**-*adj*	waterproof
8241	**inéluctable**-*adj*	inevitable| ineluctable
8242	**hâtif**-*adj*	hasty

8246	**antiquaire**-*adj; m/f*	antiquarian; antiquarian
8252	**haineux**-*adj*	hateful
8253	**glauque**-*adj*	glaucous
8255	**visqueux**-*adj*	viscous| slimy
8261	**relatif**-*adj; m*	relative; relative
8264	**chirurgical**-*adj*	surgical
8265	**ovale**-*adj; m*	oval; oval
8272	**fouineur**-*m; adj*	snoop; prying
8282	**déraisonnable**-*adj*	unreasonable
8283	**impétueux**-*adj*	impetuous
8291	**bestial**-*adj*	bestial
8293	**ancestral**-*adj*	ancestral
8294	**enclin**-*adj*	inclined
8301	**rangé**-*adj*	tidy
8307	**méticuleux**-*adj*	meticulous| painstaking
8309	**droitier**-*m; adj*	right-hander; right-handed
8313	**frigide**-*adj*	frigid
8316	**renégat**-*adj; m*	renegade; renegade
8317	**occulte**-*adj*	occult
8326	**persuasif**-*adj*	persuasive
8333	**immuable**-*adj*	immuable
8338	**laquais**-*m; adj*	lackey; menial
8342	**cupide**-*adj*	greedy
8343	**piteux**-*adj*	sorry
8352	**négociable**-*adj*	negotiable
8364	**autocollant**-*m; adj*	sticker; self-sealing
8368	**obsolète**-*adj*	obsolete
8369	**côtier**-*adj*	coastal
8373	**télépathique**-*adj*	telepathic
8374	**galeux**-*adj*	mangy
8375	**émouvant**-*adj*	moving| touching
8382	**impartial**-*adj*	impartial| unbiased
8389	**écœurant**-*adj*	disgusting| sickening
8394	**bagarreur**-*m; adj*	brawler; feisty
8405	**nomade**-*adj; m/f*	nomadic; nomad
8406	**irréparable**-*adj*	irreparable
8407	**nettoyeur**-*m; adj*	cleaner; cleaning
8410	**imparfait**-*adj; m*	imperfect; imperfect
8416	**gonflable**-*adj*	inflatable
8418	**illogique**-*adj*	illogical
8422	**traînant**-*adj*	shuffling
8423	**rescapé**-*m; adj*	survivor; surviving
8430	**désirable**-*adj*	desirable| likeable
8437	**nautique**-*adj*	nautical
8439	**inquiétant**-*adj*	worrying; bothering
8445	**basique**-*adj*	basic
8449	**théâtral**-*adj*	theatrical
8470	**poltron**-*m; adj*	coward; cowardly
8476	**yiddish**-*adj; m*	Yiddish; Yiddish
8480	**mormon**-*adj; m*	Mormon; Mormon
8481	**digital**-*adj*	digital
8484	**foulé**-*adj*	trodden
8489	**maure**-*adj*	Moorish
8496	**abject**-*adj*	abject
8498	**préoccupé**-*adj*	concerned
8506	**majuscule**-*adj; f*	capital; capital
8508	**écrasant**-*adj*	crushing| overwhelming;
8515	**horizontal**-*adj*	horizontal
8520	**nordiste**-*adj*	northern
8529	**somali**-*adj; m/f; mpl*	Somali; Somali
8537	**inflammable**-*adj*	flammable
8541	**envieux**-*adj*	green-eyed
8544	**gouvernemental**-*adj*	governmental
8546	**communautaire**-*adj*	communal
8548	**frontal**-*adj*	frontal
8558	**baroque**-*adj; m*	baroque; baroque
8561	**systématique**-*adj; f*	systematic; systematics
8576	**pleurnichard**-*m; adj*	crybaby; whingeing
8593	**hypnotique**-*adj; m*	hypnotic; hypnotic
8596	**rigoureux**-*adj*	rigorous
8600	**importun**-*adj; m*	unwelcome; intruder
8606	**athlétique**-*adj*	athletic
8608	**indolore**-*adj*	painless
8610	**ténébreux**-*adj*	gloomy
8615	**passionnel**-*adj*	passionate
8623	**logistique**-*f; adj*	logistics; logistical
8624	**céramique**-*adj; f*	ceramic; ceramics
8626	**ricain**-*adj*	Yank
8629	**carnivore**-*adj*	carnivorous
8634	**hospitalier**-*adj*	hospital
8642	**vénérable**-*adj*	venerable
8648	**prompt**-*adj*	prompt
8650	**maussade**-*adj*	sulky| surly
8652	**surhumain**-*adj*	superhuman
8653	**fervent**-*adj; m*	fervent; enthusiast
8658	**postérieur**-*adj; m*	posterior; posterior
8661	**contradictoire**-*adj*	contradictory

8662	**véridique**-*adj*	truthful
8673	**volcanique**-*adj*	volcanic
8682	**frisé**-*adj*	curly
8698	**baveux**-*adj*	runny
8700	**inconvenant**-*adj*	improper
8704	**ambulant**-*adj; m*	traveling; traveler
8713	**maboul**-*adj*	crazy| nuts
8715	**irrespectueux**-*adj*	disrespectful
8725	**relaxant**-*adj*	relaxing
8727	**intraveineux**-*adj*	intravenous
8728	**arbitraire**-*adj*	arbitrary
8733	**incendiaire**-*adj; m/f*	incendiary; arsonist
8752	**inspirant**-*adj*	inspiring
8758	**abondant**-*adj; m*	abundant; affluent
8759	**illisible**-*adj*	illegible
8762	**inébranlable**-*adj*	unwavering| steadfast
8763	**chevelu**-*adj*	haired| hairy
8764	**condescendant**-*adj*	patronizing
8765	**arménien**-*adj; m*	Armenian; Armenian
8773	**captif**-*adj; m*	captive; captive
8774	**contemporain**-*adj; m*	contemporary| coeval; contemporary
8776	**dégradant**-*adj*	degrading
8779	**académique**-*adj*	academic
8780	**tolérant**-*adj*	tolerant| forgiving
8782	**satisfaisant**-*adj*	satisfactory
8784	**indéniable**-*adj*	undeniable
8795	**problématique**-*adj*	problematic
8801	**inné**-*adj*	innate| inborn
8802	**marquant**-*adj*	outstanding| remarkable
8812	**tonique**-*adj; f*	tonic; tonic
8813	**intrigant**-*adj; m*	intriguing; intriguer
8815	**soupçonneux**-*adj*	suspicious
8818	**fondant**-*m; adj*	fondant; melting
8819	**catégorique**-*adj*	categorical
8824	**coquet**-*adj*	pretty| stylish
8825	**californien**-*adj*	Californian
8826	**lubrique**-*adj*	lewd| lustful
8833	**difforme**-*adj*	misshapen
8834	**pluvieux**-*adj*	rainy| wet
8836	**sophistiqué**-*adj*	sophisticated
8840	**pragmatique**-*adj*	pragmatic
8850	**lauréat**-*adj; m*	laureate; laureate
8852	**aride**-*adj*	arid
8854	**régulateur**-*m; adj*	regulator; control

8856	**vénéneux**-*adj*	poisonous
8857	**disciplinaire**-*adj*	disciplinary
8865	**thérapeutique**-*adj; f*	therapeutic; therapeutics
8867	**interstellaire**-*adj*	interstellar
8871	**saoudien**-*adj*	Saudi
8873	**pluriel**-*adj; m*	plural; plural
8880	**dérangeant**-*adj*	unpalatable
8881	**perçant**-*adj*	piercing| shrill
8884	**glouton**-*adj; m*	gluttonous; glutton
8893	**étouffant**-*adj*	stifling
8899	**confiant**-*adj*	confident
8904	**femmelette**-*adj*	wimp| sissy
8906	**métaphysique**-*adj; f*	metaphysical; metaphysics
8915	**aryen**-*adj*	Aryan
8916	**sabbatique**-*adj*	sabbatical
8926	**obsessionnel**-*adj*	obsessive
8932	**kaki**-*adj; m*	khaki; khaki
8936	**rayonnant**-*adj*	radiant| shining
8952	**négligeable**-*adj*	negligible
8959	**avantageux**-*adj*	advantageous
8965	**nuisible**-*adj*	harmful| injurious
8966	**alarmant**-*adj*	alarming
8967	**angélique**-*adj*	angelic
8968	**dorsal**-*adj*	dorsal
8969	**fraternel**-*adj*	fraternal
8972	**moqueur**-*m; adj*	mocker; derisive
8982	**inflexible**-*adj*	inflexible| unyielding
8986	**fantaisiste**-*adj; m/f*	fanciful; joker
8991	**rance**-*adj*	rancid
8994	**névrosé**-*adj*	neurotic
8997	**minutieux**-*adj*	thorough
8999	**paranormal**-*adj*	paranormal
9005	**aéroporté**-*adj*	airborne
9006	**aphrodisiaque**-*adj; m*	aphrodisiac; aphrodisiac
9011	**variable**-*adj; f*	variable; variable
9020	**crédule**-*adj*	credulous
9026	**indésirable**-*adj*	undesirable
9032	**éloquent**-*adj*	eloquent
9044	**poseur**-*m; adj*	poseur; phony
9048	**dérisoire**-*adj*	derisory| paltry
9055	**nationaliste**-*adj; m/f*	nationalist; nationalist
9058	**révélateur**-*m; adj*	developer; revealing
9070	**syndical**-*adj*	union| labor

9076	**tendu**-*adj*	tense| tight
9080	**correspondant**-*adj; m*	corresponding; correspondent
9082	**chatouilleux**-*adj*	ticklish
9090	**atténuant**-*adj*	attenuating
9091	**exécrable**-*adj*	execrable
9093	**risible**-*adj*	ludicrous
9096	**consciencieux**-*adj*	conscientious
9099	**canin**-*adj*	canine
9100	**photographique**-*adj*	photographic
9101	**opportuniste**-*adj; m/f*	opportunistic; opportunist
9104	**inédit**-*adj*	novel
9108	**citadin**-*m; adj*	city dweller; city dwelling
9115	**éventuel**-*adj*	prospective
9126	**naissant**-*adj*	nascent
9127	**jésuite**-*m; adj*	Jesuit; Jesuit
9128	**spacieux**-*adj*	spacious
9130	**troyen**-*adj*	Trojan
9133	**génital**-*adj*	genital
9135	**papal**-*adj*	papal
9137	**précaire**-*adj*	precarious
9141	**dévastateur**-*adj*	devastating
9152	**tordu**-*adj; m*	twisted; crackpot
9153	**dévergondé**-*adj*	wanton
9155	**frêle**-*adj*	frail
9156	**généalogique**-*adj*	genealogical
9157	**latéral**-*adj*	lateral
9161	**inexcusable**-*adj*	inexcusable
9162	**distinct**-*adj*	separate
9164	**significatif**-*adj*	significant
9168	**battant**-*m; adj*	clapper| fighter; swinging
9169	**subversif**-*adj*	subversive
9170	**suppliant**-*adj; m*	begging; suppliant
9174	**immaculé**-*adj*	immaculate
9180	**soyeux**-*adj*	silky| silk
9203	**mensuel**-*adj*	monthly
9204	**aborigène**-*adj; m/f*	aboriginal; aborigine
9207	**pornographique**-*adj*	pornographic
9209	**compulsif**-*adj*	compulsive
9211	**androïde**-*adj; m*	android; android
9232	**romanesque**-*adj*	dreamy| fictional
9241	**vraisemblable**-*adj*	similar
9248	**attribut**-*m; adj*	attribute; predicate
9249	**chaste**-*adj*	chaste
9250	**insecticide**-*m; adj*	insecticide; insecticidal
9255	**provincial**-*adj; m*	provincial; provincial
9256	**ignare**-*m/f; adj*	ignoramus; clueless
9257	**bulgare**-*adj; m*	Bulgarian; Bulgarian
9263	**impérialiste**-*adj; m/f*	imperialist; imperialist
9267	**moelleux**-*adj; m*	soft; mellowness
9269	**atmosphérique**-*adj*	atmospheric
9270	**constipé**-*adj*	constipated
9271	**dignitaire**-*m; adj*	dignitary; genual
9272	**refoulé**-*adj*	discharged| repressed
9274	**réjouissant**-*adj*	cheerful
9277	**volage**-*adj*	flighty
9278	**imprenable**-*adj*	impregnable
9281	**désinvolte**-*adj*	casual
9282	**platonique**-*adj*	platonic
9283	**rancunier**-*adj*	spiteful
9285	**harpie**-*f; adj*	harpy; harpy
9291	**pedigree**-*adj; m*	pedigree; pedigree
9294	**chiqué**-*adj*	sham| airs
9296	**progressiste**-*adj; m/f*	progressive; progressive
9301	**marginal**-*adj; m*	marginal; dropout
9305	**austère**-*adj*	austere
9306	**pivot**-*m; adj*	pivot; pivotal
9317	**éditorial**-*adj; m*	editorial; editorial
9318	**affectif**-*adj*	affective
9321	**déconcertant**-*adj*	disconcerting
9330	**pilleur**-*m; adj*	looter; deceitful
9340	**immunitaire**-*adj*	immune
9341	**thoracique**-*adj*	thoracic
9343	**écologique**-*adj*	ecological
9346	**Bengale**-*m; adj*	Bengal; Bengal
9349	**comestible**-*adj*	edible
9351	**passade**-*adj*	fancy
9354	**inquisiteur**-*m; adj*	inquisitor; inquisitive
9355	**prolongé**-*adj*	extended
9357	**menaçant**-*adj*	threatening| menacing
9360	**gréviste**-*m/f; adj*	striker; striking
9361	**précipité**-*adj*	rushed
9367	**illettré**-*adj*	illiterate
9369	**paradisiaque**-*adj*	heavenly
9373	**pathologique**-*adj*	pathological
9376	**crème**-*adj; f*	cream; cream

9380	**flexible**-*adj*	flexible
9382	**isolé**-*adj; m*	isolated| insulated; isolated person
9390	**angulaire**-*adj*	angular
9396	**piéton**-*m; adj*	pedestrian; pedestrian
9402	**parlementaire**-*adj; m/f*	parliamentary; parliamentarian
9412	**sismique**-*adj*	seismic
9415	**crânien**-*adj*	cranial
9425	**provocateur**-*adj; m*	challenging; agitator
9431	**forcené**-*m; adj*	madman| gunner; fanatical
9433	**captivant**-*adj*	captivating
9434	**fortuné**-*adj*	wealthy
9435	**mousseux**-*adj*	sparkling| foamy
9445	**autochtone**-*m/f; adj*	native; native
9454	**turquoise**-*f; adj*	turquoise; turquoise
9458	**beurré**-*adj*	plastered| buttered
9464	**intégral**-*adj*	integral
9471	**pectoral**-*adj; m*	pectoral; pectoral
9485	**argenté**-*adj*	silver
9494	**lourdaud**-*adj; m*	clumsy| heavy; oaf
9499	**photogénique**-*adj*	photogenic
9502	**farfelu**-*m; adj*	wacky; crazy
9505	**louable**-*adj*	commendable| rentable
9508	**interurbain**-*adj*	interurban
9510	**débordant**-*adj*	boundless
9514	**moustachu**-*adj*	moustached
9515	**magnanime**-*adj*	magnanimous
9520	**rustique**-*adj*	rustic| country
9524	**pygmée**-*f; adj*	Pygmy; pygmy
9530	**imaginatif**-*adj*	imaginative
9536	**fonctionnel**-*adj*	functional
9537	**vioque**-*adj*	wrinkly
9550	**insipide**-*adj*	tasteless
9559	**progressif**-*adj*	progressive
9561	**vacant**-*adj*	vacant
9568	**épineux**-*adj*	thorny| tricky
9572	**digestif**-*adj*	digestive
9581	**discutable**-*adj*	questionable| debatable
9582	**diagnostique**-*adj*	diagnostic
9591	**imaginable**-*adj*	imaginable
9599	**anorexique**-*adj; m/f*	anorexic; anorexic
9601	**linguistique**-*adj; f*	linguistic; linguistics
9602	**erroné**-*adj*	wrong| erroneous
9603	**idyllique**-*adj*	idyllic
9604	**hypothétique**-*adj*	hypothetical
9606	**lyrique**-*adj; f*	lyrical; lyric
9607	**fiévreux**-*adj*	feverish| hectic
9608	**suave**-*adj*	sweet
9609	**brouillon**-*m; adj*	draft; untidy
9612	**nette**-*adj*	clear| frank
9631	**pointilleux**-*adj*	punctilious
9637	**ardu**-*adj*	difficult| arduous
9643	**utilisable**-*adj*	usable| serviceable
9645	**médiéval**-*adj*	medieval
9646	**finlandais**-*adj*	Finnish
9647	**brisant**-*adj; m*	breaking; breaker
9649	**inopportun**-*adj*	inappropriate
9653	**salarié**-*adj; m*	salaried; wage earner
9654	**dansant**-*adj*	dancing
9656	**toscan**-*adj*	Tuscan
9657	**vestimentaire**-*adj*	dress| clothing
9658	**ambigu**-*adj*	ambiguous
9660	**pédagogique**-*adj*	educational| pedagogical
9668	**futuriste**-*adj; m/f*	futuristic; futurist
9669	**iranien**-*adj; m*	Iranian; Iranian
9672	**activiste**-*m/f; adj*	activist; smart
9676	**notable**-*adj; m*	notable| worthy; worthy
9681	**plaisantin**-*m; adj*	joker; bantering
9683	**arriviste**-*adj; m/f*	pushy; go-getter
9684	**boutonneux**-*adj*	spotty
9699	**énigmatique**-*adj*	enigmatic
9714	**harmonieux**-*adj*	harmonious
9716	**frénétique**-*adj*	frantic
9721	**réceptif**-*adj*	receptive
9722	**jugulaire**-*adj; f*	jugular; chinstrap
9734	**indisponible**-*adj*	unavailable
9736	**multinational**-*adj*	multinational
9759	**abordable**-*adj*	affordable
9767	**apaisant**-*adj*	soothing
9768	**gérant**-*m; adj*	manager; managing
9773	**adorateur**-*m; adj*	adorer; worshipful
9774	**blême**-*adj*	pale
9777	**arbitrage**-*m; adj*	arbitrage; arbitral
9780	**arsenic**-*adj; m*	arsenic; arsenic
9782	**calcaire**-*m; adj*	limestone; calcareous
9784	**thaïlandais**-*adj; mpl*	Thai

9787	**septique**-*adj*	septic
9791	**ombilical**-*adj*	umbilical
9792	**psychédélique**-*adj*	psychedelic
9796	**pubien**-*adj*	pubic
9802	**posthume**-*adj*	posthumous
9806	**illicite**-*adj*	illicit
9809	**fringant**-*adj*	frisky
9811	**invulnérable**-*adj*	invulnerable
9815	**indiscutable**-*adj*	indisputable
9817	**retiré**-*adj*	withdrawn| retired
9823	**pompette**-*adj*	tipsy
9824	**incontestable**-*adj*	indisputable
9832	**espiègle**-*adj; m/f*	playful| impish; imp
9839	**percepteur**-*m; adj*	collector; percipient
9847	**persan**-*adj; m*	Persian; Persian
9850	**inexact**-*adj*	incorrect| inexact
9851	**intentionnel**-*adj*	intentional
9856	**anesthésique**-*adj*	anesthetic
9863	**itinérant**-*adj; m*	itinerant; itinerant
9870	**libanais**-*adj; mpl*	Lebanese
9872	**intergalactique**-*adj*	intergalactic
9878	**pesticide**-*m; adj*	pesticide; pesticidal
9882	**cordial**-*adj; m*	cordial; cordial
9884	**libéré**-*adj*	released
9886	**gémissant**-*adj*	moaning| groaning
9893	**fanfaron**-*m; adj*	braggart; boastful
9894	**teint**-*adj; m*	dyed; color
9899	**déporté**-*m; adj*	deportee; deported
9903	**mélodramatique**-*adj*	melodramatic
9904	**vingtième**-*adj*	twentieth| twentieth
9905	**aigre**-*adj*	sour
9906	**invaincu**-*adj*	unbeaten
9909	**altruiste**-*adj; m/f*	altruistic; altruist
9914	**asthmatique**-*adj; m/f*	asthmatic; asthmatic
9915	**calculateur**-*adj*	calculating
9916	**angoissant**-*adj*	scary
9919	**bâti**-*adj; m*	built; bed
9930	**imitateur**-*m; adj*	imitator; mimic
9934	**prude**-*m/f; adj*	prude; prudish
9938	**détergent**-*adj; m*	detergent; cleanser
9944	**ukrainien**-*adj; m|mpl*	Ukrainian; Ukrainian
9950	**duveteux**-*adj*	fluffy
9951	**oblong**-*adj*	oblong
9952	**prolétaire**-*m/f; adj*	proletarian; prolete
9961	**fourni**-*adj*	provided
9964	**vantard**-*adj; m*	boastful; braggart
9966	**physiologique**-*adj*	physiological
9968	**nécessiteux**-*adj; m/f*	needy; needy person
9975	**impayable**-*adj*	priceless
9986	**charnel**-*adj*	carnal
9988	**bouleversant**-*adj*	upsetting
9995	**navrant**-*adj*	heartbreaking
9996	**constructif**-*adj*	constructive
9999	**dièse**-*adj; m*	sharp; sharp
10004	**dominateur**-*adj; m*	domineering; ruler
10006	**obtus**-*adj*	obtuse| thick
10008	**aveuglant**-*adj*	blinding
10009	**cancéreux**-*adj*	cancerous
10014	**arrivant**-*adj; m*	incoming; arrival
10021	**décadent**-*adj; m*	decadent; decadent
10023	**fétide**-*adj*	fetid| rank

Adverbs

Rank	French-*PoS*	Translation
7521	**mystérieusement**-*adv*	darkly
7566	**inconsciemment**-*adv*	unconsciously
7584	**intentionnellement**-*adv*	intentionally
7598	**quotidiennement**-*adv*	daily
7698	**radicalement**-*adv*	radically
7721	**joyeusement**-*adv*	merrily
7762	**grièvement**-*adv*	severely
7766	**logiquement**-*adv*	logically
7779	**bis**-*m; adv; adj*	bis; twice; repeat
7806	**partiellement**-*adv*	partially
7811	**injustement**-*adv*	unfairly
7839	**fidèlement**-*adv*	faithfully
7899	**spontanément**-*adv*	spontaneously
7965	**mortellement**-*adv*	fatally| mortally
7977	**provisoirement**-*adv*	tentatively
8005	**professionnellement**-*adv*	professionally
8053	**étonnement**-*m; adv*	astonishment; surprisingly
8061	**respectueusement**-*adv*	with respect
8101	**miraculeusement**-*adv*	miraculously
8102	**vraisemblablement**-*adv*	in all likelihood
8116	**cordialement**-*adv*	cordially
8185	**précipitamment**-*adv*	hastily| precipitately
8190	**remarquablement**-*adv*	remarkably
8202	**ardemment**-*adv*	ardently
8228	**prochainement**-*adv*	shortly
8337	**généreusement**-*adv*	generously
8350	**efficacement**-*adv*	effectively
8366	**prématurément**-*adv*	prematurely
8429	**froidement**-*adv*	coldly
8485	**individuellement**-*adv*	individually
8486	**inévitablement**-*adv*	inevitably
8511	**agréablement**-*adv*	pleasantly
8536	**activement**-*adv*	busily
8556	**aveuglément**-*adv*	blindly
8645	**cruellement**-*adv*	cruelly
8649	**raisonnablement**-*adv*	reasonably
8664	**étroitement**-*adv*	closely
8688	**exceptionnellement**-*adv*	exceptionally
8702	**brillamment**-*adv*	brilliantly
8718	**courageusement**-*adv*	courageously
8755	**décemment**-*adv*	decently
8761	**humainement**-*adv*	humanly
8838	**délicieusement**-*adv*	deliciously
8883	**gaiement**-*adv*	gladly
8953	**indirectement**-*adv*	indirectly
8954	**loyalement**-*adv*	loyally
9192	**excessivement**-*adv*	excessively
9210	**catégoriquement**-*adv*	categorically
9230	**silencieusement**-*adv*	silently
9265	**instinctivement**-*adv*	instinctively
9268	**globalement**-*adv*	overall
9280	**positivement**-*adv*	positively
9312	**mondialement**-*adv*	worldwide
9324	**intérieurement**-*adv*	internally
9364	**royalement**-*adv*	royally
9383	**visuellement**-*adv*	visually
9384	**minutieusement**-*adv*	thoroughly
9397	**distinctement**-*adv*	distinctly| audibly
9419	**tragiquement**-*adv*	tragically
9424	**clandestinement**-*adv*	clandestinely
9448	**anciennement**-*adv*	formerly
9555	**gracieusement**-*adv*	graciously| free of charge
9558	**solidement**-*adv*	firmly
9664	**communément**-*adv*	commonly
9711	**extraordinairement**-*adv*	extraordinarily
9732	**virtuellement**-*adv*	virtually
9742	**superbement**-*adv*	magnificently
9834	**indubitablement**-*adv*	undoubtedly
9840	**sciemment**-*adv*	knowingly
9876	**traditionnellement**-*adv*	traditionally
9956	**obligatoirement**-*adv*	inevitably
9969	**habilement**-*adv*	skilfully| cleverly
9974	**admirablement**-*adv*	admirably

Numerals

Rank	**French**-*PoS*	Translation	
7535	**troisièmement**-*num*	thirdly	num
8848	**douzième**-*num*	twelfth	num
9825	**centième**-*num*	hundredth	num
9960	**treizième**-*num*	thirteenth	num

Nouns

Rank	French-PoS	Translation
7503	**synthétique**-*adj; m*	synthetic; synthetic
7505	**cynisme**-*m*	cynicism
7508	**paternité**-*f*	paternity
7509	**trompeur**-*adj; m*	misleading; deceiver
7510	**artisan**-*m*	artisan
7511	**lésion**-*f*	lesion
7512	**téléviseur**-*m*	TV
7513	**sodomie**-*f*	sodomy
7514	**charrue**-*f*	plow
7515	**lande**-*f*	moor
7516	**négociateur**-*m*	negotiator
7518	**bourdonnement**-*m*	buzz| hum
7520	**troc**-*m*	barter| bartering
7523	**dessinateur**-*m*	designer| draftsman
7525	**pamplemousse**-*m*	grapefruit
7527	**autruche**-*f*	ostrich
7528	**courroux**-*m*	wrath
7529	**magnat**-*m*	magnate
7530	**corpus**-*m*	corpus
7532	**imposture**-*f*	imposture| fraud
7536	**gendarmerie**-*f*	police
7537	**grognon**-*adj; m*	grumpy; grumbler
7539	**anchois**-*m*	anchovy
7541	**esquive**-*f*	dodge
7543	**postérité**-*f*	posterity
7544	**pignon**-*m*	pinion| gear
7545	**cornet**-*m*	horn| screw
7547	**charte**-*f*	charter| convention
7549	**qualification**-*f*	qualification
7550	**cacao**-*m*	cocoa
7552	**condor**-*m*	condor
7553	**constructeur**-*m*	builder
7554	**intégration**-*f*	integration
7560	**algèbre**-*f*	algebra
7561	**dénouement**-*m*	outcome
7564	**dépotoir**-*m; vb*	dumping ground; refuse dump
7565	**tunique**-*f*	tunic
7567	**patio**-*m*	patio
7570	**berge**-*f*	bank
7572	**ballot**-*m; adj*	bundle; clownish
7575	**brasserie**-*f*	brewery
7576	**fiole**-*f*	flask
7578	**mite**-*f*	moth
7579	**éveil**-*m*	awakening
7580	**émoi**-*m*	stir| emotion
7581	**texture**-*f*	texture
7583	**geôlier**-*m*	jailer
7589	**entorse**-*f*	sprain| strain
7591	**mets**-*m*	dish
7592	**garrot**-*m*	tourniquet
7595	**libido**-*f*	libido
7596	**cortex**-*m*	cortex
7597	**fertilité**-*f*	fertility
7599	**cadran**-*m*	dial
7603	**inquisition**-*f*	inquisition
7604	**trinité**-*f*	trinity
7605	**buveur**-*m*	drinker
7606	**paillasson**-*m*	mat
7607	**renouveau**-*m*	renewal
7608	**corbeille**-*f*	basket
7611	**mufle**-*m; adj*	oaf; caddish
7612	**diversité**-*f*	diversity
7613	**math**-*m*	math
7615	**alchimie**-*f; adj*	alchemy; alchemic
7616	**anarchiste**-*adj; m/f*	anarchist; anarchist
7618	**canif**-*m*	penknife
7620	**allocation**-*f*	allocation| allowance
7621	**rééducation**-*f*	re-education
7622	**guérillero**-*m*	guerrilla
7624	**répercussion**-*f*	repercussion
7626	**monologue**-*m*	monologue
7627	**icône**-*f*	icon
7631	**militant**-*m*	activist
7632	**électrochoc**-*m*	electroshock
7633	**herpès**-*m*	herpes
7634	**pipeline**-*m*	pipeline
7635	**perfusion**-*f*	drip
7636	**pollen**-*m*	pollen
7637	**grève**-*f*	strike
7639	**échelon**-*m*	echelon
7640	**saligaud**-*m*	bleeder| creep
7642	**circulaire**-*adj; f*	circular; circular
7643	**centenaire**-*adj; m/f*	centenary; centenary
7644	**sérénade**-*f*	serenade
7645	**prêche**-*m*	preaching
7646	**imprimeur**-*m*	printer
7647	**aubaine**-*f*	boon| windfall
7649	**puma**-*m*	puma
7650	**lux**-*m*	lux

7651	**zeppelin**-*m*	zeppelin
7653	**coqueluche**-*f*	whooping cough
7654	**acre**-*m*	acre
7655	**alto**-*adj; m*	alto; alto
7656	**limier**-*m*	bloodhound
7657	**gothique**-*adj; m*	Gothic; Gothic
7659	**museau**-*m*	muzzle
7660	**ponte**-*f*	spawn
7663	**titulaire**-*m/f; adj*	holder; titular
7664	**hebdomadaire**-*adj; m*	weekly; weekly
7665	**préoccupation**-*f*	concern| preoccupation
7668	**épileptique**-*adj; m/f*	epileptic; epileptic person
7669	**pagaie**-*f*	paddle
7670	**folklore**-*m*	folklore
7671	**décadence**-*f*	decadence| decay
7672	**protestant**-*adj; m*	Protestant; Protestant
7673	**dinar**-*m*	dinar
7674	**absolution**-*f*	absolution
7675	**intérimaire**-*adj; m/f*	interim; deputy
7676	**tranquillisant**-*m; adj*	tranquilizer; tranquilizing
7680	**remise**-*f*	delivery| remission
7681	**usure**-*f*	wear
7682	**gîte**-*m*	home| shelter
7683	**lasso**-*m*	lasso| noose
7686	**maxime**-*f*	maxim
7687	**bijoutier**-*m*	jeweler
7689	**escapade**-*f*	escapade
7690	**amande**-*f*	almond
7692	**typhus**-*m*	typhus
7693	**colosse**-*m; adj*	colossus; colossal
7694	**narcotique**-*adj; m*	narcotic; narcotic
7696	**carrelage**-*m*	tiles
7697	**albinos**-*m*	albino
7700	**genèse**-*f*	genesis
7701	**éphémère**-*adj; m*	ephemeral; ephemeral
7702	**destinée**-*f*	destiny
7703	**prouesse**-*f*	prowess
7704	**intoxication**-*f*	poisoning| addiction
7705	**alcoolisme**-*m*	alcoholism
7706	**chaman**-*m*	shaman
7708	**appendicite**-*f*	appendicitis
7710	**Antéchrist**-*m*	Antichrist
7711	**oméga**-*m*	omega
7712	**joug**-*m*	yoke
7713	**purification**-*f*	purification
7714	**insubordination**-*f*	insubordination
7717	**prédicateur**-*m*	preacher
7720	**transfusion**-*f*	transfusion
7722	**extradition**-*f*	extradition
7723	**hippodrome**-*m*	hippodrome
7724	**couturière**-*f*	seamstress
7725	**garnement**-*m*	rascal
7727	**vitalité**-*f*	vitality| vigor
7728	**bastion**-*m*	bastion
7731	**Siam**-*m*	Siam
7732	**hippopotame**-*m*	hippopotamus
7733	**abstrait**-*adj; m*	abstract; abstract
7734	**pétrolier**-*m*	tanker| oilman
7736	**profane**-*adj; m/f*	profane; layman
7737	**suspens**-*m*	suspense
7738	**disgrâce**-*f*	disgrace
7741	**bureaucrate**-*m/f*	bureaucrat
7744	**corsage**-*m*	blouse| corsage
7746	**béret**-*m*	beret
7748	**psychanalyse**-*f*	psychoanalysis
7749	**pesanteur**-*f*	gravity
7751	**phosphore**-*m*	phosphorus
7753	**aspiration**-*f*	aspiration
7754	**débit**-*m*	debit| output
7755	**souplesse**-*f*	flexibility| suppleness
7756	**rapprochement**-*m*	reconciliation| link
7757	**toxico**-*m/f*	junkie
7759	**simulateur**-*m*	simulator
7760	**habitat**-*m*	habitat
7764	**législation**-*f*	legislation
7767	**attirail**-*m*	paraphernalia
7769	**festivité**-*f*	festivity
7770	**timidité**-*f*	timidity
7772	**accroc**-*m*	snag| infraction
7773	**pavé**-*adj; m*	paved; pavement
7774	**saga**-*f*	saga
7776	**injure**-*f*	insult| affront
7779	**bis**-*m; adv; adj*	bis; twice; repeat
7780	**myope**-*adj; m/f*	short-sighted; myope
7781	**perversion**-*f*	perversion
7782	**mégère**-*f*	shrew| vixen
7783	**toison**-*f*	fleece

7784	**bouilloire**-*f*	kettle
7785	**hamac**-*m*	hammock
7787	**bénéficiaire**-*m/f; adj*	beneficiary; profitable
7788	**rizière**-*f*	paddy field
7789	**déviation**-*f*	deviation
7791	**designer**-*m*	designer
7793	**cavité**-*f*	cavity
7794	**napalm**-*m*	napalm
7795	**vandalisme**-*m*	vandalism
7796	**inceste**-*m*	incest
7798	**rempart**-*m*	rampart
7800	**persécution**-*f*	persecution
7801	**faucheur**-*m*	mower| reaper
7802	**précepteur**-*m*	tutor
7803	**macaroni**-*m*	macaroni
7805	**logeur**-*m*	landlord
7808	**fautif**-*adj; m*	incorrect| culprit
7809	**amulette**-*f*	amulet
7810	**assignation**-*f*	summons| subpoena
7813	**prélèvement**-*m; adj*	sample; compensatory
7814	**chapelet**-*m*	beads| rosary
7815	**asticot**-*m*	maggot
7817	**tapisserie**-*f*	tapestry
7818	**contravention**-*f*	violation
7819	**blocus**-*m*	blockade
7820	**caddie**-*m*	caddy| trolley
7821	**tombola**-*f*	raffle
7822	**sillage**-*m*	wake
7823	**croupier**-*m*	croupier
7824	**cellier**-*m*	cellar
7827	**remous**-*m*	swirl
7828	**cloison**-*f*	partition
7829	**instantané**-*adj; m*	instant; snapshot
7830	**dissertation**-*f*	dissertation
7831	**miaou**-*m*	meow
7832	**improvisation**-*f*	improvisation
7833	**broyeur**-*m*	crusher
7834	**cocon**-*m*	cocoon
7835	**rocker**-*m*	rock musician
7836	**échographie**-*f*	ultrasound| scan
7837	**bordure**-*f*	border
7840	**galère**-*f*	galley
7841	**surréaliste**-*m/f*	surrealist
7842	**incitation**-*f*	incitement
7843	**donation**-*f*	donation
7844	**guirlande**-*f*	garland| string
7846	**saxo**-*m*	sax
7849	**scierie**-*f*	sawmill
7853	**messagerie**-*f*	messaging| courier service
7854	**indicateur**-*m*	indicator
7855	**rumba**-*f*	rumba
7856	**triade**-*f*	triad
7857	**écuyer**-*m*	squire
7858	**armurerie**-*f*	armory
7859	**confrère**-*m*	colleague
7861	**braqueur**-*m*	raider| robber
7862	**détritus**-*m*	litter
7863	**transmetteur**-*m*	transmitter
7864	**clarinette**-*f*	clarinet
7865	**clavicule**-*f*	clavicle
7866	**chevreuil**-*m*	roe| deer
7868	**opposant**-*adj; m*	opponent; oppositionist
7871	**cachemire**-*m*	cashmere
7872	**immersion**-*f*	immersion| diving
7876	**interface**-*f*	interface
7877	**convenance**-*f*	convenience
7878	**amorce**-*f*	bait
7880	**ténor**-*m*	tenor
7882	**sonate**-*f*	sonata
7883	**niais**-*m; adj*	simpleton; simple
7884	**hirondelle**-*f*	swallow
7885	**capitulation**-*f*	capitulation
7888	**pardessus**-*m*	overcoat
7889	**nuance**-*f*	shade| nuance
7890	**caboche**-*f*	noggin
7893	**carillon**-*m*	carillon
7894	**pat**-*adj; m*	stalemate; stalemate
7896	**originalité**-*f*	originality
7897	**sténo**-*f*	shorthand| stenographer
7901	**verge**-*f*	yard| rod
7904	**bulldozer**-*m*	bulldozer
7909	**revendeur**-*m*	dealer
7911	**malt**-*m*	malt
7912	**gospel**-*m*	gospel
7913	**rave**-*f*	rave
7914	**administratif**-*adj; m*	administrative; executive
7916	**fourneau**-*m*	furnace
7918	**flatterie**-*f*	flattery

7922 **hindou**-*adj; m* Hindu; Hindu
7923 **féministe**-*adj; m/f* feminist; feminist
7924 **surcharge**-*f* overload
7926 **lavette**-*f; adj* mop; wet
7927 **hyène**-*f* hyena
7930 **ingénierie**-*f* engineering
7932 **armistice**-*m* armistice| truce
7934 **piraterie**-*f* piracy
7935 **estrade**-*f* platform| stage
7936 **fonte**-*f* melting| font
7938 **choucroute**-*f* sauerkraut
7940 **assemblage**-*m* assembly
7944 **spéculation**-*f* speculation
7945 **loch**-*m* loch
7952 **assureur**-*m* insurer
7953 **bit**-*m* bit
7954 **hémisphère**-*m* hemisphere
7955 **exterminateur**-*m; adj* exterminator; exterminating
7957 **traceur**-*m* stud| teat
7958 **mamelon**-*m* nipple| hill
7961 **averse**-*f* shower
7964 **épouvante**-*f* dread
7967 **bureaucratie**-*f* bureaucracy
7971 **gangrène**-*f* gangrene
7973 **jugeote**-*f* savvy| gumption
7974 **blizzard**-*m* blizzard
7976 **bifteck**-*m* steak
7978 **désobéissance**-*f* disobedience
7980 **acrobate**-*m/f* acrobat
7981 **pillard**-*m; adj* plunderer; predatory
7983 **guilde**-*f* guild
7984 **paperasserie**-*f* red tape
7986 **podium**-*m* podium
7987 **recyclage**-*m* recycling
7988 **serpillière**-*f* mop| swab
7989 **expérimentation**-*f* experimentation
7990 **thorax**-*m; f* thorax; bust
7992 **fornication**-*f* fornication
7993 **exorciste**-*m* exorcist
7994 **marqueur**-*m* marker| scorer
7995 **clonage**-*m* cloning
7996 **orque**-*m/f* orc| orca
7997 **videur**-*m* bouncer
7998 **écolier**-*m* schoolboy
7999 **contrefaçon**-*f* counterfeit
8000 **matou**-*m* tomcat
8001 **Chypre**-*f* Cyprus
8002 **traîtrise**-*f* treachery
8003 **tentacule**-*m* tentacle
8006 **faisan**-*m* pheasant
8007 **essayage**-*m* fitting
8008 **romancier**-*m* novelist
8009 **chimère**-*f* chimera
8010 **affirmation**-*f* affirmation
8012 **spasme**-*m* spasm
8013 **parodie**-*f* parody| skit
8014 **géomètre**-*m/f* land surveyor
8017 **confiserie**-*f* confectionery
8018 **globule**-*m* globule
8022 **aboi**-*m* barking
8023 **populace**-*f* populace| mob
8024 **salve**-*f* salvo| salute
8028 **parloir**-*m* parlor
8029 **requête**-*f* request
8030 **chalumeau**-*m* blowtorch
8031 **biologiste**-*m/f* biologist
8033 **appendice**-*m* appendix
8034 **roumain**-*adj; m* Romanian; Romanian
8035 **sodium**-*m* sodium
8036 **gamelle**-*f* lunch box
8039 **acné**-*f* acne
8040 **bâtonnet**-*m* rod
8041 **changeur**-*m* converter
8042 **beagle**-*m* beagle
8043 **stratagème**-*m* stratagem| ploy
8044 **rayonnement**-*m* influence| radiance
8046 **stimulation**-*f* stimulation
8049 **rénovation**-*f* renovation
8050 **camionneur**-*m* truck driver
8051 **prothèse**-*f* prosthesis
8053 **étonnement**-*m; adv* astonishment; surprisingly
8055 **boueux**-*adj; m* muddy; bin man
8057 **faille**-*f* break
8059 **pensionnaire**-*m/f* boarder| pensionary
8062 **iode**-*m* iodine
8063 **adoration**-*f* worship
8065 **échafaud**-*m* scaffold
8066 **saucisson**-*m* sausage
8068 **botanique**-*adj; f* botanical; botany
8069 **furet**-*m* ferret

8073	**tabou**-*adj; m*	taboo; taboo
8074	**vicomte**-*m*	viscount
8075	**turban**-*m*	turban
8077	**pompon**-*m*	tassel| cake
8078	**négresse**-*f*	nigger
8080	**désinfectant**-*adj; m*	disinfectant; disinfectant
8081	**astre**-*m*	star
8082	**framboise**-*f*	raspberry
8083	**incarcération**-*f*	incarceration
8084	**infériorité**-*f*	inferiority
8085	**astronome**-*m/f*	astronomer
8086	**poivron**-*m*	pepper
8087	**irrationnel**-*adj; m*	irrational; irrational
8088	**déodorant**-*m*	deodorant
8090	**lupus**-*m*	lupus
8092	**conduite**-*f*	conduct| driving
8093	**mousson**-*m*	monsoon
8095	**bolide**-*m*	bolide| high end car
8096	**vandale**-*adj; m/f*	vandal; vandal
8097	**mélodrame**-*m*	melodrama
8098	**acceptation**-*f*	acceptance
8099	**dégradation**-*f*	degradation| deterioration
8100	**insinuation**-*f*	insinuation
8103	**breuvage**-*m*	beverage
8104	**veto**-*m*	veto
8105	**recueil**-*m*	collection
8106	**aimant**-*m*	magnet
8107	**boursier**-*m*	scholar| stock market
8108	**carafe**-*f*	carafe| jug
8109	**légèreté**-*f*	lightness
8110	**mélasse**-*f*	treacle| molasses
8111	**tisonnier**-*m*	poker
8112	**hache**-*f*	ax
8113	**archéologie**-*f*	archeology
8114	**transcription**-*f*	transcription
8115	**corrida**-*f*	bullfight
8117	**java**-*f*	rave
8118	**recteur**-*m; adj*	rector; rectorial
8120	**accoutrement**-*m*	regalia
8121	**argot**-*m*	slang
8123	**pacifiste**-*m/f*	pacifist
8125	**mandarin**-*m*	Mandarin
8127	**passoire**-*f*	strainer
8128	**ballerine**-*f*	ballerina
8129	**verdure**-*f*	greenery| greenness
8131	**cerisier**-*m*	cherry
8132	**compression**-*f*	compression
8134	**rapace**-*adj; m*	rapacious; predator
8137	**croustillant**-*adj; m*	crispy; crispness
8138	**contusion**-*f*	contusion
8139	**mémorial**-*m*	memorial
8142	**déménageur**-*m*	mover
8143	**moisissure**-*f*	mold| mouldiness
8146	**jonction**-*f*	junction
8147	**éminence**-*f*	eminence| height
8149	**mutilation**-*f*	mutilation
8150	**cylindre**-*m*	cylinder
8151	**styliste**-*m/f*	stylist
8152	**jaquette**-*f*	jacket
8154	**menuisier**-*m*	carpenter
8157	**médiocrité**-*f*	mediocrity
8158	**balourd**-*m; adj*	oaf; awkward
8159	**abîme**-*m*	abyss| gulf
8160	**documentation**-*f*	documentation
8161	**veilleur**-*m; adj*	watchman; watchful
8162	**déchéance**-*f*	decline
8163	**alouette**-*f*	lark
8165	**moue**-*f*	pout
8166	**mausolée**-*m*	mausoleum
8168	**tuyauterie**-*f*	piping
8169	**fable**-*f*	fable
8171	**appréciation**-*f*	appreciation
8172	**grossièreté**-*f*	rudeness
8174	**ineptie**-*f*	ineptitude
8175	**commanditaire**-*m*	silent partner| sponsor
8176	**arcade**-*f*	arcade
8178	**questionnaire**-*m*	questionnaire
8179	**faussaire**-*m/f*	forger
8180	**dactylo**-*m/f*	typist
8182	**scarabée**-*m*	beetle
8183	**shah**-*m*	shah
8186	**abruti**-*m; adj*	jerk; stupid
8187	**métabolisme**-*m*	metabolism
8191	**unisson**-*m*	unison
8192	**préservation**-*f*	preservation
8194	**vallon**-*m*	small valley
8196	**hibernation**-*f*	hibernation
8197	**pathologie**-*f*	pathology
8198	**dioxyde**-*m*	dioxide

8199	**enchaînement**-*m*	sequence| linking
8204	**canasson**-*m*	nag
8206	**bazooka**-*m*	bazooka
8207	**nervosité**-*f*	nervousness
8208	**yogi**-*m*	yogi
8209	**charisme**-*m*	charisma
8211	**exécuteur**-*m*	executor
8212	**rousseur**-*f*	redness
8214	**groom**-*m*	bellhop| page
8216	**bretzel**-*m*	pretzel
8217	**obligeance**-*f*	helpfulness
8221	**natte**-*f*	mat| braid
8222	**babiole**-*f*	bauble
8223	**textile**-*adj; m*	textile; textile
8224	**asperge**-*f*	asparagus
8225	**linceul**-*m*	shroud| grave clothes
8226	**curé**-*m*	priest
8227	**carrure**-*f*	shoulders| build
8230	**arithmétique**-*adj; f*	arithmetic; arithmetic
8231	**buanderie**-*f*	utility room
8232	**cigogne**-*f*	stork
8233	**éleveur**-*m*	farmer
8234	**Bolchevik**-*m/f*	Bolshevik
8235	**ingéniosité**-*f*	ingenuity
8236	**rafale**-*f*	gust| flurry
8237	**avènement**-*m*	advent
8238	**toge**-*f*	toga
8239	**thermos**-*m; adj*	thermos; thermos
8243	**potassium**-*m*	potassium
8244	**réglisse**-*f*	licorice
8246	**antiquaire**-*adj; m/f*	antiquarian; antiquarian
8247	**récidiviste**-*m/f*	recidivist
8249	**arrosage**-*m*	spray
8251	**orbite**-*f*	orbit
8256	**parachutiste**-*m/f*	parachutist
8257	**convalescence**-*f*	recovery
8258	**ouvrage**-*m*	handiwork
8259	**virtuose**-*m/f*	virtuoso
8260	**vicaire**-*m*	vicar
8261	**relatif**-*adj; m*	relative; relative
8262	**intimidation**-*f*	intimidation
8263	**continuité**-*f*	continuity
8265	**ovale**-*adj; m*	oval; oval
8266	**enzyme**-*f*	enzyme
8267	**vecteur**-*m*	vector
8268	**végétation**-*f*	vegetation
8269	**éraflure**-*f*	scratch| score
8270	**contraction**-*f*	contraction
8272	**fouineur**-*m; adj*	snoop; prying
8273	**lamentation**-*f*	lamentation
8275	**cône**-*m*	cone
8276	**connaisseur**-*m*	connoisseur
8277	**métropole**-*f*	metropolis
8280	**gaine**-*f*	sheath
8281	**lucidité**-*f*	lucidity
8284	**forestier**-*m*	forester
8285	**greffier**-*m*	clerk| registrar
8286	**altercation**-*f*	altercation
8289	**relief**-*m*	relief
8290	**gâble**-*m*	gable| spring
8292	**digestion**-*f*	digestion
8295	**cierge**-*m*	candle
8297	**céleri**-*m*	celery
8298	**ressentiment**-*m*	resentment
8299	**allumeur**-*m*	igniter
8303	**subvention**-*f*	grant| subsidy
8304	**méprise**-*f*	mistake| misunderstanding
8305	**recruteur**-*m*	recruiter
8306	**rationnement**-*m*	rationing
8309	**droitier**-*m; adj*	right-hander; right-handed
8310	**insécurité**-*f*	insecurity
8311	**perceur**-*m*	piercer
8312	**microphone**-*m*	microphone
8314	**quadrant**-*m*	quadrant
8316	**renégat**-*adj; m*	renegade; renegade
8318	**compère**-*m*	accomplice
8320	**éloquence**-*f*	eloquence
8321	**désarroi**-*m*	disarray
8322	**montant**-*m*	amount| post
8323	**échine**-*f*	spine
8324	**anémie**-*f*	anemia
8325	**indignation**-*f*	indignation
8328	**nageoire**-*f*	fin
8329	**trapèze**-*m*	trapeze
8330	**fret**-*m*	freight| freight charges
8334	**pénalité**-*f*	penalty
8335	**gueux**-*m*	beggar
8338	**laquais**-*m; adj*	lackey; menial

8339	**minuteur**-*m*	timer
8340	**narration**-*f*	narration
8341	**crucifixion**-*f*	crucifixion
8344	**rente**-*m; f*	annuity; income
8345	**insistance**-*f*	insistence
8348	**fard**-*m*	make-up
8349	**Capricorne**-*m*	Capricorn
8351	**camaraderie**-*f*	comeradeship
8353	**professionnalisme**-*m*	professionalism
8354	**récession**-*f*	recession
8355	**anthropologie**-*f*	anthropology
8356	**enregistreur**-*m*	recorder
8357	**kleenex**-*m*	tissue
8358	**suppression**-*f*	removal
8359	**instabilité**-*f*	instability
8361	**plancton**-*m*	plankton
8362	**déroulement**-*m*	progress
8363	**ménopause**-*f*	menopause
8364	**autocollant**-*m; adj*	sticker; self-sealing
8365	**accouplement**-*m*	coupling
8367	**syllabe**-*f*	syllable
8370	**mascara**-*m*	mascara
8371	**amygdale**-*f*	tonsil| amygdala
8377	**laurier**-*m*	laurel
8378	**gué**-*m*	ford
8380	**lubie**-*f*	whim| freak
8381	**bouillotte**-*f*	hot-water bag
8384	**leurre**-*m*	lure
8385	**immensité**-*f*	immensity
8387	**gosier**-*m*	throat| gullet
8388	**cantique**-*m*	canticle| song
8390	**dispensaire**-*m*	dispensary
8391	**tirade**-*f*	tirade
8392	**variation**-*f*	variation| change
8393	**émir**-*m*	emir
8394	**bagarreur**-*m; adj*	brawler; feisty
8396	**tweed**-*m*	tweed
8398	**aisance**-*f*	ease
8399	**baignade**-*f*	bathing
8400	**piédestal**-*m*	pedestal
8401	**anévrisme**-*m*	aneurism
8403	**dissimulation**-*f*	concealment
8405	**nomade**-*adj; m/f*	nomadic; nomad
8407	**nettoyeur**-*m; adj*	cleaner; cleaning
8408	**consortium**-*m*	consortium
8409	**zèbre**-*m*	zebra
8410	**imparfait**-*adj; m*	imperfect; imperfect
8411	**rétroviseur**-*m*	mirror
8412	**niaiserie**-*m*	silliness
8413	**latex**-*m*	latex
8414	**minibus**-*m*	minibus
8415	**hépatite**-*f*	hepatitis
8417	**apport**-*m*	contribution
8419	**beuverie**-*f*	carousal| boozer
8420	**contrebandier**-*m*	smuggler
8421	**quatuor**-*m*	quartet
8423	**rescapé**-*m; adj*	survivor; surviving
8426	**galanterie**-*f*	gallantry
8427	**paroissien**-*m*	parishioner
8428	**saxophone**-*m*	saxophone
8431	**discothèque**-*f*	disco| nightclub
8432	**facette**-*f*	facet
8433	**auditoire**-*m*	audience
8436	**psyché**-*f*	psyche
8438	**chanvre**-*m*	hemp
8440	**carrosserie**-*f*	body
8442	**arôme**-*m*	aroma| flavoring
8443	**équitation**-*f*	horse riding
8450	**banquise**-*f*	pack ice
8451	**allégresse**-*f*	glee
8452	**déclarant**-*m*	declarer
8453	**armurier**-*m*	gunsmith| armourer
8456	**pendule**-*f*	pendulum
8461	**archange**-*m*	archangel
8462	**manivelle**-*f*	crank
8463	**ingratitude**-*f*	ingratitude
8464	**jouissance**-*f*	enjoyment
8466	**entraide**-*f*	mutual aid
8468	**braille**-*m*	braille
8470	**poltron**-*m; adj*	coward; cowardly
8471	**interphone**-*m*	intercom
8472	**cycliste**-*m*	cyclist
8473	**névrose**-*f*	neurosis
8474	**biscotte**-*f*	biscuit
8475	**déséquilibre**-*m*	imbalance
8476	**yiddish**-*adj; m*	Yiddish; Yiddish
8477	**cuisson**-*f*	baking
8478	**gynécologue**-*m/f*	gynecologist
8479	**prévention**-*f*	prevention
8480	**mormon**-*adj; m*	Mormon; Mormon
8482	**mangue**-*f*	mango

8488	**fossoyeur**-*m*	gravedigger
8490	**teinturier**-*m*	dry cleaner
8491	**sbire**-*m*	myrmidon| henchman
8492	**chevalerie**-*f*	chivalry
8494	**ovation**-*f*	ovation
8495	**hachis**-*m*	hash
8500	**broyer**-*vb; m*	grind; grinder
8501	**imprudence**-*f*	imprudence| recklessness
8503	**renom**-*m*	renown
8504	**impertinence**-*f*	impertinence| impudence
8506	**majuscule**-*adj; f*	capital; capital
8507	**réfectoire**-*m*	refectory
8509	**essor**-*m*	development
8510	**fougue**-*f*	fire| spirit
8512	**rosier**-*m*	rosebush
8513	**credo**-*m*	creed| belief
8517	**pale**-*f*	blade
8518	**aïeux**-*m|mpl*	forefathers
8522	**bavure**-*f*	smudge| blur
8523	**sève**-*f*	sap
8524	**amphétamine**-*f*	amphetamine
8525	**dosage**-*m*	dosage
8527	**méthane**-*m*	methane
8528	**primate**-*m*	primate
8529	**somali**-*adj; m/f; mpl*	Somali; Somali
8530	**eunuque**-*m*	eunuch
8531	**hymen**-*m*	hymen| marriage
8532	**processeur**-*m*	processor
8538	**veille**-*f*	eve| day before
8542	**créancier**-*m*	creditor
8543	**suspicion**-*f*	suspicion
8545	**résidu**-*m*	residue
8547	**amiante**-*f*	asbestos
8549	**guigne**-*f*	hoodoo| bad luck
8551	**bicarbonate**-*m*	bicarbonate
8553	**fétiche**-*m*	fetish
8554	**arrivage**-*m*	shipment
8555	**attelage**-*m*	coupling| hitch
8557	**acharnement**-*m*	fury| stubbornness
8558	**baroque**-*adj; m*	baroque; baroque
8559	**gredin**-*m*	rascal
8560	**perturbation**-*f*	disturbance
8561	**systématique**-*adj; f*	systematic; systematics
8562	**abcès**-*m*	abscess
8563	**entêtement**-*m*	stubbornness
8567	**panorama**-*m*	panorama| overview
8568	**cyclope**-*m*	Cyclops
8570	**pédiatre**-*m/f*	pediatrician
8571	**raffinerie**-*f*	refinery
8572	**luge**-*f*	sled
8574	**presbytère**-*m*	presbytery| rectory
8575	**confessionnal**-*m*	confessional
8576	**pleurnichard**-*m; adj*	crybaby; whingeing
8577	**toxine**-*f*	toxin
8578	**chrome**-*m*	chrome
8579	**container**-*m*	bowl
8580	**sono**-*f*	sound system
8581	**paon**-*m*	peacock
8582	**ailier**-*m*	wing
8584	**grosseur**-*f*	size| thickness
8585	**crissement**-*m*	screech
8586	**silo**-*m*	silo
8588	**mégot**-*m*	butt| cigarette end
8589	**falsifier**-*vb; m*	falsify; falsifier
8590	**pruneau**-*m*	prune
8591	**sommation**-*f*	summons
8592	**euthanasie**-*f*	euthanasia
8593	**hypnotique**-*adj; m*	hypnotic; hypnotic
8594	**précipice**-*m*	drop
8595	**euphorie**-*f*	euphoria
8597	**demeure**-*f*	residence| abode
8598	**plouf**-*m*	plonk| splash
8599	**blason**-*m*	blazon| shield
8600	**importun**-*adj; m*	unwelcome; intruder
8601	**électrode**-*f*	electrode
8602	**croupe**-*f*	rump| croup
8603	**cambrousse**-*f*	outback
8604	**matador**-*m*	matador
8605	**lèpre**-*f*	leprosy
8607	**tibia**-*m*	tibia
8611	**parabole**-*f*	parable
8613	**boîtier**-*m*	housing
8614	**pistache**-*f*	pistachio
8616	**avarice**-*f*	greed| stinginess
8617	**vieillissement**-*m*	aging
8618	**courroie**-*f*	belt
8619	**lobby**-*m*	lobby
8622	**souveraineté**-*f*	sovereignty
8623	**logistique**-*f; adj*	logistics; logistical

8624	**céramique**-*adj; f*	ceramic; ceramics
8627	**foreuse**-*f*	drill
8628	**gnome**-*m*	gnome
8630	**kebab**-*m*	kebab
8631	**infrastructure**-*f*	infrastructure
8632	**télex**-*m*	telex
8633	**berline**-*f*	sedan| tramcar
8638	**fève**-*f*	bean
8639	**sauveteur**-*m*	rescuer| wrecker
8640	**malice**-*f*	malice| mischief
8641	**longitude**-*f*	longitude
8643	**impudence**-*f*	impudence
8646	**solstice**-*m*	solstice
8647	**périphérie**-*f*	periphery
8653	**fervent**-*adj; m*	fervent; enthusiast
8654	**duvet**-*m*	duvet
8657	**fermeté**-*f*	firmness
8658	**postérieur**-*adj; m*	posterior; posterior
8660	**plaidoirie**-*f*	pleading
8665	**brouette**-*f*	wheelbarrow
8669	**rémission**-*f*	remission
8671	**aversion**-*f*	aversion
8675	**jarre**-*f*	jar
8677	**calmar**-*m*	squid
8679	**obscénité**-*f*	obscenity
8680	**photocopie**-*f*	photocopy
8681	**blanchiment**-*m*	whitening
8683	**pyromane**-*m/f*	pyromaniac
8684	**frappeur**-*m*	striker
8685	**utilisateur**-*m*	user
8686	**baiseur**-*m*	fucker
8687	**internement**-*m*	detention
8691	**harpon**-*m*	harpoon
8693	**lampadaire**-*m*	floor lamp
8694	**agrandissement**-*m*	enlargement
8695	**déchirure**-*f*	tear| tearing
8697	**rhumatisme**-*m*	rheumatism
8699	**cécité**-*f*	blindness
8701	**standardiste**-*m/f*	operator
8703	**vermouth**-*m*	vermouth
8704	**ambulant**-*adj; m*	traveling; traveler
8705	**entendement**-*m*	understanding
8706	**chenil**-*m*	kennel
8707	**absinthe**-*f*	absinthe
8708	**enfantillage**-*m*	childishness
8709	**tignasse**-*f*	wig
8710	**invisibilité**-*f*	invisibility
8711	**chapelier**-*m*	milliner
8714	**barde**-*m*	bard
8716	**désertion**-*f*	desertion
8719	**commère**-*f*	tattletale
8720	**finaliste**-*m/f*	finalist
8721	**rythme**-*m*	pace| rhythm
8722	**jeunot**-*m*	youngster
8724	**importation**-*f*	import
8729	**pépite**-*f*	nugget
8730	**opus**-*m*	opus
8731	**épitaphe**-*f*	epitaph
8732	**bicoque**-*f*	shanty| shack
8733	**incendiaire**-*adj; m/f*	incendiary; arsonist
8734	**rachat**-*m*	redemption| buying back
8735	**bricoleur**-*m*	handyman
8736	**albatros**-*m*	albatross
8737	**magnétisme**-*m*	magnetism
8738	**bricolage**-*m*	do-it-yourself
8739	**fresque**-*f*	fresco
8740	**litière**-*f*	litter
8741	**commerce**-*m*	trade| business
8742	**rasta**-*m*	rasta
8743	**apesanteur**-*f*	weightlessness
8744	**corner**-*m; vb*	corner; honk
8745	**configuration**-*f*	configuration
8746	**ancienneté**-*f*	seniority
8747	**variole**-*f*	smallpox
8749	**vaseline**-*f*	petroleum jelly
8750	**tuile**-*f*	tile
8751	**fraude**-*f*	fraud
8754	**indiscrétion**-*f*	indiscretion
8756	**liquidation**-*f*	liquidation
8757	**piazza**-*f*	piazza
8758	**abondant**-*adj; m*	abundant; affluent
8760	**convocation**-*f*	convocation
8765	**arménien**-*adj; m*	Armenian; Armenian
8766	**traînée**-*f*	trail| drag
8767	**impolitesse**-*f*	rudeness
8768	**soupe**-*f*	soup
8770	**idylle**-*f*	idyll
8772	**capuche**-*f*	hoodie
8773	**captif**-*adj; m*	captive; captive

8774	**contemporain**-*adj; m*	contemporary| coeval; contemporary
8777	**speech**-*m*	speech
8778	**douanier**-*m*	customs officer
8783	**gravier**-*m*	gravel
8785	**gibet**-*m*	gallows
8786	**sobriété**-*f*	sobriety
8787	**rosaire**-*m*	rosary
8788	**pénombre**-*f*	penumbra
8791	**délinquance**-*f*	delinquency
8792	**volupté**-*f*	sensuousness
8793	**gigot**-*m*	leg
8796	**trognon**-*m*	core
8797	**asphalte**-*m*	asphalt
8798	**déminage**-*m*	sweeping
8799	**capuchon**-*m*	cap| hood
8800	**calice**-*m*	chalice
8804	**grincement**-*m*	grinding| squeak
8805	**théologie**-*f*	theology
8806	**séchoir**-*m*	dryer
8807	**pulsation**-*f*	pulsation
8809	**malfaiteur**-*m*	malefactor| wrongdoer
8810	**obstination**-*f*	obstinacy
8811	**ducat**-*m*	ducat
8812	**tonique**-*adj; f*	tonic; tonic
8813	**intrigant**-*adj; m*	intriguing; intriguer
8814	**garniture**-*f*	topping| filling
8816	**dresseur**-*m*	trainer
8817	**lavement**-*m*	enema| washing
8818	**fondant**-*m; adj*	fondant; melting
8822	**boudoir**-*m*	boudoir
8828	**ébullition**-*f*	boiling
8829	**glas**-*m*	knell
8830	**raffinement**-*m*	refinement| sophistication
8831	**normalité**-*f*	normality
8832	**caille**-*f*	quail
8835	**agilité**-*f*	agility
8837	**utopie**-*f*	Utopia
8839	**réglage**-*m*	setting
8841	**interlocuteur**-*m*	interlocutor
8842	**aria**-*f*	aria
8843	**treuil**-*m*	winch| hoist
8844	**appartenance**-*f*	membership
8845	**cime**-*f*	top| crown
8846	**chaînon**-*m*	link
8847	**dépravation**-*f*	depravity
8849	**régent**-*m*	regent
8850	**lauréat**-*adj; m*	laureate; laureate
8854	**régulateur**-*m; adj*	regulator; control
8855	**arbalète**-*f*	crossbow
8858	**verrue**-*f*	wart
8859	**réchaud**-*m*	stove
8860	**teigne**-*f*	ringworm
8861	**secouriste**-*m/f*	rescuer| paramedic
8863	**négociant**-*m*	merchant
8864	**expiration**-*f*	expiry
8865	**thérapeutique**-*adj; f*	therapeutic; therapeutics
8866	**rebond**-*m*	rebound
8868	**bâillon**-*m*	gag
8870	**dysfonctionnement**-*m*	dysfunction
8872	**gourdin**-*m*	club| mace
8873	**pluriel**-*adj; m*	plural; plural
8874	**circonscription**-*f*	district| riding
8875	**canalisation**-*f*	piping
8876	**faction**-*f*	faction
8877	**goupille**-*f*	pin
8878	**hémorroïde**-*f*	hemorrhoid
8879	**perspicacité**-*f*	insight
8882	**neurologue**-*m/f*	neurologist
8884	**glouton**-*adj; m*	gluttonous; glutton
8885	**poterie**-*f*	pottery
8886	**froideur**-*f*	coldness| ice
8887	**fiacre**-*m*	carriage
8890	**panoplie**-*f*	range| toolbox
8892	**pitre**-*m*	clown
8894	**notoriété**-*f*	notoriety
8897	**caricature**-*f*	caricature
8898	**basilic**-*m*	basil
8900	**intolérance**-*f*	intolerance
8901	**crinière**-*f*	mane
8902	**mécène**-*m*	sponsor
8905	**collation**-*f*	collation| snack
8906	**métaphysique**-*adj; f*	metaphysical; metaphysics
8908	**cellophane**-*m*	cellophane
8909	**psaume**-*m*	psalm
8910	**scrutin**-*m*	ballot| polling
8911	**exactitude**-*f*	accuracy
8912	**catcheur**-*m*	wrestler

8917	**tourelle**-*f*	turret
8918	**perdrix**-*f*	partridge
8921	**naïveté**-*f*	naivete
8922	**concepteur**-*m*	designer
8923	**spiritualité**-*f*	spirituality
8924	**cardigan**-*m*	cardigan
8925	**inconscience**-*f*	unconsciousness
8927	**volley**-*m*	volleyball
8928	**écaille**-*f*	scale
8929	**calotte**-*f*	cap| dome
8930	**essaim**-*m*	swarm
8931	**malabar**-*m*	bruiser
8932	**kaki**-*adj; m*	khaki; khaki
8933	**projectile**-*m*	projectile
8934	**compresseur**-*m*	compressor
8935	**échauffement**-*m*	heating
8937	**dissection**-*f*	dissection
8938	**caïman**-*m*	caiman
8940	**ménagerie**-*f*	menagerie
8943	**phonographe**-*m*	phonograph
8945	**fonderie**-*f*	foundry
8946	**cardiologue**-*m/f*	cardiologist
8948	**bagatelle**-*f*	trifle
8955	**tétanos**-*m*	tetanus
8956	**soupirant**-*m*	suitor
8958	**vagabondage**-*m*	vagrancy
8961	**aristocratie**-*f*	aristocracy
8962	**lionne**-*f*	lioness
8964	**trésorerie**-*f*	treasury
8971	**manille**-*m*	shackle
8972	**moqueur**-*m; adj*	mocker; derisive
8973	**flamenco**-*m*	flamenco
8974	**irrigation**-*f*	irrigation
8975	**similitude**-*f*	similitude
8976	**dureté**-*f*	hardness| toughness
8978	**articulation**-*f*	joint| speech
8979	**chope**-*f*	mug
8980	**astrologie**-*f*	astrology
8983	**armoiries**-*fpl*	arms
8984	**crescendo**-*m*	crescendo
8985	**motte**-*f*	sod| clump
8986	**fantaisiste**-*adj; m/f*	fanciful; joker
8988	**confédération**-*f*	confederation
8989	**recensement**-*m*	census| count
8990	**varicelle**-*f*	varicella
8992	**suzerain**-*m*	suzerain
8995	**fouillis**-*m*	mess
8996	**paprika**-*m*	paprika
8998	**rangement**-*m*	arrangement
9000	**milligramme**-*m*	milligram
9001	**filière**-*f*	die| sector
9002	**gencive**-*f*	gum
9003	**filleul**-*m*	godson
9004	**exportation**-*f*	export
9006	**aphrodisiaque**-*adj; m*	aphrodisiac; aphrodisiac
9007	**safran**-*m*	saffron
9009	**racer**-*m*	racer
9010	**verseau**-*m*	Aquarius
9011	**variable**-*adj; f*	variable; variable
9012	**pancréas**-*m*	pancreas
9013	**hypothermie**-*f*	hypothermia
9014	**impérialisme**-*m*	imperialism
9015	**anthrax**-*m*	anthrax
9016	**latte**-*f*	lath| latte
9017	**affliction**-*f*	affliction
9018	**proclamation**-*f*	proclamation
9019	**démarche**-*f*	step| gait
9022	**infortune**-*f*	misfortune
9025	**étendard**-*m*	standard
9027	**paravent**-*m*	screen
9028	**chrétienté**-*f*	Christendom
9029	**causette**-*f*	rap| chat
9030	**ébauche**-*f*	draft
9031	**mobilisation**-*f*	mobilization
9033	**imperfection**-*f*	imperfection
9034	**catalyseur**-*m*	catalyst
9036	**parieur**-*m*	gambler
9037	**cartable**-*m*	satchel
9038	**florin**-*m*	florin
9039	**rapt**-*m*	abduction| kidnapping
9040	**justification**-*f*	justification
9041	**palissade**-*f*	palisade
9043	**collet**-*m*	collar| neck
9044	**poseur**-*m; adj*	poseur; phony
9046	**exclusion**-*f*	exclusion
9047	**tourneur**-*m*	turner
9049	**bourbier**-*m*	quagmire| slough
9050	**penseur**-*m*	thinker
9051	**bosquet**-*m*	grove
9053	**sarcophage**-*m*	sarcophagus
9054	**anticorps**-*m*	antibody

9055	**nationaliste**-*adj; m/f*	nationalist; nationalist
9056	**accrochage**-*m*	hanging| coupling
9057	**microfilm**-*m*	microfilm
9058	**révélateur**-*m; adj*	developer; revealing
9059	**gril**-*m*	grill
9060	**abstraction**-*f*	abstraction
9061	**biopsie**-*f*	biopsy
9063	**management**-*m*	management
9065	**proton**-*m*	proton
9066	**prélude**-*m*	prelude
9067	**animosité**-*f*	animosity
9068	**concessionnaire**-*m*	dealer
9069	**jante**-*f*	rim
9072	**sensualité**-*f*	sensuality
9073	**halo**-*m*	halo
9074	**perdition**-*f*	perdition
9078	**vérole**-*f*	pox
9080	**correspondant**-*adj; m*	corresponding; correspondent
9081	**chenapan**-*m*	scoundrel
9083	**discernement**-*m*	discernment
9086	**pore**-*f*	pore
9088	**canicule**-*f*	heat wave
9089	**sprint**-*m*	sprint
9092	**bourde**-*f*	howler| blunder
9094	**fana**-*m/f*	addict| fanatic
9097	**fourreau**-*m*	sheath
9098	**impresario**-*m*	impresario
9101	**opportuniste**-*adj; m/f*	opportunistic; opportunist
9102	**empêchement**-*m*	impediment
9103	**ténacité**-*f*	tenacity
9105	**néon**-*m*	neon
9106	**monarque**-*m*	monarch
9107	**régénération**-*f*	regeneration
9108	**citadin**-*m; adj*	city dweller; city dwelling
9109	**spiritisme**-*m*	spiritism
9112	**chignon**-*m*	bun| catfight
9113	**cathédrale**-*f*	cathedral
9114	**pivert**-*m*	woodpecker
9116	**bénédicité**-*f*	benediction
9117	**embarcadère**-*f; m*	jetty; wharf
9119	**exhibition**-*f*	display
9120	**brasse**-*f*	fathom
9121	**almanach**-*m*	almanac
9122	**vertèbre**-*f*	vertebra
9124	**idéalisme**-*m*	idealism
9125	**luciole**-*f*	firefly
9127	**jésuite**-*m; adj*	Jesuit; Jesuit
9129	**urbanisme**-*m*	town planning
9131	**neutron**-*m*	neutron
9132	**mégatonne**-*f*	megaton
9134	**anaconda**-*m*	anaconda
9138	**Mongolie**-*f*	Mongolia
9139	**sinus**-*m*	sinus
9142	**embolie**-*f*	embolism
9143	**tricherie**-*f*	cheating
9144	**chaux**-*f*	lime| whitewash
9145	**stature**-*f*	stature
9146	**prologue**-*m*	prologue
9149	**frigidaire**-*m*	fridge
9150	**étau**-*m*	vice| stranglehold
9151	**ramassage**-*m*	collection| gathering
9152	**tordu**-*adj; m*	twisted; crackpot
9154	**tambourin**-*m*	tambourine
9158	**baryton**-*m*	baritone
9160	**mésaventure**-*f*	misadventure
9163	**vestibule**-*m*	vestibule
9166	**jurisprudence**-*f*	jurisprudence
9167	**fourmilière**-*f*	anthill
9168	**battant**-*m; adj*	clapper| fighter; swinging
9170	**suppliant**-*adj; m*	begging; suppliant
9171	**maladresse**-*f*	clumsiness
9172	**teneur**-*f*	content
9176	**résonance**-*f*	resonance
9178	**pastille**-*f*	pellet| chip
9179	**tintement**-*m*	ringing
9181	**esthéticien**-*m*	beautician
9182	**corniche**-*f*	cornice| ledge
9184	**fusilier**-*m*	rifleman
9185	**rixe**-*f*	brawl
9187	**hiéroglyphe**-*m*	hieroglyph
9191	**récipient**-*m*	container
9193	**gisement**-*m*	deposit
9195	**calcium**-*m*	calcium
9196	**frénésie**-*f*	frenzy
9197	**échiquier**-*m*	chessboard
9199	**rondelle**-*f*	washer
9200	**plaignant**-*m*	plaintiff
9201	**citoyenneté**-*f*	citizenship

9204	**aborigène**-*adj; m/f*	aboriginal; aborigine
9205	**athlétisme**-*m*	athletics
9206	**ségrégation**-*f*	segregation
9208	**empathie**-*f*	empathy
9211	**androïde**-*adj; m*	android; android
9212	**percussion**-*f*	percussion
9213	**ajustement**-*m*	adjustment
9214	**régression**-*f*	regression
9215	**sédition**-*f*	sedition| rebellion
9216	**guépard**-*m*	cheetah
9217	**hameau**-*m*	hamlet
9219	**bouille**-*f*	mug| face
9220	**attelle**-*f*	brace| splint
9221	**pronostic**-*m*	prognosis
9222	**soviet**-*m*	Soviet
9224	**pelage**-*m*	coat| fur
9225	**continuation**-*f*	continuation
9226	**habitation**-*f*	home| habitation
9227	**rafraîchissement**-*m*	refreshment
9228	**lest**-*m*	ballast
9229	**beigne**-*f*	donut
9231	**sciure**-*f*	sawdust
9233	**palourde**-*f*	clam
9234	**tsarine**-*f*	tsarina
9235	**croquet**-*m*	croquet
9236	**royauté**-*f*	royalty
9237	**toboggan**-*m*	slide
9239	**acrobatie**-*f*	acrobatics
9240	**dérision**-*f*	derision| mockery
9242	**modération**-*f*	moderation
9243	**salopette**-*f*	overalls
9244	**gravitation**-*f*	gravitation
9246	**chaufferie**-*f*	boiler room
9247	**mathématicien**-*m*	mathematician
9248	**attribut**-*m; adj*	attribute; predicate
9250	**insecticide**-*m; adj*	insecticide; insecticidal
9251	**tremplin**-*m*	springboard
9254	**craquement**-*m*	crack
9255	**provincial**-*adj; m*	provincial; provincial
9256	**ignare**-*m/f; adj*	ignoramus; clueless
9257	**bulgare**-*adj; m*	Bulgarian; Bulgarian
9258	**cloaque**-*m*	cesspool
9259	**friction**-*f*	friction
9260	**cliquetis**-*m*	clatter| rattle
9261	**traction**-*f*	traction
9262	**trempette**-*f*	dip
9263	**impérialiste**-*adj; m/f*	imperialist; imperialist
9264	**éjaculation**-*f*	ejaculation
9266	**orbe**-*m*	orb
9267	**moelleux**-*adj; m*	soft; mellowness
9271	**dignitaire**-*m; adj*	dignitary; genual
9275	**mante**-*f*	mantis
9276	**mécontentement**-*m*	discontent
9279	**affluent**-*m*	tributary
9284	**trappeur**-*m*	trapper
9285	**harpie**-*f; adj*	harpy; harpy
9287	**pommier**-*m*	apple
9288	**cabanon**-*m*	shed
9289	**dysenterie**-*f*	dysentery
9290	**géologue**-*m/f*	geologist
9291	**pedigree**-*adj; m*	pedigree; pedigree
9292	**droiture**-*f*	righteousness
9293	**acquittement**-*m*	acquittal
9295	**crémaillère**-*f*	rack
9296	**progressiste**-*adj; m/f*	progressive; progressive
9297	**élocution**-*f*	speech
9298	**diction**-*f*	diction
9299	**frange**-*f*	fringe
9300	**laïus**-*m*	speech| spiel
9301	**marginal**-*adj; m*	marginal; dropout
9302	**couturier**-*m*	fashion designer
9303	**steppe**-*f*	steppe
9306	**pivot**-*m; adj*	pivot; pivotal
9308	**suie**-*f*	soot
9309	**prémonition**-*f*	premonition
9310	**devis**-*m*	quotation
9313	**grief**-*m*	grievance
9316	**oxyde**-*m*	oxide
9317	**éditorial**-*adj; m*	editorial; editorial
9319	**planification**-*f*	planning
9320	**diadème**-*m*	tiara
9322	**rot**-*m*	burp
9323	**sparadrap**-*m*	plaster| band-aid
9325	**astrologue**-*m/f*	astrologer
9326	**poirier**-*m*	pear tree| handstand
9327	**labrador**-*m*	Labrador dog
9330	**pilleur**-*m; adj*	looter; deceitful
9331	**recouvrement**-*m*	recovery| collection
9332	**boomerang**-*m*	boomerang

9333	**blablabla**-*m*	blah
9334	**druide**-*m*	druid
9335	**lobotomie**-*f*	lobotomy
9336	**spoon**-*m*	spoon
9337	**strudel**-*m*	strudel
9338	**oubliette**-*f*	oubliette
9339	**brouillage**-*m*	interference
9342	**nationalisme**-*m*	nationalism
9345	**prieuré**-*m*	priory
9346	**Bengale**-*m; adj*	Bengal; Bengal
9347	**sauvagerie**-*f*	savagery
9350	**dédommagement**-*m*	compensation
9352	**roseau**-*m*	reed
9353	**rectum**-*m*	rectum
9354	**inquisiteur**-*m; adj*	inquisitor; inquisitive
9359	**servitude**-*f*	servitude
9360	**gréviste**-*m/f; adj*	striker; striking
9363	**barmaid**-*f*	barmaid
9366	**brocoli**-*m*	broccoli
9368	**pépée**-*f*	chick| babe
9370	**amputation**-*f*	amputation
9371	**monotonie**-*f*	monotony
9372	**hachoir**-*m*	chopper
9374	**déportation**-*f*	deportation
9375	**toupie**-*f*	top
9376	**crème**-*adj; f*	cream; cream
9377	**chenal**-*m*	channel
9378	**toxicomane**-*m/f*	addict
9379	**freinage**-*m*	braking
9381	**braise**-*f*	embers
9382	**isolé**-*adj; m*	isolated| insulated; isolated person
9385	**douve**-*f*	stave| moat
9386	**rancœur**-*f*	rancor
9387	**blindage**-*m*	shield
9388	**manipulateur**-*m*	manipulator
9389	**ralliement**-*m*	rally
9391	**épopée**-*f*	epic
9392	**tumulte**-*m*	tumult
9393	**notice**-*f*	notice
9395	**nitroglycérine**-*f*	nitroglycerine
9396	**piéton**-*m; adj*	pedestrian; pedestrian
9398	**malhonnêteté**-*f*	dishonesty
9399	**urticaire**-*f*	urticaria| hives

9400	**marteau-piqueur**-*m*	jackhammer
9401	**transparence**-*f*	transparency
9402	**parlementaire**-*adj; m/f*	parliamentary; parliamentarian
9403	**persil**-*m*	parsley
9404	**stratège**-*m*	strategist
9405	**golfeur**-*m*	golfer
9406	**gourmet**-*m*	gourmet
9407	**incinérateur**-*m*	incinerator
9408	**vésicule**-*f*	vesicle
9409	**impossibilité**-*f*	impossibility
9410	**embargo**-*m*	embargo
9411	**propagation**-*f*	spread
9413	**polio**-*f*	polio
9414	**conditionnement**-*m*	packaging
9416	**circoncision**-*f*	circumcision
9417	**judaïsme**-*m*	Judaism
9418	**criquet**-*m*	locust
9421	**mixture**-*f*	mixture
9422	**artefact**-*m*	artifact
9423	**orifice**-*m*	orifice
9425	**provocateur**-*adj; m*	challenging; agitator
9426	**illustration**-*f*	illustration
9428	**benêt**-*m*	dullard
9430	**seigle**-*m*	rye
9431	**forcené**-*m; adj*	madman| gunner; fanatical
9432	**massue**-*f*	mace
9436	**fêtard**-*m*	roisterer| rounder
9437	**saindoux**-*m*	lard
9439	**traquenard**-*m*	trap| booby trap
9440	**bienséance**-*f*	propriety
9441	**inertie**-*f*	inertia
9443	**privation**-*f*	deprivation
9444	**rugissement**-*m*	roaring
9445	**autochtone**-*m/f; adj*	native; native
9446	**insouciance**-*f*	recklessness
9447	**aisselle**-*f*	armpit
9449	**caveau**-*m*	vault
9450	**gringalet**-*m*	weakling
9451	**mousquet**-*m*	musket
9454	**turquoise**-*f; adj*	turquoise; turquoise
9457	**flore**-*f*	flora
9459	**longévité**-*f*	longevity
9460	**épi**-*m*	ear| cob
9462	**dissolution**-*f*	dissolution
9466	**bribe**-*f*	scrap

9467	**sonde**-*f*	probe
9468	**apathie**-*f*	apathy
9469	**magnésium**-*m*	magnesium
9470	**revêtement**-*m*	coating| lining
9471	**pectoral**-*adj; m*	pectoral; pectoral
9472	**dépannage**-*m*	help| fixing
9473	**narcissisme**-*m*	narcissism
9474	**pédiatrie**-*f*	pediatrics
9477	**squash**-*m*	squash
9479	**conservation**-*f*	preservation
9480	**palpitation**-*f*	palpitation| flutter
9481	**orchestre**-*m*	orchestra
9483	**brindille**-*f*	twig
9486	**pickpocket**-*m/f*	pickpocket
9488	**abattage**-*m*	slaughter| felling
9489	**moucheron**-*m*	gnat
9490	**zigzag**-*m*	zigzag
9492	**intendance**-*f*	stewardship
9493	**marchandage**-*m*	bargaining
9494	**lourdaud**-*adj; m*	clumsy| heavy; oaf
9495	**dédain**-*m*	disdain
9497	**fiel**-*m*	gall
9498	**gravure**-*f*	engraving| print
9500	**haltère**-*m*	dumbbell
9501	**tutu**-*m*	tutu
9502	**farfelu**-*m; adj*	wacky; crazy
9503	**boniment**-*m*	pitch
9504	**chandelier**-*m*	candlestick
9507	**dormeur**-*m*	sleeper
9509	**nullité**-*f*	nullity| nonentity
9512	**sauce**-*f*	sauce
9513	**revirement**-*m*	turn-around
9516	**cornemuse**-*f*	bagpipe
9517	**diagramme**-*m*	diagram
9518	**aviron**-*m*	rowing| oar
9519	**dompteur**-*m*	tamer
9521	**opossum**-*m*	opossum
9522	**spontanéité**-*f*	spontaneity
9523	**jérémiade**-*f*	complaint
9524	**pygmée**-*f; adj*	Pygmy; pygmy
9525	**fragilité**-*f*	fragility
9526	**éboulement**-*m*	landslide
9527	**fuselage**-*m*	fuselage
9528	**ramoneur**-*m*	chimney sweep
9529	**dégel**-*m*	thaw
9531	**panthéon**-*m*	pantheon
9532	**agriculteur**-*m*	farmer
9534	**vernissage**-*m*	varnishing| opening
9535	**receleur**-*m*	fence
9538	**transplantation**-*f*	transplantation
9539	**hydromel**-*m*	mead
9540	**interaction**-*f*	interaction
9541	**chromosome**-*m*	chromosome
9542	**diminution**-*f*	decrease
9543	**incinération**-*f*	incineration
9544	**charognard**-*m*	scavenger
9545	**équité**-*f*	equity
9547	**millet**-*m*	millet
9549	**shaker**-*m*	shaker
9554	**liane**-*f*	liana
9560	**symétrie**-*f*	symmetry
9562	**nouba**-*f*	party
9564	**agrément**-*m*	approval
9570	**mocassin**-*m*	moccasin
9571	**bouledogue**-*m*	bulldog
9573	**espadon**-*m*	swordfish
9574	**adhésion**-*f*	membership
9576	**pupitre**-*m*	desk
9577	**ronflement**-*m*	snoring| roar
9578	**déclenchement**-*m*	release
9580	**plastic**-*m*	plastic explosive
9583	**comptine**-*f*	nursery rhyme
9585	**embryon**-*m*	embryo
9589	**respirateur**-*m*	respirator
9590	**tournesol**-*m*	sunflower
9593	**spoutnik**-*m*	sputnik
9594	**mobylette**-*f*	moped
9596	**triton**-*m*	triton| merman
9597	**stéréotype**-*m*	stereotype
9598	**ciboire**-*m*	ciborium
9599	**anorexique**-*adj; m/f*	anorexic; anorexic
9600	**hindi**-*m*	Hindi
9601	**linguistique**-*adj; f*	linguistic; linguistics
9605	**catacombe**-*f*	catacomb
9606	**lyrique**-*adj; f*	lyrical; lyric
9609	**brouillon**-*m; adj*	draft; untidy
9610	**repassage**-*m*	ironing
9611	**lacune**-*f*	gap
9613	**objectivité**-*f*	objectivity
9614	**rajah**-*m*	rajah
9615	**souillon**-*m*	slut| slob
9618	**tandem**-*m*	tandem

9619	**chroniqueur**-*m*	chronicler| journalist
9620	**animalerie**-*f*	pet shop
9621	**aliénation**-*f*	alienation
9624	**remake**-*m*	remake
9625	**totem**-*m*	totem
9626	**enclume**-*f*	anvil
9627	**frusques**-*fpl*	thread
9628	**bique**-*f*	nanny-goat
9630	**gifle**-*f*	slap| cuff
9633	**cancan**-*m*	cancan| dirt
9634	**plant**-*m*	plant| seedling
9635	**arête**-*f*	arete
9636	**chloroforme**-*m*	chloroform
9638	**cireur**-*m*	polisher
9640	**palette**-*f*	palette| paddle
9641	**oppresseur**-*m*	oppressor
9642	**hennissement**-*m*	neigh
9644	**tantinet**-*m*	mite
9647	**brisant**-*adj; m*	breaking; breaker
9648	**sursaut**-*m*	start| spurt
9651	**dragueur**-*m*	dredger| player
9652	**rétention**-*f*	retention
9653	**salarié**-*adj; m*	salaried; wage earner
9655	**contagion**-*f*	contagion
9659	**inflammation**-*f*	inflammation
9661	**alliage**-*m*	alloy| mixture
9663	**relativité**-*f*	relativity
9665	**glucose**-*m*	glucose
9666	**rotule**-*f*	patella
9667	**campeur**-*m*	camper
9668	**futuriste**-*adj; m/f*	futuristic; futurist
9669	**iranien**-*adj; m*	Iranian; Iranian
9670	**hurleur**-*m*	howler| squealer
9672	**activiste**-*m/f; adj*	activist; smart
9673	**stoppeur**-*m*	stopper
9674	**syntaxe**-*f*	syntax
9675	**malveillance**-*f*	malice| malignancy
9676	**notable**-*adj; m*	notable| worthy; worthy
9677	**agitateur**-*m*	agitator
9680	**glissade**-*f*	slip| slide
9681	**plaisantin**-*m; adj*	joker; bantering
9682	**huis**-*m*	door
9683	**arriviste**-*adj; m/f*	pushy; go-getter
9685	**recel**-*f*	concealment
9688	**pichet**-*m*	pitcher
9689	**abnégation**-*f*	denial| self-sacrifice
9691	**poireau**-*m*	leek
9692	**bamboula**-*m; f*	negro; tamboula
9693	**prononciation**-*f*	pronunciation
9695	**désarmement**-*m*	disarmament
9696	**exclamation**-*f*	exclamation
9697	**vaillance**-*f*	valour
9698	**satyre**-*m*	Satyr
9700	**fifre**-*m*	fife
9701	**timonier**-*m*	helmsman
9702	**transpiration**-*f*	transpiration
9703	**bougeotte**-*f*	wanderlust
9704	**dégagement**-*m*	clearance| disengagement
9705	**panne**-*f*	breakdown
9706	**pétunia**-*m*	petunia
9708	**sangle**-*f*	strap
9709	**saphir**-*m*	sapphire
9710	**substitution**-*f*	substitution
9712	**réélection**-*f*	re-election
9713	**ortie**-*f*	nettle
9715	**retouche**-*f*	retouch
9717	**courbette**-*f*	bowing
9718	**tendon**-*m*	tendon
9719	**profiteur**-*m*	profiteer
9720	**infusion**-*f*	infusion
9722	**jugulaire**-*adj; f*	jugular; chinstrap
9723	**éponge**-*f*	sponge
9724	**braconnier**-*m*	poacher
9725	**juron**-*m*	oath| profanity
9726	**garagiste**-*m/f*	mechanic
9728	**marmelade**-*f*	marmelade
9729	**surveillant**-*m*	supervisor
9730	**marxiste**-*m/f*	Marxist
9731	**corniaud**-*m; m*	mutt; analogy
9733	**individualité**-*f*	individuality
9735	**chimiothérapie**-*f*	chemotherapy
9738	**galon**-*m*	braid| stripe
9739	**sympathisant**-*m*	sympathizer
9741	**assortiment**-*m*	assortment
9743	**galipette**-*f*	somersault
9744	**joute**-*f*	joust
9746	**pommette**-*f*	cheekbone
9747	**snobisme**-*m*	snobbery
9748	**rejeton**-*m*	offshoot| kid
9750	**succursale**-*f*	branch

9751	**gribouillis**-*m*	scrawl
9752	**statuette**-*f*	small statue
9753	**exode**-*m*	exodus
9755	**inhibition**-*f*	inhibition
9756	**têtard**-*m*	tadpole
9757	**perfidie**-*f*	perfidy
9758	**accolade**-*f*	hug| accolade
9760	**remorqueur**-*m*	tug
9761	**contour**-*m*	contour| outline
9764	**ébriété**-*f*	intoxication
9765	**liège**-*m*	cork
9768	**gérant**-*m; adj*	manager; managing
9773	**adorateur**-*m; adj*	adorer; worshipful
9775	**calepin**-*m*	notebook
9776	**soudure**-*f*	welding
9777	**arbitrage**-*m; adj*	arbitrage; arbitral
9778	**conjonction**-*f*	conjunction
9779	**potiron**-*m*	pumpkin
9780	**arsenic**-*adj; m*	arsenic; arsenic
9781	**cagibi**-*m*	storage room| cupboard
9782	**calcaire**-*m; adj*	limestone; calcareous
9783	**grillon**-*m*	cricket
9784	**thaïlandais**-*adj; mpl*	Thai
9785	**expiation**-*f*	atonement
9786	**thriller**-*m*	thriller
9789	**aménagement**-*m*	planning
9790	**conque**-*f*	conch
9793	**cellulite**-*f*	cellulite
9794	**godemiché**-*m*	dildo
9795	**survêtement**-*m*	track suit
9797	**walkman**-*m*	walkman
9798	**apartheid**-*f*	apartheid
9799	**aberration**-*f*	aberration
9800	**malnutrition**-*f*	malnutrition
9801	**hypertension**-*f*	hypertension
9803	**chuchotement**-*m*	whisper
9808	**réjouissance**-*f*	rejoicing
9812	**paillasse**-*f*	pallet
9813	**cuivre**-*m*	copper
9814	**dramaturge**-*m/f*	dramatist
9818	**laudanum**-*m*	laudanum
9820	**clopinettes**-*fpl*	peanuts
9821	**butée**-*f*	toe
9822	**chiffe**-*f*	spineless individual
9827	**condescendance**-*f*	condescension
9828	**képi**-*m*	cap
9829	**électrocution**-*f*	electrocution
9830	**menuiserie**-*f*	carpentry
9831	**broutille**-*f*	trifle
9832	**espiègle**-*adj; m/f*	playful| impish; imp
9835	**voyance**-*f*	clairvoyance
9836	**agrafe**-*f*	clip
9837	**litige**-*m*	litigation
9838	**subtilité**-*f*	subtlety
9839	**percepteur**-*m; adj*	collector; percipient
9841	**amirauté**-*f*	admiralty
9842	**bistouri**-*m*	scalpel
9843	**caillot**-*m*	clot
9844	**embouchure**-*f*	mouth| outlet
9845	**suffisance**-*f*	sufficiency
9846	**zeste**-*m*	zest
9847	**persan**-*adj; m*	Persian; Persian
9848	**bourgeon**-*m*	bud
9849	**diphtérie**-*f*	diphtheria
9852	**gond**-*m*	hinge
9853	**broderie**-*f*	embroidery
9854	**insomniaque**-*m/f*	insomniac
9855	**prolongement**-*m*	extension| prolongation
9858	**belette**-*f*	weasel
9859	**guetteur**-*m*	watchman| look-out
9860	**poncho**-*m*	poncho
9862	**maléfice**-*m*	devilry
9863	**itinérant**-*adj; m*	itinerant; itinerant
9865	**kayak**-*m*	kayak
9866	**engrenage**-*m*	gearing
9868	**déformation**-*f*	deformation| distortion
9869	**anéantissement**-*m*	annihilation
9870	**libanais**-*adj; mpl*	Lebanese
9871	**pubis**-*m*	pubis
9873	**migration**-*f*	migration
9874	**supérette**-*f*	minimarket
9875	**subterfuge**-*m*	subterfuge
9877	**engouement**-*m*	infatuation
9878	**pesticide**-*m; adj*	pesticide; pesticidal
9879	**multiplication**-*f*	multiplication
9880	**verso**-*m*	back| reverse
9881	**faubourg**-*m*	suburb
9882	**cordial**-*adj; m*	cordial; cordial
9885	**moquerie**-*f*	mockery
9887	**cueillette**-*f*	picking

9891	**poudrier**-*m*	powder compact
9893	**fanfaron**-*m; adj*	braggart; boastful
9894	**teint**-*adj; m*	dyed; color
9895	**tricycle**-*m*	tricycle
9896	**plumard**-*m*	sack
9897	**réglementation**-*f*	regulation
9898	**colonisation**-*f*	colonization
9899	**déporté**-*m; adj*	deportee; deported
9900	**crible**-*m*	screen| riddle
9907	**bidet**-*m*	bidet
9909	**altruiste**-*adj; m/f*	altruistic; altruist
9911	**immoralité**-*f*	immorality
9912	**rami**-*m*	rummy
9914	**asthmatique**-*adj; m/f*	asthmatic; asthmatic
9917	**bru**-*f*	daughter-in-law
9918	**mors**-*m*	bit
9919	**bâti**-*adj; m*	built; bed
9920	**feuillage**-*m*	foliage
9922	**appréhension**-*f*	apprehension
9923	**jarretelle**-*f*	garter
9924	**abolition**-*f*	abolition
9925	**relaxation**-*f*	relaxation
9927	**monticule**-*m*	mound
9928	**sternum**-*m*	sternum
9929	**flambeur**-*m*	high-roller
9930	**imitateur**-*m; adj*	imitator; mimic
9931	**quiétude**-*f*	quietude
9932	**cerne**-*m*	circle
9933	**génisse**-*f*	young cow
9934	**prude**-*m/f; adj*	prude; prudish
9935	**palmarès**-*m*	prize list
9936	**perversité**-*f*	perversity
9938	**détergent**-*adj; m*	detergent; cleanser
9939	**négation**-*f*	negation
9940	**œillet**-*m*	eyelet
9941	**nécrologie**-*f*	obituary
9942	**quiche**-*f*	quiche
9943	**disponibilité**-*f*	availability
9944	**ukrainien**-*adj; m/mpl*	Ukrainian; Ukrainian
9945	**urinoir**-*m*	urinal
9946	**émancipation**-*f*	emancipation
9947	**lotissement**-*m*	allotment| project
9948	**magma**-*m*	magma
9949	**tabard**-*m*	tabard
9952	**prolétaire**-*m/f; adj*	proletarian; prolete
9954	**pélican**-*m*	pelican
9955	**convoitise**-*f*	greed| desire
9958	**calife**-*m*	caliph
9962	**trombe**-*f*	whirlwind
9963	**plénitude**-*f*	fullness
9964	**vantard**-*adj; m*	boastful; braggart
9965	**aubergine**-*f*	eggplant
9968	**nécessiteux**-*adj; m/f*	needy; needy person
9971	**nymphe**-*f*	nymph
9972	**linotte**-*f*	linnet
9976	**intégralité**-*f*	entirety
9979	**torero**-*m*	bullfighter
9980	**médiateur**-*m*	mediator
9984	**favoritisme**-*m*	favoritism
9985	**destinataire**-*m*	recipient| addressee
9989	**clameur**-*f*	clamor| shouting
9990	**tarentule**-*f*	tarantula
9991	**affolement**-*m*	panic
9992	**cloître**-*m*	cloister| enclosure
9993	**rattrapage**-*m*	picking up
9994	**hydravion**-*m*	seaplane
9997	**briseur**-*m*	breaker
9999	**dièse**-*adj; m*	sharp; sharp
10000	**aveuglement**-*m*	blindness
10001	**illégalité**-*f*	illegality
10004	**dominateur**-*adj; m*	domineering; ruler
10005	**camomille**-*f*	chamomile
10007	**betterave**-*f*	beet
10011	**vinaigrette**-*f*	vinaigrette
10012	**arachide**-*f*	peanut
10013	**dividende**-*m*	dividend
10014	**arrivant**-*adj; m*	incoming; arrival
10015	**poulpe**-*m*	octopus
10016	**banalité**-*f*	banality| ordinariness
10017	**risotto**-*m*	risotto
10018	**carême**-*m*	fast
10019	**strangulation**-*f*	strangulation
10020	**insuffisance**-*f*	insufficiency
10021	**décadent**-*adj; m*	decadent; decadent
10022	**cabriolet**-*m*	convertible
10024	**pater**-*m*	pater
10025	**prolongation**-*f*	extension| prolongation

Verbs

Rank	French-*PoS*	Translation
7501	**irriter**-*vb*	irritate
7504	**trotter**-*vb*	trot
7517	**pâturer**-*vb*	graze
7519	**déraper**-*vb*	skid
7522	**attrister**-*vb*	sadden
7524	**éradiquer**-*vb*	eradicate
7526	**ravager**-*vb*	ravage| destroy
7531	**formuler**-*vb*	formulate| express
7533	**transpercer**-*vb*	pierce| penetrate
7534	**embobiner**-*vb*	bamboozle
7538	**épingler**-*vb*	pin
7540	**stabiliser**-*vb*	stabilize
7542	**hospitaliser**-*vb*	hospitalize
7546	**fourcher**-*vb*	pitchfork
7548	**jaillir**-*vb*	flow
7557	**survoler**-*vb*	fly| fly over
7558	**argenter**-*vb*	silver
7559	**border**-*vb*	border| rim
7562	**dissiper**-*vb*	dispel| clear
7564	**dépotoir**-*m; vb*	dumping ground; refuse dump
7569	**empester**-*vb*	stink
7573	**mûrir**-*vb*	mature| ripen
7574	**froisser**-*vb*	offend| crease
7577	**certifier**-*vb*	certify
7582	**dérailler**-*vb*	derail
7590	**rebondir**-*vb*	bounce| start up
7600	**enfler**-*vb*	swell| inflate
7601	**stipuler**-*vb*	stipulate
7614	**interférer**-*vb*	interfere
7623	**pourchasser**-*vb*	chase
7625	**métamorphoser**-*vb*	metamorphose
7630	**sélectionner**-*vb*	select
7648	**dompter**-*vb*	tame
7658	**alléger**-*vb*	alleviate
7661	**équivaloir**-*vb*	amount
7662	**privilégier**-*vb*	privilege
7666	**amadouer**-*vb*	coax
7667	**bouder**-*vb*	sulk
7677	**émerger**-*vb*	emerge
7679	**varier**-*vb*	vary
7688	**soudoyer**-*vb*	bribe| tamper
7695	**lacer**-*vb*	lace
7709	**tresser**-*vb*	braid| twine
7715	**dédommager**-*vb*	compensate
7718	**balayer**-*vb*	sweep| scan
7729	**geindre**-*vb*	whine| moan
7735	**défigurer**-*vb*	disfigure
7740	**immigrer**-*vb*	immigrate
7742	**reconsidérer**-*vb*	reconsider
7743	**tricoter**-*vb*	knit
7745	**tartiner**-*vb*	spread
7761	**renier**-*vb*	deny| renounce
7765	**neiger**-*vb*	snow
7768	**assortir**-*vb*	set
7777	**épanouir**-*vb*	light up
7778	**insérer**-*vb*	insert| slot
7786	**klaxonner**-*vb*	honk| sound
7790	**réintégrer**-*vb*	reinstate
7792	**clignoter**-*vb*	flash
7797	**circoncire**-*vb*	circumcise
7799	**recourir**-*vb*	resort
7807	**déjouer**-*vb*	foil
7816	**dissoudre**-*vb*	dissolve| deactivate
7826	**scier**-*vb*	saw
7847	**languir**-*vb*	languish
7848	**décliner**-*vb*	decline| refuse
7850	**consentir**-*vb*	consent
7851	**divulguer**-*vb*	disclose
7867	**lyncher**-*vb*	lynch
7870	**amender**-*vb*	amend
7875	**survenir**-*vb*	occur| arise
7879	**emplir**-*vb*	fill
7891	**saper**-*vb*	undermine
7892	**murmurer**-*vb*	murmur
7895	**humer**-*vb*	smell
7898	**repêcher**-*vb*	recover
7905	**déguster**-*vb*	savor
7910	**décontracter**-*vb*	relax
7915	**enlacer**-*vb*	embrace
7917	**recaler**-*vb*	fail
7920	**flamber**-*vb*	blaze| flame
7925	**approfondir**-*vb*	deepen
7928	**fracasser**-*vb*	smash
7929	**déporter**-*vb*	deport
7939	**administrer**-*vb*	administer
7941	**retoucher**-*vb*	retouch| touch
7942	**succéder**-*vb*	succeed
7943	**incomber**-*vb*	behove

7946	**farcir**-*vb*	stuff
7947	**immatriculer**-*vb*	register
7948	**confédérer**-*vb*	confederate
7956	**restreindre**-*vb*	restrict| narrow
7959	**sniffer**-*vb*	sniff
7963	**peupler**-*vb*	populate
7966	**calligraphier**-*vb*	calligraph
7969	**vadrouiller**-*vb*	bum around
7970	**désapprouver**-*vb*	disapprove
7975	**démentir**-*vb*	deny| contradict
7979	**éclore**-*vb*	hatch
7991	**gazer**-*vb*	zap| gas
8004	**aiguiser**-*vb*	whet| hone
8011	**gravir**-*vb*	climb| ascend
8015	**déformer**-*vb*	deform| distort
8016	**implanter**-*vb*	implant
8026	**chronométrer**-*vb*	time
8027	**dispenser**-*vb*	dispense| exempt
8047	**engourdir**-*vb*	numb
8048	**endurcir**-*vb*	harden
8052	**consumer**-*vb*	consume
8054	**différer**-*vb*	differ| vary
8058	**mimer**-*vb*	mimic| gesture
8064	**conférer**-*vb*	confer| lend
8072	**révolter**-*vb*	appal| revolt
8079	**orienter**-*vb*	guide| orient
8089	**fusionner**-*vb*	merge
8122	**asperger**-*vb*	spray
8135	**traumatiser**-*vb*	traumatize
8136	**trimballer**-*vb*	cart around
8140	**habiliter**-*vb*	empower| enable
8145	**pulvériser**-*vb*	spray| pulverize
8167	**dépraver**-*vb*	pervert
8170	**agacer**-*vb*	annoy| aggravate
8189	**cligner**-*vb*	wink| blink
8193	**incinérer**-*vb*	incinerate
8195	**accoupler**-*vb*	mate
8200	**dégueuler**-*vb*	puke
8205	**simplifier**-*vb*	simplify
8210	**opprimer**-*vb*	oppress| grind
8215	**escroquer**-*vb*	defraud| cheat
8218	**rétrécir**-*vb*	shrink
8219	**accroître**-*vb*	increase| enhance
8245	**méduser**-*vb*	daze| paralyze
8248	**retracer**-*vb*	trace| recount
8250	**ressortir**-*vb*	stand out
8254	**exalter**-*vb*	exalt| extoll
8271	**expier**-*vb*	atone for
8274	**immiscer**-*vb*	interfere
8278	**gratifier**-*vb*	gratify
8279	**encombrer**-*vb*	encumber
8287	**dérouiller**-*vb*	stretch| whack
8288	**discréditer**-*vb*	discredit
8296	**résulter**-*vb*	result
8300	**commenter**-*vb*	comment| commentate
8302	**gaver**-*vb*	stuff
8308	**cloquer**-*vb*	blister
8315	**platiner**-*vb*	platinize
8319	**abréger**-*vb*	shorten
8327	**écorcher**-*vb*	skin
8331	**mobiliser**-*vb*	mobilize| enlist
8332	**innocenter**-*vb*	clear| find not guilty
8336	**adoucir**-*vb*	soften
8346	**brider**-*vb*	bridle
8347	**courtiser**-*vb*	court
8360	**peler**-*vb*	peel| rind
8372	**devancer**-*vb*	forestall| outstrip
8376	**déloger**-*vb*	dislodge
8379	**hypnotiser**-*vb*	hypnotize
8383	**jacasser**-*vb*	chatter| jabber
8386	**diagnostiquer**-*vb*	diagnose
8395	**subvenir**-*vb*	support
8397	**sangloter**-*vb*	sob
8402	**conformer**-*vb*	comply with| conform
8404	**réapparaître**-*vb*	reappear
8424	**rayonner**-*vb*	beam| radiate
8425	**jauger**-*vb*	gauge
8434	**jongler**-*vb*	juggle
8435	**solliciter**-*vb*	solicit| ask
8441	**colorer**-*vb*	color
8444	**renommer**-*vb*	rename| reappoint
8446	**labourer**-*vb*	plow| till
8447	**élucider**-*vb*	clarify
8448	**diaphragmer**-*vb*	screen
8454	**engloutir**-*vb*	engulf| swallow
8455	**tranquilliser**-*vb*	calm| ease
8457	**déplorer**-*vb*	deplore
8458	**nuancer**-*vb*	nuance
8459	**immobiliser**-*vb*	immobilize
8460	**souder**-*vb*	weld
8465	**volatiliser**-*vb*	volatilize

8467	**débaucher**-*vb*	unblock| cork off
8469	**réformer**-*vb*	reform
8483	**envoûter**-*vb*	voodoo
8487	**adhérer**-*vb*	join| adhere
8493	**retentir**-*vb*	sound| resound
8497	**chantonner**-*vb*	hum
8499	**éplucher**-*vb*	peel| clean
8500	**broyer**-*vb; m*	grind; grinder
8502	**déchiqueter**-*vb*	shred
8505	**perpétuer**-*vb*	perpetuate
8514	**ébranler**-*vb*	shake| undermine
8516	**gigoter**-*vb*	wriggle
8519	**apprivoiser**-*vb*	tame
8521	**aliéner**-*vb*	alienate
8526	**uriner**-*vb*	urinate
8533	**rainer**-*vb*	groove
8534	**nouer**-*vb*	establish
8535	**gicler**-*vb*	spurt| spew
8539	**châtier**-*vb*	chasten| smite
8540	**parfumer**-*vb*	perfume| flavor
8550	**fourguer**-*vb*	flog| fence
8552	**émaner**-*vb*	emanate
8564	**hâter**-*vb*	hasten| accelerate
8565	**endetter**-*vb*	put into debt
8566	**capituler**-*vb*	capitulate
8569	**favoriser**-*vb*	promote| foster
8573	**draper**-*vb*	drape
8583	**sculpter**-*vb*	sculpt| carve
8587	**abonner**-*vb*	subscribe
8589	**falsifier**-*vb; m*	falsify; falsifier
8609	**éternuer**-*vb*	sneeze
8612	**tortiller**-*vb*	twirl| twist round
8620	**surchauffer**-*vb*	overheat
8621	**enrouler**-*vb*	wrap
8625	**disqualifier**-*vb*	disqualify
8635	**minimiser**-*vb*	minimize| play down
8636	**subsister**-*vb*	subsist| remain
8637	**graisser**-*vb*	grease
8644	**débaucher**-*vb*	poach| harass
8651	**exceller**-*vb*	excel
8655	**épier**-*vb*	spy
8656	**modeler**-*vb*	shape| model
8659	**braver**-*vb*	brave
8663	**parader**-*vb*	show
8666	**électrocuter**-*vb*	electrocute
8667	**galoper**-*vb*	gallop
8668	**meubler**-*vb*	furnish
8670	**fredonner**-*vb*	hum
8672	**grincer**-*vb*	squeak| grind
8674	**arrondir**-*vb*	round
8676	**déstabiliser**-*vb*	shake
8678	**déconnecter**-*vb*	disconnect
8689	**polluer**-*vb*	pollute| taint
8690	**couver**-*vb*	smolder| brood
8692	**dévisager**-*vb*	stare at
8696	**raviver**-*vb*	revive| rekindle
8712	**rafler**-*vb*	grab
8717	**rénover**-*vb*	renovate| restore
8723	**sauvegarder**-*vb*	safeguard
8726	**engraisser**-*vb*	fatten| grow fat
8744	**corner**-*m; vb*	corner; honk
8748	**discipliner**-*vb*	discipline
8753	**broder**-*vb*	embroider
8769	**illustrer**-*vb*	illustrate
8771	**siroter**-*vb*	sip
8775	**altérer**-*vb*	alter
8781	**spéculer**-*vb*	speculate
8789	**remorquer**-*vb*	tow
8790	**attendrir**-*vb*	tenderize| pound
8794	**postuler**-*vb*	apply| postulate
8803	**forer**-*vb*	drill| sink
8808	**vidanger**-*vb*	drain
8820	**interposer**-*vb*	interpose
8821	**sommeiller**-*vb*	sleep| doze
8823	**entraver**-*vb*	impede| hamper
8827	**stimuler**-*vb*	stimulate
8851	**déséquilibrer**-*vb*	unbalance
8853	**éblouir**-*vb*	dazzle
8862	**visualiser**-*vb*	visualize
8869	**rembobiner**-*vb*	rewind
8888	**accumuler**-*vb*	accumulate
8889	**lamenter**-*vb*	lament
8891	**mousser**-*vb*	foam| froth
8895	**ratisser**-*vb*	rake| comb
8896	**flâner**-*vb*	stroll| loiter
8903	**soustraire**-*vb*	subtract| remove
8907	**militer**-*vb*	militate
8913	**magouiller**-*vb*	fiddle
8914	**canarder**-*vb*	snipe
8919	**rajeunir**-*vb*	rejuvenate
8920	**récapituler**-*vb*	summarize| recapitulate

8939	**dégrader**-*vb*	degrade| deteriorate
8941	**équivoquer**-*vb*	equivocate
8942	**susciter**-*vb*	create| arouse
8944	**surestimer**-*vb*	overestimate
8947	**défavoriser**-*vb*	disadvantage
8949	**incruster**-*vb*	inlay| insert
8950	**ressasser**-*vb*	turn over
8951	**replonger**-*vb*	relapse
8957	**resservir**-*vb*	serve again
8960	**longer**-*vb*	follow
8963	**désinfecter**-*vb*	disinfect
8970	**rapatrier**-*vb*	repatriate
8977	**regrouper**-*vb*	regroup| gather
8981	**paître**-*vb*	graze| feed
8987	**persévérer**-*vb*	persevere
8993	**balafrer**-*vb*	slash| scar
9008	**recycler**-*vb*	recycle
9021	**séjourner**-*vb*	stay
9023	**restituer**-*vb*	return| restore
9024	**inaugurer**-*vb*	inaugurate
9035	**empocher**-*vb*	pocket
9042	**puiser**-*vb*	draw
9045	**aplatir**-*vb*	flatten
9052	**rêvasser**-*vb*	daydream
9062	**photocopier**-*vb*	photocopy
9064	**castrer**-*vb*	castrate
9071	**friser**-*vb*	curl
9075	**opter**-*vb*	opt
9077	**convulser**-*vb*	convulse
9079	**frissonner**-*vb*	shiver| tremble
9084	**éparpiller**-*vb*	scatter
9085	**roussir**-*vb*	scorch| brown
9087	**arnaquer**-*vb*	rip off
9095	**infester**-*vb*	infest| be infested
9110	**démêler**-*vb*	untangle| tease
9111	**décerner**-*vb*	award
9118	**malter**-*vb*	malt
9123	**pétrifier**-*vb*	petrify| stone
9136	**appâter**-*vb*	bait
9140	**foudroyer**-*vb*	blast
9147	**mutiler**-*vb*	mutilate| maim
9148	**affliger**-*vb*	afflict
9159	**mitrailler**-*vb*	volley
9165	**réincarner**-*vb*	reincarnate
9173	**immuniser**-*vb*	immunize
9175	**rabattre**-*vb*	tilt| turn down
9177	**laquer**-*vb*	lacquer
9183	**extirper**-*vb*	remove
9186	**réélire**-*vb*	re-elect
9188	**reluquer**-*vb*	ogle
9189	**réfuter**-*vb*	refute| disprove
9190	**bercer**-*vb*	rock
9194	**baratiner**-*vb*	sweet talk
9202	**référer**-*vb*	refer
9218	**nitrater**-*vb*	nitrate
9223	**ajourner**-*vb*	adjourn| postpone
9238	**clipper**-*vb*	clip
9245	**taxer**-*vb*	tax
9252	**râper**-*vb*	grate
9253	**procréer**-*vb*	procreate
9273	**réprimer**-*vb*	repress
9286	**faiblir**-*vb*	weaken
9304	**corser**-*vb*	lace
9307	**émigrer**-*vb*	emigrate
9311	**approvisionner**-*vb*	provision| store
9314	**accabler**-*vb*	overwhelm
9315	**perfectionner**-*vb*	improve
9328	**ravitailler**-*vb*	supply
9329	**cravacher**-*vb*	whip
9344	**scotcher**-*vb*	tape
9348	**amasser**-*vb*	amass| pile
9356	**persécuter**-*vb*	persecute
9358	**ériger**-*vb*	erect
9362	**atténuer**-*vb*	mitigate| ease
9365	**décompresser**-*vb*	decompress
9394	**rebrousser**-*vb*	turn back
9420	**tisser**-*vb*	weave
9427	**débusquer**-*vb*	flush
9429	**converser**-*vb*	converse
9438	**accoster**-*vb*	land| dock
9442	**appareiller**-*vb*	pair
9452	**canaliser**-*vb*	channel
9453	**dorloter**-*vb*	pamper| mother
9455	**carboniser**-*vb*	carbonize| char
9456	**brouter**-*vb*	graze| chatter
9461	**langer**-*vb*	swaddle
9463	**divaguer**-*vb*	ramble| rave
9465	**dédicacer**-*vb*	autograph
9475	**dîmer**-*vb*	tithe
9476	**suffoquer**-*vb*	suffocate
9478	**actionner**-*vb*	activate
9482	**malmener**-*vb*	bully| manhandle

9484	**invétérer**-*vb*	ingrain
9487	**instaurer**-*vb*	establish| instigate
9491	**chiffonner**-*vb*	crumple| ruffle
9496	**culbuter**-*vb*	tumble
9506	**roupiller**-*vb*	saw wood
9511	**camoufler**-*vb*	camouflage
9533	**palper**-*vb*	feel
9546	**scintiller**-*vb*	twinkle| sparkle
9548	**gondoler**-*vb*	warp
9551	**obliquer**-*vb*	skew
9552	**saturer**-*vb*	saturate
9553	**courber**-*vb*	bend
9556	**rétrograder**-*vb*	demote| downgrade
9557	**empailler**-*vb*	stuff
9563	**désintéresser**-*vb*	pay off
9565	**consolider**-*vb*	consolidate
9566	**assoupir**-*vb*	dull
9567	**réanimer**-*vb*	resuscitate
9569	**asservir**-*vb*	enslave
9575	**siéger**-*vb*	sit
9579	**sermonner**-*vb*	lecture| sermonize
9584	**assimiler**-*vb*	assimilate| absorb
9586	**entasser**-*vb*	pile| pile up
9587	**décomposer**-*vb*	decompose
9588	**surgeler**-*vb*	quick-freeze
9592	**écrémer**-*vb*	skim| separate
9595	**unifier**-*vb*	unify| standardize
9616	**répartir**-*vb*	allocate| divide
9617	**débiter**-*vb*	debit| cut
9622	**extorquer**-*vb*	extort| exact
9623	**ahurir**-*vb*	astound
9629	**panser**-*vb*	dress
9632	**tutoyer**-*vb*	tutoyer
9639	**bouillonner**-*vb*	bubble| boil
9650	**surexciter**-*vb*	overexcite
9662	**obtempérer**-*vb*	obey
9671	**fausser**-*vb*	distort| skew
9678	**profaner**-*vb*	defile
9679	**incorporer**-*vb*	mix| weave
9686	**affranchir**-*vb*	enfranchise| frank
9687	**cribler**-*vb*	sift| riddle
9690	**estomper**-*vb*	blur
9694	**marmonner**-*vb*	mumble
9707	**surmener**-*vb*	overwork
9727	**pieuter**-*vb*	sleep
9737	**démanteler**-*vb*	dismantle
9740	**tanguer**-*vb*	pitch| sway
9745	**essouffler**-*vb*	make breathless
9749	**plomber**-*vb*	seal
9754	**broncher**-*vb*	stumble
9762	**dépeindre**-*vb*	depict
9763	**gargouiller**-*vb*	gurgle
9766	**discerner**-*vb*	discern| detect
9769	**contrecarrer**-*vb*	thwart| oppose
9770	**attester**-*vb*	certify| attest
9771	**sursauter**-*vb*	jump up
9772	**compresser**-*vb*	compress
9788	**ricaner**-*vb*	sneer
9804	**ensanglanter**-*vb*	cover in blood
9805	**munir**-*vb*	provide| fit
9807	**télégraphier**-*vb*	telegraph
9810	**dessécher**-*vb*	dry out
9816	**abasourdir**-*vb*	stun| dumbfound
9819	**frémir**-*vb*	tremble| shudder
9826	**façonner**-*vb*	shape| fashion
9833	**assaillir**-*vb*	assail
9857	**déboussoler**-*vb*	confuse
9861	**décimer**-*vb*	decimate
9864	**imbiber**-*vb*	soak
9867	**allaiter**-*vb*	breast-feed| nurse
9883	**induire**-*vb*	induce
9888	**incriminer**-*vb*	incriminate
9889	**ébruiter**-*vb*	spread
9890	**perpétrer**-*vb*	perpetrate
9892	**esquisser**-*vb*	sketch| outline
9901	**révolutionner**-*vb*	revolutionize
9902	**abolir**-*vb*	abolish| lift
9908	**vacciner**-*vb*	vaccinate| inject
9910	**délaisser**-*vb*	abandon| neglect
9913	**enthousiasmer**-*vb*	enthuse
9921	**décommander**-*vb*	cancel
9926	**éreinter**-*vb*	hammer| exhaust
9937	**préconiser**-*vb*	advocate
9953	**surcharger**-*vb*	overload| overburden
9957	**enivrer**-*vb*	intoxicate| get drunk
9959	**terrasser**-*vb*	crush
9967	**ébattre**-*vb*	frolic
9970	**perforer**-*vb*	perforate
9973	**périmer**-*vb*	expire
9977	**concocter**-*vb*	concoct
9978	**communier**-*vb*	communicate
9981	**érafler**-*vb*	scratch| scuff

9982	**exténuer**-*vb*	exhaust
9983	**débiner**-*vb*	run down
9987	**évaporer**-*vb*	evaporate
9998	**replacer**-*vb*	replace
10002	**réorganiser**-*vb*	reorganize| reorder
10003	**pirouetter**-*vb*	pirouette
10010	**distancer**-*vb*	distance| outrun

Alphabetical order

Rank	French-PoS	Translation
9816	**abasourdir**-*vb*	stun| dumbfound
9488	**abattage**-*m*	slaughter| felling
8562	**abcès**-*m*	abscess
9799	**aberration**-*f*	aberration
8159	**abîme**-*m*	abyss| gulf
8496	**abject**-*adj*	abject
9689	**abnégation**-*f*	denial| self-sacrifice
8022	**aboi**-*m*	barking
9902	**abolir**-*vb*	abolish| lift
9924	**abolition**-*f*	abolition
8758	**abondant**-*adj; m*	abundant; affluent
8587	**abonner**-*vb*	subscribe
9759	**abordable**-*adj*	affordable
9204	**aborigène**-*adj; m/f*	aboriginal; aborigine
8319	**abréger**-*vb*	shorten
8186	**abruti**-*m; adj*	jerk; stupid
8707	**absinthe**-*f*	absinthe
7674	**absolution**-*f*	absolution
9060	**abstraction**-*f*	abstraction
7733	**abstrait**-*adj; m*	abstract; abstract
8779	**académique**-*adj*	academic
9314	**accabler**-*vb*	overwhelm
8098	**acceptation**-*f*	acceptance
7812	**accidentel**-*adj*	accidental| incidental
9758	**accolade**-*f*	hug| accolade
9438	**accoster**-*vb*	land| dock
8365	**accouplement**-*m*	coupling
8195	**accoupler**-*vb*	mate
8120	**accoutrement**-*m*	regalia
9056	**accrochage**-*m*	hanging| coupling
7772	**accroc**-*m*	snag| infraction
8219	**accroître**-*vb*	increase| enhance
8888	**accumuler**-*vb*	accumulate
8557	**acharnement**-*m*	fury| stubbornness
8039	**acné**-*f*	acne
9293	**acquittement**-*m*	acquittal
7654	**acre**-*m*	acre
7980	**acrobate**-*m/f*	acrobat
9239	**acrobatie**-*f*	acrobatics
9478	**actionner**-*vb*	activate
8536	**activement**-*adv*	busily
9672	**activiste**-*m/f; adj*	activist; smart
8487	**adhérer**-*vb*	join| adhere
9574	**adhésion**-*f*	membership
7914	**administratif**-*adj; m*	administrative; executive
7939	**administrer**-*vb*	administer
9974	**admirablement**-*adv*	admirably
9773	**adorateur**-*m; adj*	adorer; worshipful
8063	**adoration**-*f*	worship
8336	**adoucir**-*vb*	soften
9005	**aéroporté**-*adj*	airborne
8229	**affecté**-*adj*	affected
9318	**affectif**-*adj*	affective
8010	**affirmation**-*f*	affirmation
9017	**affliction**-*f*	affliction
9148	**affliger**-*vb*	afflict
9279	**affluent**-*m*	tributary
9991	**affolement**-*m*	panic
9686	**affranchir**-*vb*	enfranchise| frank
8170	**agacer**-*vb*	annoy| aggravate
8835	**agilité**-*f*	agility
9677	**agitateur**-*m*	agitator
9836	**agrafe**-*f*	clip
8694	**agrandissement**-*m*	enlargement
8511	**agréablement**-*adv*	pleasantly
9564	**agrément**-*m*	approval
9532	**agriculteur**-*m*	farmer
9623	**ahurir**-*vb*	astound
8518	**aïeux**-*m/mpl*	forefathers
9905	**aigre**-*adj*	sour
7902	**aigri**-*adj*	embittered
8004	**aiguiser**-*vb*	whet| hone
8582	**ailier**-*m*	wing
8106	**aimant**-*m*	magnet
8398	**aisance**-*f*	ease
9447	**aisselle**-*f*	armpit
9223	**ajourner**-*vb*	adjourn| postpone
9213	**ajustement**-*m*	adjustment
8966	**alarmant**-*adj*	alarming
8736	**albatros**-*m*	albatross
7697	**albinos**-*m*	albino
7615	**alchimie**-*f; adj*	alchemy; alchemic
7705	**alcoolisme**-*m*	alcoholism
7560	**algèbre**-*f*	algebra
9621	**aliénation**-*f*	alienation
8521	**aliéner**-*vb*	alienate
9867	**allaiter**-*vb*	breast-feed| nurse
7658	**alléger**-*vb*	alleviate

8451	**allégresse**-*f*	glee
9661	**alliage**-*m*	alloy| mixture
7620	**allocation**-*f*	allocation| allowance
8299	**allumeur**-*m*	igniter
9121	**almanach**-*m*	almanac
8163	**alouette**-*f*	lark
7617	**alphabétique**-*adj*	alphabetical| alphabet
8286	**altercation**-*f*	altercation
8775	**altérer**-*vb*	alter
8148	**alternatif**-*adj*	alternative
7655	**alto**-*adj; m*	alto; alto
9909	**altruiste**-*adj; m/f*	altruistic; altruist
7666	**amadouer**-*vb*	coax
7690	**amande**-*f*	almond
9348	**amasser**-*vb*	amass| pile
9658	**ambigu**-*adj*	ambiguous
8704	**ambulant**-*adj; m*	traveling; traveler
9789	**aménagement**-*m*	planning
7870	**amender**-*vb*	amend
8547	**amiante**-*f*	asbestos
9841	**amirauté**-*f*	admiralty
7878	**amorce**-*f*	bait
8524	**amphétamine**-*f*	amphetamine
9370	**amputation**-*f*	amputation
7809	**amulette**-*f*	amulet
8371	**amygdale**-*f*	tonsil| amygdala
9134	**anaconda**-*m*	anaconda
7960	**anal**-*adj*	anal
7616	**anarchiste**-*adj; m/f*	anarchist; anarchist
8293	**ancestral**-*adj*	ancestral
7539	**anchois**-*m*	anchovy
9448	**anciennement**-*adv*	formerly
8746	**ancienneté**-*f*	seniority
9211	**androïde**-*adj; m*	android; android
9869	**anéantissement**-*m*	annihilation
8324	**anémie**-*f*	anemia
9856	**anesthésique**-*adj*	anesthetic
8401	**anévrisme**-*m*	aneurism
8967	**angélique**-*adj*	angelic
9916	**angoissant**-*adj*	scary
9390	**angulaire**-*adj*	angular
9620	**animalerie**-*f*	pet shop
9067	**animosité**-*f*	animosity
9599	**anorexique**-*adj; m/f*	anorexic; anorexic
7710	**Antéchrist**-*m*	Antichrist
9015	**anthrax**-*m*	anthrax
8355	**anthropologie**-*f*	anthropology
9054	**anticorps**-*m*	antibody
8246	**antiquaire**-*adj; m/f*	antiquarian; antiquarian
9767	**apaisant**-*adj*	soothing
9798	**apartheid**-*f*	apartheid
9468	**apathie**-*f*	apathy
8743	**apesanteur**-*f*	weightlessness
9006	**aphrodisiaque**-*adj; m*	aphrodisiac; aphrodisiac
9045	**aplatir**-*vb*	flatten
9442	**appareiller**-*vb*	pair
8844	**appartenance**-*f*	membership
9136	**appâter**-*vb*	bait
8033	**appendice**-*m*	appendix
7708	**appendicite**-*f*	appendicitis
7951	**appétissant**-*adj*	appetizing
8417	**apport**-*m*	contribution
8171	**appréciation**-*f*	appreciation
9922	**appréhension**-*f*	apprehension
8519	**apprivoiser**-*vb*	tame
7925	**approfondir**-*vb*	deepen
9311	**approvisionner**-*vb*	provision| store
10012	**arachide**-*f*	peanut
8855	**arbalète**-*f*	crossbow
9777	**arbitrage**-*m; adj*	arbitrage; arbitral
8728	**arbitraire**-*adj*	arbitrary
8176	**arcade**-*f*	arcade
8461	**archange**-*m*	archangel
8113	**archéologie**-*f*	archeology
8202	**ardemment**-*adv*	ardently
9637	**ardu**-*adj*	difficult| arduous
9635	**arête**-*f*	arete
9485	**argenté**-*adj*	silver
7558	**argenter**-*vb*	silver
8121	**argot**-*m*	slang
8842	**aria**-*f*	aria
8852	**aride**-*adj*	arid
8961	**aristocratie**-*f*	aristocracy
8230	**arithmétique**-*adj; f*	arithmetic; arithmetic
8765	**arménien**-*adj; m*	Armenian; Armenian
7932	**armistice**-*m*	armistice| truce
8983	**armoiries**-*fpl*	arms
7858	**armurerie**-*f*	armory
8453	**armurier**-*m*	gunsmith| armourer
9087	**arnaquer**-*vb*	rip off
8442	**arôme**-*m*	aroma| flavoring

8554	**arrivage**-*m*	shipment
10014	**arrivant**-*adj; m*	incoming; arrival
9683	**arriviste**-*adj; m/f*	pushy; go-getter
8674	**arrondir**-*vb*	round
8249	**arrosage**-*m*	spray
9780	**arsenic**-*adj; m*	arsenic; arsenic
9422	**artefact**-*m*	artifact
7750	**artériel**-*adj*	arterial
8978	**articulation**-*f*	joint| speech
7510	**artisan**-*m*	artisan
8915	**aryen**-*adj*	Aryan
8224	**asperge**-*f*	asparagus
8122	**asperger**-*vb*	spray
8797	**asphalte**-*m*	asphalt
7753	**aspiration**-*f*	aspiration
9833	**assaillir**-*vb*	assail
7940	**assemblage**-*m*	assembly
9569	**asservir**-*vb*	enslave
7810	**assignation**-*f*	summons| subpoena
9584	**assimiler**-*vb*	assimilate| absorb
9741	**assortiment**-*m*	assortment
7768	**assortir**-*vb*	set
9566	**assoupir**-*vb*	dull
7952	**assureur**-*m*	insurer
9914	**asthmatique**-*adj; m/f*	asthmatic; asthmatic
7815	**asticot**-*m*	maggot
8081	**astre**-*m*	star
8980	**astrologie**-*f*	astrology
9325	**astrologue**-*m/f*	astrologer
8085	**astronome**-*m/f*	astronomer
8606	**athlétique**-*adj*	athletic
9205	**athlétisme**-*m*	athletics
9269	**atmosphérique**-*adj*	atmospheric
8555	**attelage**-*m*	coupling| hitch
9220	**attelle**-*f*	brace| splint
8790	**attendrir**-*vb*	tenderize| pound
9090	**atténuant**-*adj*	attenuating
9362	**atténuer**-*vb*	mitigate| ease
9770	**attester**-*vb*	certify| attest
7767	**attirail**-*m*	paraphernalia
9248	**attribut**-*m; adj*	attribute; predicate
7522	**attrister**-*vb*	sadden
7647	**aubaine**-*f*	boon| windfall
9965	**aubergine**-*f*	eggplant
8433	**auditoire**-*m*	audience
9305	**austère**-*adj*	austere
9445	**autochtone**-*m/f; adj*	native; native
8364	**autocollant**-*m; adj*	sticker; self-sealing
8060	**autrichien**-*adj*	Austrian
7527	**autruche**-*f*	ostrich
8959	**avantageux**-*adj*	advantageous
8616	**avarice**-*f*	greed| stinginess
8237	**avènement**-*m*	advent
7961	**averse**-*f*	shower
8671	**aversion**-*f*	aversion
10008	**aveuglant**-*adj*	blinding
8556	**aveuglément**-*adv*	blindly
10000	**aveuglement**-*m*	blindness
9518	**aviron**-*m*	rowing| oar

B

8222	**babiole**-*f*	bauble
8394	**bagarreur**-*m; adj*	brawler; feisty
8948	**bagatelle**-*f*	trifle
8399	**baignade**-*f*	bathing
8868	**bâillon**-*m*	gag
8686	**baiseur**-*m*	fucker
8993	**balafrer**-*vb*	slash| scar
7718	**balayer**-*vb*	sweep| scan
8128	**ballerine**-*f*	ballerina
7572	**ballot**-*m; adj*	bundle; clownish
8158	**balourd**-*m; adj*	oaf; awkward
9692	**bamboula**-*m; f*	negro; tamboula
10016	**banalité**-*f*	banality| ordinariness
8450	**banquise**-*f*	pack ice
9194	**baratiner**-*vb*	sweet talk
8714	**barde**-*m*	bard
9363	**barmaid**-*f*	barmaid
8558	**baroque**-*adj; m*	baroque; baroque
9158	**baryton**-*m*	baritone
8898	**basilic**-*m*	basil
8445	**basique**-*adj*	basic
7728	**bastion**-*m*	bastion
9919	**bâti**-*adj; m*	built; bed
8040	**bâtonnet**-*m*	rod
9168	**battant**-*m; adj*	clapper| fighter; swinging
8698	**baveux**-*adj*	runny
8522	**bavure**-*f*	smudge| blur
8206	**bazooka**-*m*	bazooka

8042	**beagle**-*m*	beagle
9229	**beigne**-*f*	donut
9858	**belette**-*f*	weasel
9116	**bénédicité**-*f*	benediction
7787	**bénéficiaire**-*m/f; adj*	beneficiary; profitable
9428	**benêt**-*m*	dullard
9346	**Bengale**-*m; adj*	Bengal; Bengal
9190	**bercer**-*vb*	rock
7746	**béret**-*m*	beret
7570	**berge**-*f*	bank
8633	**berline**-*f*	sedan| tramcar
8291	**bestial**-*adj*	bestial
10007	**betterave**-*f*	beet
9458	**beurré**-*adj*	plastered| buttered
8419	**beuverie**-*f*	carousal| boozer
8551	**bicarbonate**-*m*	bicarbonate
8732	**bicoque**-*f*	shanty| shack
9907	**bidet**-*m*	bidet
9440	**bienséance**-*f*	propriety
7976	**bifteck**-*m*	steak
8181	**bigleux**-*adj*	cross-eyed| four-eyed
7687	**bijoutier**-*m*	jeweler
8031	**biologiste**-*m/f*	biologist
9061	**biopsie**-*f*	biopsy
9628	**bique**-*f*	nanny-goat
8474	**biscotte**-*f*	biscuit
7779	**bis**-*m; adv; adj*	bis; twice; repeat
9842	**bistouri**-*m*	scalpel
7953	**bit**-*m*	bit
9333	**blablabla**-*m*	blah
8681	**blanchiment**-*m*	whitening
8599	**blason**-*m*	blazon| shield
9774	**blême**-*adj*	pale
9387	**blindage**-*m*	shield
7974	**blizzard**-*m*	blizzard
7819	**blocus**-*m*	blockade
8613	**boîtier**-*m*	housing
8234	**Bolchevik**-*m/f*	Bolshevik
8095	**bolide**-*m*	bolide| high end car
9503	**boniment**-*m*	pitch
9332	**boomerang**-*m*	boomerang
7559	**border**-*vb*	border| rim
7837	**bordure**-*f*	border
9051	**bosquet**-*m*	grove
8068	**botanique**-*adj; f*	botanical; botany
7667	**bouder**-*vb*	sulk
8822	**boudoir**-*m*	boudoir
8055	**boueux**-*adj; m*	muddy; bin man
9703	**bougeotte**-*f*	wanderlust
9219	**bouille**-*f*	mug| face
7784	**bouilloire**-*f*	kettle
9639	**bouillonner**-*vb*	bubble| boil
8381	**bouillotte**-*f*	hot-water bag
9571	**bouledogue**-*m*	bulldog
9988	**bouleversant**-*adj*	upsetting
9049	**bourbier**-*m*	quagmire| slough
9092	**bourde**-*f*	howler| blunder
7518	**bourdonnement**-*m*	buzz| hum
9848	**bourgeon**-*m*	bud
8107	**boursier**-*m*	scholar| stock market
9684	**boutonneux**-*adj*	spotty
9724	**braconnier**-*m*	poacher
8468	**braille**-*m*	braille
9381	**braise**-*f*	embers
7861	**braqueur**-*m*	raider| robber
9120	**brasse**-*f*	fathom
7575	**brasserie**-*f*	brewery
8659	**braver**-*vb*	brave
8216	**bretzel**-*m*	pretzel
8103	**breuvage**-*m*	beverage
9466	**bribe**-*f*	scrap
8738	**bricolage**-*m*	do-it-yourself
8735	**bricoleur**-*m*	handyman
8346	**brider**-*vb*	bridle
8702	**brillamment**-*adv*	brilliantly
9483	**brindille**-*f*	twig
9647	**brisant**-*adj; m*	breaking; breaker
9997	**briseur**-*m*	breaker
9366	**brocoli**-*m*	broccoli
9853	**broderie**-*f*	embroidery
8753	**broder**-*vb*	embroider
9754	**broncher**-*vb*	stumble
8665	**brouette**-*f*	wheelbarrow
9339	**brouillage**-*m*	interference
9609	**brouillon**-*m; adj*	draft; untidy
9456	**brouter**-*vb*	graze| chatter
9831	**broutille**-*f*	trifle
8500	**broyer**-*vb; m*	grind; grinder
7833	**broyeur**-*m*	crusher
9917	**bru**-*f*	daughter-in-law
8231	**buanderie**-*f*	utility room

9257	**bulgare**-*adj; m*	Bulgarian; Bulgarian
7904	**bulldozer**-*m*	bulldozer
7741	**bureaucrate**-*m/f*	bureaucrat
7967	**bureaucratie**-*f*	bureaucracy
9821	**butée**-*f*	toe
7605	**buveur**-*m*	drinker

C

9288	**cabanon**-*m*	shed
7890	**caboche**-*f*	noggin
10022	**cabriolet**-*m*	convertible
7550	**cacao**-*m*	cocoa
7871	**cachemire**-*m*	cashmere
7820	**caddie**-*m*	caddy| trolley
7599	**cadran**-*m*	dial
9781	**cagibi**-*m*	storage room| cupboard
8832	**caille**-*f*	quail
9843	**caillot**-*m*	clot
8938	**caïman**-*m*	caiman
9782	**calcaire**-*m; adj*	limestone; calcareous
9195	**calcium**-*m*	calcium
9915	**calculateur**-*adj*	calculating
9775	**calepin**-*m*	notebook
8800	**calice**-*m*	chalice
9958	**calife**-*m*	caliph
8825	**californien**-*adj*	Californian
7966	**calligraphier**-*vb*	calligraph
8677	**calmar**-*m*	squid
8929	**calotte**-*f*	cap| dome
8351	**camaraderie**-*f*	comeradeship
8603	**cambrousse**-*f*	outback
8050	**camionneur**-*m*	truck driver
10005	**camomille**-*f*	chamomile
9511	**camoufler**-*vb*	camouflage
9667	**campeur**-*m*	camper
8875	**canalisation**-*f*	piping
9452	**canaliser**-*vb*	channel
8914	**canarder**-*vb*	snipe
8204	**canasson**-*m*	nag
9633	**cancan**-*m*	cancan| dirt
10009	**cancéreux**-*adj*	cancerous
9088	**canicule**-*f*	heat wave
7618	**canif**-*m*	penknife
9099	**canin**-*adj*	canine
8388	**cantique**-*m*	canticle| song
7885	**capitulation**-*f*	capitulation
8566	**capituler**-*vb*	capitulate
8349	**Capricorne**-*m*	Capricorn
8773	**captif**-*adj; m*	captive; captive
9433	**captivant**-*adj*	captivating
8772	**capuche**-*f*	hoodie
8799	**capuchon**-*m*	cap| hood
8108	**carafe**-*f*	carafe| jug
9455	**carboniser**-*vb*	carbonize| char
8924	**cardigan**-*m*	cardigan
8946	**cardiologue**-*m/f*	cardiologist
10018	**carême**-*m*	fast
8897	**caricature**-*f*	caricature
7893	**carillon**-*m*	carillon
8629	**carnivore**-*adj*	carnivorous
7696	**carrelage**-*m*	tiles
8440	**carrosserie**-*f*	body
8227	**carrure**-*f*	shoulders| build
9037	**cartable**-*m*	satchel
9064	**castrer**-*vb*	castrate
9605	**catacombe**-*f*	catacomb
9034	**catalyseur**-*m*	catalyst
8912	**catcheur**-*m*	wrestler
8819	**catégorique**-*adj*	categorical
9210	**catégoriquement**-*adv*	categorically
9113	**cathédrale**-*f*	cathedral
9029	**causette**-*f*	rap| chat
9449	**caveau**-*m*	vault
7793	**cavité**-*f*	cavity
8699	**cécité**-*f*	blindness
8297	**céleri**-*m*	celery
7824	**cellier**-*m*	cellar
8908	**cellophane**-*m*	cellophane
9793	**cellulite**-*f*	cellulite
7643	**centenaire**-*adj; m/f*	centenary; centenary
9825	**centième**-*num*	hundredth
8624	**céramique**-*adj; f*	ceramic; ceramics
8131	**cerisier**-*m*	cherry
9932	**cerne**-*m*	circle
7577	**certifier**-*vb*	certify
8846	**chaînon**-*m*	link
8030	**chalumeau**-*m*	blowtorch
7706	**chaman**-*m*	shaman
9504	**chandelier**-*m*	candlestick

8041	**changeur**-*m*	converter
8497	**chantonner**-*vb*	hum
8438	**chanvre**-*m*	hemp
7931	**chaotique**-*adj*	chaotic
7814	**chapelet**-*m*	beads| rosary
8711	**chapelier**-*m*	milliner
8209	**charisme**-*m*	charisma
9986	**charnel**-*adj*	carnal
9544	**charognard**-*m*	scavenger
7514	**charrue**-*f*	plow
7547	**charte**-*f*	charter| convention
9249	**chaste**-*adj*	chaste
8539	**châtier**-*vb*	chasten| smite
9082	**chatouilleux**-*adj*	ticklish
9246	**chaufferie**-*f*	boiler room
9144	**chaux**-*f*	lime| whitewash
9377	**chenal**-*m*	channel
9081	**chenapan**-*m*	scoundrel
8706	**chenil**-*m*	kennel
8492	**chevalerie**-*f*	chivalry
8763	**chevelu**-*adj*	haired| hairy
7866	**chevreuil**-*m*	roe| deer
9822	**chiffe**-*f*	spineless individual
9491	**chiffonner**-*vb*	crumple| ruffle
9112	**chignon**-*m*	bun| catfight
8009	**chimère**-*f*	chimera
9735	**chimiothérapie**-*f*	chemotherapy
9294	**chiqué**-*adj*	sham| airs
8264	**chirurgical**-*adj*	surgical
9636	**chloroforme**-*m*	chloroform
8979	**chope**-*f*	mug
7938	**choucroute**-*f*	sauerkraut
9028	**chrétienté**-*f*	Christendom
8578	**chrome**-*m*	chrome
9541	**chromosome**-*m*	chromosome
9619	**chroniqueur**-*m*	chronicler| journalist
8026	**chronométrer**-*vb*	time
9803	**chuchotement**-*m*	whisper
8001	**Chypre**-*f*	Cyprus
9598	**ciboire**-*m*	ciborium
8295	**cierge**-*m*	candle
8232	**cigogne**-*f*	stork
8845	**cime**-*f*	top| crown
7797	**circoncire**-*vb*	circumcise
9416	**circoncision**-*f*	circumcision
8874	**circonscription**-*f*	district| riding
7642	**circulaire**-*adj; f*	circular; circular
9638	**cireur**-*m*	polisher
9108	**citadin**-*m; adj*	city dweller; city dwelling
9201	**citoyenneté**-*f*	citizenship
9989	**clameur**-*f*	clamor| shouting
9424	**clandestinement**-*adv*	clandestinely
7864	**clarinette**-*f*	clarinet
8141	**claustrophobe**-*adj*	claustrophobic
7865	**clavicule**-*f*	clavicle
8189	**cligner**-*vb*	wink| blink
7792	**clignoter**-*vb*	flash
9238	**clipper**-*vb*	clip
9260	**cliquetis**-*m*	clatter| rattle
9258	**cloaque**-*m*	cesspool
7828	**cloison**-*f*	partition
9992	**cloître**-*m*	cloister| enclosure
7995	**clonage**-*m*	cloning
9820	**clopinettes**-*fpl*	peanuts
8308	**cloquer**-*vb*	blister
7834	**cocon**-*m*	cocoon
8905	**collation**-*f*	collation| snack
9043	**collet**-*m*	collar| neck
7739	**colonial**-*adj*	colonial
9898	**colonisation**-*f*	colonization
8441	**colorer**-*vb*	color
7972	**colossal**-*adj*	colossal| huge
7693	**colosse**-*m; adj*	colossus; colossal
9349	**comestible**-*adj*	edible
8175	**commanditaire**-*m*	silent partner| sponsor
8300	**commenter**-*vb*	comment| commentate
8741	**commerce**-*m*	trade| business
8719	**commère**-*f*	tattletale
8546	**communautaire**-*adj*	communal
9664	**communément**-*adv*	commonly
9978	**communier**-*vb*	communicate
8318	**compère**-*m*	accomplice
9772	**compresser**-*vb*	compress
8934	**compresseur**-*m*	compressor
8132	**compression**-*f*	compression
9583	**comptine**-*f*	nursery rhyme
9209	**compulsif**-*adj*	compulsive
8922	**concepteur**-*m*	designer
9068	**concessionnaire**-*m*	dealer

9977	**concocter**-*vb*	concoct
9827	**condescendance**-*f*	condescension
8764	**condescendant**-*adj*	patronizing
9414	**conditionnement**-*m*	packaging
7552	**condor**-*m*	condor
8092	**conduite**-*f*	conduct| driving
8275	**cône**-*m*	cone
8988	**confédération**-*f*	confederation
7948	**confédérer**-*vb*	confederate
8064	**conférer**-*vb*	confer| lend
8575	**confessionnal**-*m*	confessional
8899	**confiant**-*adj*	confident
8745	**configuration**-*f*	configuration
8017	**confiserie**-*f*	confectionery
8402	**conformer**-*vb*	comply with| conform
7859	**confrère**-*m*	colleague
9778	**conjonction**-*f*	conjunction
8276	**connaisseur**-*m*	connoisseur
9790	**conque**-*f*	conch
9096	**consciencieux**-*adj*	conscientious
7850	**consentir**-*vb*	consent
9479	**conservation**-*f*	preservation
9565	**consolider**-*vb*	consolidate
8408	**consortium**-*m*	consortium
9270	**constipé**-*adj*	constipated
7553	**constructeur**-*m*	builder
9996	**constructif**-*adj*	constructive
8052	**consumer**-*vb*	consume
9655	**contagion**-*f*	contagion
8579	**container**-*m*	bowl
8774	**contemporain**-*adj; m*	contemporary| coeval; contemporary
9225	**continuation**-*f*	continuation
8263	**continuité**-*f*	continuity
9761	**contour**-*m*	contour| outline
8270	**contraction**-*f*	contraction
8661	**contradictoire**-*adj*	contradictory
7818	**contravention**-*f*	violation
8420	**contrebandier**-*m*	smuggler
9769	**contrecarrer**-*vb*	thwart| oppose
7999	**contrefaçon**-*f*	counterfeit
8138	**contusion**-*f*	contusion
8257	**convalescence**-*f*	recovery
7877	**convenance**-*f*	convenience
9429	**converser**-*vb*	converse
8760	**convocation**-*f*	convocation
9955	**convoitise**-*f*	greed| desire
9077	**convulser**-*vb*	convulse
7653	**coqueluche**-*f*	whooping cough
8824	**coquet**-*adj*	pretty| stylish
7608	**corbeille**-*f*	basket
9882	**cordial**-*adj; m*	cordial; cordial
8116	**cordialement**-*adv*	cordially
9516	**cornemuse**-*f*	bagpipe
8744	**corner**-*m; vb*	corner; honk
7545	**cornet**-*m*	horn| screw
9731	**corniaud**-*m; m*	mutt; analogy
9182	**corniche**-*f*	cornice| ledge
7530	**corpus**-*m*	corpus
9080	**correspondant**-*adj; m*	corresponding; correspondent
8115	**corrida**-*f*	bullfight
7744	**corsage**-*m*	blouse| corsage
9304	**corser**-*vb*	lace
7596	**cortex**-*m*	cortex
8369	**côtier**-*adj*	coastal
8718	**courageusement**-*adv*	courageously
9553	**courber**-*vb*	bend
9717	**courbette**-*f*	bowing
8618	**courroie**-*f*	belt
7528	**courroux**-*m*	wrath
8347	**courtiser**-*vb*	court
7724	**couturière**-*f*	seamstress
9302	**couturier**-*m*	fashion designer
8690	**couver**-*vb*	smolder| brood
9415	**crânien**-*adj*	cranial
9254	**craquement**-*m*	crack
9329	**cravacher**-*vb*	whip
8542	**créancier**-*m*	creditor
8513	**credo**-*m*	creed| belief
9020	**crédule**-*adj*	credulous
9295	**crémaillère**-*f*	rack
9376	**crème**-*adj; f*	cream; cream
8984	**crescendo**-*m*	crescendo
9900	**crible**-*m*	screen| riddle
9687	**cribler**-*vb*	sift| riddle
8901	**crinière**-*f*	mane
9418	**criquet**-*m*	locust
8585	**crissement**-*m*	screech
9235	**croquet**-*m*	croquet
8602	**croupe**-*f*	rump| croup

7823	**croupier**-*m*	croupier
8137	**croustillant**-*adj; m*	crispy; crispness
8341	**crucifixion**-*f*	crucifixion
8645	**cruellement**-*adv*	cruelly
9887	**cueillette**-*f*	picking
8477	**cuisson**-*f*	baking
9813	**cuivre**-*m*	copper
9496	**culbuter**-*vb*	tumble
8342	**cupide**-*adj*	greedy
8226	**curé**-*m*	priest
8472	**cycliste**-*m*	cyclist
8568	**cyclope**-*m*	Cyclops
8150	**cylindre**-*m*	cylinder
7505	**cynisme**-*m*	cynicism

D

8180	**dactylo**-*m/f*	typist
9654	**dansant**-*adj*	dancing
8644	**débaucher**-*vb*	poach| harass
9983	**débiner**-*vb*	run down
9617	**débiter**-*vb*	debit| cut
7754	**débit**-*m*	debit| output
9510	**débordant**-*adj*	boundless
8467	**déboucher**-*vb*	unblock| cork off
9857	**déboussoler**-*vb*	confuse
9427	**débusquer**-*vb*	flush
7671	**décadence**-*f*	decadence| decay
10021	**décadent**-*adj; m*	decadent; decadent
8755	**décemment**-*adv*	decently
9111	**décerner**-*vb*	award
8162	**déchéance**-*f*	decline
8502	**déchiqueter**-*vb*	shred
8695	**déchirure**-*f*	tear| tearing
9861	**décimer**-*vb*	decimate
8452	**déclarant**-*m*	declarer
9578	**déclenchement**-*m*	release
7848	**décliner**-*vb*	decline| refuse
9921	**décommander**-*vb*	cancel
9587	**décomposer**-*vb*	decompose
9365	**décompresser**-*vb*	decompress
9321	**déconcertant**-*adj*	disconcerting
8678	**déconnecter**-*vb*	disconnect
7910	**décontracter**-*vb*	relax
9495	**dédain**-*m*	disdain
9465	**dédicacer**-*vb*	autograph
9350	**dédommagement**-*m*	compensation
7715	**dédommager**-*vb*	compensate
8947	**défavoriser**-*vb*	disadvantage
7735	**défigurer**-*vb*	disfigure
9868	**déformation**-*f*	deformation| distortion
8015	**déformer**-*vb*	deform| distort
9704	**dégagement**-*m*	clearance| disengagement
9529	**dégel**-*m*	thaw
8776	**dégradant**-*adj*	degrading
8099	**dégradation**-*f*	degradation| deterioration
8939	**dégrader**-*vb*	degrade| deteriorate
8200	**dégueuler**-*vb*	puke
7905	**déguster**-*vb*	savor
7807	**déjouer**-*vb*	foil
9910	**délaisser**-*vb*	abandon| neglect
8838	**délicieusement**-*adv*	deliciously
8791	**délinquance**-*f*	delinquency
8376	**déloger**-*vb*	dislodge
8213	**déloyal**-*adj*	unfair| disloyal
9737	**démanteler**-*vb*	dismantle
9019	**démarche**-*f*	step| gait
9110	**démêler**-*vb*	untangle| tease
8142	**déménageur**-*m*	mover
7975	**démentir**-*vb*	deny| contradict
8597	**demeure**-*f*	residence| abode
8798	**déminage**-*m*	sweeping
7561	**dénouement**-*m*	outcome
8088	**déodorant**-*m*	deodorant
9472	**dépannage**-*m*	help| fixing
9762	**dépeindre**-*vb*	depict
7602	**déplorable**-*adj*	deplorable
8457	**déplorer**-*vb*	deplore
9374	**déportation**-*f*	deportation
9899	**déporté**-*m; adj*	deportee; deported
7929	**déporter**-*vb*	deport
7564	**dépotoir**-*m; vb*	dumping ground; refuse dump
8847	**dépravation**-*f*	depravity
8167	**dépraver**-*vb*	pervert
7582	**dérailler**-*vb*	derail
8282	**déraisonnable**-*adj*	unreasonable
8880	**dérangeant**-*adj*	unpalatable
7519	**déraper**-*vb*	skid
9240	**dérision**-*f*	derision| mockery

9048	**dérisoire**-*adj*	derisory| paltry
8287	**dérouiller**-*vb*	stretch| whack
8362	**déroulement**-*m*	progress
7747	**déroutant**-*adj*	disconcerting
7970	**désapprouver**-*vb*	disapprove
9695	**désarmement**-*m*	disarmament
8321	**désarroi**-*m*	disarray
8475	**déséquilibre**-*m*	imbalance
8851	**déséquilibrer**-*vb*	unbalance
8716	**désertion**-*f*	desertion
7791	**designer**-*m*	designer
8080	**désinfectant**-*adj; m*	disinfectant; disinfectant
8963	**désinfecter**-*vb*	disinfect
9563	**désintéresser**-*vb*	pay off
9281	**désinvolte**-*adj*	casual
8430	**désirable**-*adj*	desirable| likeable
7775	**désireux**-*adj*	eager
7978	**désobéissance**-*f*	disobedience
9810	**dessécher**-*vb*	dry out
7523	**dessinateur**-*m*	designer| draftsman
8676	**déstabiliser**-*vb*	shake
9985	**destinataire**-*m*	recipient| addressee
7702	**destinée**-*f*	destiny
9938	**détergent**-*adj; m*	detergent; cleanser
7862	**détritus**-*m*	litter
8372	**devancer**-*vb*	forestall| outstrip
9141	**dévastateur**-*adj*	devastating
9153	**dévergondé**-*adj*	wanton
7789	**déviation**-*f*	deviation
8692	**dévisager**-*vb*	stare at
9310	**devis**-*m*	quotation
9320	**diadème**-*m*	tiara
9582	**diagnostique**-*adj*	diagnostic
8386	**diagnostiquer**-*vb*	diagnose
9517	**diagramme**-*m*	diagram
8448	**diaphragmer**-*vb*	screen
9298	**diction**-*f*	diction
9999	**dièse**-*adj; m*	sharp; sharp
8054	**différer**-*vb*	differ| vary
8833	**difforme**-*adj*	misshapen
9572	**digestif**-*adj*	digestive
8292	**digestion**-*f*	digestion
8481	**digital**-*adj*	digital
9271	**dignitaire**-*m; adj*	dignitary; genual
9475	**dîmer**-*vb*	tithe
9542	**diminution**-*f*	decrease
7673	**dinar**-*m*	dinar
8198	**dioxyde**-*m*	dioxide
9849	**diphtérie**-*f*	diphtheria
9083	**discernement**-*m*	discernment
9766	**discerner**-*vb*	discern| detect
8857	**disciplinaire**-*adj*	disciplinary
8748	**discipliner**-*vb*	discipline
8431	**discothèque**-*f*	disco| nightclub
8288	**discréditer**-*vb*	discredit
9581	**discutable**-*adj*	questionable| debatable
7738	**disgrâce**-*f*	disgrace
8390	**dispensaire**-*m*	dispensary
8027	**dispenser**-*vb*	dispense| exempt
9943	**disponibilité**-*f*	availability
8625	**disqualifier**-*vb*	disqualify
8937	**dissection**-*f*	dissection
7830	**dissertation**-*f*	dissertation
8403	**dissimulation**-*f*	concealment
7562	**dissiper**-*vb*	dispel| clear
9462	**dissolution**-*f*	dissolution
7816	**dissoudre**-*vb*	dissolve| deactivate
10010	**distancer**-*vb*	distance| outrun
9162	**distinct**-*adj*	separate
9397	**distinctement**-*adv*	distinctly| audibly
7919	**distingué**-*adj*	distinguished
9463	**divaguer**-*vb*	ramble| rave
7612	**diversité**-*f*	diversity
10013	**dividende**-*m*	dividend
8094	**divisionnaire**-*adj*	divisional
7851	**divulguer**-*vb*	disclose
8160	**documentation**-*f*	documentation
7887	**dominant**-*adj*	dominant
10004	**dominateur**-*adj; m*	domineering; ruler
7648	**dompter**-*vb*	tame
9519	**dompteur**-*m*	tamer
7843	**donation**-*f*	donation
7685	**doré**-*adj*	golden| coated
9453	**dorloter**-*vb*	pamper| mother
9507	**dormeur**-*m*	sleeper
8968	**dorsal**-*adj*	dorsal
8525	**dosage**-*m*	dosage
8778	**douanier**-*m*	customs officer
9385	**douve**-*f*	stave| moat
8848	**douzième**-*num*	twelfth

9651	**dragueur**-*m*	dredger| player
9814	**dramaturge**-*m/f*	dramatist
8573	**draper**-*vb*	drape
8816	**dresseur**-*m*	trainer
8309	**droitier**-*m; adj*	right-hander; right-handed
9292	**droiture**-*f*	righteousness
9334	**druide**-*m*	druid
8811	**ducat**-*m*	ducat
8976	**dureté**-*f*	hardness| toughness
9950	**duveteux**-*adj*	fluffy
8654	**duvet**-*m*	duvet
9289	**dysenterie**-*f*	dysentery
8870	**dysfonctionnement**-*m*	dysfunction

E

9967	**ébattre**-*vb*	frolic
9030	**ébauche**-*f*	draft
8853	**éblouir**-*vb*	dazzle
9526	**éboulement**-*m*	landslide
8514	**ébranler**-*vb*	shake| undermine
9764	**ébriété**-*f*	intoxication
9889	**ébruiter**-*vb*	spread
8828	**ébullition**-*f*	boiling
8928	**écaille**-*f*	scale
8065	**échafaud**-*m*	scaffold
8935	**échauffement**-*m*	heating
7639	**échelon**-*m*	echelon
8323	**échine**-*f*	spine
9197	**échiquier**-*m*	chessboard
7836	**échographie**-*f*	ultrasound| scan
7979	**éclore**-*vb*	hatch
8389	**écœurant**-*adj*	disgusting| sickening
7998	**écolier**-*m*	schoolboy
9343	**écologique**-*adj*	ecological
8327	**écorcher**-*vb*	skin
8508	**écrasant**-*adj*	crushing| overwhelming;
9592	**écrémer**-*vb*	skim| separate
7857	**écuyer**-*m*	squire
9317	**éditorial**-*adj; m*	editorial; editorial
7825	**éducatif**-*adj*	educative
8350	**efficacement**-*adv*	effectively
9264	**éjaculation**-*f*	ejaculation
7632	**électrochoc**-*m*	electroshock
8666	**électrocuter**-*vb*	electrocute
9829	**électrocution**-*f*	electrocution
8601	**électrode**-*f*	electrode
7593	**électromagnétique**-*adj*	electromagnetic
8233	**éleveur**-*m*	farmer
9297	**élocution**-*f*	speech
8320	**éloquence**-*f*	eloquence
9032	**éloquent**-*adj*	eloquent
8447	**élucider**-*vb*	clarify
9946	**émancipation**-*f*	emancipation
8552	**émaner**-*vb*	emanate
9117	**embarcadère**-*f; m*	jetty; wharf
9410	**embargo**-*m*	embargo
7534	**embobiner**-*vb*	bamboozle
9142	**embolie**-*f*	embolism
9844	**embouchure**-*f*	mouth| outlet
9585	**embryon**-*m*	embryo
7677	**émerger**-*vb*	emerge
9307	**émigrer**-*vb*	emigrate
8147	**éminence**-*f*	eminence| height
8393	**émir**-*m*	emir
7580	**émoi**-*m*	stir| emotion
8375	**émouvant**-*adj*	moving| touching
9557	**empailler**-*vb*	stuff
9208	**empathie**-*f*	empathy
9102	**empêchement**-*m*	impediment
7569	**empester**-*vb*	stink
7879	**emplir**-*vb*	fill
9035	**empocher**-*vb*	pocket
8199	**enchaînement**-*m*	sequence| linking
8294	**enclin**-*adj*	inclined
9626	**enclume**-*f*	anvil
8279	**encombrer**-*vb*	encumber
8565	**endetter**-*vb*	put into debt
8048	**endurcir**-*vb*	harden
8203	**énergique**-*adj*	energetic
7507	**énervant**-*adj*	annoying
8708	**enfantillage**-*m*	childishness
7726	**enfantin**-*adj*	infantile
7600	**enfler**-*vb*	swell| inflate
8454	**engloutir**-*vb*	engulf| swallow
9877	**engouement**-*m*	infatuation
8047	**engourdir**-*vb*	numb
8726	**engraisser**-*vb*	fatten| grow fat
9866	**engrenage**-*m*	gearing

9699	**énigmatique**-*adj*	enigmatic
9957	**enivrer**-*vb*	intoxicate| get drunk
7915	**enlacer**-*vb*	embrace
8356	**enregistreur**-*m*	recorder
8621	**enrouler**-*vb*	wrap
9804	**ensanglanter**-*vb*	cover in blood
9586	**entasser**-*vb*	pile| pile up
8705	**entendement**-*m*	understanding
8563	**entêtement**-*m*	stubbornness
9913	**enthousiasmer**-*vb*	enthuse
7589	**entorse**-*f*	sprain| strain
8466	**entraide**-*f*	mutual aid
8823	**entraver**-*vb*	impede| hamper
8541	**envieux**-*adj*	green-eyed
8483	**envoûter**-*vb*	voodoo
8266	**enzyme**-*f*	enzyme
7777	**épanouir**-*vb*	light up
9084	**éparpiller**-*vb*	scatter
7701	**éphémère**-*adj; m*	ephemeral; ephemeral
8655	**épier**-*vb*	spy
7668	**épileptique**-*adj; m/f*	epileptic; epileptic person
9460	**épi**-*m*	ear| cob
9568	**épineux**-*adj*	thorny| tricky
7538	**épingler**-*vb*	pin
7860	**épique**-*adj*	epic
8731	**épitaphe**-*f*	epitaph
8499	**éplucher**-*vb*	peel| clean
9723	**éponge**-*f*	sponge
9391	**épopée**-*f*	epic
7964	**épouvante**-*f*	dread
7691	**éprouvant**-*adj*	testing
8443	**équitation**-*f*	horse riding
9545	**équité**-*f*	equity
7661	**équivaloir**-*vb*	amount
8941	**équivoquer**-*vb*	equivocate
7524	**éradiquer**-*vb*	eradicate
9981	**érafler**-*vb*	scratch| scuff
8269	**éraflure**-*f*	scratch| score
9926	**éreinter**-*vb*	hammer| exhaust
9358	**ériger**-*vb*	erect
9602	**erroné**-*adj*	wrong| erroneous
7689	**escapade**-*f*	escapade
8215	**escroquer**-*vb*	defraud| cheat
9573	**espadon**-*m*	swordfish
9832	**espiègle**-*adj; m/f*	playful| impish; imp

9892	**esquisser**-*vb*	sketch| outline
7541	**esquive**-*f*	dodge
8930	**essaim**-*m*	swarm
8007	**essayage**-*m*	fitting
8509	**essor**-*m*	development
9745	**essouffler**-*vb*	make breathless
9181	**esthéticien**-*m*	beautician
9690	**estomper**-*vb*	blur
7935	**estrade**-*f*	platform| stage
8240	**étanche**-*adj*	waterproof
9150	**étau**-*m*	vice| stranglehold
9025	**étendard**-*m*	standard
8609	**éternuer**-*vb*	sneeze
7873	**ethnique**-*adj*	ethnic
7949	**étiré**-*adj*	spread| stretch
8053	**étonnement**-*m; adv*	astonishment; surprisingly
8893	**étouffant**-*adj*	stifling
8664	**étroitement**-*adv*	closely
8530	**eunuque**-*m*	eunuch
8595	**euphorie**-*f*	euphoria
8592	**euthanasie**-*f*	euthanasia
9987	**évaporer**-*vb*	evaporate
7579	**éveil**-*m*	awakening
9115	**éventuel**-*adj*	prospective
8911	**exactitude**-*f*	accuracy
8254	**exalter**-*vb*	exalt| extoll
8651	**exceller**-*vb*	excel
8688	**exceptionnellement**-*adv*	exceptionally
9192	**excessivement**-*adv*	excessively
9696	**exclamation**-*f*	exclamation
9046	**exclusion**-*f*	exclusion
9091	**exécrable**-*adj*	execrable
8211	**exécuteur**-*m*	executor
9119	**exhibition**-*f*	display
7719	**exigeant**-*adj*	demanding| exacting
9753	**exode**-*m*	exodus
7993	**exorciste**-*m*	exorcist
7989	**expérimentation**-*f*	experimentation
9785	**expiation**-*f*	atonement
8271	**expier**-*vb*	atone for
8864	**expiration**-*f*	expiry
9004	**exportation**-*f*	export
9982	**exténuer**-*vb*	exhaust
7955	**exterminateur**-*m; adj*	exterminator; exterminating

9183	**extirper**-*vb*	remove
9622	**extorquer**-*vb*	extort| exact
7722	**extradition**-*f*	extradition
9711	**extraordinairement**-*adv*	extraordinarily
7886	**extravagant**-*adj*	extravagant

F

8169	**fable**-*f*	fable
8432	**facette**-*f*	facet
9826	**façonner**-*vb*	shape| fashion
8876	**faction**-*f*	faction
9286	**faiblir**-*vb*	weaken
8057	**faille**-*f*	break
8006	**faisan**-*m*	pheasant
8589	**falsifier**-*vb; m*	falsify; falsifier
9094	**fana**-*m/f*	addict| fanatic
9893	**fanfaron**-*m; adj*	braggart; boastful
8986	**fantaisiste**-*adj; m/f*	fanciful; joker
7946	**farcir**-*vb*	stuff
8348	**fard**-*m*	make-up
9502	**farfelu**-*m; adj*	wacky; crazy
9881	**faubourg**-*m*	suburb
7801	**faucheur**-*m*	mower| reaper
8179	**faussaire**-*m/f*	forger
9671	**fausser**-*vb*	distort| skew
7808	**fautif**-*adj; m*	incorrect| culprit
8569	**favoriser**-*vb*	promote| foster
9984	**favoritisme**-*m*	favoritism
7923	**féministe**-*adj; m/f*	feminist; feminist
8904	**femmelette**-*adj*	wimp| sissy
8657	**fermeté**-*f*	firmness
7597	**fertilité**-*f*	fertility
8653	**fervent**-*adj; m*	fervent; enthusiast
7769	**festivité**-*f*	festivity
9436	**fêtard**-*m*	roisterer| rounder
8553	**fétiche**-*m*	fetish
10023	**fétide**-*adj*	fetid| rank
9920	**feuillage**-*m*	foliage
8638	**fève**-*f*	bean
8887	**fiacre**-*m*	carriage
8153	**fictif**-*adj*	fictional
7839	**fidèlement**-*adv*	faithfully
9497	**fiel**-*m*	gall
9607	**fiévreux**-*adj*	feverish| hectic
9700	**fifre**-*m*	fife
9001	**filière**-*f*	die| sector
9003	**filleul**-*m*	godson
8720	**finaliste**-*m/f*	finalist
9646	**finlandais**-*adj*	Finnish
7576	**fiole**-*f*	flask
7920	**flamber**-*vb*	blaze| flame
9929	**flambeur**-*m*	high-roller
8973	**flamenco**-*m*	flamenco
8896	**flâner**-*vb*	stroll| loiter
7918	**flatterie**-*f*	flattery
9380	**flexible**-*adj*	flexible
9457	**flore**-*f*	flora
9038	**florin**-*m*	florin
7670	**folklore**-*m*	folklore
9536	**fonctionnel**-*adj*	functional
8818	**fondant**-*m; adj*	fondant; melting
8945	**fonderie**-*f*	foundry
7936	**fonte**-*f*	melting| font
9431	**forcené**-*m; adj*	madman| gunner; fanatical
8803	**forer**-*vb*	drill| sink
8284	**forestier**-*m*	forester
8627	**foreuse**-*f*	drill
7531	**formuler**-*vb*	formulate| express
7992	**fornication**-*f*	fornication
9434	**fortuné**-*adj*	wealthy
8488	**fossoyeur**-*m*	gravedigger
9140	**foudroyer**-*vb*	blast
8510	**fougue**-*f*	fire| spirit
8995	**fouillis**-*m*	mess
8272	**fouineur**-*m; adj*	snoop; prying
8484	**foulé**-*adj*	trodden
7546	**fourcher**-*vb*	pitchfork
8550	**fourguer**-*vb*	flog| fence
9167	**fourmilière**-*f*	anthill
7916	**fourneau**-*m*	furnace
9961	**fourni**-*adj*	provided
9097	**fourreau**-*m*	sheath
7928	**fracasser**-*vb*	smash
9525	**fragilité**-*f*	fragility
8082	**framboise**-*f*	raspberry
9299	**frange**-*f*	fringe
8684	**frappeur**-*m*	striker
8969	**fraternel**-*adj*	fraternal
8751	**fraude**-*f*	fraud

8670	**fredonner**-*vb*	hum
9379	**freinage**-*m*	braking
9155	**frêle**-*adj*	frail
9819	**frémir**-*vb*	tremble| shudder
9196	**frénésie**-*f*	frenzy
9716	**frénétique**-*adj*	frantic
8739	**fresque**-*f*	fresco
8330	**fret**-*m*	freight| freight charges
9259	**friction**-*f*	friction
9149	**frigidaire**-*m*	fridge
8313	**frigide**-*adj*	frigid
9809	**fringant**-*adj*	frisky
8682	**frisé**-*adj*	curly
9071	**friser**-*vb*	curl
9079	**frissonner**-*vb*	shiver| tremble
7641	**frivole**-*adj*	frivolous
8429	**froidement**-*adv*	coldly
8886	**froideur**-*f*	coldness| ice
7574	**froisser**-*vb*	offend| crease
8548	**frontal**-*adj*	frontal
9627	**frusques**-fpl	thread
8069	**furet**-*m*	ferret
8126	**furtif**-*adj*	furtive| slinking
9527	**fuselage**-*m*	fuselage
9184	**fusilier**-*m*	rifleman
8089	**fusionner**-*vb*	merge
9668	**futuriste**-*adj; m/f*	futuristic; futurist

G

8290	**gâble**-*m*	gable| spring
7937	**gaga**-*adj*	gaga
8883	**gaiement**-*adv*	gladly
8280	**gaine**-*f*	sheath
8426	**galanterie**-*f*	gallantry
7840	**galère**-*f*	galley
8374	**galeux**-*adj*	mangy
9743	**galipette**-*f*	somersault
9738	**galon**-*m*	braid| stripe
8667	**galoper**-*vb*	gallop
8036	**gamelle**-*f*	lunch box
7971	**gangrène**-*f*	gangrene
9726	**garagiste**-*m/f*	mechanic
9763	**gargouiller**-*vb*	gurgle
7725	**garnement**-*m*	rascal
8814	**garniture**-*f*	topping| filling
7592	**garrot**-*m*	tourniquet
8302	**gaver**-*vb*	stuff
7991	**gazer**-*vb*	zap| gas
7729	**geindre**-*vb*	whine| moan
9886	**gémissant**-*adj*	moaning| groaning
9002	**gencive**-*f*	gum
7536	**gendarmerie**-*f*	police
9156	**généalogique**-*adj*	genealogical
8337	**généreusement**-*adv*	generously
7700	**genèse**-*f*	genesis
9933	**génisse**-*f*	young cow
9133	**génital**-*adj*	genital
7583	**geôlier**-*m*	jailer
9290	**géologue**-*m/f*	geologist
8014	**géomètre**-*m/f*	land surveyor
9768	**gérant**-*m; adj*	manager; managing
8785	**gibet**-*m*	gallows
8535	**gicler**-*vb*	spurt| spew
9630	**gifle**-*f*	slap| cuff
8516	**gigoter**-*vb*	wriggle
8793	**gigot**-*m*	leg
9193	**gisement**-*m*	deposit
7682	**gîte**-*m*	home| shelter
8829	**glas**-*m*	knell
8253	**glauque**-*adj*	glaucous
9680	**glissade**-*f*	slip| slide
9268	**globalement**-*adv*	overall
8018	**globule**-*m*	globule
8884	**glouton**-*adj; m*	gluttonous; glutton
9665	**glucose**-*m*	glucose
8628	**gnome**-*m*	gnome
9794	**godemiché**-*m*	dildo
9405	**golfeur**-*m*	golfer
9852	**gond**-*m*	hinge
9548	**gondoler**-*vb*	warp
8416	**gonflable**-*adj*	inflatable
8387	**gosier**-*m*	throat| gullet
7912	**gospel**-*m*	gospel
7657	**gothique**-*adj; m*	Gothic; Gothic
8877	**goupille**-*f*	pin
8872	**gourdin**-*m*	club| mace
9406	**gourmet**-*m*	gourmet
8544	**gouvernemental**-*adj*	governmental
9555	**gracieusement**-*adv*	graciously| free of charge

8637	**graisser**-*vb*	grease
8278	**gratifier**-*vb*	gratify
8783	**gravier**-*m*	gravel
8011	**gravir**-*vb*	climb| ascend
9244	**gravitation**-*f*	gravitation
9498	**gravure**-*f*	engraving| print
8559	**gredin**-*m*	rascal
8285	**greffier**-*m*	clerk| registrar
7637	**grève**-*f*	strike
9360	**gréviste**-*m/f; adj*	striker; striking
9751	**gribouillis**-*m*	scrawl
9313	**grief**-*m*	grievance
7762	**grièvement**-*adv*	severely
9783	**grillon**-*m*	cricket
9059	**gril**-*m*	grill
8804	**grincement**-*m*	grinding| squeak
8672	**grincer**-*vb*	squeak| grind
9450	**gringalet**-*m*	weakling
7537	**grognon**-*adj; m*	grumpy; grumbler
8214	**groom**-*m*	bellhop| page
8584	**grosseur**-*f*	size| thickness
8172	**grossièreté**-*f*	rudeness
8378	**gué**-*m*	ford
9216	**guépard**-*m*	cheetah
7622	**guérillero**-*m*	guerrilla
9859	**guetteur**-*m*	watchman| look-out
8335	**gueux**-*m*	beggar
8549	**guigne**-*f*	hoodoo| bad luck
7983	**guilde**-*f*	guild
7844	**guirlande**-*f*	garland| string
8478	**gynécologue**-*m/f*	gynecologist

H

9969	**habilement**-*adv*	skilfully| cleverly
8140	**habiliter**-*vb*	empower| enable
9226	**habitation**-*f*	home| habitation
7760	**habitat**-*m*	habitat
8112	**hache**-*f*	ax
8495	**hachis**-*m*	hash
9372	**hachoir**-*m*	chopper
8252	**haineux**-*adj*	hateful
9073	**halo**-*m*	halo
9500	**haltère**-*m*	dumbbell
7785	**hamac**-*m*	hammock
9217	**hameau**-*m*	hamlet
7763	**hardi**-*adj*	bold| daring
9714	**harmonieux**-*adj*	harmonious
9285	**harpie**-*f; adj*	harpy; harpy
8691	**harpon**-*m*	harpoon
8564	**hâter**-*vb*	hasten| accelerate
8242	**hâtif**-*adj*	hasty
7664	**hebdomadaire**-*adj; m*	weekly; weekly
7954	**hémisphère**-*m*	hemisphere
8878	**hémorroïde**-*f*	hemorrhoid
9642	**hennissement**-*m*	neigh
8415	**hépatite**-*f*	hepatitis
7633	**herpès**-*m*	herpes
8196	**hibernation**-*f*	hibernation
9187	**hiéroglyphe**-*m*	hieroglyph
9600	**hindi**-*m*	Hindi
7922	**hindou**-*adj; m*	Hindu; Hindu
7723	**hippodrome**-*m*	hippodrome
7732	**hippopotame**-*m*	hippopotamus
7884	**hirondelle**-*f*	swallow
8515	**horizontal**-*adj*	horizontal
8634	**hospitalier**-*adj*	hospital
7542	**hospitaliser**-*vb*	hospitalize
9682	**huis**-*m*	door
8761	**humainement**-*adv*	humanly
7895	**humer**-*vb*	smell
9670	**hurleur**-*m*	howler| squealer
9994	**hydravion**-*m*	seaplane
9539	**hydromel**-*m*	mead
7927	**hyène**-*f*	hyena
7985	**hygiénique**-*adj*	hygienic
8531	**hymen**-*m*	hymen| marriage
9801	**hypertension**-*f*	hypertension
8593	**hypnotique**-*adj; m*	hypnotic; hypnotic
8379	**hypnotiser**-*vb*	hypnotize
9013	**hypothermie**-*f*	hypothermia
9604	**hypothétique**-*adj*	hypothetical

7627	**icône**-*f*	icon
9124	**idéalisme**-*m*	idealism
8770	**idylle**-*f*	idyll
9603	**idyllique**-*adj*	idyllic
9256	**ignare**-*m/f; adj*	ignoramus; clueless
10001	**illégalité**-*f*	illegality

9367	**illettré**-*adj*	illiterate
9806	**illicite**-*adj*	illicit
8759	**illisible**-*adj*	illegible
8418	**illogique**-*adj*	illogical
9426	**illustration**-*f*	illustration
8769	**illustrer**-*vb*	illustrate
9591	**imaginable**-*adj*	imaginable
9530	**imaginatif**-*adj*	imaginative
9864	**imbiber**-*vb*	soak
9930	**imitateur**-*m; adj*	imitator; mimic
9174	**immaculé**-*adj*	immaculate
7947	**immatriculer**-*vb*	register
8385	**immensité**-*f*	immensity
7872	**immersion**-*f*	immersion| diving
7740	**immigrer**-*vb*	immigrate
8274	**immiscer**-*vb*	interfere
8459	**immobiliser**-*vb*	immobilize
9911	**immoralité**-*f*	immorality
8333	**immuable**-*adj*	immuable
9173	**immuniser**-*vb*	immunize
9340	**immunitaire**-*adj*	immune
8410	**imparfait**-*adj; m*	imperfect; imperfect
8382	**impartial**-*adj*	impartial| unbiased
9975	**impayable**-*adj*	priceless
9033	**imperfection**-*f*	imperfection
9014	**impérialisme**-*m*	imperialism
9263	**impérialiste**-*adj; m/f*	imperialist; imperialist
8504	**impertinence**-*f*	impertinence| impudence
8283	**impétueux**-*adj*	impetuous
8016	**implanter**-*vb*	implant
8767	**impolitesse**-*f*	rudeness
8724	**importation**-*f*	import
8600	**importun**-*adj; m*	unwelcome; intruder
9409	**impossibilité**-*f*	impossibility
7532	**imposture**-*f*	imposture| fraud
9278	**imprenable**-*adj*	impregnable
9098	**impresario**-*m*	impresario
7646	**imprimeur**-*m*	printer
7832	**improvisation**-*f*	improvisation
8501	**imprudence**-*f*	imprudence| recklessness
8643	**impudence**-*f*	impudence
7684	**inapte**-*adj*	unfit
8045	**inaudible**-*adj*	inaudible
9024	**inaugurer**-*vb*	inaugurate
8083	**incarcération**-*f*	incarceration
8733	**incendiaire**-*adj; m/f*	incendiary; arsonist
7796	**inceste**-*m*	incest
9407	**incinérateur**-*m*	incinerator
9543	**incinération**-*f*	incineration
8193	**incinérer**-*vb*	incinerate
7842	**incitation**-*f*	incitement
7943	**incomber**-*vb*	behove
7628	**incomplet**-*adj*	incomplete
7968	**incompris**-*adj*	misunderstood
7566	**inconsciemment**-*adv*	unconsciously
8925	**inconscience**-*f*	unconsciousness
9824	**incontestable**-*adj*	indisputable
8700	**inconvenant**-*adj*	improper
9679	**incorporer**-*vb*	mix| weave
7900	**incorrect**-*adj*	incorrect
9888	**incriminer**-*vb*	incriminate
8949	**incruster**-*vb*	inlay| insert
7568	**indécent**-*adj*	indecent| improper
8784	**indéniable**-*adj*	undeniable
8201	**indescriptible**-*adj*	indescribable
9026	**indésirable**-*adj*	undesirable
7854	**indicateur**-*m*	indicator
8325	**indignation**-*f*	indignation
8953	**indirectement**-*adv*	indirectly
8754	**indiscrétion**-*f*	indiscretion
9815	**indiscutable**-*adj*	indisputable
9734	**indisponible**-*adj*	unavailable
9733	**individualité**-*f*	individuality
8485	**individuellement**-*adv*	individually
8608	**indolore**-*adj*	painless
9834	**indubitablement**-*adv*	undoubtedly
9883	**induire**-*vb*	induce
8762	**inébranlable**-*adj*	unwavering| steadfast
9104	**inédit**-*adj*	novel
8071	**inefficace**-*adj*	ineffective| inefficient
8241	**inéluctable**-*adj*	inevitable| ineluctable
8174	**ineptie**-*f*	ineptitude
9441	**inertie**-*f*	inertia
8486	**inévitablement**-*adv*	inevitably
9850	**inexact**-*adj*	incorrect| inexact
9161	**inexcusable**-*adj*	inexcusable

8084	**inferiorité**-*f*	inferiority
9095	**infester**-*vb*	infest| be infested
8537	**inflammable**-*adj*	flammable
9659	**inflammation**-*f*	inflammation
8982	**inflexible**-*adj*	inflexible| unyielding
9022	**infortune**-*f*	misfortune
8631	**infrastructure**-*f*	infrastructure
9720	**infusion**-*f*	infusion
7930	**ingénierie**-*f*	engineering
8235	**ingéniosité**-*f*	ingenuity
8463	**ingratitude**-*f*	ingratitude
9755	**inhibition**-*f*	inhibition
7776	**injure**-*f*	insult| affront
7811	**injustement**-*adv*	unfairly
8801	**inné**-*adj*	innate| inborn
8332	**innocenter**-*vb*	clear| find not guilty
9649	**inopportun**-*adj*	inappropriate
8439	**inquiétant**-*adj*	worrying; bothering
9354	**inquisiteur**-*m; adj*	inquisitor; inquisitive
7603	**inquisition**-*f*	inquisition
7588	**insaisissable**-*adj*	elusive
7881	**insatiable**-*adj*	insatiable
9250	**insecticide**-*m; adj*	insecticide; insecticidal
8310	**insécurité**-*f*	insecurity
7778	**insérer**-*vb*	insert| slot
8100	**insinuation**-*f*	insinuation
9550	**insipide**-*adj*	tasteless
8345	**insistance**-*f*	insistence
9854	**insomniaque**-*m/f*	insomniac
9446	**insouciance**-*f*	recklessness
8752	**inspirant**-*adj*	inspiring
8359	**instabilité**-*f*	instability
7829	**instantané**-*adj; m*	instant; snapshot
9487	**instaurer**-*vb*	establish| instigate
9265	**instinctivement**-*adv*	instinctively
7714	**insubordination**-*f*	insubordination
10020	**insuffisance**-*f*	insufficiency
9464	**intégral**-*adj*	integral
9976	**intégralité**-*f*	entirety
7554	**intégration**-*f*	integration
9492	**intendance**-*f*	stewardship
9851	**intentionnel**-*adj*	intentional
7584	**intentionnellement**-*adv*	intentionally
9540	**interaction**-*f*	interaction
7876	**interface**-*f*	interface
7614	**interférer**-*vb*	interfere
9872	**intergalactique**-*adj*	intergalactic
9324	**intérieurement**-*adv*	internally
7629	**intérim**-*adj*	interim
7675	**intérimaire**-*adj; m/f*	interim; deputy
8841	**interlocuteur**-*m*	interlocutor
8687	**internement**-*m*	detention
8471	**interphone**-*m*	intercom
8820	**interposer**-*vb*	interpose
8867	**interstellaire**-*adj*	interstellar
9508	**interurbain**-*adj*	interurban
8262	**intimidation**-*f*	intimidation
8900	**intolérance**-*f*	intolerance
7704	**intoxication**-*f*	poisoning| addiction
8727	**intraveineux**-*adj*	intravenous
8813	**intrigant**-*adj; m*	intriguing; intriguer
9906	**invaincu**-*adj*	unbeaten
9484	**invétérer**-*vb*	ingrain
8710	**invisibilité**-*f*	invisibility
7652	**invraisemblable**-*adj*	unlikely| incredible
9811	**invulnérable**-*adj*	invulnerable
8062	**iode**-*m*	iodine
7758	**irakien**-*adj*	Iraqi
9669	**iranien**-*adj; m*	Iranian; Iranian
8087	**irrationnel**-*adj; m*	irrational; irrational
8119	**irréfutable**-*adj*	irrefutable
8406	**irréparable**-*adj*	irreparable
8715	**irrespectueux**-*adj*	disrespectful
8173	**irréversible**-*adj*	irreversible
8974	**irrigation**-*f*	irrigation
7501	**irriter**-*vb*	irritate
7874	**islamique**-*adj*	Islamic
9382	**isolé**-*adj; m*	isolated| insulated; isolated person
9863	**itinérant**-*adj; m*	itinerant; itinerant

J

8383	**jacasser**-*vb*	chatter| jabber
7548	**jaillir**-*vb*	flow
9069	**jante**-*f*	rim
8152	**jaquette**-*f*	jacket
8675	**jarre**-*f*	jar
9923	**jarretelle**-*f*	garter
8425	**jauger**-*vb*	gauge
8117	**java**-*f*	rave

9523	**jérémiade**-*f*	complaint
9127	**jésuite**-*m; adj*	Jesuit; Jesuit
8722	**jeunot**-*m*	youngster
8146	**jonction**-*f*	junction
8434	**jongler**-*vb*	juggle
7712	**joug**-*m*	yoke
8464	**jouissance**-*f*	enjoyment
9744	**joute**-*f*	joust
7721	**joyeusement**-*adv*	merrily
9417	**judaïsme**-*m*	Judaism
7973	**jugeote**-*f*	savvy| gumption
9722	**jugulaire**-*adj; f*	jugular; chinstrap
9166	**jurisprudence**-*f*	jurisprudence
9725	**juron**-*m*	oath| profanity
9040	**justification**-*f*	justification
7771	**juvénile**-*adj*	juvenile

K

8932	**kaki**-*adj; m*	khaki; khaki
9865	**kayak**-*m*	kayak
8630	**kebab**-*m*	kebab
9828	**képi**-*m*	cap
7786	**klaxonner**-*vb*	honk| sound
8357	**kleenex**-*m*	tissue

8446	**labourer**-*vb*	plow| till
9327	**labrador**-*m*	Labrador dog
7695	**lacer**-*vb*	lace
9611	**lacune**-*f*	gap
9300	**laïus**-*m*	speech| spiel
8273	**lamentation**-*f*	lamentation
8889	**lamenter**-*vb*	lament
8693	**lampadaire**-*m*	floor lamp
7515	**lande**-*f*	moor
9461	**langer**-*vb*	swaddle
7847	**languir**-*vb*	languish
8338	**laquais**-*m; adj*	lackey; menial
9177	**laquer**-*vb*	lacquer
7683	**lasso**-*m*	lasso| noose
9157	**latéral**-*adj*	lateral
8413	**latex**-*m*	latex
9016	**latte**-*f*	lath| latte
9818	**laudanum**-*m*	laudanum
8850	**lauréat**-*adj; m*	laureate; laureate
8377	**laurier**-*m*	laurel
8817	**lavement**-*m*	enema| washing
7926	**lavette**-*f; adj*	mop; wet
8109	**légèreté**-*f*	lightness
7764	**législation**-*f*	legislation
8605	**lèpre**-*f*	leprosy
7511	**lésion**-*f*	lesion
9228	**lest**-*m*	ballast
8384	**leurre**-*m*	lure
9554	**liane**-*f*	liana
9870	**libanais**-*adj; mpl*	Lebanese
9884	**libéré**-*adj*	released
7595	**libido**-*f*	libido
9765	**liège**-*m*	cork
7656	**limier**-*m*	bloodhound
8225	**linceul**-*m*	shroud| grave clothes
9601	**linguistique**-*adj; f*	linguistic; linguistics
9972	**linotte**-*f*	linnet
8962	**lionne**-*f*	lioness
8756	**liquidation**-*f*	liquidation
8740	**litière**-*f*	litter
9837	**litige**-*m*	litigation
8619	**lobby**-*m*	lobby
9335	**lobotomie**-*f*	lobotomy
7945	**loch**-*m*	loch
7805	**logeur**-*m*	landlord
7766	**logiquement**-*adv*	logically
8623	**logistique**-*f; adj*	logistics; logistical
8960	**longer**-*vb*	follow
9459	**longévité**-*f*	longevity
8641	**longitude**-*f*	longitude
9947	**lotissement**-*m*	allotment| project
9505	**louable**-*adj*	commendable| rentable
9494	**lourdaud**-*adj; m*	clumsy| heavy; oaf
8954	**loyalement**-*adv*	loyally
8380	**lubie**-*f*	whim| freak
8826	**lubrique**-*adj*	lewd| lustful
8281	**lucidité**-*f*	lucidity
9125	**luciole**-*f*	firefly
7707	**lucratif**-*adj*	lucrative
8572	**luge**-*f*	sled
7556	**lunatique**-*adj*	lunatic
8090	**lupus**-*m*	lupus
7650	**lux**-*m*	lux

7867	**lyncher**-*vb*	lynch
9606	**lyrique**-*adj; f*	lyrical; lyric

M

8713	**maboul**-*adj*	crazy| nuts
7803	**macaroni**-*m*	macaroni
9948	**magma**-*m*	magma
9515	**magnanime**-*adj*	magnanimous
7529	**magnat**-*m*	magnate
9469	**magnésium**-*m*	magnesium
8737	**magnétisme**-*m*	magnetism
8913	**magouiller**-*vb*	fiddle
8130	**majestueux**-*adj*	majestic| stately
8506	**majuscule**-*adj; f*	capital; capital
8931	**malabar**-*m*	bruiser
9171	**maladresse**-*f*	clumsiness
7678	**malchanceux**-*adj*	unlucky| unfortunate
9862	**maléfice**-*m*	devilry
8809	**malfaiteur**-*m*	malefactor| wrongdoer
9398	**malhonnêteté**-*f*	dishonesty
8640	**malice**-*f*	malice| mischief
9482	**malmener**-*vb*	bully| manhandle
9800	**malnutrition**-*f*	malnutrition
9118	**malter**-*vb*	malt
7911	**malt**-*m*	malt
9675	**malveillance**-*f*	malice| malignancy
7958	**mamelon**-*m*	nipple| hill
9063	**management**-*m*	management
8125	**mandarin**-*m*	Mandarin
8482	**mangue**-*f*	mango
8971	**manille**-*m*	shackle
9388	**manipulateur**-*m*	manipulator
8462	**manivelle**-*f*	crank
8133	**manquant**-*adj*	missing
9275	**mante**-*f*	mantis
9493	**marchandage**-*m*	bargaining
9301	**marginal**-*adj; m*	marginal; dropout
9728	**marmelade**-*f*	marmelade
9694	**marmonner**-*vb*	mumble
8802	**marquant**-*adj*	outstanding| remarkable
7994	**marqueur**-*m*	marker| scorer
9400	**marteau-piqueur**-*m*	jackhammer
9730	**marxiste**-*m/f*	Marxist
8370	**mascara**-*m*	mascara
9432	**massue**-*f*	mace
8604	**matador**-*m*	matador
9247	**mathématicien**-*m*	mathematician
7613	**math**-*m*	math
8000	**matou**-*m*	tomcat
8489	**maure**-*adj*	Moorish
8166	**mausolée**-*m*	mausoleum
8650	**maussade**-*adj*	sulky| surly
7686	**maxime**-*f*	maxim
8902	**mécène**-*m*	sponsor
9276	**mécontentement**-*m*	discontent
9980	**médiateur**-*m*	mediator
9645	**médiéval**-*adj*	medieval
8157	**médiocrité**-*f*	mediocrity
8245	**méduser**-*vb*	daze| paralyze
9132	**mégatonne**-*f*	megaton
7782	**mégère**-*f*	shrew| vixen
8588	**mégot**-*m*	butt| cigarette end
8110	**mélasse**-*f*	treacle| molasses
9903	**mélodramatique**-*adj*	melodramatic
8097	**mélodrame**-*m*	melodrama
8139	**mémorial**-*m*	memorial
9357	**menaçant**-*adj*	threatening| menacing
8940	**ménagerie**-*f*	menagerie
8363	**ménopause**-*f*	menopause
9203	**mensuel**-*adj*	monthly
9830	**menuiserie**-*f*	carpentry
8154	**menuisier**-*m*	carpenter
8304	**méprise**-*f*	mistake| misunderstanding
9160	**mésaventure**-*f*	misadventure
7853	**messagerie**-*f*	messaging| courier service
8187	**métabolisme**-*m*	metabolism
7625	**métamorphoser**-*vb*	metamorphose
8906	**métaphysique**-*adj; f*	metaphysical; metaphysics
8527	**méthane**-*m*	methane
8307	**méticuleux**-*adj*	meticulous| painstaking
8277	**métropole**-*f*	metropolis
7591	**mets**-*m*	dish
8668	**meubler**-*vb*	furnish
7831	**miaou**-*m*	meow
9057	**microfilm**-*m*	microfilm
8312	**microphone**-*m*	microphone
9873	**migration**-*f*	migration

7631	**militant**-*m*	activist
8907	**militer**-*vb*	militate
9547	**millet**-*m*	millet
9000	**milligramme**-*m*	milligram
8058	**mimer**-*vb*	mimic| gesture
8414	**minibus**-*m*	minibus
8635	**minimiser**-*vb*	minimize| play down
8339	**minuteur**-*m*	timer
9384	**minutieusement**-*adv*	thoroughly
8997	**minutieux**-*adj*	thorough
8101	**miraculeusement**-*adv*	miraculously
7578	**mite**-*f*	moth
9159	**mitrailler**-*vb*	volley
7852	**mixte**-*adj*	mixed
9421	**mixture**-*f*	mixture
9031	**mobilisation**-*f*	mobilization
8331	**mobiliser**-*vb*	mobilize| enlist
9594	**mobylette**-*f*	moped
9570	**mocassin**-*m*	moccasin
8656	**modeler**-*vb*	shape| model
9242	**modération**-*f*	moderation
9267	**moelleux**-*adj; m*	soft; mellowness
8143	**moisissure**-*f*	mold| mouldiness
8184	**moite**-*adj*	moist
9106	**monarque**-*m*	monarch
9312	**mondialement**-*adv*	worldwide
9138	**Mongolie**-*f*	Mongolia
7626	**monologue**-*m*	monologue
9198	**mono**-*-pfx*	mono-
9371	**monotonie**-*f*	monotony
8322	**montant**-*m*	amount| post
9927	**monticule**-*m*	mound
9885	**moquerie**-*f*	mockery
8972	**moqueur**-*m; adj*	mocker; derisive
8480	**mormon**-*adj; m*	Mormon; Mormon
8070	**morose**-*adj*	morose
9918	**mors**-*m*	bit
7965	**mortellement**-*adv*	fatally| mortally
7838	**mortuaire**-*adj*	mortuary
8985	**motte**-*f*	sod| clump
9489	**moucheron**-*m*	gnat
8165	**moue**-*f*	pout
9451	**mousquet**-*m*	musket
8891	**mousser**-*vb*	foam| froth
9435	**mousseux**-*adj*	sparkling| foamy
8093	**mousson**-*m*	monsoon
9514	**moustachu**-*adj*	moustached
7611	**mufle**-*m; adj*	oaf; caddish
9736	**multinational**-*adj*	multinational
9879	**multiplication**-*f*	multiplication
9805	**munir**-*vb*	provide| fit
7573	**mûrir**-*vb*	mature| ripen
7892	**murmurer**-*vb*	murmur
7659	**museau**-*m*	muzzle
8149	**mutilation**-*f*	mutilation
9147	**mutiler**-*vb*	mutilate| maim
7780	**myope**-*adj; m/f*	short-sighted; myope
7521	**mystérieusement**-*adv*	darkly
8037	**mythique**-*adj*	mythical

N

8328	**nageoire**-*f*	fin
9126	**naissant**-*adj*	nascent
8921	**naïveté**-*f*	naivete
7794	**napalm**-*m*	napalm
8091	**narcissique**-*adj*	narcissistic
9473	**narcissisme**-*m*	narcissism
7694	**narcotique**-*adj; m*	narcotic; narcotic
8340	**narration**-*f*	narration
9342	**nationalisme**-*m*	nationalism
9055	**nationaliste**-*adj; m/f*	nationalist; nationalist
8221	**natte**-*f*	mat| braid
8437	**nautique**-*adj*	nautical
9995	**navrant**-*adj*	heartbreaking
7586	**nébuleux**-*adj*	nebulous
9968	**nécessiteux**-*adj; m/f*	needy; needy person
9941	**nécrologie**-*f*	obituary
8188	**néfaste**-*adj*	harmful
9939	**négation**-*f*	negation
8952	**négligeable**-*adj*	negligible
8352	**négociable**-*adj*	negotiable
8863	**négociant**-*m*	merchant
7516	**négociateur**-*m*	negotiator
8078	**négresse**-*f*	nigger
7765	**neiger**-*vb*	snow
9105	**néon**-*m*	neon
8207	**nervosité**-*f*	nervousness
9612	**nette**-*adj*	clear| frank

8407	**nettoyeur**-*m; adj*	cleaner; cleaning
8882	**neurologue**-*m/f*	neurologist
9131	**neutron**-*m*	neutron
8994	**névrosé**-*adj*	neurotic
8473	**névrose**-*f*	neurosis
8412	**niaiserie**-*m*	silliness
7883	**niais**-*m; adj*	simpleton; simple
9218	**nitrater**-*vb*	nitrate
9395	**nitroglycérine**-*f*	nitroglycerine
8405	**nomade**-*adj; m/f*	nomadic; nomad
8520	**nordiste**-*adj*	northern
8831	**normalité**-*f*	normality
8025	**normand**-*adj*	Norman
9676	**notable**-*adj; m*	notable| worthy; worthy
9393	**notice**-*f*	notice
8894	**notoriété**-*f*	notoriety
9562	**nouba**-*f*	party
8534	**nouer**-*vb*	establish
8019	**nuageux**-*adj*	cloudy| misty
7889	**nuance**-*f*	shade| nuance
8458	**nuancer**-*vb*	nuance
8965	**nuisible**-*adj*	harmful| injurious
9509	**nullité**-*f*	nullity| nonentity
9971	**nymphe**-*f*	nymph

O

9613	**objectivité**-*f*	objectivity
9956	**obligatoirement**-*adv*	inevitably
8217	**obligeance**-*f*	helpfulness
9551	**obliquer**-*vb*	skew
9951	**oblong**-*adj*	oblong
8679	**obscénité**-*f*	obscenity
8926	**obsessionnel**-*adj*	obsessive
8368	**obsolète**-*adj*	obsolete
8810	**obstination**-*f*	obstinacy
9662	**obtempérer**-*vb*	obey
10006	**obtus**-*adj*	obtuse| thick
8317	**occulte**-*adj*	occult
9940	**œillet**-*m*	eyelet
9791	**ombilical**-*adj*	umbilical
7711	**oméga**-*m*	omega
9521	**opossum**-*m*	opossum
9101	**opportuniste**-*adj; m/f*	opportunistic; opportunist
7868	**opposant**-*adj; m*	opponent; oppositionist
9641	**oppresseur**-*m*	oppressor
8210	**opprimer**-*vb*	oppress| grind
9075	**opter**-*vb*	opt
8730	**opus**-*m*	opus
9266	**orbe**-*m*	orb
8251	**orbite**-*f*	orbit
9481	**orchestre**-*m*	orchestra
8079	**orienter**-*vb*	guide| orient
9423	**orifice**-*m*	orifice
7896	**originalité**-*f*	originality
7903	**originel**-*adj*	original
7996	**orque**-*m/f*	orc| orca
9713	**ortie**-*f*	nettle
7908	**osseux**-*adj*	bony| angular
9338	**oubliette**-*f*	oubliette
8258	**ouvrage**-*m*	handiwork
8265	**ovale**-*adj; m*	oval; oval
8494	**ovation**-*f*	ovation
9316	**oxyde**-*m*	oxide

P

8123	**pacifiste**-*m/f*	pacifist
7669	**pagaie**-*f*	paddle
9812	**paillasse**-*f*	pallet
7606	**paillasson**-*m*	mat
8981	**paître**-*vb*	graze| feed
8517	**pale**-*f*	blade
9640	**palette**-*f*	palette| paddle
9041	**palissade**-*f*	palisade
9935	**palmarès**-*m*	prize list
9233	**palourde**-*f*	clam
9533	**palper**-*vb*	feel
9480	**palpitation**-*f*	palpitation| flutter
7525	**pamplemousse**-*m*	grapefruit
9012	**pancréas**-*m*	pancreas
9705	**panne**-*f*	breakdown
8890	**panoplie**-*f*	range| toolbox
8567	**panorama**-*m*	panorama| overview
7921	**panoramique**-*adj*	panoramic
9629	**panser**-*vb*	dress
9531	**panthéon**-*m*	pantheon
8581	**paon**-*m*	peacock
9135	**papal**-*adj*	papal

7984	**paperasserie**-*f*	red tape
8996	**paprika**-*m*	paprika
8611	**parabole**-*f*	parable
8256	**parachutiste**-*m/f*	parachutist
8663	**parader**-*vb*	show
9369	**paradisiaque**-*adj*	heavenly
8999	**paranormal**-*adj*	paranormal
9027	**paravent**-*m*	screen
7888	**pardessus**-*m*	overcoat
8540	**parfumer**-*vb*	perfume| flavor
9036	**parieur**-*m*	gambler
8020	**parisien**-*adj*	Parisian
9402	**parlementaire**-*adj; m/f*	parliamentary; parliamentarian
8028	**parloir**-*m*	parlor
8013	**parodie**-*f*	parody| skit
8427	**paroissien**-*m*	parishioner
7806	**partiellement**-*adv*	partially
9351	**passade**-*adj*	fancy
8615	**passionnel**-*adj*	passionate
8127	**passoire**-*f*	strainer
9178	**pastille**-*f*	pellet| chip
7894	**pat**-*adj; m*	stalemate; stalemate
10024	**pater**-*m*	pater
7508	**paternité**-*f*	paternity
8197	**pathologie**-*f*	pathology
9373	**pathologique**-*adj*	pathological
7567	**patio**-*m*	patio
7517	**pâturer**-*vb*	graze
7619	**paumé**-*adj*	lost| godforsaken
7773	**pavé**-*adj; m*	paved; pavement
9471	**pectoral**-*adj; m*	pectoral; pectoral
9660	**pédagogique**-*adj*	educational| pedagogical
8570	**pédiatre**-*m/f*	pediatrician
9474	**pédiatrie**-*f*	pediatrics
9291	**pedigree**-*adj; m*	pedigree; pedigree
9224	**pelage**-*m*	coat| fur
8360	**peler**-*vb*	peel| rind
9954	**pélican**-*m*	pelican
8334	**pénalité**-*f*	penalty
8456	**pendule**-*f*	pendulum
7610	**pénitentiaire**-*adj*	penitentiary
8788	**pénombre**-*f*	penumbra
9050	**penseur**-*m*	thinker
8059	**pensionnaire**-*m/f*	boarder| pensionary
9368	**pépée**-*f*	chick| babe
8729	**pépite**-*f*	nugget
8881	**perçant**-*adj*	piercing| shrill
9839	**percepteur**-*m; adj*	collector; percipient
8311	**perceur**-*m*	piercer
9212	**percussion**-*f*	percussion
9074	**perdition**-*f*	perdition
8918	**perdrix**-*f*	partridge
9315	**perfectionner**-*vb*	improve
9757	**perfidie**-*f*	perfidy
9970	**perforer**-*vb*	perforate
7635	**perfusion**-*f*	drip
9973	**périmer**-*vb*	expire
8647	**périphérie**-*f*	periphery
9890	**perpétrer**-*vb*	perpetrate
7982	**perpétuel**-*adj*	perpetual
8505	**perpétuer**-*vb*	perpetuate
9847	**persan**-*adj; m*	Persian; Persian
9356	**persécuter**-*vb*	persecute
7800	**persécution**-*f*	persecution
8987	**persévérer**-*vb*	persevere
9403	**persil**-*m*	parsley
8879	**perspicacité**-*f*	insight
8326	**persuasif**-*adj*	persuasive
8560	**perturbation**-*f*	disturbance
7781	**perversion**-*f*	perversion
9936	**perversité**-*f*	perversity
7749	**pesanteur**-*f*	gravity
9878	**pesticide**-*m; adj*	pesticide; pesticidal
9123	**pétrifier**-*vb*	petrify| stone
7734	**pétrolier**-*m*	tanker| oilman
9706	**pétunia**-*m*	petunia
7963	**peupler**-*vb*	populate
8156	**phénoménal**-*adj*	phenomenal
8032	**philosophique**-*adj*	philosophical
8943	**phonographe**-*m*	phonograph
7751	**phosphore**-*m*	phosphorus
8680	**photocopie**-*f*	photocopy
9062	**photocopier**-*vb*	photocopy
9499	**photogénique**-*adj*	photogenic
9100	**photographique**-*adj*	photographic
9966	**physiologique**-*adj*	physiological
8757	**piazza**-*f*	piazza
9688	**pichet**-*m*	pitcher
9486	**pickpocket**-*m/f*	pickpocket
8400	**piédestal**-*m*	pedestal
9396	**piéton**-*m; adj*	pedestrian; pedestrian

9727	**pieuter**-*vb*	sleep
7544	**pignon**-*m*	pinion| gear
7981	**pillard**-*m; adj*	plunderer; predatory
9330	**pilleur**-*m; adj*	looter; deceitful
7634	**pipeline**-*m*	pipeline
7934	**piraterie**-*f*	piracy
10003	**pirouetter**-*vb*	pirouette
8614	**pistache**-*f*	pistachio
8343	**piteux**-*adj*	sorry
8892	**pitre**-*m*	clown
9114	**pivert**-*m*	woodpecker
9306	**pivot**-*m; adj*	pivot; pivotal
8660	**plaidoirie**-*f*	pleading
9200	**plaignant**-*m*	plaintiff
9681	**plaisantin**-*m; adj*	joker; bantering
8361	**plancton**-*m*	plankton
9319	**planification**-*f*	planning
9634	**plant**-*m*	plant| seedling
9580	**plastic**-*m*	plastic explosive
8315	**platiner**-*vb*	platinize
9282	**platonique**-*adj*	platonic
9963	**plénitude**-*f*	fullness
8576	**pleurnichard**-*m; adj*	crybaby; whingeing
9749	**plomber**-*vb*	seal
8598	**plouf**-*m*	plonk| splash
9896	**plumard**-*m*	sack
8873	**pluriel**-*adj; m*	plural; plural
8834	**pluvieux**-*adj*	rainy| wet
7986	**podium**-*m*	podium
9631	**pointilleux**-*adj*	punctilious
9691	**poireau**-*m*	leek
9326	**poirier**-*m*	pear tree| handstand
8086	**poivron**-*m*	pepper
9413	**polio**-*f*	polio
7636	**pollen**-*m*	pollen
8689	**polluer**-*vb*	pollute| taint
8470	**poltron**-*m; adj*	coward; cowardly
9746	**pommette**-*f*	cheekbone
9287	**pommier**-*m*	apple
9823	**pompette**-*adj*	tipsy
8076	**pompeux**-*adj*	pompous
8077	**pompon**-*m*	tassel| cake
9860	**poncho**-*m*	poncho
7638	**ponctuel**-*adj*	punctual
7660	**ponte**-*f*	spawn
8023	**populace**-*f*	populace| mob
9086	**pore**-*f*	pore
9207	**pornographique**-*adj*	pornographic
8144	**posé**-*adj*	laid
9044	**poseur**-*m; adj*	poseur; phony
9280	**positivement**-*adv*	positively
8658	**postérieur**-*adj; m*	posterior; posterior
7543	**postérité**-*f*	posterity
9802	**posthume**-*adj*	posthumous
8794	**postuler**-*vb*	apply| postulate
8243	**potassium**-*m*	potassium
8885	**poterie**-*f*	pottery
9779	**potiron**-*m*	pumpkin
9891	**poudrier**-*m*	powder compact
10015	**poulpe**-*m*	octopus
7623	**pourchasser**-*vb*	chase
7869	**poussiéreux**-*adj*	dusty
8840	**pragmatique**-*adj*	pragmatic
9137	**précaire**-*adj*	precarious
7802	**précepteur**-*m*	tutor
7645	**prêche**-*m*	preaching
8594	**précipice**-*m*	drop
8185	**précipitamment**-*adv*	hastily| precipitately
9361	**précipité**-*adj*	rushed
9937	**préconiser**-*vb*	advocate
7717	**prédicateur**-*m*	preacher
8067	**préhistorique**-*adj*	prehistoric
7813	**prélèvement**-*m; adj*	sample; compensatory
9066	**prélude**-*m*	prelude
8366	**prématurément**-*adv*	prematurely
9309	**prémonition**-*f*	premonition
7665	**préoccupation**-*f*	concern| preoccupation
8498	**préoccupé**-*adj*	concerned
8574	**presbytère**-*m*	presbytery| rectory
8192	**préservation**-*f*	preservation
7907	**présomptueux**-*adj*	presumptuous
7585	**préventif**-*adj*	preventive
8479	**prévention**-*f*	prevention
9345	**prieuré**-*m*	priory
8528	**primate**-*m*	primate
9443	**privation**-*f*	deprivation
7662	**privilégier**-*vb*	privilege
8795	**problématique**-*adj*	problematic
8532	**processeur**-*m*	processor
8228	**prochainement**-*adv*	shortly
9018	**proclamation**-*f*	proclamation

9253	**procréer**-*vb*	procreate
7736	**profane**-*adj; m/f*	profane; layman
9678	**profaner**-*vb*	defile
8353	**professionnalisme**-*m*	professionalism
8005	**professionnellement**-*adv*	professionally
9719	**profiteur**-*m*	profiteer
9559	**progressif**-*adj*	progressive
9296	**progressiste**-*adj; m/f*	progressive; progressive
8933	**projectile**-*m*	projectile
9952	**prolétaire**-*m/f; adj*	proletarian; prolete
9146	**prologue**-*m*	prologue
10025	**prolongation**-*f*	extension| prolongation
9355	**prolongé**-*adj*	extended
9855	**prolongement**-*m*	extension| prolongation
8648	**prompt**-*adj*	prompt
9693	**prononciation**-*f*	pronunciation
9221	**pronostic**-*m*	prognosis
9411	**propagation**-*f*	spread
7672	**protestant**-*adj; m*	Protestant; Protestant
8051	**prothèse**-*f*	prosthesis
9065	**proton**-*m*	proton
7703	**prouesse**-*f*	prowess
9255	**provincial**-*adj; m*	provincial; provincial
7977	**provisoirement**-*adv*	tentatively
9425	**provocateur**-*adj; m*	challenging; agitator
9934	**prude**-*m/f; adj*	prude; prudish
8590	**pruneau**-*m*	prune
8909	**psaume**-*m*	psalm
7748	**psychanalyse**-*f*	psychoanalysis
9792	**psychédélique**-*adj*	psychedelic
8436	**psyché**-*f*	psyche
9796	**pubien**-*adj*	pubic
9871	**pubis**-*m*	pubis
9042	**puiser**-*vb*	draw
8807	**pulsation**-*f*	pulsation
8145	**pulvériser**-*vb*	spray| pulverize
7649	**puma**-*m*	puma
9576	**pupitre**-*m*	desk
7713	**purification**-*f*	purification
9524	**pygmée**-*f; adj*	Pygmy; pygmy
8683	**pyromane**-*m/f*	pyromaniac

Q

8314	**quadrant**-*m*	quadrant
7549	**qualification**-*f*	qualification
8421	**quatuor**-*m*	quartet
8178	**questionnaire**-*m*	questionnaire
9942	**quiche**-*f*	quiche
9931	**quiétude**-*f*	quietude
7598	**quotidiennement**-*adv*	daily

R

9175	**rabattre**-*vb*	tilt| turn down
9009	**racer**-*m*	racer
8734	**rachat**-*m*	redemption| buying back
7698	**radicalement**-*adv*	radically
8236	**rafale**-*f*	gust| flurry
8830	**raffinement**-*m*	refinement| sophistication
8571	**raffinerie**-*f*	refinery
8712	**rafler**-*vb*	grab
9227	**rafraîchissement**-*m*	refreshment
8533	**rainer**-*vb*	groove
8649	**raisonnablement**-*adv*	reasonably
9614	**rajah**-*m*	rajah
8919	**rajeunir**-*vb*	rejuvenate
9389	**ralliement**-*m*	rally
9151	**ramassage**-*m*	collection| gathering
9912	**rami**-*m*	rummy
9528	**ramoneur**-*m*	chimney sweep
8991	**rance**-*adj*	rancid
9386	**rancœur**-*f*	rancor
9283	**rancunier**-*adj*	spiteful
8301	**rangé**-*adj*	tidy
8998	**rangement**-*m*	arrangement
8134	**rapace**-*adj; m*	rapacious; predator
8970	**rapatrier**-*vb*	repatriate
9252	**râper**-*vb*	grate
7756	**rapprochement**-*m*	reconciliation| link
9039	**rapt**-*m*	abduction| kidnapping
8742	**rasta**-*m*	rasta
8306	**rationnement**-*m*	rationing
8895	**ratisser**-*vb*	rake| comb

9993	**rattrapage**-*m*	picking up
7526	**ravager**-*vb*	ravage| destroy
7913	**rave**-*f*	rave
9328	**ravitailler**-*vb*	supply
8696	**raviver**-*vb*	revive| rekindle
8936	**rayonnant**-*adj*	radiant| shining
8044	**rayonnement**-*m*	influence| radiance
8424	**rayonner**-*vb*	beam| radiate
9567	**réanimer**-*vb*	resuscitate
8404	**réapparaître**-*vb*	reappear
7590	**rebondir**-*vb*	bounce| start up
8866	**rebond**-*m*	rebound
9394	**rebrousser**-*vb*	turn back
7917	**recaler**-*vb*	fail
8920	**récapituler**-*vb*	summarize| recapitulate
9535	**receleur**-*m*	fence
9685	**recel**-*f*	concealment
8989	**recensement**-*m*	census| count
9721	**réceptif**-*adj*	receptive
8354	**récession**-*f*	recession
8859	**réchaud**-*m*	stove
8247	**récidiviste**-*m/f*	recidivist
9191	**récipient**-*m*	container
7742	**reconsidérer**-*vb*	reconsider
7799	**recourir**-*vb*	resort
9331	**recouvrement**-*m*	recovery| collection
8305	**recruteur**-*m*	recruiter
8118	**recteur**-*m; adj*	rector; rectorial
9353	**rectum**-*m*	rectum
8105	**recueil**-*m*	collection
7987	**recyclage**-*m*	recycling
9008	**recycler**-*vb*	recycle
7621	**rééducation**-*f*	re-education
9712	**réélection**-*f*	re-election
9186	**réélire**-*vb*	re-elect
8507	**réfectoire**-*m*	refectory
9202	**référer**-*vb*	refer
8469	**réformer**-*vb*	reform
9272	**refoulé**-*adj*	discharged| repressed
9189	**réfuter**-*vb*	refute| disprove
9107	**régénération**-*f*	regeneration
8849	**régent**-*m*	regent
8839	**réglage**-*m*	setting
7906	**réglementaire**-*adj*	regulation
9897	**réglementation**-*f*	regulation
8244	**réglisse**-*f*	licorice
9214	**régression**-*f*	regression
8977	**regrouper**-*vb*	regroup| gather
8854	**régulateur**-*m; adj*	regulator; control
9165	**réincarner**-*vb*	reincarnate
7790	**réintégrer**-*vb*	reinstate
9748	**rejeton**-*m*	offshoot| kid
9808	**réjouissance**-*f*	rejoicing
9274	**réjouissant**-*adj*	cheerful
8261	**relatif**-*adj; m*	relative; relative
9663	**relativité**-*f*	relativity
8725	**relaxant**-*adj*	relaxing
9925	**relaxation**-*f*	relaxation
8289	**relief**-*m*	relief
9188	**reluquer**-*vb*	ogle
9624	**remake**-*m*	remake
8190	**remarquablement**-*adv*	remarkably
8869	**rembobiner**-*vb*	rewind
7680	**remise**-*f*	delivery| remission
8669	**rémission**-*f*	remission
8789	**remorquer**-*vb*	tow
9760	**remorqueur**-*m*	tug
7827	**remous**-*m*	swirl
7798	**rempart**-*m*	rampart
8316	**renégat**-*adj; m*	renegade; renegade
7761	**renier**-*vb*	deny| renounce
8503	**renom**-*m*	renown
8444	**renommer**-*vb*	rename| reappoint
7607	**renouveau**-*m*	renewal
8049	**rénovation**-*f*	renovation
8717	**rénover**-*vb*	renovate| restore
8344	**rente**-*m; f*	annuity; income
10002	**réorganiser**-*vb*	reorganize| reorder
9616	**répartir**-*vb*	allocate| divide
9610	**repassage**-*m*	ironing
7898	**repêcher**-*vb*	recover
7624	**répercussion**-*f*	repercussion
9998	**replacer**-*vb*	replace
8951	**replonger**-*vb*	relapse
9273	**réprimer**-*vb*	repress
7502	**répugnant**-*adj*	repugnant
8177	**réputé**-*adj*	renowned| reputed
8029	**requête**-*f*	request
8423	**rescapé**-*m; adj*	survivor; surviving
8545	**résidu**-*m*	residue

7555	**résistant**-*adj*	resistant
9176	**résonance**-*f*	resonance
8061	**respectueusement**-*adv*	with respect
9589	**respirateur**-*m*	respirator
7730	**resplendissant**-*adj*	resplendent
8950	**ressasser**-*vb*	turn over
8298	**ressentiment**-*m*	resentment
8957	**resservir**-*vb*	serve again
8250	**ressortir**-*vb*	stand out
9023	**restituer**-*vb*	return| restore
7956	**restreindre**-*vb*	restrict| narrow
8296	**résulter**-*vb*	result
9652	**rétention**-*f*	retention
8493	**retentir**-*vb*	sound| resound
9817	**retiré**-*adj*	withdrawn| retired
9715	**retouche**-*f*	retouch
7941	**retoucher**-*vb*	retouch| touch
8248	**retracer**-*vb*	trace| recount
8218	**rétrécir**-*vb*	shrink
9556	**rétrograder**-*vb*	demote| downgrade
8411	**rétroviseur**-*m*	mirror
9052	**rêvasser**-*vb*	daydream
9058	**révélateur**-*m; adj*	developer; revealing
7909	**revendeur**-*m*	dealer
9470	**revêtement**-*m*	coating| lining
9513	**revirement**-*m*	turn-around
8072	**révolter**-*vb*	appal| revolt
8164	**révolu**-*adj*	gone
9901	**révolutionner**-*vb*	revolutionize
8697	**rhumatisme**-*m*	rheumatism
8626	**ricain**-*adj*	Yank
9788	**ricaner**-*vb*	sneer
8596	**rigoureux**-*adj*	rigorous
9093	**risible**-*adj*	ludicrous
10017	**risotto**-*m*	risotto
9185	**rixe**-*f*	brawl
7788	**rizière**-*f*	paddy field
7835	**rocker**-*m*	rock musician
8008	**romancier**-*m*	novelist
9232	**romanesque**-*adj*	dreamy| fictional
9199	**rondelle**-*f*	washer
9577	**ronflement**-*m*	snoring| roar
8787	**rosaire**-*m*	rosary
9352	**roseau**-*m*	reed
8512	**rosier**-*m*	rosebush
9322	**rot**-*m*	burp
9666	**rotule**-*f*	patella
8034	**roumain**-*adj; m*	Romanian; Romanian
9506	**roupiller**-*vb*	saw wood
8212	**rousseur**-*f*	redness
9085	**roussir**-*vb*	scorch| brown
9364	**royalement**-*adv*	royally
9236	**royauté**-*f*	royalty
9444	**rugissement**-*m*	roaring
7855	**rumba**-*f*	rumba
9520	**rustique**-*adj*	rustic| country
8721	**rythme**-*m*	pace| rhythm

S

8916	**sabbatique**-*adj*	sabbatical
9007	**safran**-*m*	saffron
7774	**saga**-*f*	saga
9437	**saindoux**-*m*	lard
9653	**salarié**-*adj; m*	salaried; wage earner
7640	**saligaud**-*m*	bleeder| creep
9243	**salopette**-*f*	overalls
8024	**salve**-*f*	salvo| salute
9708	**sangle**-*f*	strap
8397	**sangloter**-*vb*	sob
8871	**saoudien**-*adj*	Saudi
7891	**saper**-*vb*	undermine
9709	**saphir**-*m*	sapphire
9053	**sarcophage**-*m*	sarcophagus
8056	**satanique**-*adj*	satanic| ghoulish
8782	**satisfaisant**-*adj*	satisfactory
9552	**saturer**-*vb*	saturate
9698	**satyre**-*m*	Satyr
9512	**sauce**-*f*	sauce
8066	**saucisson**-*m*	sausage
9347	**sauvagerie**-*f*	savagery
8723	**sauvegarder**-*vb*	safeguard
8639	**sauveteur**-*m*	rescuer| wrecker
7551	**savoureux**-*adj*	tasty| savory
7846	**saxo**-*m*	sax
8428	**saxophone**-*m*	saxophone
8491	**sbire**-*m*	myrmidon| henchman
8182	**scarabée**-*m*	beetle
7752	**schizophrène**-*adj*	schizophrenic
9840	**sciemment**-*adv*	knowingly
7849	**scierie**-*f*	sawmill

7826	**scier**-*vb*	saw
9546	**scintiller**-*vb*	twinkle| sparkle
9231	**sciure**-*f*	sawdust
9344	**scotcher**-*vb*	tape
8910	**scrutin**-*m*	ballot| polling
8583	**sculpter**-*vb*	sculpt| carve
8806	**séchoir**-*m*	dryer
8861	**secouriste**-*m/f*	rescuer| paramedic
9215	**sédition**-*f*	sedition| rebellion
9206	**ségrégation**-*f*	segregation
9430	**seigle**-*m*	rye
9021	**séjourner**-*vb*	stay
7630	**sélectionner**-*vb*	select
9072	**sensualité**-*f*	sensuality
7962	**sensuel**-*adj*	sensual
9787	**septique**-*adj*	septic
7644	**sérénade**-*f*	serenade
9579	**sermonner**-*vb*	lecture| sermonize
7988	**serpillière**-*f*	mop| swab
7933	**serviable**-*adj*	helpful
9359	**servitude**-*f*	servitude
8523	**sève**-*f*	sap
8124	**sexiste**-*adj*	sexist
8183	**shah**-*m*	shah
9549	**shaker**-*m*	shaker
7731	**Siam**-*m*	Siam
9575	**siéger**-*vb*	sit
9164	**significatif**-*adj*	significant
9230	**silencieusement**-*adv*	silently
7822	**sillage**-*m*	wake
8586	**silo**-*m*	silo
8975	**similitude**-*f*	similitude
8205	**simplifier**-*vb*	simplify
7759	**simulateur**-*m*	simulator
9139	**sinus**-*m*	sinus
8771	**siroter**-*vb*	sip
9412	**sismique**-*adj*	seismic
7959	**sniffer**-*vb*	sniff
9747	**snobisme**-*m*	snobbery
8786	**sobriété**-*f*	sobriety
8035	**sodium**-*m*	sodium
7513	**sodomie**-*f*	sodomy
7571	**solennel**-*adj*	solemn
8021	**solidaire**-*adj*	solidary
9558	**solidement**-*adv*	firmly
8435	**solliciter**-*vb*	solicit| ask
8646	**solstice**-*m*	solstice
8529	**somali**-*adj; m/f; mpl*	Somali; Somali
8591	**sommation**-*f*	summons
8821	**sommeiller**-*vb*	sleep| doze
7882	**sonate**-*f*	sonata
9467	**sonde**-*f*	probe
8580	**sono**-*f*	sound system
8836	**sophistiqué**-*adj*	sophisticated
8460	**souder**-*vb*	weld
7688	**soudoyer**-*vb*	bribe| tamper
9776	**soudure**-*f*	welding
9615	**souillon**-*m*	slut| slob
8815	**soupçonneux**-*adj*	suspicious
8768	**soupe**-*f*	soup
8956	**soupirant**-*m*	suitor
7755	**souplesse**-*f*	flexibility| suppleness
8903	**soustraire**-*vb*	subtract| remove
8622	**souveraineté**-*f*	sovereignty
9222	**soviet**-*m*	Soviet
9180	**soyeux**-*adj*	silky| silk
9128	**spacieux**-*adj*	spacious
9323	**sparadrap**-*m*	plaster| band-aid
8038	**spartiate**-*adj*	Spartan
8012	**spasme**-*m*	spasm
7944	**spéculation**-*f*	speculation
8781	**spéculer**-*vb*	speculate
8777	**speech**-*m*	speech
9109	**spiritisme**-*m*	spiritism
8923	**spiritualité**-*f*	spirituality
9522	**spontanéité**-*f*	spontaneity
7899	**spontanément**-*adv*	spontaneously
9336	**spoon**-*m*	spoon
9593	**spoutnik**-*m*	sputnik
9089	**sprint**-*m*	sprint
9477	**squash**-*m*	squash
7540	**stabiliser**-*vb*	stabilize
8701	**standardiste**-*m/f*	operator
9752	**statuette**-*f*	small statue
9145	**stature**-*f*	stature
7897	**sténo**-*f*	shorthand| stenographer
9303	**steppe**-*f*	steppe
9597	**stéréotype**-*m*	stereotype
9928	**sternum**-*m*	sternum
8046	**stimulation**-*f*	stimulation
8827	**stimuler**-*vb*	stimulate

7601	**stipuler**-*vb*	stipulate
9673	**stoppeur**-*m*	stopper
10019	**strangulation**-*f*	strangulation
8043	**stratagème**-*m*	stratagem| ploy
9404	**stratège**-*m*	strategist
9337	**strudel**-*m*	strudel
8151	**styliste**-*m/f*	stylist
9608	**suave**-*adj*	sweet
8636	**subsister**-*vb*	subsist| remain
9710	**substitution**-*f*	substitution
9875	**subterfuge**-*m*	subterfuge
9838	**subtilité**-*f*	subtlety
8395	**subvenir**-*vb*	support
8303	**subvention**-*f*	grant| subsidy
9169	**subversif**-*adj*	subversive
7942	**succéder**-*vb*	succeed
8220	**succulent**-*adj*	succulent
9750	**succursale**-*f*	branch
9845	**suffisance**-*f*	sufficiency
9476	**suffoquer**-*vb*	suffocate
9308	**suie**-*f*	soot
9742	**superbement**-*adv*	magnificently
9874	**supérette**-*f*	minimarket
9170	**suppliant**-*adj; m*	begging; suppliant
7563	**supportable**-*adj*	bearable| tolerable
8358	**suppression**-*f*	removal
7924	**surcharge**-*f*	overload
9953	**surcharger**-*vb*	overload| overburden
8620	**surchauffer**-*vb*	overheat
8944	**surestimer**-*vb*	overestimate
9650	**surexciter**-*vb*	overexcite
9588	**surgeler**-*vb*	quick-freeze
8652	**surhumain**-*adj*	superhuman
9707	**surmener**-*vb*	overwork
7841	**surréaliste**-*m/f*	surrealist
9771	**sursauter**-*vb*	jump up
9648	**sursaut**-*m*	start| spurt
9729	**surveillant**-*m*	supervisor
7875	**survenir**-*vb*	occur| arise
9795	**survêtement**-*m*	track suit
7557	**survoler**-*vb*	fly| fly over
8942	**susciter**-*vb*	create| arouse
7737	**suspens**-*m*	suspense
8543	**suspicion**-*f*	suspicion
8992	**suzerain**-*m*	suzerain
8367	**syllabe**-*f*	syllable
9560	**symétrie**-*f*	symmetry
9739	**sympathisant**-*m*	sympathizer
8155	**symphonique**-*adj*	symphonic
9070	**syndical**-*adj*	union| labor
9674	**syntaxe**-*f*	syntax
7503	**synthétique**-*adj; m*	synthetic; synthetic
8561	**systématique**-*adj; f*	systematic; systematics

T

9949	**tabard**-*m*	tabard
8073	**tabou**-*adj; m*	taboo; taboo
9154	**tambourin**-*m*	tambourine
7716	**tamisé**-*adj*	screened| sifted
9618	**tandem**-*m*	tandem
7950	**tangible**-*adj*	tangible
9740	**tanguer**-*vb*	pitch| sway
9644	**tantinet**-*m*	mite
7817	**tapisserie**-*f*	tapestry
9990	**tarentule**-*f*	tarantula
7745	**tartiner**-*vb*	spread
9245	**taxer**-*vb*	tax
7594	**Tchao!**-*int*	Ciao!
8860	**teigne**-*f*	ringworm
9894	**teint**-*adj; m*	dyed; color
8490	**teinturier**-*m*	dry cleaner
9807	**télégraphier**-*vb*	telegraph
8373	**télépathique**-*adj*	telepathic
7512	**téléviseur**-*m*	TV
8632	**télex**-*m*	telex
9103	**ténacité**-*f*	tenacity
9718	**tendon**-*m*	tendon
9076	**tendu**-*adj*	tense| tight
8610	**ténébreux**-*adj*	gloomy
9172	**teneur**-*f*	content
7880	**ténor**-*m*	tenor
8003	**tentacule**-*m*	tentacle
9959	**terrasser**-*vb*	crush
8955	**tétanos**-*m*	tetanus
9756	**têtard**-*m*	tadpole
8223	**textile**-*adj; m*	textile; textile
7581	**texture**-*f*	texture
9784	**thaïlandais**-*adj; mpl*	Thai
8449	**théâtral**-*adj*	theatrical
8805	**théologie**-*f*	theology

8865	**thérapeutique**-*adj; f*	therapeutic; therapeutics
8239	**thermos**-*m; adj*	thermos; thermos
9341	**thoracique**-*adj*	thoracic
7990	**thorax**-*m; f*	thorax; bust
9786	**thriller**-*m*	thriller
8607	**tibia**-*m*	tibia
8709	**tignasse**-*f*	wig
7770	**timidité**-*f*	timidity
9701	**timonier**-*m*	helmsman
9179	**tintement**-*m*	ringing
8391	**tirade**-*f*	tirade
8111	**tisonnier**-*m*	poker
9420	**tisser**-*vb*	weave
7663	**titulaire**-*m/f; adj*	holder; titular
9237	**toboggan**-*m*	slide
8238	**toge**-*f*	toga
7783	**toison**-*f*	fleece
8780	**tolérant**-*adj*	tolerant| forgiving
7821	**tombola**-*f*	raffle
8812	**tonique**-*adj; f*	tonic; tonic
9152	**tordu**-*adj; m*	twisted; crackpot
9979	**torero**-*m*	bullfighter
8612	**tortiller**-*vb*	twirl| twist round
9656	**toscan**-*adj*	Tuscan
9625	**totem**-*m*	totem
9375	**toupie**-*f*	top
8917	**tourelle**-*f*	turret
9590	**tournesol**-*m*	sunflower
9047	**tourneur**-*m*	turner
7757	**toxico**-*m/f*	junkie
9378	**toxicomane**-*m/f*	addict
8577	**toxine**-*f*	toxin
7957	**traceur**-*m*	stud| teat
9261	**traction**-*f*	traction
9876	**traditionnellement**-*adv*	traditionally
9419	**tragiquement**-*adv*	tragically
8422	**traînant**-*adj*	shuffling
8766	**traînée**-*f*	trail| drag
8002	**traîtrise**-*f*	treachery
7676	**tranquillisant**-*m; adj*	tranquilizer; tranquilizing
8455	**tranquilliser**-*vb*	calm| ease
8114	**transcription**-*f*	transcription
7720	**transfusion**-*f*	transfusion
7863	**transmetteur**-*m*	transmitter
9401	**transparence**-*f*	transparency
7533	**transpercer**-*vb*	pierce| penetrate
9702	**transpiration**-*f*	transpiration
9538	**transplantation**-*f*	transplantation
8329	**trapèze**-*m*	trapeze
9284	**trappeur**-*m*	trapper
9439	**traquenard**-*m*	trap| booby trap
7506	**traumatique**-*adj*	traumatic
8135	**traumatiser**-*vb*	traumatize
9960	**treizième**-*num*	thirteenth
9262	**trempette**-*f*	dip
9251	**tremplin**-*m*	springboard
8964	**trésorerie**-*f*	treasury
7709	**tresser**-*vb*	braid| twine
8843	**treuil**-*m*	winch| hoist
7856	**triade**-*f*	triad
9143	**tricherie**-*f*	cheating
7743	**tricoter**-*vb*	knit
9895	**tricycle**-*m*	tricycle
8136	**trimballer**-*vb*	cart around
7604	**trinité**-*f*	trinity
9596	**triton**-*m*	triton| merman
7520	**troc**-*m*	barter| bartering
8796	**trognon**-*m*	core
7535	**troisièmement**-*num*	thirdly
9962	**trombe**-*f*	whirlwind
7509	**trompeur**-*adj; m*	misleading; deceiver
7504	**trotter**-*vb*	trot
9130	**troyen**-*adj*	Trojan
9234	**tsarine**-*f*	tsarina
8750	**tuile**-*f*	tile
9392	**tumulte**-*m*	tumult
7565	**tunique**-*f*	tunic
8075	**turban**-*m*	turban
9454	**turquoise**-*f; adj*	turquoise; turquoise
9632	**tutoyer**-*vb*	tutoyer
9501	**tutu**-*m*	tutu
8168	**tuyauterie**-*f*	piping
8396	**tweed**-*m*	tweed
7692	**typhus**-*m*	typhus

U

9944	**ukrainien**-*adj; m/mpl*	Ukrainian; Ukrainian
7609	**unanime**-*adj*	unanimous

9595 **unifier**-*vb* unify| standardize
8191 **unisson**-*m* unison
9129 **urbanisme**-*m* town planning
8526 **uriner**-*vb* urinate
9945 **urinoir**-*m* urinal
9399 **urticaire**-*f* urticaria| hives
7681 **usure**-*f* wear
9643 **utilisable**-*adj* usable| serviceable
8685 **utilisateur**-*m* user
8837 **utopie**-*f* Utopia

V

9561 **vacant**-*adj* vacant
9908 **vacciner**-*vb* vaccinate| inject
7969 **vadrouiller**-*vb* bum around
8958 **vagabondage**-*m* vagrancy
9697 **vaillance**-*f* valour
8194 **vallon**-*m* small valley
8096 **vandale**-*adj; m/f* vandal; vandal
7795 **vandalisme**-*m* vandalism
9964 **vantard**-*adj; m* boastful; braggart
9011 **variable**-*adj; f* variable; variable
8392 **variation**-*f* variation| change
8990 **varicelle**-*f* varicella
7679 **varier**-*vb* vary
8747 **variole**-*f* smallpox
8749 **vaseline**-*f* petroleum jelly
8267 **vecteur**-*m* vector
8268 **végétation**-*f* vegetation
8538 **veille**-*f* eve| day before
8161 **veilleur**-*m; adj* watchman; watchful
8856 **vénéneux**-*adj* poisonous
8642 **vénérable**-*adj* venerable
7587 **venimeux**-*adj* venomous
8129 **verdure**-*f* greenery| greenness
7901 **verge**-*f* yard| rod
8662 **véridique**-*adj* truthful
8703 **vermouth**-*m* vermouth
9534 **vernissage**-*m* varnishing| opening
9078 **vérole**-*f* pox
8858 **verrue**-*f* wart
9010 **verseau**-*m* Aquarius
9880 **verso**-*m* back| reverse
9122 **vertèbre**-*f* vertebra
7699 **vertical**-*adj* vertical
9408 **vésicule**-*f* vesicle
9163 **vestibule**-*m* vestibule
9657 **vestimentaire**-*adj* dress| clothing
8104 **veto**-*m* veto
8260 **vicaire**-*m* vicar
8074 **vicomte**-*m* viscount
8808 **vidanger**-*vb* drain
7997 **videur**-*m* bouncer
8617 **vieillissement**-*m* aging
7804 **vigoureux**-*adj* vigorous
10011 **vinaigrette**-*f* vinaigrette
9904 **vingtième**-*adj* twentieth| twentieth
9537 **vioque**-*adj* wrinkly
9732 **virtuellement**-*adv* virtually
8259 **virtuose**-*m/f* virtuoso
8255 **visqueux**-*adj* viscous| slimy
8862 **visualiser**-*vb* visualize
9383 **visuellement**-*adv* visually
7727 **vitalité**-*f* vitality| vigor
7845 **Vlan!**-*int* Whack!
9277 **volage**-*adj* flighty
8465 **volatiliser**-*vb* volatilize
8673 **volcanique**-*adj* volcanic
8927 **volley**-*m* volleyball
8792 **volupté**-*f* sensuousness
9835 **voyance**-*f* clairvoyance
9241 **vraisemblable**-*adj* similar
8102 **vraisemblablement**-*adv* in all likelihood

W

9797 **walkman**-*m* walkman

Y

8476 **yiddish**-*adj; m* Yiddish; Yiddish
8208 **yogi**-*m* yogi

Z

8409 **zèbre**-*m* zebra
7651 **zeppelin**-*m* zeppelin
9846 **zeste**-*m* zest
9490 **zigzag**-*m* zigzag

Contact, Further Reading and Resources

For more tools, tips & tricks visit our site www.mostusedwords.com. We publish various language learning resources.

If you have a great idea you want to pitch us, please send an e-mail to info@mostusedwords.com.

Frequency Dictionaries

Frequency Dictionaries in this series:

French Frequency Dictionary 1 – Essential Vocabulary – 2500 Most Common French Words
French Frequency Dictionary 2 - Intermediate Vocabulary – 2501-5000 Most Common French Words
French Frequency Dictionary 3 - Advanced Vocabulary – 5001-7500 Most Common French Words
French Frequency Dictionary 4 - Master Vocabulary – 7501-10000 Most Common French Words

Please visit our website www.mostusedwords.com/frequency-dictionary/french-english for more information.

Our goal is to provide language learners with frequency dictionaries for every major and minor language worldwide. You can view our selection on www.mostusedwords.com/frequency-dictionary

Bilingual books

We're creating a selection of parallel texts, and our selection is ever expanding.

To help you in your language learning journey, all our bilingual books come with a dictionary included, created for that particular book.

Current bilingual books available are English, Spanish, Portuguese, Italian, German, and French.

For more information, check www.mostusedwords.com/parallel-texts. Check back regularly for new books and languages.

Other language learning methods

You'll find reviews of other 3rd party language learning applications, software, audio courses, and apps. There are so many available, and some are (much) better than others.

Check out our reviews at www.mostusedwords.com/reviews.

Contact

If you have any questions, you can contact us through e-mail info@mostusedwords.com.

Made in the USA
Lexington, KY
31 May 2019